MULTI-LEVEL ISSUES IN ORGANIZATIONS AND TIME

RESEARCH IN MULTI-LEVEL ISSUES

Series Editors: Fred Dansereau and
Francis J. Yammarino

RESEARCH IN MULTI-LEVEL ISSUES   VOLUME 6

MULTI-LEVEL ISSUES IN ORGANIZATIONS AND TIME

EDITED BY

FRED DANSEREAU

State University of New York at Buffalo, USA

FRANCIS J. YAMMARINO

State University of New York at Binghamton, USA

ELSEVIER
JAI

Amsterdam – Boston – Heidelberg – London – New York – Oxford
Paris – San Diego – San Francisco – Singapore – Sydney – Tokyo

JAI Press is an imprint of Elsevier

JAI Press is an imprint of Elsevier
Linacre House, Jordan Hill, Oxford OX2 8DP, UK
Radarweg 29, PO Box 211, 1000 AE Amsterdam, The Netherlands
525 B Street, Suite 1900, San Diego, CA 92101-4495, USA

First edition 2007

British Library Cataloguing in Publication Data
A catalogue record for this book is available from the British Library

ISBN: 978-0-7623-1434-8
ISSN: 1475-9144 (Series)

For information on all JAI Press publications
visit our website at books.elsevier.com

Printed and bound in the United Kingdom

07 08 09 10 11 10 9 8 7 6 5 4 3 2 1

Working together to grow
libraries in developing countries ·

www.elsevier.com | www.bookaid.org | www.sabre.org

ELSEVIER   BOOK AID International   Sabre Foundation

CONTENTS

LIST OF CONTRIBUTORS

Joseph A. Alutto	Ohio State University, USA
Maureen L. Ambrose	University of Central Florida, USA
Adam D. Bailey	Texas Tech University, USA
Michael Bashshur	University of Illinois at Urbana-Champaign, USA
Allen C. Bluedorn	University of Missouri-Columbia, USA
J. Christian Broberg	Texas Tech University, USA
C. Shawn Burke	University of Central Florida, USA
Jennifer L. Burke	University of South Florida, USA
Jan Cannon-Bowers	University of Central Florida, USA
Jeffrey M. Conte	San Diego State University, USA
Michael D. Coovert	University of South Florida, USA
Russell Cropanzano	University of Arizona, USA
Fred Dansereau	State University of New York at Buffalo, USA
Gerald F. Goodwin	U.S. Army Research Institute, USA
James G. (Jerry) Hunt	Texas Tech University, USA
Keith James	Portland State University, USA
Kimberly S. Jaussi	State University of New York at Binghamton, USA
Joan H. Johnston	NAVAIR Orlando Training Systems Division, USA
Andrew Li	University of Arizona, USA

Hui Liao	Rutgers, The State University of New Jersey, USA
Sara A. McComb	University of Massachusetts-Amherst, USA
Heather A. Priest	University of Central Florida, USA
Richard Reeves-Ellington	State University of New York at Binghamton, USA
Joan R. Rentsch	University of Tennessee, USA
Michael A. Rosen	University of Central Florida, USA
Deborah E. Rupp	University of Illinois at Urbana-Champaign, USA
Eduardo Salas	University of Central Florida, USA
Marshall Schminke	University of Central Florida, USA
John F. Sherry	University of Notre Dame, USA
Erika E. Small	University of Tennessee, USA
Kevin C. Stagl	Assessment Technologies Group, USA
Mary J. Waller	University of Maastricht, The Netherlands
Francis J. Yammarino	State University of New York at Binghamton, USA

ABOUT THE EDITORS

Fred Dansereau, PhD, is professor of Organization and Human Resources and associate dean for Research in the School of Management at the State University of New York at Buffalo. He received his PhD from the Labor and Industrial Relations Institute at the University of Illinois with a specialization in Organizational Behavior. Dr. Dansereau has extensive research experience in the areas of leadership and managing at the individual, dyad, group, and collective levels of analysis. Along with others, he has developed a theoretical and empirical approach to theorizing and testing at multiple levels of analysis. He has served on the editorial review boards of the *Academy of Management Review, Group and Organization Management*, and *Leadership Quarterly*. He is a fellow of the American Psychological Association and the American Psychological Society. He has authored 10 books and over 80 articles and is a consultant to numerous organizations, including the Bank of Chicago, Occidental, St. Joe Corp., Sears, TRW, the United States Army and Navy, Worthington Industries, and various educational institutions.

Francis J. Yammarino, PhD, is SUNY distinguished professor of Management and director and fellow of the Center for Leadership Studies at the State University of New York at Binghamton. He received his PhD in Organizational Behavior (Management) from the State University of New York at Buffalo. Dr. Yammarino has extensive research experience in the areas of superior–subordinate relationships, leadership, self–other agreement processes, and multiple levels of analysis issues. He has served on the editorial review boards of seven scholarly journals, including the *Academy of Management Journal, Journal of Applied Psychology*, and *Leadership Quarterly*. He is a fellow of the American Psychological Society and the Society for Industrial and Organizational Psychology. He is the author of 11 books and has published over 100 articles. Dr. Yammarino has served as a consultant to numerous organizations, including IBM, Textron, TRW, Lockheed Martin, Medtronic, United Way, Skills Net, and the US Army, Navy, Air Force, and Department of Education.

OVERVIEW: MULTI-LEVEL ISSUES IN ORGANIZATIONS AND TIME

Francis J. Yammarino and Fred Dansereau

INTRODUCTION

"Multi-Level Issues in Organizations and Time" is Volume 6 of *Research in Multi-Level Issues*, an annual series that provides an outlet for the discussion of multi-level problems and solutions across a variety of fields of study. Using a scientific debate format of a key scholarly essay followed by two commentaries and a rebuttal, we present, in this series, theoretical work, significant empirical studies, methodological developments, analytical techniques, and philosophical treatments to advance the field of multi-level studies, regardless of disciplinary perspective.

Similar to Volumes 1 through 5 (Yammarino & Dansereau, 2002, 2004, 2006; Dansereau & Yammarino, 2003, 2005), this volume, Volume 6, contains five major essays with commentaries and rebuttals that cover a range of topics, but in the realms of organizations and time. In particular, the five "critical essays" offer extensive literature reviews, new model developments, methodological advancements, and some data for the study of distributed teams, team mental models, dimensions of time, timescapes, and justice climate. While each of the major essays, and associated commentaries and rebuttals, is unique in orientation, they show a common bond in raising and addressing multi-level issues or discussing problems and solutions that involve multiple levels of analysis in organizations and time.

Multi-Level Issues in Organizations and Time
Research in Multi-Level Issues, Volume 6, 1–8
Copyright © 2007 by Elsevier Ltd.
All rights of reproduction in any form reserved
ISSN: 1475-9144/doi:10.1016/S1475-9144(07)06023-7

DISTRIBUTED TEAMS

In the first essay, Stagl, Salas, Rosen, Priest, Burke, Goodwin, and Johnston present a multi-level review and conceptualization of distributed team performance with key implications for decision making at the individual, team, and organizational levels of analysis. They begin their review by acknowledging that distributed teams are not a panacea, but rather provide a number of benefits *and* challenges for teamwork. Stagl et al. then provide a multi-level heuristic of distribution, demography/culture, and decision making, not as a testable model, but as an organizing framework for their review. In terms of decision making, Stagl et al. consider both how people *do* make decisions and how people *should* make decisions; i.e., description and prescription for individual, team, and organizational decision making as well as their precursors and consequences at multiple levels of analysis. Specifically, they examine the impact of "distribution" as well as "cultural demography" on multi-level decision making and its underlying processes. Stagl et al. conclude their review with some practical implications for team leadership, training and development, and information technology.

In his commentary, Alutto makes the point that most of Stagl et al.'s work seems to focus on lower (e.g., intra-person and interpersonal) levels of analysis rather than on the higher organizational level. He indicates that the interactional effects of distributed teams and organizational-level phenomena and processes require greater attention. In particular, Alutto discusses the different implications of distributed teams as well as their performance and decision making for service-centric firms as compared to product-centric firms.

In their commentary, Coovert and Burke highlight, and provide a different perspective on, the key contributions of Stagl et al. They then offer a new conceptual model as an extension to the work of Stagl et al. In particular, Coovert and Burke's tetrahedral model of capacity in distributed systems captures the influence of time, space, and technology – three dimensions of distributedness – on individual, team, and organizational levels of capacity for effective performance. The three dimensions of distribution are a continuum along which individuals, teams, and organizations can vary.

In their reply, Stagl, Salas, Rosen, Priest, Burke, Goodwin, and Johnston acknowledge the contributions of Alutto, and Coovert and Burke for continuing the dialogue on distributed team performance and providing additional directions for future research. Stagl et al. respond to some issues raised in the commentaries by Alutto, and Coovert and Burke and then raise further research directions for distributed team performance. They conclude with a call for cooperative, interdisciplinary and multi-level research in this emerging field of study.

MENTAL MODELS IN TEAMS

In the second essay, McComb develops an approach to mental model convergence, an emergent process that occurs when team members interact, to describe the shift across levels of analysis from being an individual to being a team member. She notes that team members' individual mental models (both content and structure) evolve into shared mental models via a cognitive shift in an individual's focal level of analysis. In particular, an individual must shift his/her focus from thinking about the team from an individual perspective to thinking about the team from a team perspective. This occurs through a three-stage process of orientation toward the team domain, differentiation of the different perspectives of team members, and integration of these views into a team perspective. Relying on group development and information processing research, McComb presents a framework of mental model convergence that explains how individuals transform into team members over time. In addition, she examines the role of mental model contents on the convergence process, how converged models relate to team functioning and performance, and presents some preliminary data for high-performing project teams to support her views.

In her commentary, Cannon-Bowers focuses on fostering team mental model convergence through training. She begins by acknowledging the integrative work of McComb to specify a model of convergence. Cannon-Bowers then addresses the issues of consciousness of the convergence process by team members as well as volition and motivation of team members and the enhancement of these notions via training. In particular, she discusses how team members can be (1) made aware of the convergence process and induced to exert control over it; (2) motivated to effectively and efficiently converge their mental models; and (3) ensured to possess the knowledge, skills, and attitudes necessary to optimize the convergence process. Quite simply, for all three issues, the solution lies in team training.

In their commentary, Rentsch and Small acknowledge the contributions of McComb in highlighting the theoretical and methodological challenges in the study of cognition in teams. They then address many of those challenges and offer an extension to McComb's work. In particular, Rentsch and Small, in commenting on the abstract and complex nature of team cognition, provide and elaborate a model of team cognition that includes multiple types of cognitive similarity configurations.

In her reply, McComb acknowledges the comments of Cannon-Bowers, Rentsch, and Small and uses the similar, divergent, and complementary views of convergence to demonstrate how scholarship is analogous to mental model convergence processes. Specifically, she shows how her mental-model convergence framework can be applied to research scholarship in a variety of fields. McComb offers several examples of how a research field progresses through the three phases of mental model convergence but in opposite order to typical convergence processes; i.e., from integration to differentiation to orientation, and with suitable feedback loops.

DIMENSIONS OF TIME

In the third essay, Bluedorn and Jaussi focus on organizationally relevant dimensions of time. In particular, they address the temporal dimensions of polychronicity, speed, punctuality, and temporal depth, as well as the temporal phenomenon of entrainment and its insights to the other dimensions. In their in-depth treatment of polychronicity and speed, Bluedorn and Jaussi offer four task-engagement strategies and a variety of propositions regarding these temporal dimensions and their links to other organizational constructs at multiple levels of analysis (i.e., individual, group, and organization). They also specify propositions regarding punctuality and temporal depth, primarily at the individual and organizational levels of analysis. In their conceptualization, Bluedorn and Jaussi view entrainment (in various forms) as a "meta-dimension" that impacts the other temporal dimensions of polychronicity, speed, punctuality, and temporal depth. They also offer various cautions, challenges, and implications for addressing temporal issues from a multi-level perspective.

In his commentary, Conte acknowledges the contributions of Bluedorn and Jaussi and then extends their work to the measurement of temporal constructs across multiple levels of analysis. In particular, he examines measures that are available, and speculates about those still to be developed, for the levels of analysis relevant for the temporal dimensions of polychronicity, speed, punctuality, and temporal depth. Conte's focus is on the individual, group, and organizational levels with additional discussion of higher levels (e.g., industry, country, national culture).

In her commentary, Waller focuses on polychronicity, the preference to attend to more than one task simultaneously; and multitasking, its behavioral counterpart, at the individual, group, and organizational levels. She makes the point that polychronicity and multitasking are linked inextricably, but that high levels of the former do not necessarily lead to productive and effective levels of the latter. Beyond clarifying the differences and connections between polychronicity and multitasking, Waller explores the role of task performance strategies in multitasking behavior at multiple levels of analysis.

In their reply, Bluedorn and Jaussi address the challenges of temporal concepts, including their clear definitions and precise measurement. After acknowledging the new research directions raised by Conte and Waller, they explore further the dimensionality of polychronicity, contextual effects on temporal variables, and the implications of temporal variables interacting with one another. In addition, Bluedorn and Jaussi discuss process issues associated with temporal concepts.

TIMESCAPES

In the fourth essay, Reeves-Ellington introduces the concept of "timescapes" as a multi-level approach for understanding the use of time in complex organizations. In particular, he develops two phenotypes – timescapes of business time and social time, each with different functions and applications – that are defined by six dimensions (type, movement, actions, use, management, and work habits), each with a social and a business time parameter. For the social timescape, the parameters are qualitative, cyclical, polychromic climate, symmetric power, and moral, respectively; while, for business time the parameters are quantitative, linear, monochromic, counterfactual, asymmetric power, and amoral, respectively. To develop a multi-level conceptualization for understanding time use, Reeves-Ellington then combines these timescapes and parameters with both levels of management (senior, middle, and entry) and levels of analysis (self, dyadic, and social/group). He then uses his framework and conceptualization in conjunction with a grounded, anthropological research methodology to review and understand timescapes and time use throughout a 20-year history of the Proctor & Gamble Company. Reeves-Ellington's insightful multi-level analysis of P&G frames the company's timescape understanding and use from a practitioner perspective.

In their commentary, Broberg, Bailey, and Hunt take a systems-dynamic perspective on timescapes in organizations. In particular, using "data" from Reeves-Ellington's P&G case analysis, Broberg et al. does a constructive replication and extension at different hierarchical levels via systems dynamics, a multi-level simulation approach. They begin with a particular set of assumptions and the notion that senior management level plays a key role in determining the timescape that dominates. The Broberg et al.'s systems-dynamics model did not support a key idea of Reeves-Ellington that organization performance diminishes when there is a lack of fit between senior-management timescapes and those at lower levels of management. Focusing on temporality and feedback, Broberg et al. note that longer time frames are needed for these effects to be manifested and that environmental consumer demand, not considered by Reeves-Ellington, affect the performance measures beyond the timescape fit.

In his commentary, Sherry uses Reeves-Ellington's timescape notion to describe how marketing managers have responded to consumers' lived experience of time. In particular, he focuses on the retail "retroscape" as a source of meaning for consumers. Sherry accounts for consumers' temporal orientation displayed by both clock time and cosmic time. He also provides some interesting insights on "pluritemporality" in postmodern culture. This commentary holds the *RMLI* record for the most words not recognized by the spell-checker – a tribute to Sherry's creativity.

In his reply, Reeves-Ellington uses a multi-tiered research model to reinterpret the P&G case data and address the various issues raised by Broberg et al. and Sherry. He discusses a complex research model that employs qualitative organizational learning methods to formulate research questions that can be addressed via quantitative methodologies. Using this approach, he responds to the concerns of Broberg et al. and Sherry and offers an approach that permits theory building rather than simply theorizing. Reeves-Ellington notes that this work is both descriptive and prescriptive as well as bridges science and practice.

JUSTICE CLIMATE

In the fifth essay, Rupp, Bashshur, and Liao present models of the structure and emergence of justice climate. In this work on multi-level organizational justice, they provide some historical context, discuss organizational-level antecedents (culture and structure) to individual-level justice perceptions for the study of justice climate. Rupp et al. also explore the process of justice climate emergence from both bottom-up and top-down perspectives. In their model, individual differences and environmental characteristics interact to influence justice judgments in organizations. These processes of emergence and judgments are based on information sharing, unique and shared experiences, and interactions among group members. As such, Rupp et al. have gone well beyond individual-level work and proposed a uniquely multi-level (individual, unit, organization, and cultural) model of justice climate in organizations.

In their commentary, Ambrose and Schminke focus on issues of fit, simplicity, and content for justice climate. They discuss polynomial regression and response surface methodology as an approach to examine climate fit, offer a simplified view of justice climate, and develop a framework to examine a climate that promotes fair behavior in organizations. As such, Ambrose and Schminke address the important issues of modeling climate strength, degree of complexity in modeling justice climate, and alternative conceptualizations of justice climate.

In their commentary, Cropanzano, Li, and James address both intra-unit and inter-unit justice and focus on the people who experience such justice. They first use social identity theory and social categorization theory to understand what it means to be an individual when justice is experienced as a team member. Next, Cropanzano et al. elaborate intra-unit justice (group perception about how team members treat one another) and inter-unit justice (perception about how one group treats another) as new multi-level justice manifestations. They close their work with a four-cell taxonomy of the various multi-level justice concepts.

In their reply, Rupp, Bashshur, and Liao focus around the issues of source, target, type, specificity, and emergence of justice climate in their responses to Ambrose and Schminke, and Cropanzano et al. These five issues offer Rupp et al. an opportunity to integrate and extend the commentaries and provide additional multi-level justice climate propositions. Like their commentators, Rupp et al. acknowledge the importance of moving toward multi-level testing of justice climate in future research.

CONCLUSIONS

The essays, commentaries, and replies in this book illustrate the kind of issues that arise in dealing with multiple levels of analysis in organizations and time. The definitions of concepts (albeit, distributed teams, mental models in teams, dimensions of time, timescapes, and justice climate) change depending on what combination of levels of analysis are involved and added to them. The nuances of analytical methods (albeit, multi-level quantitative or qualitative in nature) change when one moves from one level of analysis to multiple levels of analysis. Moreover, although different paradigms may guide different scholars' theories and research methods and techniques, levels of analysis issues must be resolved to have a viable paradigm (albeit, traditional or novel). We believe that the demonstration of these issues in organizations and for time shows that these insights, applications, and advances will apply to numerous areas of scholarly investigation.

The authors in this volume have challenged theorists, researchers, and methodologists to raise and address multi-level issues in all their disciplinary and interdisciplinary work. If you would like to be a part of contributing ideas to this scholarly endeavor, please contact us directly or visit our website at: www.levelsofanalysis.com.

ACKNOWLEDGEMENTS

The publication of the *Research in Multi-Level Issues* annual series and this volume have been greatly facilitated by Julie Walker, Joanna Scott, Mary Malin, Philip Tite at Elsevier in the United Kingdom, and the production team of Macmillan India Limited. Closer to home, we thank our Schools of Management, the Center for Leadership Studies at Binghamton, the Jacobs Management Center at Buffalo, our secretaries, Marie Iobst, and Cheryl Tubisz, as well as our copy-editor, Jill Hobbs, for their help in preparing this book for publication. Finally and perhaps most importantly, we offer our sincere thanks to our contributors. The authors of the essays, commentaries, and rebuttals in this volume have provided new ideas and insights for unraveling the challenges of dealing with multiple levels of analysis and multi-level issues in a wide variety of areas. Thank you all.

REFERENCES

Dansereau, F., & Yammarino, F. J. (Eds). (2003). *Multi-level issues in organizational behavior and strategy (Vol. 2 of Research in multi-level issues)*. Oxford, UK: Elsevier.

Dansereau, F., & Yammarino, F. J. (Eds). (2005). *Multi-level issues in strategy and methods (Vol. 4 of Research in multi-level issues)*. Oxford, UK: Elsevier.

Yammarino, F. J., & Dansereau, F. (Eds). (2002). *The many faces of multi-level issues (Vol. 1 of Research in multi-level issues)*. Oxford, UK: Elsevier.

Yammarino, F. J., & Dansereau, F. (Eds). (2004). *Multi-level issues in organizational behavior and processes (Vol. 3 of Research in multi-level issues)*. Oxford, UK: Elsevier.

Yammarino, F. J., & Dansereau, F. (Eds). (2006). *Multi-level issues in social systems (Vol. 5 of Research in multi-level issues)*. Oxford, UK: Elsevier.

PART I:
DISTRIBUTED TEAMS

DISTRIBUTED TEAM PERFORMANCE: A MULTI-LEVEL REVIEW OF DISTRIBUTION, DEMOGRAPHY, AND DECISION MAKING

Kevin C. Stagl, Eduardo Salas, Michael A. Rosen,
Heather A. Priest, C. Shawn Burke,
Gerald F. Goodwin and Joan H. Johnston

ABSTRACT

Distributed performance arrangements are increasingly used by organizations to structure dyadic and team interactions. Unfortunately, distributed teams are no panacea. This chapter reviews some of the advantages and disadvantages associated with the geographical and temporal distribution of team members. An extended discussion of the implications of distributed team performance for individual, team, and organizational decision making is provided, with particular attention paid to selected cultural factors. Best practices and key points are advanced for those stakeholders charged with offsetting the performance decrements in decision making that can result from distribution and culture.

Multi-Level Issues in Organizations and Time
Research in Multi-Level Issues, Volume 6, 11–58
Copyright © 2007 by Elsevier Ltd.
ISSN: 1475-9144/doi:10.1016/S1475-9144(07)06001-8

INTRODUCTION

Emerging markets, growing international and domestic competition, and rapid technological development are driving organizations to make more effective use of their human capital to accomplish their mission. With the dual aims of increasing profitability and ensuring viability, institutions of all sizes are changing their strategies, structures, and systems in response to the realities of operating in this challenging environment. One manifestation of this changing reality in organizations is witnessed in the increasing reliance on teams to take responsibility for diverse, often complex tasks. Teams are rapidly becoming ubiquitous in modern organizations in part because they are uniquely able to call upon a deep reservoir of resources and thereby be more responsive, adaptive, and effective at a wide range of processes, including decision making.

Until recently, the interdependencies inherent to dyadic- and team-level interaction have required teammates to be physically collocated. Increasingly, however, advancements in information technology have provided the technological infrastructure to allow teams to function more easily across traditional temporal and geographic boundaries (Priest, Stagl, Klein, Salas, & Burke, 2006). Reports of the prevalence of distributed teams can be found in both the lay press and professional literature, documenting the facts that a majority of large companies are utilizing distributed teams and more professional-class workers are being members of a distributed team than not (de Lisser, 1999; Kanawattanachai & Yoo, 2002).

Despite the growing use of distributed performance arrangements to organize work in public and private sector organizations, distributed teams are no panacea (Bell & Kozlowski, 2002; Driskell, Radtke, & Salas, 2003; Thompson & Coovert, 2006). In fact, distributed team performance is a double-edged sword: While distributed teamwork offers tangible and attractive benefits, it also introduces a host of challenges for team members, teams, and the organizations in which they are embedded. Illuminating both the upside and downside factors associated with the geographic and temporal distribution of team members is important because, like all interventions, the adoption of this strategy must result in a return on investment (Levenson & Cohen, 2003).

This multi-level review seeks to advance the current understanding of distributed teams by addressing some of the benefits and challenges of distributed teamwork. The remainder of this chapter is organized around Fig. 1, which illustrates a multi-level heuristic of distribution, demography, and decision making. This framework is not advanced as a testable model

Fig. 1. A Multi-Level Framework of Distribution, Demography, and Decision Making.

but rather as a convenient means of quickly framing the issues discussed herein. This review emphasizes the implications of distribution and culture for decision making.

Most, if not all, of the previous research on distributed teams contrasts teams whose members are all in one location with teams where each member is isolated from all other members, calling the latter case the "distributed team." In business and the military, this is less frequently the case for real teams. More common are teams that are partially distributed, where several individuals are co-located with the team leader and clusters of team members reside in other locations. Most of the propositions advanced in this chapter are based on this idealistic but not wholly encompassing contrast between distributed and co-located teams.

The chapter begins with a discussion of the nature of distributed teams and a brief review of several contexts in which distributed teamwork is increasingly found. Next, the inherent challenges of distributed teamwork are discussed, with an extended discussion of the implications of distributed team performance for individual, team, and organizational decision making, with particular attention being paid to selected cultural factors. Several "best practices" related to distributed teamwork are then identified for those stakeholders charged with offsetting the performance decrements in decision making that result from distribution and culture. The chapter concludes with a set of take-away points deemed most critical by the authors.

DISTRIBUTED TEAMS

Teams have been defined as a distinguishable set of two or more individuals who interact dynamically, adaptively, and interdependently; who share common goals or purposes; and who each serve in specific roles or perform unique functions (Salas, Dickinson, Converse, & Tannenbaum, 1992). Additionally, teams are often hierarchically structured, have a limited lifespan, and are typically embedded within an organizational context that influences, and is influenced by, the team (Salas, Stagl, Burke, & Goodwin, in press). Of particular note, this definition makes no supposition about the geographic or temporal proximity of team members during performance. In addition to possessing these characteristics, distributed teams are further distinguished as interdependent entities where "members' primary interaction is through some combination of electronic communication systems, such as telephone, fax machine, e-mail, and computer-based video conferencing" (Townsend, DeMarie, & Hendrickson, 1996, p. 122), whereby teammates "are mediated by time, distance, or technology" (Driskell et al., 2003, p. 3).

The same features of distributed teams are also widely used in the literature to characterize entities termed "virtual teams." Despite popular use of the term "virtual" to describe teams with distributed members, we find it to be inaccurate (Salas, Stagl, & Burke, 2004; Zaccaro & Bader, 2003). Specifically, Merriam-Webster's (2005) online dictionary provides the relevant definition of virtual as "being such in essence or effect though not formally recognized or admitted" (www.m-w.com). Software programs that emulate a separate, functional computer are appropriately labeled "virtual machines" as they are a machine – specifically a computer – in effect or essence but not in reality. Distributed team members often interact via information technology, but they remain a team in reality – not simply in essence or effect – regardless of their geographic or temporal distribution. Although the authors object to the use of this term to describe distributed teams, those teams labeled elsewhere as "virtual" are likely to belong to the class of teams that we identify as distributed.

Distributed teams are not a team type, in the sense intended by Sundstrom and colleagues (Sundstrom, McIntyre, Halfhill, & Richards, 2000). Their characterization of team types was largely based on the tasks and functions being performed by the team, rather than a description of the structure of the team. In this sense, distribution is perhaps best viewed as a characteristic of teams, ranging from physical and temporal co-location (i.e., not distributed); through a state of partial distribution, in which some team members are distributed physically, temporally, or both; to a state of full distribution, in which all team members are distributed physically, temporally, or both.

As a performance arrangement, distribution both offers advantages and presents challenges that are differentially important relative to those inherent to co-located teamwork. Some of the benefits of distribution are discussed next. Following this discussion, some of the challenges of distributed teamwork are addressed. Of particular importance are the challenges distribution holds for individual, team, and organizational decision making.

WHERE ARE THEY? ORGANIZATIONAL CONTEXTS OF DISTRIBUTED TEAMS

A variety of reasons explain the attraction of fostering effective distributed teamwork. For example, the recent increase in utilization of telework by organizations (International Telework Association and Council, 2004) has both organizational benefits and personal benefits for employees. Telework better enables employees to manage the time regularly lost to commuting, which can be a significant portion of time in some areas. In turn, telework is one enabler of distributed teams, specifically in regard to developing the aspects of organizational culture and personnel skills related to handling workers who are distributed across geographic sites. Distribution also produces some utilitarian benefits. For example, GTECH reports savings of $3 million from improving the manageability of its manufacturing process via the use of telework and distributed teams (Gaspar, 2001). These are, however, far from the only benefits of distribution.

Global Organizations

In June 2005, Asia's largest computer maker, Lenovo, purchased a controlling interest in IBM's personal computer business through a $1.75 billion deal dubbed "Big Red." The alliance is expected to both quadruple Lenovo's sales and add 10,000 of Big Blue's employees to the firm's current roster of 9,000 workers. Approximately 25% of those 10,000 incumbents are currently based in the United States, and 4,000 live in China. The remaining 3,500 employees largely comprise a global distribution and sales network that operates out of 160 countries worldwide.

Realizing the potential synergies between Beijing-based Lenovo and New York-based IBM depends in no small part on the art and science of effectively utilizing distributed, multicultural personnel. In fact, most large-scale, multinational mergers and acquisitions ultimately result in the use of distributed multicultural teams in an effort to capitalize on the merging of similar functions across worksites without physically relocating personnel. This outcome is preferred because distribution can reduce the costs associated with securing or developing (e.g., real estate, buildings, parking space) and operating (e.g., rent, heat, electricity, maintenance) workplace facilities. Distributed performance arrangements can also reduce the financial and productivity costs associated with travel between Asia and North America, such as those incurred from airline transportation, lodging, miscellaneous expenditures, and daylong transcontinental flights.

Distributed performance arrangements will also allow Lenovo's and IBM's team members more flexibility in scheduling their time and efforts. By fitting the system to the team, rather than asking the team to fit the system, distributed teamwork reduces role overload, job-induced stress, and proximal and distal strain. By curtailing workplace stressors, team member perceptions of stress, and subsequent employee strain, these two organizations can contribute to a happy and healthy workforce during what is already a major transition. Routinely avoiding airport hassles and unfamiliar hotel accommodations should thus serve to markedly increase incumbent satisfaction at both Lenovo and IBM. Alleviating incumbent stress and strain should also decrease recurring medical costs, insurance premiums, and turnover for both organizations. In fact, a 1997 World Bank study suggested that employees who travel file 300% more insurance claims for psychological and stress-related problems than do their nontraveling associates.

Organizations Adapting to Change

The deal by IBM described in the preceding section is just one in a series of moves aimed at transforming the company's organizational strategy. In light of current macroeconomic forces, IBM is moving away from its historical focus on being a cost leader in manufacturing computers, software, storage, and microelectronics. As part of its new role, IBM is transitioning toward adopting an innovator strategy that is grounded in inventing and developing information technologies and subsequently translating those breakthroughs into business-to-business (B2B) solutions and consulting services. In the long run, this is likely to be a fortuitous realignment by IBM – a view echoed by Bennis (1999), who believes that system success is contingent upon whether internal organizational changes match the pace of external environmental changes.

Realizing its overarching vision of becoming a global purveyor of e-business and consulting services is no small endeavor, however, as IBM currently has $109 billion in assets under management to protect and employs 329,000 individuals (www.ibm.com). Success breeds entrenchment, and even a willing monolith does not change course quickly. Change is a difficult process in part because it requires disconfirmation as a primer to unfreeze a system in preparation for adaptation (Lewin, 1951). Although there is an intuitive appeal to repeating solutions that were successful in the past, today's winning strategies tend to become progressively less effective – even obsolete – over time (Bennis, 1999). Fortunately, key stakeholders at IBM know "obsolescence has a way of sneaking up on us all. The better we have been, the sneakier the condition becomes ... the prescriptive pill is change, but for most of us, it is a hard pill to swallow – even tougher when things seem to be going pretty good" (Harback & Keller, 1995, p. 30).

Similar to its joint venture discussed in the previous subsection, the ultimate success of IBM's strategic realignment is contingent in part on the long-term effective use of distributed customer service, technical support, and service development teams. Fortunately, distributed performance arrangements have much to contribute in the way of giving IBM the means and the motive to seize a share of emerging markets that might otherwise be more difficult to capture.

Two such benefits afforded by distribution are an increase in adaptive capacity and an expanded base of social capital (Zaccaro & Bader, 2003). Both of these competitive advantages flow in part from the capabilities that are created by attracting, recruiting, securing, utilizing, and retaining team members with a broad repertoire of capacities, experiences, and networks. For example, the use of distributed teams will allow IBM to identify and utilize the talents of the best people irrespective of their location. Moreover, because distributed teams can be geographically dispersed, they can be purposefully composed to leverage a wider range of localized social networks. Composing distributed teams with members who possess specialized cultural knowledge, skills, and connections affords IBM the insight needed to customize its IT solution and business service offerings to better fit the needs of its local clientele. Empowered distributed team members will also be able to detect, frame, and act upon a wider range of cues signaling the need for change faster than co-located team members could. These decentralized team members are better positioned to dynamically adapt to changing circumstances.

Multinational Political and Military Coalitions

In the last decade, substantive changes in the geopolitical environment and technological advances have led to new concepts of warfare. These concepts, as recently articulated in "Joint Vision 2020" (U.S. Department of Defense,

2000), are commonly referred to within the U.S. military as network-centric warfare and coalition warfare. Each of these concepts, individually and jointly, relies heavily on team concepts, but particularly those related to distributed team decision making.

In its fundamental essence, network-centric warfare is the incorporation of communication technology into the command and control, surveillance, and decision-making processes, with the goal of allowing decision makers to have faster and more complete access to the information needed to decisively win in combat. Network-centric warfare is primarily about information, and specifically about moving information to the right individuals at, or before, the right time. The ultimate, and perhaps unachievable, goal of network-centric warfare is to lift the "fog of war" and give decision makers the most complete and accurate information possible, as quickly as possible.

One critical aspect of the current geopolitical environment is that in political confrontation, one facet of which is the employment of military force, no nation acts alone. In U.S. talks with North Korea related to nuclear weapons development, a variety of other nations are involved, including Japan, China, and South Korea. On similar concerns related to Iran, several members of the European Union have taken the lead. In the employment of military force in Afghanistan and Iraq, the United States has a number of coalition partners that are contributing personnel and resources. All nations, the United States included, are in the process of shifting their force employment strategies to incorporate the realities of taking action as a part of a multinational coalition. As a result, many of the United States' coalition-partner nations are developing network-enabling concepts in parallel with the U.S. effort on network-centric warfare. The Canadian concept, termed network-enabled operations, is somewhat broader than the U.S. concept and focuses on operations other than war as well as major combat operations. The British concept, called network-enabled capability, goes a step further to focus on military capabilities rather than military actions. Although military theorists sometimes disagree regarding the extent of similarities, differences, and compatibility of these concepts, for the purposes of this chapter the end result is the same: Military decision makers will often be widely distributed in time and space, and often must rely heavily on newly developed technologies to send and receive information necessary for prosecuting their piece of military operations. Thus the success of modern warfare ultimately depends on the decision-making abilities of widely distributed but highly interdependent personnel.

This section addressed some of the benefits inherent to distributed team performance and discussed some of the contexts in which these benefits were being reaped. While distributed teams can be more efficient and effective than co-located teams, they are by nature subject to a host of challenges that may, if left unchecked, ultimately result in performance decrements and, therefore, inefficiencies and ineffectiveness. Co-located teams face these same challenges, but some obstacles are relatively more important to navigate to facilitate effective distributed teamwork. A sample of some of these challenges is presented next.

GENERAL CHALLENGES OF DISTRIBUTION

The use of distributed performance arrangements results in a distributed coordination space in which interdependent interaction can occur almost anytime and anywhere (Fiore, Salas, Cuevas, & Bowers, 2003). On-demand coordination is not, however, without its drawbacks, as distributed team members must face an increased level of abstraction, ambiguity, or team opacity (Fiore et al., 2003). Team opacity is the decrease in team member situation awareness that results from the loss of cues in distributed teams. Member awareness is suppressed because distributed environments have few paralinguistic, nonverbal, and other sensory cues (e.g., touch, smell). Perceptual cues that are abundant in co-located contexts are absent or must be interpreted via information technologies in distributed teams. Thus distribution affects how team members send, receive, interpret, and react to information (Thompson & Coovert, 2006).

Distributed team members seldom interact with one another on a face-to-face basis and, therefore, must deal with a plethora of challenges. Previous research efforts have qualitatively and quantitatively addressed the myriad of implications that distribution holds for individuals, teams, and organizations (e.g., Cascio & Shurygailo, 2002; Kahai, Sosik, & Avolio, 2003). For example, one interview study suggests that organizations are likely to experience problems with building trust, cohesion, and team identity, as well as overcoming the debilitating effects of social isolation, when implementing distributed performance arrangements (Kirkman, Rosen, Gibson, Tesluk, & McPherson, 2002). In regard to first of these issues, researchers have recently advanced a theoretical model of distributed team development that highlights the role of leaders in developing trust (Avolio, Kahai, Dumdum, & Sivasubramaniam, 2001). The formation and maintenance of trust is a critical issue for distributed teams because physical dispersion can result is less trust (Jarvenpaa & Leidner, 1999; Moon, 1999) and thereby lower levels of innovation (Lynn & Reilly, 2002). A recent theoretical review highlighted the effects of computer-mediated communication on team phenomena such as cohesiveness, feedback, counter-normative behavior, and social loafing (Driskell et al., 2003). Cohesion is essential to facilitating effective team-work, but especially so when team members are distributed in space and time. In fact, a mounting body of empirical evidence suggests that distributed teams have lower levels of cohesiveness than traditional co-located teams (Straus, 1997; Warkentin, Sayeed, & Hightower, 1997). This point is particularly important, because meta-analytic results suggest cohesive teams interact more and demonstrate higher levels of performance than less cohesive teams (Mullen & Cooper, 1994).

In addition to the problems inherent to distribution noted earlier, this review specifically emphasizes the challenges that distributed teamwork holds for individual, team, and organizational decision making. Because distribution affects how team members process and exchange information (Griffith & Neale, 2001), it also influences how team members make decisions. Moreover, given that team members are embedded in teams, and teams are embedded in organizations, distribution affects not only the enactment of individual-level processes but also the decision-making processes that entire teams and organizations engage in. The results of multiple meta-analyses suggest distributed teams take longer to reach decisions (Hollingshead & McGrath, 1995; McLeod, 1992). However, one of these meta-analytic investigations found that distributed teams make better-quality decisions (McLeod, 1992), while another found that primary studies showed mixed results in regard to the differences in decision quality between computer-mediated and co-located groups (Hollingshead & McGrath, 1995). Clearly, much remains to be learned about distribution and decision making.

DISTRIBUTION AND DECISION MAKING

The technologically augmented environment in which decision making in the modern workplace often occurs can be characterized as having increasing levels of complexity, abstraction, and severity of repercussions for decision errors (Cannon-Bowers, Salas, & Pruitt, 1996). Because decision-making products are critical to achieving targeted levels of team performance outcomes (Ilgen, Major, Hollenbeck, & Sego, 1993), and because distribution is an increasingly common characteristic of teams, understanding the effects of distribution on decision-making processes and team outcomes is essential to the design of technological collaborative environments and to the management of distributed teams.

Broadly defined, decision making in the work environment is "the ability to gather and integrate information, use sound judgment, identify alternatives, select the best solution, and evaluate the consequences" (Cannon-Bowers, Tannenbaum, Salas, & Volpe, 1995, p. 346). This general process is similar for individuals, groups, and teams (e.g., quality circles, task forces, and action teams; see Guzzo & Dickson, 1996). Moreover, recent theoretical work has begun to illuminate the processes inherent in organizational decision making (Beach, 1997).

In general, the study of decision making seeks to answer two questions: How *do* people make decisions? and How *should* people make decisions? It is rare for both questions to be examined concurrently. In fact, these two questions divide the study of decision making into two separate traditions or approaches: descriptive research and prescriptive research. Descriptive research seeks to develop models of decision making based on observations of expert decision makers facing real problems in fluid environments. In contrast, prescriptive research attempts to explain human decision making in terms of deviations from optimal mathematical models.

Traditionally, the prescriptive perspective has dominated decision-making research, as witnessed by the sheer volume of work addressing classical decision theory, modern behavioral decision theory, and judgment theory (e.g., Payne, Bettman, & Johnson, 1992; Mellers, Schwartz, & Cooke, 1998). Within the last 20 years, however, the field has undergone a paradigm shift as theoreticians have attempted to elucidate how decisions are made by workers in context (Cannon-Bowers et al., 1996). This emerging perspective is descriptive and has been labeled naturalistic decision making (NDM) (Klein, 1993). As a descriptive approach to understanding decision making "in the wild," NDM is underpinned by five core assumptions: (1) decision makers are task proficient, (2) decision rules should match a specific situation to a specific action, (3) decision making is contextually bound, (4) decision making is a process, and (5) methods should focus on empirical-based prescription (Lipshitz, Klein, Orasanu, & Salas, 2001).

Many researchers who prefer a prescriptive approach criticize NDM, stating that it is too vulnerable to the naturalistic fallacy, or accepting the way things are as the way things should be. Similarly, members of the descriptive camp criticize prescriptive decision research as being inapplicable to real-world situations, as its mathematical models emphasize a rationalism that seldom resembles the complexities of many natural decision-making settings. This section first reviews the theoretical basis and evidence for prescriptive and descriptive research on decision making at the individual, team, and organizational levels of analysis. However, because the majority of research to date has been conducted with co-located teams, this section closes by advancing propositions about the effects of distribution on decision making at each level.

Prescriptive Decision Making at the Individual, Team, and Organizational Levels

The research reviewed in this subsection asks questions concerning how people *should* or *ought* to make decisions; that is, the starting point is an optimal and analytically derived decision outcome against which actual decision making is compared. At the individual level, this review highlights the body of dynamic decision-making research, as it is unique in its consideration of distribution on individuals. At the team level, this review addresses the lens model approach to hierarchical team decision making. Finally, at the organizational level, policy making is discussed.

Dynamic Decision Making at the Individual Level

Although dynamic decision making began as a purely prescriptive approach based on the decision maker's subjective estimations of utility (Edwards, 1962), there are problems with mathematically representing the complexity of truly dynamic real-world situations. The nature of many real-world tasks – such as military command and control, industrial process control, and air-traffic control – has served as the impetus for research into dynamic decision making.

This subfield of decision research focuses on decision-making activities with four core identifying characteristics. First, multiple decisions are made in a series (Edwards, 1962); the decision maker works toward a goal of control over a system in a continuous cycle of evaluation and action (Brehmer, 1992). Second, decisions are not independent; any one decision is made on an assessment of the environment and the information generated by the previous decision (Edwards, 1962). Third, the decision environment changes through the decision maker's actions, variables outside of the decision maker's control, or both (Edwards, 1962). Fourth, decisions must be made in real time (Brehmer, 1992). As the system is constantly changing, the decision maker must constantly adapt and is not granted the luxury of dictating the time scale for decision making. Dynamic decision making is therefore a process in which the decision maker seeks control over the decision space as he or she incrementally works toward a goal.

A number of factors drive performance in dynamic decision-making tasks. First, the structure and temporal characteristics of the feedback cycle between the decision maker and the decision environment significantly affect decision effectiveness. The feedback structure is one of three main types: outcome, feedforward, or cognitive. Outcome feedback focuses on changes in the environment after the decision action. Feedforward feedback is generated when the decision maker is provided with a model of the task before the task begins. Cognitive feedback consists of information concerning relations in the environment, the decision maker's perception of the relations in the environment, and relations between the environment and the decision maker's perceptions. Outcome feedback is considered the least effective because it does not provide enough information for the decision maker to draw conclusions about relationships in the environment (Brehmer, 1990). Cognitive feedback is considered the most effective because it facilitates the development of accurate models of the task (Sengupta & Abdel-Hamid, 1993; Beroggi & Wallace, 1997). It should be noted, however, that findings from research investigating this matter are inconclusive, as some studies suggest feedforward feedback produces significantly higher increases in decision effectiveness (Gonzalez, 2005).

Second, the temporal aspects of information in the decision space affect decision quality. Feedback delays are inherent in complex systems, as the consequences of a decision are seldom immediately available to the decision maker. Specifically, time constraints involved with executing the action of a decision, and the time it takes to learn about the decision's effects temporally, disperse a course of action and its outcomes in the decision environment. Therefore, the decision maker needs to understand the temporal characteristics of a system to make effective decisions.

As different types of feedback delays will demand different strategies, the decision maker will need to develop a mental model of the task and its temporal characteristics (Brehmer, 1996). In general, longer feedback delays are associated with poorer performance in dynamic decision tasks. This relationship is attributed to decision makers' insufficient mental models of complex feedback processes and their poor skills at inferring causality in nonlinear dynamic environments (Diehl & Sterman, 1995). This last point is echoed by Jensen and Brehmer (2003), who argue that quality decision making in such environments calls for effective systems thinking skills (see Senge, 1990). Systems thinking skills have been defined as "understanding how system behavior over time is generated by interactions between its parts, identifying stocks, flows and feedback relationships, nonlinearities and delays within the system, and understanding their impact on system behavior" (Jensen & Brehmer, 2003, p. 120).

Hierarchical Decision Making at the Team Level
Teams in the workplace often have members with unequal status (i.e., the team is hierarchically structured) as well as variations in task-relevant expertise. To capture this complexity, Hollenbeck et al. (1995) presented a model of team decision making for teams with these characteristics. Their model is based on a lens approach, whereby individual team members perceive cues representing aspects of the decision environment and then generate beliefs and judgments about the state of the environment and possible courses of action. The leader interacts with each of the team members individually, at which time the team member communicates his or her judgment. Based on this input, the leader forms a belief about that team member's decision quality or the predictive validity of that team member's judgment in the specific decision context. The leader then weights the decision inputs of individual team members according to his or her judgment of the individual team member's decision quality (i.e., the team leader's assessment of the team member's task-relevant expertise).

Three major factors dictate decision effectiveness in this model. First, a greater degree of access to all cues relevant to the decision at hand for all team members is associated with more effective decisions. Put succinctly, the more informed the team members are, the better their decisions will be. Second, higher levels of expertise at the team member level yield better decisions at the team level. Higher levels of expertise allow individual team members to better translate decision cues into accurate judgments and, in turn, enhance the team decision outcome. Finally, the leader's assessment and weighting of the team members' individual decisions is a significant driver of the effectiveness of the overall team decision. The leader's ability to correctly weight the decision input of a team member according to that member's expertise is crucial to effective team decision making. In addition to these core factors, decision-making performance increases when team members are given process feedback about these three factors in comparison to outcome feedback (Hollenbeck, Ilgen, LePine, Colquitt, & Hedlund, 1998b).

Empirical findings support the idea that the ability of a team to correctly identify the expertise of its members is essential for effective decision making in hierarchical teams regardless of the degree of team member role specialization (Hollenbeck, Colquitt, Ilgen, LePine, & Hedlund, 1998a). Research findings also suggest the ability to identify expertise interacts with the type of task, such that the identification of member expertise grows in importance as the task becomes more complex and involves a variety of subtasks (Libby, Trotman, & Zimmer, 1987). In addition to expertise, individual characteristics such as general mental ability and conscientiousness have been linked to hierarchical team decision-making effectiveness (LePine, Hollenbeck, Ilgen, & Hedlund, 1997).

Policy at the Organizational Level
A policy is a means for an organization to make an important decision once and then apply that decision repeatedly as deemed necessary for subsequent situations (Beach, 1997). In relation to organizations consisting of distributed teams, two aspects of policy beg a closer inspection: How does distribution affect policy making? and How does distribution affect the enactment of policy?

First, the policy-making process is likely complicated by distribution in the same way as general individual and team decision making are, because policies are decisions arrived at by individuals and teams working as agents of the organization. Moreover, distribution likely interferes with the enactment of policy in at least three ways: (1) the flow of policy meaning or its intent may be degraded by technological mediation, (2) the assessment of a distal situation and subsequently its relationship to policy may be degraded, and (3) policies may be completely ignored by distributed entities when no mechanisms are in place to ensure the oversight and enforcement of policy compliance. That is, technology mediation can interfere with the processes of disseminating a clear vision of the intent behind a policy and, therefore, the ability of distributed elements of the organization to effectively apply that policy. Similarly, an individual or team charged with the task of assessing the degree to which a situation fits within the bounds of a policy is given access to a limited set of situational cues (i.e., only those afforded by the collaborative technology about the situation) on which to make a decision.

Descriptive Decision Making at the Individual, Team, and Organizational Levels

The decision-making research presented in this subsection is based on descriptive studies and seeks to answer questions concerning what people actually do while making decisions in context. The contexts studied in NDM research are often characterized by ill-structured problems and goals, uncertain dynamic environments, time stress, multiple players, outcomes that have high stakes for the decision maker, and the presence of multiple and sometimes competing organizational influences (e.g., goals and norms; see Orasanu & Connolly, 1993). Because NDM models are bound closely to the context in which the observations upon which they are formed were made (Lipshitz et al., 2001), numerous contextualized models have been advanced. This section reviews one unique model – the recognition-primed decisions (RPD) model – at the individual, team, and organizational level of analysis.

Recognition-Primed Decisions at the Individual Level
The RPD model (Klein, 1993, 1997, 1998) describes an expert's decision-making process as comprising two general subprocesses: (1) cue and pattern recognition and (2) mental simulation of courses of action. First, a decision maker senses cues in the environment and attempts to match the pattern of cues in the decision environment with past experiences. If the match for the present problem is found, the decision maker retrieves four pieces of information: (1) associated expectancies about the problem, (2) possible courses of action that are likely to be effective, (3) a set of cues that are most relevant to the problem, and (4) goals for the situation. If a reasonable match is not immediately found, the expert decision maker engages in a more exhaustive diagnosis of the situation, which involves gathering more informational cues about the problem.

Once the situation has been assessed and relevant information retrieved from memories of similar past experiences, the expert decision maker mentally simulates a course of action to determine whether the solution will work given the contextual constraints that characterize the current situation. The decision maker's mental simulation results in either adoption of the original course of action, modification of particular aspects of the retrieved course of action so that it becomes more effective in the present situation, or rejection of the course of action in lieu of retrieval and mental simulation of an alternate course of action.

The RPD model makes explicit the crucial role of situation assessment and situation awareness in expert decision-making processes in natural real-world settings. Endsley (1997) proposes that the three levels of situation awareness (i.e., perception of elements in the environment, comprehension of the current situation, projection of future status) are the inputs to the decision-making process. That is, processes culminating in an understanding of the current and likely future states of the environment feed directly into the decision-making process. This approach is represented in the RPD model, for which the first stage of the model is labeled "Experience the Situation in a Changing Context" (Klein, 1998, p. 25). This stage is essential to the subsequent cue recognition and retrieval of expectancies, goals, relevant cue sets, and possible courses of action stages of the RPD model. Similarly, the projection of the future status of the environment stage of situation assessment likely plays a role in the mental simulation involved in RPD whereby decision makers evaluate whether a course of action will work in the present situation.

In support of the idea that situation assessment is a necessary prerequisite to high-quality decision making, Orasanu and Connolly (1993) state that "experts are distinguished from novices mainly by their situation assessment abilities, not their general reasoning skills" (p. 20). Some empirical evidence in support of this claim comes from the research of Randel, Pugh, and Reed (1996), whose findings suggest expert and novice electronic warfare technicians on U.S. Navy ships exhibited differences in decision making. Specifically, experts spent more time evaluating the current environmental situation, whereas novices spent more time evaluating the possible courses of action. Similarly, Kirlik, Walker, Fisk, and Nagel (1996) argue user interfaces that support perception and pattern recognition (i.e., situation assessment) are essential to expert decision making. Moreover, training interventions should focus on imparting trainees with heuristic strategies rather than intensely cognitive and abstract strategies (Kirlik et al., 1996).

The situation assessment stage of decision making can be conceptualized in an alternate manner than that described previously. Some researchers have asserted that in addition to the situation assessment abilities noted above, mental models of the problem are an essential component of expert decision making (Lipshitz & Ben Shaul, 1997). Mental models of the problem serve as inputs into the situation assessment process, and revised mental models are a product of situation assessment. Expert and novice decision makers are differentiated by the schemata that they use to translate situational information into representational models of the decision environment. In short, expert decision makers make better decisions because they can create more accurate and complete mental models of the problem.

The Team Mind Model of Team Decision Making

In addition to the processes present in individual-level situation assessment-based models such as the RPD model, some attributes of decision making in naturalistic contexts are unique to decisions made by teams. The metaphor of the team mind has been used to explain four properties of expert team decision making: team competencies, team identity, team cognition, and team meta-cognition (Klein, Zsambok, & Thordsen, 1993; Klein, 1998).

In this context, *team competencies* refer to the individual capabilities of team members. Individual competency is a prerequisite to expert team decision making in the team mind model. This property is similar to, but broader than, the individual expertise that serves as a driving factor of effectiveness in the hierarchical team decision-making model.

Team identity is the degree to which individual members take on the goals of the team as their own and view themselves as part of a unified team. Expert teams have a sense of themselves as a collective, rather than as just an aggregation of individuals doing related work.

Team cognition is another central aspect of the team mind model. That is, teams must work to build a shared understanding of the situation through communication of information cues and interpretations of the environment, direct their members so that all relevant information is processed, and propagate leadership intent about courses of action throughout the team. Expert decision-making teams are capable of developing accurate and complete shared understandings of the decision environment.

Team meta-cognition involves self-monitoring behaviors by which expert decision-making teams are able to monitor and adapt to problems by selecting resources and courses of action that utilize the strengths of the team (e.g., team competencies) and avoid skill deficiencies.

The decision-making process enacted by both individuals and teams is tightly associated with mental models. In fact, the shift between expert and novice decision making is explained in part through differences in mental models (Salas, Cannon-Bowers, & Johnston, 1997; Cannon-Bowers, Salas, & Converse, 1993). Orasanu (1990) showed that high-performing cockpit crews differed from poor-performing cockpit crews in that the former crews communicated in such a way as to build a shared understanding of problems, which in turn facilitated effective decision making. Such shared problem models include an understanding of the nature of the situation and the problem, an understanding of the team goals, and an understanding of the course of action being taken to solve the problem (Orasanu, 1994). These and other empirical data from high-stakes decision-making environments suggest that "reasoning is schema driven, that is, guided by the decision maker's knowledge, to search and assess information, and to build causal models of events" (Orasanu & Connolly, 1993, p. 20). Accurate mental models of the task and situation are essential components to successful individual decision making; elements of these models must be shared for quality team decision making.

Image Theory at the Organizational Level

Image theory (Beach, 1997) is an NDM theory of decision making related to RPD and other recognition-based models of individual decision making (Beach, Chi, Klein, Smith, & Vicente, 1997). In this theory, the individual level is extended to the organizational level by adopting the perspective that people as individual members of the organization make decisions, not organizations as disembodied entities (Beach, 1997). Therefore, in image theory, organizational decision making is a particular type or instance of individual-level decision making.

To make an organizational decision, a decision maker consults three knowledge structures, or images: (1) the culture image, which contains organizational values and beliefs; (2) the vision image, which contains the organization's goals; and (3) the strategy image, which contains plans for achieving the goals found in the vision image. Variations of these three images are present in individual decision making but contain information about the individual decision maker rather than information about the organization as a whole. Armed with this information, decision makers can make one of two types of decisions: an adoption decision, which adds new goals or plans to the vision or strategy images, respectively, or a progress decision, which focuses on the effectiveness of a current course of action. To make these decisions, decision makers first employ a compatibility test, a decision mechanism that effectively screens decision alternatives against the content of the three images. This process reduces the number of alternative choices available and minimizes the possibility of making a bad decision. Specifically, alternatives that do not meet the minimum requirements of the organization (e.g., an alternative may conflict with an organizational value) are eliminated early and not admitted to the post-screening pool of decision alternatives. After the screening process, the decision maker must choose between the remaining alternatives if more than one passes the compatibility test. At this point, the decision maker may use any one of a multitude of decision strategies, grouped under the heading of the profitability test, to choose the option that most benefits the organization.

The Impact of Distribution on Individual Decision Making

At the individual level, distribution implies a separation in space and time of the decision maker and the cues used during situation assessment. That is, in practical applications of the dynamic decision-making scenario (e.g., industrial control systems, piloting of unmanned aerial vehicles), the original source of the environmental cue is mediated by technology. The original cue or cue stream is somehow sensed by the information technologies that make up a system and relayed to the decision maker through visual, auditory, or haptic displays. In this sense, distribution has a significant influence on decision making, as both the representation the system imposes on cues and the inevitable feedback delays in information systems jointly affect decision-making outcomes (e.g., Adelman, Bresnick, Christian, Gualtieri, & Minionis, 1997; Kirlik et al., 1996; Nygren, 1997).

A technological interface used within a dynamic decision environment is capable of focusing the decision maker's attention on specific aspects of the problem, thereby altering the decision maker's mental model of the problem and consequently the course of action ultimately selected. In doing so, the technological interface biases certain informational cues, which can increase performance on associated tasks, albeit at the price of degrading performance on other aspects of the decision task (Adelman, Cohen, Bresnick, Chinnis, & Laskey, 1993).

These effects of feedback delay and interface design on decision making can be illustrated by considering an example from air-traffic control, a representative dynamic decision-making task. The task of finding optimal solutions to air-traffic management problems is outside the cognitive abilities of any one person; therefore, the task is subdivided and distributed to many individuals – a process that sacrifices optimal solutions in exchange for a relatively stable output of satisfactory solutions (Smith, McCoy, & Orasanu, 2001). On occasion, however, the decisions made are not satisfactory and safety within the system drops below acceptable limits. The root cause of this problem is usually a deficiency in the information available to an operator and fluctuations in the rate of information flow. Operators may not be able to make satisfactory decisions when feedback delays in the system or the availability and timeliness of information about incoming aircraft inhibit the formation of an accurate representation of the decision space.

Research on dynamic decision making leads to two propositions about the effects of distribution on individual decision making

Proposition 1. Distribution of team members in space and time introduces feedback delays and asymmetries in the temporal flow of information from disparate physical locations. As feedback delays and/or asymmetries increase, team members' interpretations of implemented courses of action and subsequent decisions made on the basis of those interpretations can become erroneous or degraded from the optimal.

Proposition 2. Distribution of team members in space and time affects the quality of decision outcomes by complicating the process of building accurate mental representations of causality in a dynamic system.

In terms of the RPD model, distribution in the form of technological mediation can interfere with the pattern-matching processes of an expert decision maker. This occurs for similar reasons as discussed earlier (i.e., feedback characteristics, feedback delays) and for an additional reason involving information order effects. Working with experienced military air defense officers, Adelman, Bresnick, Black, Marvin, and Sak (1996) showed that the order in which decision makers receive information affects their final decision. A primacy effect was observed in that the officers based their assessments on the earliest information they received, a finding also noted with Army intelligence analysts (Tolcott, Marvin, & Lehner, 1989).

The experts' cue recognition processes account not only for the informational content of a cue, but also for the temporal sequence of cues (Perrin, Barnett, & Walrath, 2001). As decision makers become distributed from environmental cues, it becomes more likely that cues from different physical spaces will arrive at the decision maker at different times. Factors such as properties of the technological system (e.g., asymmetries in speed of data transfer in different components of the network) and arbitrary or artificially imposed characteristics of the information display can cause or mediate the order in which distributed cues are presented to a decision maker. This issue, along with how best to represent environmental cues and focus the decision maker's attention, is a central concern of distributed individual decision making in light of the current understanding about decision-making processes through both prescriptive and descriptive research perspectives.

The effects of distribution on recognition-based decision making can be illustrated by examining the collision of two ships, the Coast Guard cutter *Cuyahoga* and a large freighter in the Chesapeake Bay in 1978 (Burns, 2005). In this disaster, which claimed the lives of 11 Coast Guard personnel, uncertainty about environmental cues induced by darkness led the Coast Guard Captain to erroneously interpret the lights of the oncoming freighter as those of a slow-moving fishing boat that the cutter was overtaking. The Captain then decided on a course of action that he thought would move the cutter behind the fishing boat so that he could overtake the fishing vessel and not block its access to the river channel they were approaching. Unfortunately, this course of action brought the cutter directly into the path of the oncoming freighter. Much like darkness, distribution can affect the ability of decision makers to accurately assess the situation at hand and therefore lead to the adoption of flawed courses of action. The interpretation of environmental cues becomes increasingly more difficult as context is removed and the set of cues available to the decision maker becomes more constrained.

Research on recognition-based decision making therefore leads to one proposition about the effects of distribution on decision making

Proposition 3. Distribution of team members in space and time reduces the salience of environmental cues necessary for building an accurate mental model of the decision space and, therefore, produces decrements in situation assessment, pattern matching, mental simulation, and consequently decision quality.

The Impact of Distribution on Team Decision Making

Just as the mediation of environmental cues by technology alters decision-making processes and outcomes at the individual level, so the technological mediation made necessary by the physical distribution of team members can alter decision-making processes and decision outcomes at the team level. For example, distributed team members may not be able to fully demonstrate their capabilities or expertise across the distributed interface. Moreover, the technology that enables distributed teams to function also allows for the formation of teams composed of individuals who may be initially unfamiliar to one another. In terms of the Hollenbeck et al.'s (1995) model of hierarchical team decision making, distribution is therefore likely to affect the ability of leaders to identify the expertise of individual team members, thereby degrading decision effectiveness. This assertion is supported by empirical evidence suggesting that a decision performance decrement exists when distributed teams engage in an interdependent task when the team members have no prior history of interaction (Alge, Weithoff, & Klein, 2003). In contrast, no such decrement has been observed for those distributed teams with members who have previously worked together.

Of note, even when team members are familiar with one another, they may not be able to fully demonstrate their expertise because of system limitations. Moreover, members may not be willing to share their expertise because they feel disconnected from their collective. Either case presents a challenge for leaders who are attempting to identify and integrate a diverse range of member expertise.

The effects of distribution on hierarchical team decision making can be illustrated with an example from the medical domain. Arriving at a medical diagnosis can be a complicated process that involves the contributions of many specialists. Often, the lead doctor is responsible for synthesizing information and expert opinions advanced by numerous consulting doctors, a team organization that fits Hollenbeck et al.'s (1995) hierarchical team model. In a relatively nondistributed configuration (i.e., most conferring between specialists and primary care physician is done face-to-face), the lead doctor is capable of assessing the relevance of each specialist's perspective to the problem as well as the certainty of that specialist's conclusions based on formal and informal communication. With more distributed arrangements, the primary physician may be less capable of assessing the specialist's level of certainty regarding his or her judgment due to the loss of paralinguistic cues and a constrained ability to engage in real-time communication (e.g., asking questions, providing opinions of other specialists that may alter the diagnosis). Therefore, systems designed to facilitate distributed medical diagnosis must also afford the communication of levels of certainty in expert judgment (Cicourel, 1990).

A second factor of concern involves the assessment of a team member's overall level of expertise in a given area. Specialists are indeed highly qualified, but no doubt there are variations in levels of expertise and the relevance of any one type of expertise to a specific problem; the boundaries of these variations are not always clear in complicated medical diagnoses. Therefore, in distributed medical teams, the members' ethos, or general credibility relative to others on the team, may not be known. This uncertainty complicates the issue of weighting judgment inputs for the team leader.

The preceding research leads to three propositions concerning the effects of distribution on hierarchical team decision making

Proposition 4. Distribution of teams in space and time allows the assemblage of team members who have never worked together before and consequently complicates the process of leaders identifying the expertise of their team members.

Proposition 5. Distribution of teams in space and time eliminates subtle cues used by leaders to assess the certainty of team members' judgments and consequently complicates the process of leaders weighing the input of their team members when reaching a decision.

Proposition 6. Distribution of teams in space and time eliminates subtle cues used by team members to assess the input of their fellow teammates when weighting information in an attempt to reach a decision.

According to the team mind model, highly accurate and complete shared mental models of problem-relevant information are essential for expert team decision making. Bolstad and Endsley (1999) showed that physical prox-imity allows for faster development of shared mental models in teams be-cause proximity affords an opportunity for the members of teams to communicate and observe one another. By contrast, social network distance – the amount of communication between team members – has been shown to be a significant predictor of shared mental models independent of phys-ical distance such that team members with higher levels of communication have higher levels of sharedness in mental models (Graham, Schneider, Bauer, Bessiere, & Gonzalez, 2004). This finding suggests that distributed teams are also capable of developing the shared mental models necessary for expert team decision making.

Research examining the effects of computer-mediated communication on distributed decision-making groups versus face-to-face decision-making groups, however, has produced less than optimistic findings. In fact, both a recent meta-analysis and a comprehensive qualitative review of relevant findings suggest that distributed decision-making groups produce less effec-tive decision outcomes, take longer to make decisions, and have less satisfied group members relative to face-to-face groups (Baltes, Dickson, Sherman, Bauer, & LaGanke, 2002; Martins, Gilson, & Maynard, 2004). The findings concerning member satisfaction relate to the team identity component of the team mind model of expert team decision making. Specifically, team identity is affected by distribution, with distributed teams often exhibiting low co-hesiveness (Hertel, Geister, & Konradt, 2005).

The effects of distribution and team identity on decision-making quality can be illustrated by considering Kline's (2005) description of intuitive team decision making, a process Kline identifies in numerous settings (e.g., health care, governmental agencies, consulting firms). An intuitive team decision is one that does not require explicit deliberation of response alternatives; in-stead, the decision appears to just happen on its own accord. This scenario is possible when there is a highly developed team identity, a shared under-standing of the team goals, and salient norms. Teams that do not have these characteristics are forced to deliberate about the fit between various courses of action and the team goals. As distributed teams generally have lower cohesiveness (Hertel et al., 2005), they experience process losses (e.g., ex-tended time to reach a decision) during this deliberation.

This research leads to one proposition concerning the effects of distri-bution on the team mind model of team decision making

Proposition 7. Distribution of teams in space and time complicates the formation of the highly developed team identity necessary for expert team decision making. Distribution makes it more difficult for team members to identify with the team, as the nature of distributed organizations allows for and encourages the formation of teams of individuals who are unfamiliar with one another.

The Impact of Distribution on Organizational Decision Making

According to image theory and supporting empirical evidence, people making organizational decisions will choose different options depending on the degree to which they believe those options are compatible with the organization's values, goals, and plans (Weatherly & Beach, 1998). Because image theory casts organizational decision making as a specific instance of individual decision making, this type of decision making is vulnerable to all of the effects of distribution on individual decision making. Specifically, the degree to which an organization is physically or temporally distributed should affect the degree to which knowledge content in the three images discussed earlier is shared between collaborating decision makers and the degree to which any one organizational decision maker's knowledge content (e.g., values, beliefs, goals, plans) matches that of the organization at large.

This research leads to one proposition concerning the effects of distribution on organizational decision making

Proposition 8. Distribution of teams and team members in space and time complicates the process of building sharedness of content in the culture, vision, and strategy images. Just as distribution has deleterious effects on the congruence of team-oriented knowledge structures, so the content of organizationally relevant images, or mental representations, will degrade as distribution increases.

CULTURAL DEMOGRAPHY AND DECISION MAKING

The previous section addressed some of the effects of distribution on individual, team, and organizational decision making. During this discussion, it was noted that distributed teams often include multicultural personnel. The differing implicit assumptions and values that team members from different cultures have internalized will inevitably affect their experiences and decisions. Moreover, as multicultural team members are embedded in teams, and teams are embedded in organizations, cultural assumptions also affect the decisions made by teams and on behalf of organizations. The current section discusses culture in terms of national/ethnic culture, although the principles presented here may be generalized to other forms of culture (e.g., organizational).

This section adopts a relational demography approach (see Tsui & O'Reilly, 1989) to discuss the social dynamic that emerges when a team member with one set of cultural assumptions interacts with his or her teammates who have disparate assumptions in an effort to describe how those differences affect decision making. The "basic premise of the relational approach is that the relationship of an individual's own demographic attributes to that of all the other members in a particular unit will have an impact on the individual's experience in that unit" (Tsui & Gutek, 1999, p. 23). Moreover, deep-level diversity attributes such as values, beliefs, and assumptions underlying culture become more pronounced in their effects on teamwork over time (Harrison, Price, & Bell, 1998; Harrison, Price, Gavin, & Florey, 2002).

National culture consists of the shared norms, values, assumptions, and practices of a nation (Helmreich, 2000). Culture has also been defined as the shared perception of the self and others, consisting not only of norms and behavior, but also of beliefs that provide structure for member action (Dodd, 1991). This section considers two cultural dimensions: (1) power distance and (2) individualism/collectivism. These two dimensions were chosen for review because they have considerable supporting research to anchor the following discussion.

The assumptions underlying these dimensions about the distribution of power and the priority of one's collectives ultimately affect one's decision making to the extent that differences in intrateam assumptions are salient. A team member's cultural standing becomes important when it deviates from the assumptions made by other teammates or the assumptions that have been widely accepted by the team as the correct way of thinking about or acting toward one another, a challenge that has arisen, or some other contextual event. For example, a given team member's assumptions about the proper way to distribute power are likely to be salient and, therefore, to affect both decisions made by that individual and decisions made about that individual, if the other members of the team share a different set of beliefs about power relations.

Power Distance

Power distance is defined as the extent to which less powerful members within a culture expect and accept an unequal distribution of power

(Hofstede, 1980). This construct is measured on a continuum that ranges from low to high (Robert, Probst, Martocchio, Drasgow, & Lawler, 2000). Distributed team members with higher levels of power distance will not feel comfortable speaking up to team leaders or having close, friendly relationships with leaders. For example, team members with the assumptions underlying a high level of power distance will often defer to those in power and thus will not feel comfortable approaching team leaders and offering unsolicited opinions. Such team members will likely follow orders without question and contribute less in the decision-making process unless they hold a position of power themselves.

At the other end of the spectrum, team members with assumptions that correspond to a low level of power distance are more likely to attempt to form close personal bonds with their leaders and openly speak their minds. Low-power-distance individuals often display more collegial relationships with members at all levels of the hierarchy. Such team members perceive less of a barrier between lower-ranking and higher-ranking team members. In turn, they are more inclined to offer their input and feel more comfortable about approaching team leaders with suggestions during decision making.

In sum, assumptions about the distribution of power affect individual, team, and organizational decision making in distributed teams. The next three subsections adopt a relational demography approach as a basis for discussing how intrateam differences in power distance assumptions can affect decision making at multiple levels.

Power Distance and Individual Decision Making
As an example of how the assumptions underlying power distance can influence team member decision making within a typical decision-making task, consider a distributed team of experts made up of a mix of individuals who fall on the high end of the power distance continuum and individuals who fall on the low end of the power distance continuum. Given this situation, the disparate intrateam assumptions about the distribution of power will likely affect the team's ability to make an informed decision. Specifically, the individuals who perceive a low power distance would likely dominate the discussions, because this is a distributed team for which the primary form of communication is via teleconference; being a newly formed team, clear norms for communication have yet to be established. In contrast, team members from high-power-distance cultures will be reluctant to speak up, resulting in less input from these individuals into the decision-making process. Furthermore, their reluctance to speak up may be even more pronounced due to factors such as which end of the power distance

continuum their direct supervisors fall on. Consequently, individuals from high-power-distance cultures run the risks of both being ignored and being perceived by their low-power-distance counterparts as reserved, disinterested, aloof, or incompetent. In contrast, the low-power-distance individuals may sacrifice innovation through idea generation and be perceived as being disrespectful.

The preceding example illustrates how uninformed decision making can unfold when all team members do not contribute their expertise to the decision-making process. Cultural differences in beliefs about the distribution of power affect the dyadic interactions between a team leader and a team member. In turn, these differences lead to disparate contributions and possibly the adoption of flawed courses of action. Ultimately, team effectiveness and productivity could suffer.

This example leads to one proposition about the effect of power distance on team member decision making in a distributed environment

Proposition 9. Distributed teams with members who hold disparate intrateam assumptions about the distribution of power can lead to an incomplete assessment of the situation, withheld input, and ultimately flawed or suboptimal decisions.

Power Distance and Team Decision Making
The implications of disparate intrateam assumptions about the appropriate distribution of power can also be witnessed at the team level. Specifically, referencing Hollenbeck and colleagues' (1995) model of team decision making, team leaders must assess the team members' individual decisions and weigh them appropriately for the overall team decision to be effective. In the preceding example, suppose Lee cannot effectively weigh the decision input of his subordinate Kokwan because the situation and his cultural tendency interact to constrain Kokwan's contribution. Therefore, Lee's final decision made on behalf of the team about the threat posed by a competitor's offering will not fully take advantage of all the information available.

One of the oft-noted advantages of distributed teams is that organizations can leverage the expertise of team members without regard to their location. Because he did not understand how members of different cultures go about making their unique contribution to the decision-making process nor recognize how to encourage that contribution, Lee failed to maximize this inherent advantage of distributed teams. To decrease Kokwan's anxiety about distinguishing himself from the group by approaching the leader with his own ideas, Lee could have encouraged the submission of contributions anonymously in a chat room or solicited the group members' initial opinions through one-on-one conversations.

This example leads to one proposition about the effect of power distance on team decision making in a distributed environment

> **Proposition 10.** High-power-distance team members may contribute less during the decision-making process, resulting in team leaders misbalancing their input and ultimately leading to degraded team decisions.

Power Distance and Organizational Decision Making
The prescriptive approach to decision making conceptualizes policy setting as organizational-level decision making, even though the policy makers are often team members (e.g., executive team members) and leaders of teams (e.g., chief executive officer). From this perspective, a policy is defined as the means for an organization to make an important decision once, and then apply this decision repeatedly as deemed necessary (Beach, 1997). Similar to the effects of distribution, the power distance of team leaders and team members in relation to one another can affect both the flow of policy and the assessment of a given situation in relation to policy. In fact, the effects of power distance on how leaders and members create and assess policy as organizational decision making would be even more obvious in a distributed environment. Within distributed environments, there are fewer opportunities for team members to gain offline insight into other team members' cultural preferences or to attempt to create a hybrid culture that would encompass or address individual needs.

The effects of power distance on organizational decision making can be illustrated with a hypothetical example of a leader of a distributed management team who assumes that power should be distributed hierarchically (i.e., high power distance). When this leader sets an organizational policy, one would expect the resulting policy to favor vertical (rather than horizontal) structures, downward (rather than bidirectional) communication channels, and centralized control (rather than empowerment at lower echelons of the organization). This policy, once set, would likely meet with general acceptance if the other members of the management team were of a like mind in regard to the distribution of power. If the circumstances were different, however, and the leader was a member of a team which held a common belief that sharing power is adaptive, then the leader's low-power-distance teammates might feel that neither they nor their subordinates had ample opportunity to provide their input into the policy. As a result, conflict might ensue.

In contrast to the previous example, if the leader could be characterized as being on the low end of the power distance continuum, the policies that he or she enacts would be more likely to reflect his or her belief in the value of flattened hierarchies, upward feedback streams, and cross-level coordination. Moreover, in constructing the policy, the leader would be more likely to elicit the input of his or her teammates as well as a variety of incumbents who would ultimately enforce and enact the policy. In this case, team members with low power distance would feel appreciated and included. While low-power-distance team members and subordinates might be more satisfied with the decision processes and outcomes of their low-power-distance leader, high-power-distance members would likely feel uncomfortable and lose respect for the leader. To these individuals, the leader would seem less competent for not wielding his or her power directly. The perception of incompetence would be all the more relevant because distribution impedes the communication required for team members and subordinates to socially identify with a leader.

This example leads to one proposition about the effect of power distance on organizational decision making in a distributed environment

Proposition 11. Distributed team leaders set policies on behalf of their organizations, which will likely fit with the assumptions of their own level of power distance. However, when distributed team members have levels of power distance that differ significantly from the levels perceived by their team leaders, the decisions made by the team leaders will likely be interpreted differently, and perhaps even in a negative light, by those team members.

Individualism versus Collectivism

The individualism–collectivism construct is used to describe a preference for thinking in terms of the group (i.e., collectivism) or the individual (i.e., individualism) (Triandis, Bontempo, Villareal, Asai, & Lucca, 1988).

Individualistic team members tend to place their own needs first and maintain a more distinct sense of their individual identity. Individualism implies loose ties; individualists assume one is expected to look after oneself and one's immediate family but no one else (Hofstede, 1980). Team members with individualistic beliefs typically place their own needs above the needs of the group. For example, team members from individualistic cultures prefer direct confrontation when problems occur. Furthermore, individualistic team members are motivated by individual goals and individual incentives.

Collectivist team members place the needs of the group above their own needs and tend to derive their identity from the group (Triandis, 2000). Collectivism implies that people are integrated into strong, cohesive groups that protect them in exchange for loyalty to the group. Team members with collectivistic beliefs put group needs first. For example, because group identity is so strong, team members with collectivistic assumptions will find direct confrontation rude and may be embarrassed by blunt feedback. In addition, collectivistic team members are motivated by group goals and group incentives.

The individualism–collectivism construct has important implications for teamwork. For example, collectivistic individuals often perform better when responsibility for performance and products is placed at the group level and rewards are structured to reflect this collective contribution. In contrast, team members who are individualistic will perform more effectively when they are solely responsible for their work and are rewarded as such (Markus & Kitayama, 1991). Team member assumptions related to individualism–collectivism also affect the decision-making process at the individual, team, and organizational levels. The next three subsections adopt a relational demography approach to describe how intrateam differences in the assumptions underlying individualism–collectivism can affect decision making at multiple levels.

Individualism–Collectivism and Individual Decision Making
When team members and team leaders have differing individualist–collectivistic cultural dimensions, divergent views can emerge regarding the best way to make decisions. A number of explanations can be advanced for the divergent views between these two factions about the best decision, but the one most relevant to this discussion is the differences in their underlying beliefs about to whom they are most responsible. When team members are highly individualistic, their first priority is to their own performance, reputation, and career. In contrast to highly individualistic team members, their highly collectivistic counterparts have an allegiance to the larger collective, which in the current discussion consists of the team and its employing organization.

The differences in the assumptions made by these two groups can lead them to provide different types of input to a team leader charged with making a decision. For example, if team members are asked to provide input into a decision about the continued allocation of funds to a project that is likely never to reach fruition, individualists may have a more difficult time admitting the embarrassing truth – namely, that some fundamental problems exist that are not likely rectifiable. Such individualistic team members will be driven to a greater extent than their collectivistic colleagues to save face in the situation.

This example leads to a proposition about the effects of individualism–collectivism on team member decision making in distributed environments

> **Proposition 12.** When a distributed team of highly individualistic members is directed by a collectivistic leader, the leader must be aware that the decision input provided by his or her team members may reflect a means to achieving their own goals as much as it does a means for achieving the team's goals.

Individual-Collectivism and Team Decision Making

The pattern of individualism–collectivism within a team also has implications for team decision making as it is conceptualized by the team mind theory. As previously noted, the metaphor of the team mind has been used to explain four properties of expert team decision making: team competencies, team identity, team cognition, and team meta-cognition (Klein et al., 1993; Klein, 1998). The individualism–collectivism construct is important to the development and perpetuation of the second of these four properties – team identity – because it describes a preference for thinking in terms of the group (i.e., collectivism) or the individual (i.e., individualism) (Triandis et al., 1988).

Team identity is the degree to which individual members adopt the goals of the team as their own and view themselves as part of a unified whole. Expert teams have a sense of themselves as a collective rather than as just an aggregation of individuals doing related work. This feeling of belonging to the team is likely to be further reinforced to the degree that team members are collectivistic – that is, depending on how they value and believe in the group as a source of personal identity. In turn, this sense of connection between a team member and his or her team can curtail the deliberation of response alternatives, thereby reducing decision latency by facilitating intuitive decision making (Kline, 2005).

This line of thinking leads to a proposition about the effects of individualism–collectivism on team decision making in distributed environments

> **Proposition 13.** To the degree a team member is an individualist, he or she will not be as likely to have developed a team identity and thus will take longer both to consider response alternatives in light of team goals and to

make decisions in support of team goals, relative to his or her collectivistic teammates.

Individualism–Collectivism and Organizational Decision Making
Both individualistic and collectivistic beliefs, values, and assumptions can affect policy making, a form of organizational decision making from the prescriptive paradigm of decision making. This section presents examples intended to illuminate how the individualism–collectivism construct affects the policies set to govern distributed teams and how those policies are likely to be interpreted by distributed team members who are either similar or different with respect to the policy maker's assumptions about the priority of one's collectives.

A team leader's individualistic or collectivistic beliefs are likely to affect organizational decision making because a leader often works as a representative of the organization to set policies that can be used repeatedly during the course of business operations. For example, individualistic leaders would favor policies that promote individual performance and individual rewards within the organization. Therefore, a policy structured by an individualistic leader would tend to emphasize personal responsibility. Such a policy would be welcomed by the leader's like-minded team members and subordinates. Conversely, the leader's collectivistic teammates and subordinates would likely feel uncomfortable with the emphasis placed on individual accolades.

In contrast, collectivistic leaders would tend to enact policies that would take the individual emphasis out of organizational operations. For example, rewards would be structured around team performance, with individual praise or punishment being limited. In relation to other incumbents, collectivistic team members would feel most comfortable and would likely be most productive while applying these policies. Unfortunately, individual team members would likely seek ways to distinguish themselves from their teammates and gain credit for their individual accomplishments. Ultimately, individualists would likely find shortcuts around these policies because they reject the premises upon which they are built.

Both of these examples depict situations in which the cultural assumptions of the team leader conflict with the assumptions made by that leader's team members as well as the beliefs of other members of the organization. In the short term, this conflict could lead to disharmony, with some team members emphasizing individual goals while others emphasize collective goals. In the long run, disagreements about organizational policies that are fueled by disparate intrateam assumptions about the priority of the collective could serve to impair both team and organizational viability.

Proposition 14. Disparate intrateam assumptions about the priority of one's collectives can have deleterious effects on organizational decision making and ultimately organizational and team viability because members will operate from different worldviews when setting and interpreting policy.

PRACTICAL IMPLICATIONS

Throughout this chapter, we have noted that distributed performance arrangements are a double-edged sword: While distributed teamwork has many inherent benefits, it also results in challenges for team staffing (Harvey, Novicevic, & Garrison, 2004), selection (Aguinis, Henle, & Beaty, 2001), leadership (Cascio & Shurygailo, 2002), performance measurement (Dwyer, Oser, Salas, & Fowlkes, 1999), and information visualization (Bryson, 2002). The previous sections also addressed some of the many important implications that distribution and demography hold for individual, team, and organizational decision making.

All of this discussion raises the question of what can be done to facilitate the decision-making performance of distributed, multicultural team members and teams. This section begins to answer this question by advancing a three-pronged approach to facilitating distributed team member and team performance. This approach is grounded in the use of team leadership, training, and technology as means to secure a sustainable competitive advantage via the use of distributed teams. Prior to launching into a full discussion of this approach, however, an example is offered from an incumbent of a *Fortune* 500 organization that uses distributed teams as part of its ongoing operations. The situation described here depicts the complexity of distributed teamwork and underscores the importance of intervening with team leadership, training, and technology:

> I am a member of a distributed team [that includes] negotiators, lawyers, IT staff, and psychologists. The purpose of this particular team is to negotiate with vendors in order to secure the best deal on their products and services for our organization. For example, we have geographically dispersed team members researching information on the fly and communicating it to the lead negotiator immediately. This process involves taking information gathered from an exchange with a vendor, researching it immediately on the Web or internally, communicating our findings via technology-generated notes and

graphical illustrations to the entire team on the call, coming to a quick agreement, and then feeding pertinent information to our lead negotiator. This process is very advantageous when negotiating with vendors whose team members are not in the same location and or who may not have the technology to communicate like we do.

Team Leadership

Team leaders can serve to enhance distributed team decision making by establishing the conditions that contribute to team effectiveness (Hackman, 2002; Salas, Stagl, & Burke, in press). Moreover, team leaders facilitate distributed decision making by structuring, regulating, and developing team processes and products.

For example, it has been argued that team leaders contribute to distributed team performance by influencing five team member and team processes: (1) motivational, (2) affective, (3) cognitive, (4) coordination, and (5) boundary spanning (see Zaccaro, Ardison, & Orvis, 2004; Zaccaro, Rittman, & Marks, 2001). Team leaders influence motivational processes by affecting the volitional choices of team members, such as the choice to put forth task-related effort, the amount of effort to expend, and the persistence of that effort over time. Team leaders influence affective processes by soliciting and modulating the expression of emotion and affect displayed by distributed team members. Team leaders influence cognitive processes and emergent cognitive states by facilitating collective information processing and the generation of shared or compatible knowledge structures. Team leaders influence coordination by integrating and synchronizing distributed team members' contributions to task activities. Team leaders influence boundary-spanning processes by empowering, enabling, and encouraging distributed team members to scan their performance environment for contextual changes that can potentially influence, or have already influenced, the team's objectives.

Leaders of distributed teams can influence these team members – and team-level processes, and thereby contribute to distributed team decision making, by engaging in functional behaviors and enacting functional roles. This line of thinking flows from the functional theory of leadership. The guiding philosophy of the functional approach to leadership is that a team leader's primary responsibility is to "do, or get done, whatever is not being adequately handled for group needs" (McGrath, 1962, p. 5). This philosophy has been espoused by many historically notable team leaders, including *Apollo* 13 Flight Director Eugene Kranz and four-time Super Bowl – winning Pittsburgh Steelers head coach Chuck Noll.

The functional approach to team leadership suggests that team leaders engage in four broad classes of behavior: (1) information search and structuring, (2) information use in problem solving, (3) managing personnel resources, and (4) managing material resources. For example, leaders of distributed teams search for, identify, structure, and use information during a process of sense making and sense giving (see Burke, Salas, Stagl, & Fowlkes, 2002; Weick, 1996). Specifically, team leaders can provide distributed team members with situation updates during periods of high task intensity, thereby priming members to remain cognizant of shared goal strategies and role linkages when making decisions. Another aspect of functional leadership, managing personnel resources, will be expounded upon in the next subsection of this chapter on training.

Distributed team leaders engage in these behaviors while filling functional roles. A plethora of different conceptualizations exist about the roles distributed team leaders adopt. For example, it has been suggested that distributed team leaders can adopt three roles: (1) team liaison, (2) team direction setter, and (3) team operational coordinator (Zaccaro & Bader, 2003). Moreover, research results suggest that the most important role a leader of a globally distributed team can fill is that of mentor (Kayworth & Leidner, 2002).

While intriguing, many of the roles advanced as important to distributed team leadership can be organized around two broad functional roles: task and developmental (see Kozlowski, Gully, McHugh, Salas, & Cannon-Bowers, 1996; Salas, Burke, & Stagl, 2004). The task role is filled when distributed team leaders set and monitor goals, strategies, and role expectations so as to foster the conditions necessary for effective distributed decision making. By contrast, the developmental role is filled by leaders when they act to build or recreate shared cognition, affect, and behavior (i.e., team coherence). In fact, recent meta-analytic findings support the importance of these two roles for facilitating behaviorally based team performance outcomes such as the number of decisions made correctly and overall decision latency (Burke et al., in press).

Training and Development

Creating an expert decision-making team is not as simple as assembling a team of expert decision makers (see Salas, Cannon-Bowers, Rhodenizer, & Bowers, 1999). Developing team members and teams and their decision-making processes so as to facilitate distributive performance in dynamic, complex contexts is a process wrought with challenges. At a broad level, developing distributed team members and teams consists of creating and sustaining change. Three pillars – formal training, operational assignments, and self-development – serve as enablers of this ongoing change process whereby decision-making skill is developed.

Distributed teams and their members participating in formal training, operational assignments, or self-development activities experience growth in the form of differentiation from and integration with their team and other systems of operation in which they are embedded. Specifically, distributed team members "at higher levels of development are able to use a greater number of knowledge principles to construct their experiences (differentiation), make more interconnections among these principles (integration), resulting in a broader perspective" (Day & Lance, 2004, p. 3). The growth that occurs as a result of participation in developmental activities can be framed in terms of increases in cognitive, social, or behavioral complexity. Therefore, a training program would be considered effective if participants engaged in more sophisticated decision making (i.e., behavioral complexity) because of their instructional experience.

This subsection describes some of the aspects of formal training, one of the three pillars that support the development of distributed team member and team decision making. Prior to launching into a discussion of formal training, however, another example is offered. It was provided by an incumbent of a *Fortune* 500 company that regularly conducts training. This example illustrates how large organizations can leverage advancements in technology to conduct distributed training of distributed team members and teams

> I often deliver training from here in the United States to focal points in China, Japan, India, Australia, and Singapore about the use of our selection tests. These sessions are Web-based conferences where the view of my laptop is displayed on the PC screens of focal points in different countries. These Web-based conferences are augmented by audio conferencing meeting rooms and other technology. For example, I often post private notes to trainees, highlight examples, and chat via Lotus Sametime. We also have a library of Webcasts and online training where trainees can access conferences or past training sessions; the information is at the trainee's fingertips and is on-demand.

Formal Training

Formal training is the cornerstone of team member and team development. While programs vary widely in terms of their content, tools, and methods, most involve some combination of off-site educational opportunity followed by sporadic on-site follow-up. Organizations often use formal training to develop the decision-making skills of their teams and team members. This consideration is particularly important when employees are distributed in space and time, as additional challenges are likely to be faced by teams in this environment. In the text that follows, three applications of formal training to develop decision-making skills are discussed.

One computer-based simulation that can be used to deliver decision-making training to distributed teams and team members is the Distributed Dynamic Decision-Making (DDD) game (Kleinmann & Serfaty, 1989). DDD is a flexible platform that can be programmed to present a variety of synthetic task environments that typify military command and control operations. In DDD III, the most recent iteration, trainees act as decision makers who interpret, assign meaning to, and allocate resources in response to evolving situations that are typically encountered in stability and support operations (SASO). Effective decision making in a SASO consists of allocating appropriate information-gathering resources in a timely manner.

Another example of decision-making training for distributed team members was described by Kirkman and colleagues (2002), who conducted extensive interviews with incumbents of Sabre, Inc. Sabre uses 15 training modules delivered by CD-ROM. The modules consist of exercises and scenarios intended to deliver training to the firm's distributed teams and their members. These modules require trainees to practice making a wide range of decisions, such as those typically involved in establishing a team charter, managing a meeting, engaging in conflict resolution, and selecting new team members.

A third approach to enhancing distributed team member decision making is to design instructional strategies that target the development of critical thinking skills (Cohen, Thompson, Adelman, Bresnick, & Riedel, 1999). An example of this approach is a CD-ROM-based training program that focuses on the thought processes that facilitate expert decision making. The purpose of this training is to augment critical thinking among distributed team members, which in turn enables the team members to better balance the need for initiative against the risks associated with reducing coordination in ambiguous situations. Evidence suggests that trainees who participated in this training more often developed contingency plans, used a proactive time orientation, and recognized the strategic implications of their tactical decisions (Cohen & Adelman, 2002).

Information Technology

In addition to team leadership and training serving as enablers of distributed decision making, the decision processes and outcomes of teams and team members can be enhanced via the use of information technology. A few established and emerging information technologies used as means to facilitate decision making at a distance will be described here.

Perhaps the most frequently used technology to communicate across geographical divides is audio conferencing. Audio conferencing provides a cost-efficient and effective means to engaging in synchronous communication. In fact, research results suggest synchronous communication is better for complex tasks such as those involving decision making than asynchronous modalities are (Farmer & Hyatt, 1994; Hollingshead, McGrath, & O'Connor, 1993).

The most widely used form of asynchronous communication in distributed teams is e-mail. Other forms of asynchronous communication include voicemail, pages, postal mail, bulletin board messages, and team calendars. While these modes of communication are also cost-efficient, they may not be practically viable for making important decisions, a series of decisions, or decisions that must be made in a short time frame. Moreover, when the decision-making process is complex, as is often the case in globally distributed teams, asynchronous forms of communication will result in process losses (Bell & Kozlowski, 2002).

While the previously mentioned information technologies are certainly useful, recent products have combined their varying functionality into unified collaborative technologies. For example, IBM's Lotus Workplace Team Collaboration platform combines instant messaging, presence awareness, a team library, discussion forums, and Web conferencing into a single package that can be used by distributed team members to engage in real-time decision making (www.ibm.com). Microsoft recently introduced a similar product called the Team Collaboration Tool for use by Intel to help its globally distributed product development teams make more effective decisions during the product development life cycle (www.microsoft.com). This product is touted as a means of helping to improve product development while decreasing time to market.

TAKE-AWAY POINTS

While far from exhaustive, these key take-away points quickly summarize the research presented in this chapter, which addressed some of the effects of distribution and demography for individual, team, and organizational decision making.

Change Happens

Emerging markets, growing international and domestic competition, rapid technological development, and increasing consumer wealth are all driving today's global economy. Institutions of all sizes are changing their strategy, structure, and systems in response to the realities of operating in the global marketplace. One manifestation of this continuing transformation is evident in the use of teams as a means to structure work. Teammates can now coordinate their activities at varying times or locations from the same or different office complex, metropolis, city, time zone, country, continent, or planet. In fact, 20% of the total domestic workforce engages in distributive performance on a monthly basis.

Adaptations are Imperfect

Distributed teams are conceptualized as a performance arrangement used by organizational stakeholders to structure interdependent interactions between team members who are in different geographical or temporal locations. Unfortunately, distributed team performance is a double-edged sword: While distribution offers humanitarian and utilitarian benefits, it also introduces a host of challenges to team members, teams, and the organizations in which they are embedded. Both the advantages and the disadvantages associated with the use of distributed teams must be taken into account, because – like all interventions – it must result in a return on investment.

The Crux of the Problem

The use of distributed performance arrangements results in a distributed coordination space in which interdependent interactions can occur almost anytime and anywhere. Multicultural distributed team members, however, face an increased level of abstraction, ambiguity, or team opacity; therefore, distribution affects how team members send, receive, interpret, and react to information. Because distribution affects how team members process, exchange, and act on information, it also influences how team members and teams make decisions. Illuminating and understanding the effects of distribution on decision-making processes and outcomes is essential to the design of technological collaborative environments and to the management of distributed teams.

The Quest Continues

The effects of distribution on decision making must be studied from both a prescriptive lens (i.e., how team members and teams *should* make decisions) and a descriptive lens (i.e., how team members and teams *do* make decisions). Descriptive research seeks to develop models of decision making based on observations of expert decision makers facing real problems in fluid environments. Prescriptive research attempts to explain human decision making in terms of deviations from optimal mathematical models. Similarly, a relational demography approach can be used to describe how intrateam differences in the assumptions underlying cultural dimensions such as power distance and individualism–collectivism affect decision making at multiple levels in the conceptual space.

CONCLUSION

This multi-level review was undertaken to advance the collective understanding about distributed team performance by addressing some of the inherent benefits and challenges to the use of this performance arrangement. This chapter examined some of the more pressing implications of distribution for individual, team, and organizational decision making. Moreover, given that distributed teams are increasingly used by multinational organizations to provide continuous service and production capability, the implications of cultural demography for individual, team, and organizational decision making were highlighted. Practical implications of the issues raised by this review were advanced. Ideally, this review will provide a platform from which to construct more contextualized models of decision making that jointly consider the effects of distribution and demography for decision making.

ACKNOWLEDGMENTS

The views, opinions, and findings contained in this chapter are those of the authors and should not be construed as an official Department of the Army or Department of the Navy position or policy. This work was supported by funding from the U.S. Army Research Institute for the Behavioral and Social Sciences (Contract #W74V8H-05-C-0030). We would also like to thank Damon Bryant, Francis Yammarino, and Fred Dansereau for their insightful comments on an earlier version of this work.

REFERENCES

Adelman, L., Bresnick, T., Black, P. K., Marvin, F. F., & Sak, S. G. (1996). Research with patriot air defense officers: Examining information order effects. *Human Factors, 38*, 250–262.

Adelman, L., Bresnick, T. A., Christian, M., Gualtieri, J., & Minionis, D. (1997). Demonstrating the effect of context on order effects for an army air defense task using the patriot simulator. *Journal of Behavioral Decision Making, 10*, 327–342.

Adelman, L., Cohen, M. S., Bresnick, T. A., Chinnis, J. O., & Laskey, K. B. (1993). Real-time expert system interfaces, cognitive processes, and task performance: An empirical assessment. *Human Factors, 35*(2), 243–261.

Aguinis, H., Henle, C. A., & Beaty, J. C. (2001). Virtual reality technology: A new tool for personnel selection. *International Journal of Selection and Assessment, 9*, 70–83.

Alge, B. J., Weithoff, C., & Klein, H. J. (2003). When does the medium matter? Knowledge-building experiences and opportunities in decision-making teams. *Organizational Behavior and Human Decision Processes, 91*, 26–38.

Avolio, B. J., Kahai, S., Dumdum, R., & Sivasubramaniam, N. (2001). Virtual teams: Implications for e-leadership and team development. In: M. London (Ed.), *How people evaluate others in organizations* (pp. 337–358). Mahwah, NJ: Lawrence Erlbaum Associates.

Baltes, B. B., Dickson, M. W., Sherman, M. P., Bauer, C. C., & LaGanke, J. (2002). Computer-mediated communication and group decision making: A meta-analysis. *Organizational Behavior and Human Decision Processes, 87*, 156–179.

Beach, L. R. (1997). *The psychology of decision making: People in organizations.* Thousand Oaks, CA: Sage.

Beach, L. R., Chi, M., Klein, G., Smith, P., & Vicente, K. (1997). Naturalistic decision making and related research lines. In: C. E. Zsambok & G. Klein (Eds), *Naturalistic decision making* (pp. 19–36). Mahwah, NJ: Lawrence Erlbaum Associates.

Bell, B. S., & Kozlowski, S. W. J. (2002). A typology of virtual teams: Implications for effective leadership. *Group and Organization Management, 27*, 14–49.

Bennis, W. (1999). *The leadership advantage: Leader to leader.* San Francisco, CA: Jossey-Bass.

Beroggi, G. E. G., & Wallace, W. A. (1997). *Computer supported risk management.* Dordrecht: Kluwer Academic Publishers.

Bolstad, C. A., & Endsley, M. R. (1999). Shared mental models and shared displays: An empirical evaluation of team performance. Paper presented at the Human Factors and Ergonomics Society 43rd Annual Meeting.

Brehmer, B. (1990). Strategies in real-time, dynamic decision making. In: R. M. Hogarth (Ed.), *Insights in decision making: A tribute to Hillel J. Einhorn* (pp. 262–279). Chicago, IL: University of Chicago Press.

Brehmer, B. (1992). Dynamic decision making: Human control of complex systems. *Acta Psychologica, 81*(3), 211–241.

Brehmer, B. (1996). Man as a stabilizer of systems: From static snapshots of judgment processes to dynamic decision making. *Thinking and Reasoning, 2*(2–3), 225–238.

Bryson, S. (2002). Information visualization in virtual environments. In: K. M. Stanney (Ed.), *Handbook of virtual environments.* Mahwah, NJ: Lawrence Erlbaum Associates.

Burke, C. S., Salas, E., Stagl, K. C., & Fowlkes, J. E. (2002). Leading multi-national teams. In: J. C. Ziegert & K. J. Klein (Co-chairs), *Team leadership: Current theoretical and research perspectives.* Symposium conducted at the 17th annual conference for the Society for Industrial and Organizational Psychology.

Burke, C. S., Stagl, K. C., Klein, C., Goodwin, G. F., Salas, E., & Halpin, S. M. (in press). Does leadership in teams matter? A meta-analytic integration. *Leadership Quarterly.*

Burns, K. (2005). Mental models and normal errors. In: H. Montgomery, R. Lipshitz & B. Brehmer (Eds), *How professionals make decisions* (pp. 15–28). Mahwah, NJ: Lawrence Erlbaum Associates.

Cannon-Bowers, J., Salas, E., & Converse, S. (1993). Shared mental models in expert team decision making. In: N. J. Castellna, Jr. (Ed.), *Individual and group decision making: Current issues* (pp. 221–246). Hillsdale, NJ: Lawrence Erlbaum Associates.

Cannon-Bowers, J. A., Salas, E., & Pruitt, J. S. (1996). Establishing the boundaries of a paradigm for decision-making research. *Human Factors, 38,* 193–205.

Cannon-Bowers, J. A., Tannenbaum, S. I., Salas, E., & Volpe, C. E. (1995). Defining competencies and establishing team training requirements. In: R. Guzzo & E. Salas (Eds), *Team effectiveness and decision-making in organizations.* San Francisco, CA: Jossey-Bass.

Cascio, W. F., & Shurygailo, S. (2002). E-leadership and virtual teams. *Organizational Dynamics, 31,* 362–376.

Cicourel, A. V. (1990). The integration of distributed knowledge in collaborative medical diagnosis. In: J. Galegher, R. E. Kraut & C. Egido (Eds), *Intellectual teamwork: Social and technological foundations of cooperative work* (pp. 221–242). Hillsdale, NJ: Lawrence Erlbaum Associates.

Cohen, M. S., & Adelman, L. (2002). Training critical thinking to enhance battlefield initiative. *Proceedings of the Human Factors and Ergonomics Society, 46th Annual Meeting.* Human Factors Society, Santa Monica, CA.

Cohen, M. S., Thompson, B. B., Adelman, L., Bresnick, T. A., & Riedel, S. L. (1999). *Training battlefield critical thinking and initiative. (Research # 2000–01).* Arlington, VA: Cognitive Tech.

Day, D. V., & Lance, C. E. (2004). Understanding the development of leadership complexity through latent growth modeling. In: D. Day, S. J. Zaccaro & S. M. Halpin (Eds), *Leader development for transforming organizations.* Mahwah, NJ: Lawrence Erlbaum Associates.

de Lisser, E. (1999). Update on small business: Firms with virtual environments appeal to workers. *Wall Street Journal,* June 2, p. B2.

Diehl, E., & Sterman, J. D. (1995). Effects of feedback complexity on dynamic decision making. *Organizational Behavior and Human Decision Processes, 62,* 198–215.

Dodd, C. H. (1991). *Dynamics of intercultural communication* (3rd ed.). Dubuque, IA: William C. Brown Publishers.

Driskell, J. E., Radtke, P. H., & Salas, E. (2003). Virtual teams: Effects of technological mediation on team processes. *Group Dynamics: Theory, Research, and Practice, 7,* 297–323.

Dwyer, D. J., Oser, R. L., Salas, E., & Fowlkes, J. E. (1999). Performance measurement in distributed environments: Initial results and implications for training. *Military Psychology, 11,* 189–215.

Edwards, W. (1962). Dynamic decision theory and probabilistic information processing. *Human Factors, 4,* 59–73.

Endsley, M. R. (1997). The role of situation awareness in naturalistic decision making. In: C. Zambock & G. Klein (Eds), *Naturalistic decision making* (pp. 269–284). Mahwah, NJ: Lawrence Erlbaum Associates.

Farmer, S. M., & Hyatt, C. W. (1994). Effects of task language demands and task complexity on computer-mediated work groups. *Small Group Research, 25*, 331–336.

Fiore, S. M., Salas, E., Cuevas, H. M., & Bowers, C. A. (2003). Distributed coordination space: Toward a theory of distributed team process and performance. *Theoretical Issues in Ergonomics, 4*, 340–364.

Gaspar, S. (2001). Virtual teams, real benefits. *Network World.* Retrieved December 22, 2002, from www.nwfusion.com/careers/2001/0924man.html

Gonzalez, C. (2005). Decision support for real-time, dynamic decision-making tasks. *Organizational Behavior and Human Decision Processes, 96*, 142–155.

Graham, J., Schneider, M., Bauer, A., Bessiere, K., & Gonzalez, C. (2004). Shared mental models in military command and control organizations: Effect of social network distance. Paper presented at the Human Factors and Ergonomics Society 48th Annual Meeting, New Orleans, LA.

Griffith, T. L., & Neale, M. A. (2001). Information processing in traditional, hybrid, and virtual teams: From nascent knowledge to transactive memory. In: R. Sutton & B. Staw (Eds), *Research in organizational behavior* (Vol. 23). Stamford, CT: JAI Press.

Guzzo, R. A., & Dickson, M. W. (1996). Teams in organizations: Recent research on performance and effectiveness. *Annual Review of Psychology, 47*, 307–338.

Hackman, J. R. (2002). *Leading teams: Setting the stage for great performances.* Boston: HBS Press.

Harback, H. F., & Keller, U. H. (1995). Learning leader XXI. *Military Review, 75*, 30–37.

Harrison, D. A., Price, K. H., & Bell, M. P. (1998). Beyond relational demography: Time and the effects of surface- and deep-level diversity on work group cohesion. *Academy of Management Journal, 41*, 96–107.

Harrison, D. A., Price, K. H., Gavin, J. H., & Florey, A. T. (2002). Time, teams, and task performance: Changing effects of surface- and deep-level diversity on group functioning. *Academy of Management Journal, 45*, 1029–1045.

Harvey, M., Novicevic, M., & Garrison, G. (2004). Challenges to staffing global virtual teams. *Human Resource Management Review, 14*, 275–294.

Helmreich, R. L. (2000). Culture and error in space: Implications from analog environments. *Aviation, Space, & Environmental Medicine, 71*(Sept.), A133–A139.

Hertel, G., Geister, S., & Konradt, U. (2005). Managing virtual teams: A review of current empirical research. *Human Resource Management Review, 15*, 69–95.

Hofstede, G. (1980). *Culture's consequences: International differences in work related values.* Beverly Hills, CA: Sage Publications.

Hollenbeck, J. R., Colquitt, J. A., Ilgen, D. R., LePine, J. A., & Hedlund, J. (1998a). Accuracy decomposition and team decision making: Testing theoretical boundary conditions. *Journal of Applied Psychology, 83*(3), 494–500.

Hollenbeck, J. R., Ilgen, D. R., LePine, J. A., Colquitt, J. A., & Hedlund, J. (1998b). Extending the multi-level theory of team decision making: Effects of feedback and experience in hierarchical teams. *Academy of Management Journal, 41*(3), 269–282.

Hollenbeck, J. R., Ilgen, D. R., Sego, D. J., Hedlund, J., Major, D. A., & Phillips, J. (1995). Multi-level theory of team decision making: Decision performance in teams incorporating distributed expertise. *Journal of Applied Psychology, 80*, 292–316.

Hollingshead, A. B., & McGrath, J. E. (1995). Computer-assisted groups. In: R. A. Guzzo, E. Salas & Associates (Eds), *Team effectiveness and decision-making in organizations* (pp. 46–78). San Francisco, CA: Jossey-Bass.

Hollingshead, A. B., McGrath, J. E., & O'Connor, K. M. (1993). Group task performance and communication technology: A longitudinal study of computer-mediated versus face-to-face work groups. *Small Group Research, 24*, 307–333.

Ilgen, D. R., Major, D. A., Hollenbeck, J. R., & Sego, D. J. (1993). Team research in the 1990s. In: M. M. Chemers & R. Ayman (Eds), *Leadership theory and research: Perspectives and directions* (pp. 245–269). San Diego, CA: Academic Press.

International Telework Association and Council. (2004). ITAC press release. Retrieved July 17, 2005.

Jarvenpaa, S. L., & Leidner, D. E. (1999). Communication and trust in global virtual teams. *Organization Science, 10*, 791–815.

Jensen, E., & Brehmer, B. (2003). Understanding and control of a simple dynamic system. *System Dynamics Review, 19*, 119.

Kahai, S. S., Sosik, J. J., & Avolio, B. J. (2003). Effects of leadership style, anonymity, and rewards on creativity-relevant processes and outcomes in an electronic meeting system context. *Leadership Quarterly, 14*, 499–524.

Kanawattanachai, P., & Yoo, Y. (2002). Dynamic nature of trust in virtual teams. *Journal of Strategic Information Systems, 11*, 187–213.

Kayworth, T. R., & Leidner, D. E. (2002). Leadership effectiveness in global virtual teams. *Journal of Management Information Systems, 18*, 7–40.

Kirkman, B. L., Rosen, B., Gibson, C. B., Tesluk, P. E., & McPherson, S. (2002). Five challenges to virtual team success: Lessons from Sabre, Inc. *Academy of Management Executive, 16*, 67–79.

Kirlik, A., Walker, N., Fisk, A. D., & Nagel, K. (1996). Supporting perception in the service of dynamic decision making. *Human Factors, 38*, 288–299.

Klein, G. (1993). A recognition primed decision (RPD) model of rapid decision making. In: G. Klein, J. Orasanu, R. Calderwood & C. E. Zsambok (Eds), *Decision making in action* (pp. 138–147). Norwood, NJ: Ablex.

Klein, G. (1997). The recognition-primed decision (RPD) model: Looking back, looking forward. In: C. E. Zsambok & G. Klein (Eds), *Naturalistic decision making* (pp. 285–292). Mahwah, NJ: Lawrence Erlbaum Associates.

Klein, G. (1998). *Sources of power: How people make decisions.* Cambridge, MA: MIT Press.

Klein, G., Zsambok, C. E., & Thordsen, M. L. (1993). Team decision training: Five myths and a model. *Military Review, 7*(April), 36–42.

Kleinmann, D. L., & Serfaty, D. (1989). Team performance assessment in distributed decision-making. Paper presented at the Simulation and Training Research Symposium on Interactive Networked Simulation for Training, Orlando, FL.

Kline, D. A. (2005). Intuitive team decision making. In: H. Montgomery, R. Lipshitz & B. Brehmer (Eds), *How professionals make decisions* (pp. 171–182). Mahwah, NJ: Lawrence Erlbaum Associates.

Kozlowski, S. W. J., Gully, S. M., McHugh, P. P., Salas, E., & Cannon-Bowers, J. A. (1996). A dynamic theory of leadership and team effectiveness: Developmental and task contingent leader roles. In: G. R. Ferris (Ed.), *Research in personnel and human resources management* (Vol. 14, pp. 253–305). Greenwich, CT: JAI Press.

LePine, J. A., Hollenbeck, J. R., Ilgen, D. R., & Hedlund, J. (1997). Effects of individual differences on the performance of hierarchical decision making teams: Much more than g. *Journal of Applied Psychology, 82*, 803–811.

Levenson, A., & Cohen, S. G. (2003). Meeting the performance challenge: Calculating ROI for virtual teams. In: C. B. Gibson & S. G. Cohen (Eds), *Virtual teams that work: Creating the conditions for virtual team effectiveness* (pp. 213–259). San Francisco, CA: Jossey-Bass.

Lewin, K. (1951). *Field theory in social science.* New York: Harper & Row.

Libby, R., Trotman, K. T., & Zimmer, I. (1987). Member variation, recognition of expertise, and group performance. *Journal of Applied Psychology, 72,* 81–87.

Lipshitz, R., & Ben Shaul, O. (1997). Schemata and mental models in recognition-primed decision making. In: C. E. Zsambok & G. Klein (Eds), *Naturalistic decision making* (pp. 293–303). Hillsdale, NJ: Lawrence Erlbaum Associates.

Lipshitz, R., Klein, G., Orasanu, J., & Salas, E. (2001). Taking stock of naturalistic decision making. *Journal of Behavioral Decision Making, 14,* 331–352.

Lynn, G., & Reilly, R. (2002). How to build a blockbuster. *Harvard Business Review, 80,* 18–19.

Markus, H., & Kitayama, S. (1991). Culture and the self: Implications for cognition, emotion, and motivation. *Psychological Review, 98,* 224–253.

Martins, L. L., Gilson, L. L., & Maynard, M. T. (2004). Virtual teams: What do we know and where to we go from here? *Journal of Management, 30,* 805–835.

McGrath, J. E. (1962). *Leadership behavior: Requirements for leadership training.* Prepared for U.S. Civil Service Commission Office of Career Development, Washington, DC.

McLeod, P. L. (1992). An assessment of the experimental literature on electronic support of group work: Results of a meta-analysis. *Human–Computer Interaction, 7,* 257–280.

Mellers, B. A., Schwartz, A., & Cooke, D. J. (1998). Judgment and decision making. *Annual Review of Psychology, 49,* 447–477.

Merriam-Webster. (2005). Merriam-Webster's Online Dictionary. Retrieved July 17.

Moon, Y. (1999). The effects of physical distance and response latency on persuasion in computer-mediated communication and human–computer communication. *Journal of Experimental and Human–Computer Communication, 5,* 379–392.

Mullen, B., & Cooper, C. (1994). The relation between group cohesiveness and performance: An integration. *Psychological Bulletin, 115,* 210–227.

Nygren, T. E. (1997). Framing of task performance strategies: Effects on performance in a multiattribute dynamic decision making environment. *Human Factors, 39,* 425–437.

Orasanu, J. (1990). *Shared mental models and crew decision making* (no. 46). Princeton, NJ: Princeton University, Cognitive Science Laboratory.

Orasanu, J. (1994). Shared problem models and flight crew performance. In: N. Johnston, N. McDonald & R. Fuller (Eds), *Aviation psychology in practice* (pp. 255–285). Brookfield, VT: Ashgate.

Orasanu, J., & Connolly, T. (1993). The reinvention of decision making. In: G. Klein, J. Orasanu, R. Calderwood & C. E. Zsambok (Eds), *Decision making in action: Models and methods* (pp. 3–20). Norwood, CT: Ablex.

Payne, J. W., Bettman, J. R., & Johnson, E. J. (1992). Behavioral decision research: A constructive processing perspective. *Annual Review of Psychology, 43,* 87–131.

Perrin, B. M., Barnett, B. J., & Walrath, L. (2001). Information order and outcome framing: An assessment of judgment bias in a naturalistic decision-making context. *Human Factors, 43,* 227–238.

Priest, H., Stagl, K. C., Klein, C., Salas, E., Burke, C. S. (2006). Virtual teams: Creating context for distributed teamwork. In: C. A. Bowers, E. Salas & F. Jentsch (Eds), *Creating high-tech teams: Practical guidance on work performance and technology.* Washington, DC: American Psychological Association.

Randel, J. M., Pugh, H. L., & Reed, S. K. (1996). Differences in expert and novice situation awareness in naturalistic decision making. *International Journal of Human–Computer Studies, 45,* 579–597.

Robert, C., Probst, T. M., Drasgow, F., Martocchio, J., & Lawler, J. (2000). Empowerment and continuous improvement in the U.S., Mexico, Poland, and India: Predicting fit on the basis of the dimensions of power distance and individualism. *Journal of Applied Psychology, 85,* 643–658.

Salas, E., Burke, C. S., Stagl, K. C. (2004). Developing teams and team leaders: Strategies and principles. In: D. Day, S. J. Zaccaro & S. M. Halpin (Eds), *Leader development for transforming organizations* (pp. 325–355). Mahwah, NJ: Lawrence Erlbaum Associates.

Salas, E., Cannon-Bowers, J. A., & Johnston, J. H. (1997). How can you turn a team of experts into an expert team? Emerging training strategies. In: C. E. Zsambok & G. Klein (Eds), *Naturalistic decision making* (pp. 359–370). Mahwah, NJ: Lawrence Erlbaum Associates.

Salas, E., Cannon-Bowers, J. A., Rhodenizer, L., & Bowers, C. A. (1999). Training in organizations: Myths, misconceptions, and mistaken assumptions. *Personnel and Human Resources Management, 17,* 123–161.

Salas, E., Dickinson, T. L., Converse, S. A., & Tannenbaum, S. I. (1992). Toward an understanding of team performance and training. In: R. W. Swezey & E. Salas (Eds), *Teams: Their training and performance* (pp. 3–29). Norwood, NJ: Ablex Publishing Corporation.

Salas, E., Stagl, K. C., & Burke, C. S. (2004). 25 years of team effectiveness in organizations: Research themes and emerging needs. In: C. L. Cooper & I. T. Robertson (Eds), *International review of industrial and organizational psychology.* New York: Wiley.

Salas, E., Stagl, K. C., & Burke, C. S. (in press). Best practices in team leadership: What team leaders do to facilitate team effectiveness. In: J. A. Conger & R. E. Riggio (Eds), *The practice of leadership.* New York: Wiley.

Salas, E., Stagl, K. C., Burke, C. S., & Goodwin, G. F. (in press). Fostering team effectiveness in organizations: Toward an integrative theoretical framework of team performance. In: J. W. Shuart, W. Spaulding & J. Poland, (Eds), *Modeling complex systems: Motivation, cognition and social processes, Nebraska Symposium on Motivation, 51.* Lincoln, NE: University of Nebraska Press.

Senge, P. M. (1990). *The fifth discipline: The art and practice of the learning organization.* New York: Doubleday Press.

Sengupta, K., & Abdel-Hamid, T. (1993). Alternative conceptions of feedback in dynamic environments: An experimental investigation. *Management Science, 39,* 411–428.

Smith, P. J., McCoy, C. E., & Orasanu, J. (2001). Distributed cooperative problem solving in the air traffic management system. In: E. Salas & G. Klein (Eds), *Linking expertise and naturalistic decision making* (pp. 367–382). Lawrence Mahwah, NJ: Erlbaum Associates.

Straus, S. G. (1997). Technology, group process, and group outcomes: Testing the connections in computer-mediated and face-to-face groups. *Human–Computer Interaction, 12,* 227–266.

Sundstrom, E., McIntyre, M., Halfhill, T., & Richards, H. (2000). Work groups: From the Hawthorne studies to work teams of the 1990s and beyond. *Group Dynamics, 4,* 44–67.

Thompson, L. F., & Coovert, M. D. (2006). Understanding and developing virtual computer-supported cooperative work teams. In: C. A. Bowers, E. Salas & F. Jentsch (Eds), *Creating high-tech teams: Practical guidance on work performance and technology.* Washington, DC: American Psychological Association.

Tolcott, M. A., Marvin, F. F., & Lehner, P. E. (1989). Expert decision making in evolving situations. *IEEE Transactions on Systems, Man and Cybernetics, 19,* 606–615.

Townsend, A. M., DeMarie, S. M., & Hendrickson, A. R. (1996). Are you ready for virtual teams? *HR Magazine, 41*(Sept.), 122–128.

Triandis, H. C. (2000). Culture and conflict. *International Journal of Psychology, 35*(2), 145–152.

Triandis, H. C., Bontempo, R., Villareal, M. J., Asai, M., & Lucca, N. (1988). Individualism and collectivism: Cross-cultural perspectives on self-ingroup relationships. *Journal of Personality and Social Psychology, 54*, 323–338.

Tsui, A. S., & Gutek, B. A. (1999). *Demographic differences in organizations: Current research and future directions.* New York: Lexington Books.

Tsui, A. S., & O'Reilly, C. (1989). Beyond simple demographic effects: The importance of relational demography in superior–subordinate dyads. *Academy of Management Journal, 32*, 402–423.

U.S. Department of Defense. (2000). Joint vision 2020. Retrieved July 17, 2005.

Warkentin, M. E., Sayeed, L., & Hightower, R. (1997). Virtual teams versus face-to-face teams: An exploratory study of a web-based conference system. *Decision Science, 28*, 975–996.

Weatherly, K. A., & Beach, L. R. (1998). Organizational culture and decision-making. In: L. R. Beach (Ed.), *Image theory: Theoretical and empirical foundations* (pp. 211–225). Mahwah, NJ: Lawrence Erlbaum Associates.

Weick, K. E. (1996). *Sensemaking in organizations.* Newbury Park, CA: Sage.

Zaccaro, S. J., Ardison, S. D., Orvis, K. L. (2004). Leadership in virtual teams. In: D. Day, S. J. Zaccaro & S. M. Halpin (Eds), *Leader development for transforming organizations* (pp. 267–292). Mahwah, NJ: Lawrence Erlbaum Associates.

Zaccaro, S. J., & Bader, P. (2003). E-leadership and the challenges of leading E-teams: Minimizing the bad and maximizing the good. *Organizational Dynamics, 31*, 377–387.

Zaccaro, S., Rittman, A., & Marks, M. (2001). Team leadership. *Leadership Quarterly, 12*, 1–34.

ISSUES IN DISTRIBUTED TEAM PERFORMANCE

Joseph A. Alutto

ABSTRACT

Stagl, Salas, Rosen, Priest, Burke, Goodwin, and Johnston review a series of factors determining the effectiveness of distributed team performance, thereby providing an effective overview of existing literature, particularly at the intrapersonal and interpersonal levels. Although the effort to provide guidelines for future research in the form of 14 propositions is less effective than might have been hoped, there is sufficient focus to suggest fruitful areas for future inquiry. The exploration of their work suggests that it would prove valuable to both scholars and practitioners if greater attention were concentrated on the interactive effects of distributed teams and organizational-level phenomena.

INTRODUCTION

Distributed teams are increasingly a fact of life for many organizations. While the forms of distribution and composition of such teams can vary considerably, some intrapersonal, interpersonal, and organizational-level factors consistently can and do affect the overall performance of such groups. This commentary highlights the considerable strengths found in the work of Stagl et al. (this volume). Their discussions of how intrapersonal

Multi-Level Issues in Organizations and Time
Research in Multi-Level Issues, Volume 6, 59–64
Copyright © 2007 by Elsevier Ltd.
All rights of reproduction in any form reserved
ISSN: 1475-9144/doi:10.1016/S1475-9144(07)06002-X

and interpersonal processes affect distributed team performance are extensive and organized in a fashion designed to guide future research. However, one mechanism selected to provide that guidance – namely, the formulation of propositions – is less effective than might be hoped, and the reasons for this shortcoming are discussed in this commentary. Finally, the effects of distributed group characteristics on a host of organizational-level processes remain to be explored, and this commentary makes an effort to identify some of these possible areas for future research.

SUBSTANTIVE ISSUES

To begin with, it is important to identify a bias that is undoubtedly reflected in this commentary. Given the focus of the work of Stagl, Salas, Rosen, Priest, Burke, Goodwin, and Johnston, it was reasonable to anticipate discussions of intrapersonal, interpersonal, organizational-level, and cultural-level factors critical to distributed team functioning. The intrapersonal, interpersonal, and, to some extent, cultural contexts critical to distributed team effectiveness were, indeed, carefully addressed. Nevertheless, their work appeared to lack a focus on organizational-level issues. The implications of how diversity in distributed team composition – whether in terms of mental maps, perceived expertise of members, opacity of groups, or means – can affect organizational structure and internal processing, as well as how those and other organizational-level phenomena can affect distributed team performance are dealt with only incidentally. Yet, implicit in the focus on distributed teams is the question of how such modes of interaction affect and are, in turn, affected by organizational structure and function. Thus, from at least this one perspective, the absence of adequate discussion of such issues can be seen as limiting the impact of their work.

Clearly, distributed team performance has become an increasingly important element in overall organizational effectiveness. As noted by Stagl et al., this trend has been driven by technological advances and the growth in globalization in operations for both business and public sector organizations. One might add that the expansion of service-centric firms relative to product-centric firms has generated increased interest in distributed team performance. Product-centric firms tend to have an internal *centralization dynamic* that leads to developing colocated teams for problem solving. By contrast, service-centric firms by their very nature tend to be driven by a *decentralization dynamic*, with service delivery being localized and human resources being distributed to the point of sale. As a result, for service-centric firms, growth usually means that the issue of managing distributed teams becomes increasingly complex and is critical to overall organizational effectiveness.

Thus, it is both timely and valuable that Stagl et al. provide a very effective review of the issues involved in determining the effectiveness of distributed team performance. These authors clearly and effectively identify a number of factors that must be considered in assessing the potential of distributed groups to operate effectively. They note that in reality most decision-making groups consist of both colocated and distributed members. Yet, because most existing research focuses on "pure cases," they are then unable to deal with this reality in developing propositions designed to assist in future research and practice, a limitation they clearly identify.

PROPOSITIONS AS A GUIDE FOR FUTURE INQUIRY

One strength of the approach used by Stagl et al. is that after reviewing the relevant research, they develop 14 propositions that could be used as guidelines for creating and enhancing the effectiveness of groups with distributed members. However, the authors do not provide propositional forms for a number of research directions they identify as being worthy of further assessment. For example, in discussing the economic consequences of distributed workgroups, the authors point out that eliminating the need for colocation tends to reduce the economic costs of group operation by limiting the need for real estate, travel, stress reduction, and other support costs associated with keeping people meeting at a common location. They even provide vivid examples using Lenovo and IBM as mini-cases. Given the move to service-centric activities by many firms, it would have proven valuable if they had put forward a proposition that asserted a testable hypothesis, such as "The cost of operations for distributed workteams is lower than that for colocated teams working on identical or similar problems." They chose not do so, even though the development of explicit propositions is one of the goals adopted by the authors.

While the authors do put forth 14 propositions, these proposals are often in a form that is neither clear nor immediately testable. Also, as noted previously, it is not apparent why some interpretations of data analyses are stated in propositional form, whereas other implications from research are not. For example, based on prior research, Proposition 2 states "Distribution of team members in space–time affects the quality of decision outcomes by complicating the process of building accurate mental representations of causality in a dynamic system." This proposition would be more helpful if stated in hypothesis form, as follows: "Distribution of team members in space–time will degrade or decrease the quality of decision outcomes by impeding the building of accurate mental representations of causality in a dynamic system." Such a formation would more clearly tie an independent variable (distribution of group members) first to a mediating factor (mental representations) and then to a dependent variable (quality of decision outcomes), and, finally, posit directionality to the relationships.

Interestingly, the authors tend to use the propositional form "A *can* affect Y" or "A is *likely* to affect Y" as they develop propositions. Yet, the evidence they cite for supporting the proposition clearly allows them to state that "A *will positively (or negatively)* affect Y." This is an issue in Propositions 9–12 and 14. The frequent use of phrases, such as "can," "will likely," or "may," provides ambiguous surrogates for the identification of mediating factors or directionality. The authors would have further helped to guide future inquiry had they explicitly pursued identification of mitigating factors and/or directionality of effects.

As is the case in Proposition 2, the authors tend to use the phrase "complicates" in propositions in a way that limits their value. What does "complicate" mean? Does it mean a greater investment of time, energy, or other resources is needed? If so, in which resources? Does the "complication" decrease a specific type of effectiveness or efficiency? Identification of explicit independent, mediating, and dependent variables would increase the value of the proposition for guiding both future research and action options for executives.

Having stated a concern with the focus and form of propositions developed by the authors, it is important to reaffirm that the overall effect of the chapter is very helpful and will be informative to anyone attempting to understand the dynamics underlying the performance of distributed teams. Stagl et al. make clear that there is often confusion regarding what is meant by distributed teams – confusion that is an increasingly critical issue from both research and practice perspectives. The question of what lies at the core of providing leadership for distributed teams is raised in an interesting fashion, and a careful reading suggests that there are limited data available about this issue. Given its focus on task and socioemotional activities, the discussion of supporting research suggests that the leadership role for distributed teams may not be much different from that for nondistributed teams. Of course, the specific actions supportive of task or developmental foci may be more technology mediated when distributed groups are involved, but this discrepancy may or may not constitute a fundamental process difference. It is certainly an issue worthy of future study.

OPPORTUNITIES FOR FUTURE RESEARCH

Based on this review, one concludes that there is relatively limited focused research available about the effect of distributed work teams on organizational structure and culture. For example, given what we know or infer about the requirements for effective operation of distributed teams, would we expect organizational structure to become more or less hierarchical as distributed teams proliferate? Is the answer to this question a function of the personalities of team members, which is the focus for much of the available research cited in the review, or are the effects a function of the existence of an organizational culture shaped by the reality of multilocational – particularly multigeopolitical – operations? Certainly, the confusion evident in the Ford Motor Company's vacillating approach to supporting worldwide operations suggests that both factors are important. The company's approach has been influenced both by the personalities of senior executives and by the realities of attempting to integrate worldwide operational initiatives in which distributed team operations have flourished.

As someone who travels extensively and has an opportunity to work with executives who are almost always part of one or more distributed teams, I have been impressed by the consistent view that "face-to-face" (i.e., informal) interactions are critical even if regular interactions between distant team members are technology enhanced. As noted by Stagl et al., knowing your distributed team members informally seems to be critical in developing trust, both in a predictability sense and in an affective, emotional sense. Left apparently unanswered are questions such as whether the need to develop trust among distributed group members varies according to the importance of the problem to the individual or firm, the substantive nature of the problem, the decision-making structure in which a team is embedded, the characteristics of societal and organizational cultures in which participants are embedded, or other factors. If these are important factors, under what circumstances should the organization and design of distributed teams include an assumption that face-to-face interaction must be planned for so as to achieve greater effectiveness? All of these questions flow from the issues identified by Stagl et al. in this chapter and demonstrate the intersection of open research issues and practices critical to actual organizational performance.

Finally, it seems clear from this chapter that there has been a considerable focus among academic researchers on intra- or interindividual level effects. Consequently, analyses of the effects of organizational-level phenomena on the performance of distributed teams and the effects of distributed team processes on organizational-level phenomena may prove fruitful areas of future inquiry. For example, do distributed teams work more effectively at particular hierarchical levels, across or only within given hierarchical levels? Does the existence of distributed teams allow organizations to be structured differently than those with limited or no distributed team operations? Are there limits on the number or type of distributed teams that individual executives can "lead," and what effect does this restriction have on organizational design and internal processes? Much research with theoretical and practical implications remains to be done, and the work of Stagl et al. provides a good foundation for exploring such issues.

CONCLUSION

Clearly, there is much work still to be done in exploring the effects of distributed work teams on organizations and the ways in which intrapersonal, interpersonal, organizational, and cultural factors influence team performance. As Stagl et al. demonstrate, there is a growing body of research on intrapersonal and interpersonal factors affecting distributed team performance that are reflected in the real-world actions of organizations interested in enhancing the effectiveness of such teams. Certainly, these issues are relevant for academic scholars who are concerned with core psychological, group, and sociological processes as well as organizational dynamics. But this also happens to be an area where the interests of executives and other decision makers intersect with academic interests as distributed workteams proliferate, in the process becoming increasingly critical determinates in overall organizational effectiveness. One should expect to see greater applied as well as theoretical attention being focused on these issues in the years ahead.

REFERENCE

Stagl, K., Salas, E., Rosen, M., Priest, H., Burke, C., Goodwin, G., & Johnston, J. (this volume). Distributed team performance: A multi-level review of distribution, demography, and decision making. In: F. Dansereau & F. J. Yammarino (Eds), *Multi-level issues in organizations and time* (Vol. 6). Oxford: Elsevier.

T-MoP: A TETRAHEDRAL MODEL OF PERFORMANCE

Michael D. Coovert and Jennifer L. Burke

ABSTRACT

Understanding the complexities of performance in the world of work is central for advancing science and practice. Pulling from Stagl et al.'s chapter and integrating it with the work of others and our own, we develop and propose a multi-level conceptual model depicting the influences of "distributedness" on system decision making and performance. The tetrahedral model of performance (T-MoP) illustrates how the three levels of capacity (individual, team, and organizational) are influenced by three types of distributedness (geospatial, temporal, and technological), interact with a cultural base, and subsequently lead to performance. The model can be viewed at http://www.jennyburke.com/images/T-MoP.mpeg.

INTRODUCTION

We are pleased to review the chapter written by Stagl et al. (this volume) a distinguished group of authors who have chosen topics that are both extensive and challenging. Considerable care and clarity of thought obviously went into the development of ideas and the writing of the chapter, and the authors are to be commended for a job well done.

Multi-Level Issues in Organizations and Time
Research in Multi-Level Issues, Volume 6, 65–82
Copyright © 2007 by Elsevier Ltd.
All rights of reproduction in any form reserved
ISSN: 1475-9144/doi:10.1016/S1475-9144(07)06003-1

Our task as commentators is to provide critical insight and perspective on the points made throughout Stagl et al.'s chapter. Our comments are organized in two parts. In the first part, we provide specific perspectives on the chapter to help readers consider further points or alternative perspectives from those provided by the authors. In the spirit of "playing devil's advocate," this commentary challenges some perspectives presented by Stagl et al. in hopes of having the reader think deeply about the important issues presented. The second part of the commentary introduces a model that represents some of the constructs important in this area of research and practice. This model is intended not so much as a critique of the model by Stagl et al., but rather as an attempt to facilitate enriched thinking and further consideration of the issues. These are challenging and important concepts; viewing them from multiple perspectives can only prove beneficial.

We move now to consider the issues raised by Stagl et al. (this volume). Our comments are linearly structured to follow the presentation of the authors. Again, our purpose is not to be critical of their work, as we believe these authors' perspective is worthwhile. Rather, we strive to point out potential limitations and boundary conditions on their arguments and to build on their foundation.

FURTHER CONSIDERATIONS

The chapter begins with a statement about the nature of the constructs being multi-level, and the reader is pointed to Fig. 1, which is a representational heuristic of Stagl et al.'s perspective. The use of the term "multi-level" is helpful, and certainly timely given the advances in multi-level modeling that have occurred in the past decade. Multi-level data analysis is clearly the technique of choice for analyzing any hierarchically organized system – such as that described in Stagl et al.'s chapter, in which individuals are nested within teams and teams are nested within organizations.

Distributed Teams

The authors do a fine job in describing a boundary condition on much of the distributed/colocated research that has been performed to date. Teams are rarely fully colocated or fully distributed, but rather are typically some mix of the two. By making this point explicit, the authors help us to realize that

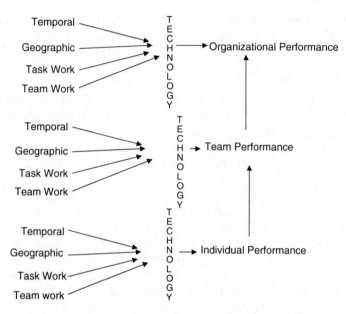

Fig. 1. Mediational Role of Technology in Distribution and Work Type, with the Hierarchical Nature of Performance.

much of the research in this area needs to be considered in light of this potential limitation. The findings in the literature based on fully colocated or fully distributed teams should be viewed cautiously when applied to the mixed distribution teams that exist in the real world.

A side point is presented regarding the use of "virtual" teams in the literature. The authors astutely point out that the use of "virtual" is inconsistent with the dictionary's current definition, and that virtual teams do, in fact, exist and are physically embodied "real" people – not computer emulations of real people. This might, however, be an instance where the dictionary's definition has yet to catch up with the colloquial use of a term. These authors reduce the potential for confusion by clearly stating that virtual teams belong to their class of "distributed" teams. We prefer the term "technologically mediated" teams, as it is more descriptive of real team members who are distributed and interact via a technological channel of some sort. "Virtual team" is catchier, which may be why it is used. "Techno-mediated" or "tech-med" might also get a few popular votes!

Other substantive issues should be considered at this juncture. When describing a job or team as "distributed" (virtual, techno-mediated), it is important to consider where the distributed label applies. Specifically, are we describing a job (or the worker) as being distributed in time or location? Consider the work of a typical project team member in his or her cubical in the organization. This individual works on a piece of project A, and then a piece of project B, and then moves on to project C or perhaps back to project A. The work is clearly distributed across time (but not individuals or location). Similarly, many individuals have more than one work location. Part of the work gets done in the "office," other work gets done in meetings at the client's location, and more work gets done at home. In this case, the work is distributed across geographic locations (but not individual workers).

Note that technology has not yet entered the picture, nor has the work been spread across individuals who are part of a team (even a nominal one). Thus, Stagl et al. begin an important dialogue by pointing out that the term "distributed" carries with it certain meanings and connotations. Technology is sometimes used to overcome geographic or temporal distributions.

But let us continue the dialogue. Indeed, the argument needs to be extended in such a fashion as to make explicit that the idea of a distributed team carries with it several implications. Individuals in a team can be distributed temporally (e.g., shifts or time zones), geographically (e.g., next to each other or on the other side of the globe), and in terms of the extent to which technology is employed to help mediate the functioning of the individuals' work (ranging from none through partial to full), individual team behaviors (e.g., coordination or backing up; ranging from none through partial to full), and use of technology to enable team members to coordinate and generate the team-level outcome. Our initial representation is presented in Fig. 1.

These distinctions really occur along a continuum – from none to partial through full (e.g., geographic distribution, technology affecting task work) – and at the individual level. Issues should be considered at this level prior to aggregation to the team or organizational level. If aggregation occurs inappropriately or if analysis occurs at the level below which concepts are considered, the research is open to the host of statistical mistakes and conceptual errors that multi-level analysis was developed to correct.

Global Organizations

Stagl et al. broach the topic of organizations operating on a global scale, and this discussion is a critical contribution made by their work. Let us consider some further implications. Readers of Thomas Friedman's *The World is Flat* (2005) certainly come away with a sense of how quickly and dramatically the world is changing toward a global economy. Technological advances have generated major shifts in the traditional barriers of time, distance, and, to some extent, culture. Global organizations are clearly the direction in which the world of work is heading.

Stagl et al. profile the takeover of IBM by the Asian company, Lenovo, and the consequences of that merger. They describe a process of, within a global organization, allowing workers "flexibility in scheduling their time and efforts." But could a global organization really survive any other way? Is this really something innovative on the part of Lenovo/IBM or merely the facts of life for doing business in today's global economy? Organizations need to fit within the demands of their clients to fulfill the clients' needs. A global organization is, by definition, widely dispersed in geography and time. It is through management via technological means that these organizations are able to act and react in a timely manner, allowing them to be competitive around the globe.

Many of today's global organizations are service based as opposed to manufacturing based. Services are typically provided at the time they are needed by the requesting client. Organizations must meet the needs of their clients, or otherwise they will not survive. It can be argued that this "flexibility" actually represents the adaptation of global organizations to the time and distance demands of their clients. Consider a call center in Bangalore, India, that operates throughout the day and night (local time) to answer calls from Europe, America, Australia, and Japan (local times). Such an organization is having its workers adapt to the client's needs. This is quite different from "fitting the system to the team." We agree with Stagl et al. that it is a good idea to fit the system to the team. Often, however, this is challenging to accomplish given the temporal, geographic, and cultural needs of the clients of global organizations.

Multinational Political and Military Coalitions

A coherent and insightful perspective is presented regarding the nature of the decision-making shift within the military. Network-centric warfare entails accumulating, filtering, and providing huge amounts of information to the individual war-fighter. (For example, see the Future Force Warrior; http://www.natick.army.mil/soldier/wsit/) The intent is to "push down" the decision-making process to the appropriate level. This goal is accomplished by providing the appropriate information to the correct war-fighter at the time it is needed. The individual war-fighter can then use this information and take the appropriate action. The future force warrior is defined as "a formidable warrior in an invincible team, able to see first, understand first, act first, and finish decisively" (http://www.natick.army.mil/soldier/wsit/).

A consequence of this definition is the need to present information in a fashion that is immediately usable to the war-fighter. One of this commentary's authors (Coovert) is reminded of an instance many years ago when he was discussing with the Navy how more data could be presented to a consol operator. An operational individual spoke up: "The last thing I need is more data – give me information!"

We strongly believe that this situation has changed yet again. Considering the tenets of information-centric warfare and the vision for fighting systems such as the future force warrior, information is not enough – and too much information can be disadvantageous. What many of today's workers need is not data or information, but *knowledge.* Information needs to be accumulated, synthesized, organized, distilled, and presented into a form that immediately makes "sense" to the individual in the present context. Knowledge is essential for today's and tomorrow's workers to be able to act and react in time-critical instances. Indeed, this situation is not unique to the war-fighter. Other jobs of this nature include stock or futures trader, emergency medical technician, physician, manager, commercial airline pilot, and reporter, among thousands of other possibilities.

Presentation of information/knowledge is equally critical, and identifying the optimal method for doing so is essential. For certain types of knowledge in certain contexts, visual presentation will be optimal. At other times, auditory presentation will be preferred, and still other contexts will demand tactile presentation. Certainly, the presentation of knowledge in multimodal forms will benefit the individual to an extent above and beyond that provided by presentation of information via any single modality.

As we use technology to increase our reach into other areas of the globe, additional issues become important as well. Consider the pilot of an unmanned aeronautical vehicle (UAV). This individual is assigned the task of piloting an aircraft in one part of the world (e.g., Afghanistan) from a console located in a trailer in another part of the world (e.g., Nevada). This task becomes especially challenging during the transition phases of flight, such as takeoffs and landings, because the pilot is viewing the world through a camera located at the front of the vehicle. This camera gives the pilot a view much like one would get looking through a soda straw (Lt. Col. Hover, pers. comm., May 19, 2006). Missing are the perceptual cues a pilot has available when in a cockpit, such as speed, scenery motion, and so forth, that are otherwise provided by the peripheral visual system. Classically trained pilots have difficulty transitioning to these jobs. The individuals who are most successful appear to be from the "Nintendo generation" and grew up controlling vehicles in virtual (gaming) environments. If we are to succeed in moving individuals to such digitally intensive jobs – distributed in space and time (even the two-second delay associated with satellite transmission qualifies as "distribution") – it is critical that we understand the different attributes of the most successful workers so that effective selection or training systems can be developed and employed.

Thus far we have considered specific portions of Stagl et al.'s chapter and have offered comments for further consideration of their arguments. We now present additional conceptual evidence bearing on the topics at hand. Specifically, we address issues relative to distribution, decision making, and performance via an alternative theoretical conceptualization. This model represents constructs as a three-sided tetrahedron with a meaningful base. Because of its complexity, it is difficult to represent the model in two dimensions. An animated version can be viewed at http://www.jennyburke.com/T-MoP.mpeg. Our model builds on the Stagl et al. perspective as well as the perspectives evinced by others working in the field by cleaving constructs we deem useful and integrating them into a unique representation. We trust the field will find our model useful and use it to further discussion, practice, and research.

AN ELABORATION ON DISTRIBUTION, DECISION MAKING, AND PERFORMANCE: THE T-MoP PERSPECTIVE

This section presents a multi-level conceptual model depicting the influences of "distributedness" on system decision making and performance. Distributed decision making and, indeed, distributed performance are largely a matter of how the individual, team, and organization deal with the communication and coordination challenges faced in distributed systems. As Stagl et al. note, the links between individual, team, and organizational decision making are influenced by many factors. Specifically, these authors cite cultural demography (collectivism and power distance) and work structure (team distribution and team "opacity") as important. We argue that distributed decision making – and ultimately performance – in a distributed system is a function of the interaction of these factors (among others) with the *capacity* of the individual, team, and organization. Culture is important, too, as it provides a base for building and understanding relationships.

Our tetrahedral model of performance (T-MoP) is rooted in the work of Burke (2006), who examined distributed teams in a field setting and tested some of the theoretical constructs and relationships outlined in Klimoski and Mohammed's (1994) framework for team performance. In her work, Burke looked at the influence of technology as a resource enabling the creation of richer-shared mental models among team members, and she proposed extending the team model to include multiple organizational levels. Our commentary allows for an opportunity to examine constructs through the model's lens and provide an assessment of the authors' perspectives from the model's facets.

Our conceptual model captures the influence of three dimensions of distributedness – time, space, and technology – on individual, team, and organizational levels of *capacity* for effective performance. These three dimensions of distribution represent a continuum along which individuals, teams, and organizations can vary.

What is Capacity?

The concept of capacity comes from Klimoski and Mohammed's (1994) framework for explaining the role of team mental models in team performance. In their seminal article, Klimoski and Mohammed use the term "team mental model" to define the shared mental model construct referred to as team cognition in Stagl et al.'s chapter. Team mental models are thought to affect decision making, team dynamics, and performance, and to enhance the quality of teamwork skills and team effectiveness. Training, team composition and life cycle, communication patterns, and cohesion are listed as determinants of team mental models. Klimoski and Mohammed placed team mental models within a framework of team performance and identified them as a factor (along with leadership) influencing performance directly and indirectly through their effects on team capacity (i.e., a team's latent potential for demonstrating effective process and performance).

The framework begins with the factors thought to determine team capacity: the individual team members' potential for performance, team composition and size, and resources available to the team. A team's capacity, or readiness, influences team process and performance to an extent contingent on the availability of some orienting factor that enables the team to harness that capacity and put it to work; team mental models and leadership are two such factors. The orienting and coordinating aspects of team mental models can create smoothly functioning teams through shared cognition. Fiore and Schooler (2004, p. 431) suggested leadership can serve as a guiding factor when that shared cognition is not possible.

> [A]bsent the availability of team mental models, a leader can serve to guide the team, serving such executive functions as assigning information gathering activities among team members, doing information integration and interpretation, adjudicating disagreements and/or directing individual team members into action.

It may be that technology can assume a leadership role (or help team members do so) by performing some of these executive functions (Coovert & Burke, 2005). Technology may benefit other team processes (communication, support/backup behaviors, situation awareness) in similar fashion. For example, giving team members access to shared workspaces using distributed technologies may increase communication clarity and effectiveness. Support/backup behaviors may occur more frequently due to quicker detection of errors and better monitoring capabilities. Team situation awareness may be enhanced by giving all team members access to previously restricted sources of information, enabling them to make projections about one another's information needs before being asked.

The Model in a Nutshell: The Tetrahedral Model of Performance

The concept of team capacity serves as the starting point for our proposed conceptual model. We see the need to consider individual capacity and organizational capacity as well to capture the multi-level nature of the system within which distributed teams must operate. Individual capacity, or readiness, includes not only levels of training and experience, but other variables that can influence performance in distributed systems, such as accessibility, adaptability, multitasking (attention switching), and utilization of social/interpersonal skills tailored to a specific technology medium. Organizational capacity includes leadership, resource allocation, and both inter- and intraorganizational coordination and cooperation. All three of these capacity levels (individual, team, and organization) are affected by the distributed nature of geospatial considerations, time, and technological resources. The interactions of these three dimensions of distribution (geospace, time, and technology), in turn, influence the latent potential for

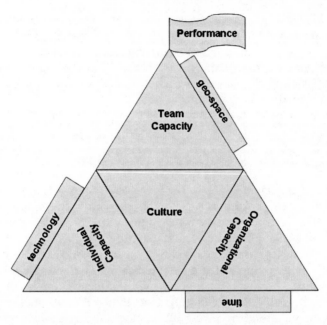

Fig. 2. Two-Dimensional Tetrahedron Model of Performance in Distributed Systems. *Note:* This Figure can be Reproduced, Cut, and Folded to Create a Paper Three-Dimensional Model.

effective process and performance (both perceived and real) of the individual, team, and organization.

In Fig. 2, the three levels of capacity are depicted as the three sides of a tetrahedron, the base of which is culture. The lines along the three sides represent the lines of distribution that affect capacity in a distributed system. (The static nature of this representation makes it difficult to capture the fact that these lines flow, and are not limited to the place they occupy between two particular sides. An animation of the model that illustrates this point more clearly can be viewed at http://www.jennyburke.com/images/T-MoP.mpeg) Note that the dimensions of cultural demography included in the Stagl et al. multi-level framework, such as power distance and individualism–collectivism, are captured in the tetrahedron base (culture). The constructs of work structure also map into the model, albeit perhaps less directly: Team distribution is presented in the T-MoP as a continuum (line of distribution), and team opacity might be reflected as an indicator of team capacity.

The Model in Detail: Individual, Team, and Organizational Capacity and Culture

Individual Capacity

What contributes to an individual's capacity for effective decision making and performance in a distributed system? Aside from the expected attributes of cognitive ability, levels of training and experience, and KSAs (knowledge, skills, and abilities) needed for a particular job, an individual's capacity may be a function of his or her adaptive ability to perform along the continuum of each of the T-MoP's lines of distribution. The distribution of individual work across different geographic settings (e.g., home, office, client's place of business) and different times (e.g., working evenings to be able to talk with people across time zones) requires increased *accessibility* on the part of the individual.

This accessibility is extended by technology. For example, an individual worker could conduct business through face-to-face contact, telephone, e-mail, and videoconference in a single day. Moreover, workers are often expected to handle several of these media at once, operating at many positions along the technology continuum simultaneously. This demand creates a need for *multitasking* and *attention-switching* abilities, and leads to a potentially frustrating capacity for those less able to function in a technology-mediated world. In a recent presentation, one professional described a business teleconference with an associate who, as the meeting progressed, spent his time answering e-mail and giving instructions to others in his office on a face-to-face basis while participating in the conference call. His attention switching from one task and medium of communication to another proved disconcerting to the teleconference participants, who were occasionally uncertain of his involvement and the persons to whom he was speaking – his colocated associates or them! Indeed, an individual's capacity may also be determined by his or her awareness of the different social/interpersonal skills required in techno-mediated work and his or her ability to transition smoothly from one type of interaction to another.

Team Capacity

In Klimoski and Mohammed's (1994) model, factors thought to determine team capacity included: (1) the individual team members' potential for performance, (2) team composition and size, and (3) resources available to the team. Other potential influences on team capacity could include the team's current work life and past work history, cohesion, group tensions, and relationships with other groups both within and outside the organization.

The team membership may be stable (e.g., an established sales team), or it may change on a regular basis (e.g., in project teams). Members may come from the same organization or from many different organizations. Other temporal factors can influence team capacity in distributed teams, such as whether the teams are assembled for a single, time-limited project or on a long-term basis; whether team members know one another and have worked together in the past; and whether they expect to have any interaction or shared work in the future.

The most challenging aspect of team capacity stems from the special challenges in communication and coordination of activities that can significantly affect team performance in distributed teams (Hinds & Bailey, 2003; Thompson & Coovert, 2003). The difficulties in establishing a shared context across distributed teams can lead to increased conflict and confusion among team members, and less satisfaction with team processes and outcomes. Communication and coordination of activities pose significant challenges to distributed teams, which can in turn affect team performance. Communication in distributed teams can suffer from the loss of information gleaned through "back channels" such as physical gestures, body language, and interaction with artifacts in the environment. Technologies that do not support transmission of contextual information are impoverished and provide less visibility and feedback, both of which are needed for establishing and maintaining mutual knowledge (i.e., knowledge that team members share and know they share) (Krauss & Fussell, 1990). Techno-mediated communication's effects on mutual knowledge are likely to be greater for tasks where individual team members possess a large quantity of unique information, and where contextual information between distributed sites differs. This problem is attenuated by high requirements for complexity, workload, and interdependence, and it can lead to confusion among team members and errors in performance (Cramton, 2001).

Coordination of activities, which requires shared awareness, or *common ground*, is difficult to achieve when team members are distributed. Indeed, it often requires more confirmatory communication, because many of the back-channel types of awareness mentioned earlier are unavailable. Successful collaboration among distributed team members requires situation awareness – ongoing awareness of what each person is doing, what the status of the task is, and how the environment is evolving (Endsley, 1995) – as well as conversational grounding – working with one another to ensure that messages are understood as intended (Clark & Marshall, 1981). Three primary sources for common ground are common group membership (which presupposes a set of common knowledge), linguistic copresence (hearing the same verbalizations), and physical copresence (inhabiting the same physical setting). Physical copresence provides multiple resources for building common ground, most prominently visual copresence.

Particularly in teams where some members are colocated and others are distributed, there is a potential for development of an in-group mentality among those who are geographically closer. This outcome may be unintentional, but the mere proximity that allows affords team members the back-channel feedback gained through physical copresence may cause problems and create tension in the distributed team setting – as is often the case when coordination problems arise due to lack of shared information or understanding.

Similarly, the temporal constraints that are present when team work asynchronously can result in greater team process loss. For example, e-mails may fly back and forth trying to get work done together that might take far less time if the team met face to face; once again, the culprit may be the lack of common ground. A team's capacity to overcome these challenges can increase with its use of technology – witness the increasingly common use of groupware, videoconferencing, and so forth. Its effectiveness is contingent, however, on team members' willingness to avail themselves of the technology and their ability to use the technology. Again, this is linked to the individual and organizational capacity for technology adoption, and it is tied to the cultural and societal norms within which the individual, team, and organization are situated.

Organizational Capacity
Organizational capacity can be viewed as a function of leadership, organizational mission, goals and objectives, and resource management. It can also include inter- and intraorganizational policies and operating strategies. These elements are affected by the lines of distribution in several ways.

As stated by Stagl et al., leadership is a key element in an organization's ability to deal with the challenges of distributed decision making. An organization's capacity to function effectively as a distributed system may require changes in leadership style or structure. For example, a global organization may have to rely on a more flattened leadership structure to accomplish its objectives and be responsive to events at the local, regional, or national level. Corporations that do not flatten the leadership structure may find themselves out of touch with the vagaries of the local market

(Hall, Bawden, & Butler, 2006). Leadership styles may also have to be altered as a result of changes in communication style – for example, can a leader be transformational over the Internet? (Kelloway, Barling, Kelley, Comtois, & Gatien, 2003). Finally, leadership's attitude toward and acceptance of new technology can be a critical determinant of the organization's capacity to effectively capitalize on the bridging advantages offered by increasingly sophisticated groupware tools and other technological resources (Lewis, Agarwal, & Sambamurthy, 2003).

In terms of the organization's mission, goals, and objectives, Stagl et al. discussed image theory as a possible way in which decision makers would examine alternatives and screen them for compatibility with their images of corporate culture, vision, and strategy. In Proposition 8, they posited that the effects of distribution on organizational decision making would complicate the process of building sharedness of content in culture, vision, and strategy images, in effect degrading an organization's images. We agree, noting that in a multinational system, organizational capacity will be affected by changes in mission, goals, and objectives that focus on a global bottom line rather than a local one – although the effects may become apparent on different levels. For example, the forced closure of a local factory may be beneficial for the organization and in line with its overall mission, goals, and objectives, but have a negative effect on teams and individuals who feel threatened by the lack of trickledown benefit to them. Moreover, the boundary spanning and blurring that take place in large-scale projects and collaborations may increase the organization's capacity by reducing costs and streamlining productivity, but at the cost of "blurring" the organization's own culture and mission values.

In another context, Stagl et al. discuss multinational political and military coalitions, saying that "no nation acts alone" in a political confrontation. Organizational capacity depends in part on the ability to collaborate as a distributed team of teams. In this sense, one could argue that a nation's capacity increases as it hones that ability.

The temporal influence on organizational capacity is portrayed in a positive light by Stagl et al. as these authors discuss the increased flexibility gained by fitting the system to the team, and the potential reduction of role overload and job-induced stress. In addition, the economic benefits of 24-hour production and availability are certainly an indicator of increased capacity. However, the temporal distribution can contribute to communication and coordination problems and breakdowns in organizations – and place further constraints on operating strategies and policies for decision makers who must now meet deadlines across time zones.

Culture

At the heart of the question of distributedness's influence on decision making and performance are the cultural differences that distribution uncovers between us at every level – individual, team, and organization. In their chapter, Stagl et al. focus on culture's effects on distributed teams and organizations through multicultural personnel, taking a relational demography approach by examining the cultural dimensions of power distance and individualism–collectivism at the individual, team, and organizational levels. Their propositions offer valuable insights and pose interesting questions that merit further study. While the authors speak primarily of national/ ethnic culture, they acknowledge the importance of organizational culture. We would add to this list the broader societal dimensions of culture as another area of consideration.

In terms of ethnic/national cultural influences, it is important to acknowledge the differences in capabilities that exist between more and less technology-enabled countries as well as the different values placed on various types of communication and interaction. These dissimilarities extend beyond the demographic constructs of individualism–collectivism and power distance, and are really more a reflection of a nation's political and economic status in the world. It is clearly a moot point whether you feel comfortable talking to your boss by e-mail when you do not have a computer in your village. Also, in communication and interaction in many national cultures, certain business rituals (e.g., small talk, inquiring about family, sharing a meal) are observed that do not necessarily mesh with the new methods of distributed communication and coordination. These are areas in which new schemas and rituals are being formed, but have not yet taken hold due to the iterative advances in technology that preclude one taking root before another new technology comes along.

Moreover, the values and traditions associated with traditional business models are not easily relinquished. Organizational cultures that demonstrate a willingness and ability to adapt and assimilate new ways of doing work do so by providing a "learning organization" setting for teams and individuals. This evolution echoes Stagl et al.'s emphasis on training and developmental leadership as key to addressing the challenges faced in distributed teaming.

Finally, the societal influences on culture – an increasingly longer-living population, the emergence of new generations for which distributedness is a given rather than an adjustment, and even the evolution of a techno-mediated world – form a backdrop that may render many of these discussions meaningless as time passes and new models of decision making and performance in distributed systems emerge.

FINAL THOUGHTS

In this commentary, we have sought to provide some critical insight and perspective on the points made by Stagl et al. in two ways. First, we have played "devil's advocate" by challenging some of the perspectives presented in the chapter in an attempt to stimulate further thought. Second, we have proposed a model that illustrates the lines of distribution along which individuals, teams, and organizations can vary in terms of their capacity for effective decision making and performance.

The T-MoP model captures the influence of three dimensions of distributedness – time, space, and technology – on individual, team, and organizational levels of capacity (readiness) for effective performance. These three dimensions of distribution represent a continuum along which individuals, teams, and organizations can vary. Klimoski and Mohammed's (1994) concept of team capacity served as the starting point for this proposed conceptual model, characterized as a function of the individual team members' potential for performance, team composition and size, and resources available to the team. The team's current work life and past work history, cohesion, group tensions, and relationships with other groups both within and outside the organization were then recognized as other factors that could determine team capacity, with the communication and coordination challenges being the most critical issues.

Next, we considered individual capacity and organizational capacity. Individual capacity includes levels of training and experience, accessibility, adaptability, multitasking (attention switching), and utilization of social/interpersonal skills tailored to a specific technology medium. Organizational capacity includes leadership, resource allocation, and both inter- and intraorganizational coordination and cooperation.

All three of these capacity levels (individual, team, and organization) are affected by the distributed nature of geospatial considerations, time, and technological resources. The interaction of these three dimensions of distribution (geospace, time, and technology) influences the latent potential for effective process and performance (both perceived and real) of the individual, team, and organization.

Stagl et al. elucidate a three-pronged approach to facilitating distributed system performance: team leadership, training, and use of information technology. We see the first two measures as ways to increase capacity of the individual, team, and organization to function effectively. Technology in the T-MoP model is a continuum along which these entities can vary in terms of distributedness; we see leadership and training as ways to move along the technology line of distribution, which exists whether we choose to embrace it or not. As Stagl et al. succinctly stated, "Change happens": Our world is getting smaller, faster, and more techno-mediated by the minute, and our adaptations are imperfect. Distribution across time, space, and technology resources affects decision making and performance at every level, and these effects need to be studied. The prescriptive, descriptive, and relational demography approaches outlined in Stagl et al.'s review are a good place to start. We would add to that a call for new models of distributed systems that foster new ways of thinking about distributed work. Clearly, it is no longer a question of *whether* we work in a distributed environment, but rather a question of *how* it is distributed.

In conclusion, we applaud Stagl et al. for their work. Their chapter illuminates some central concepts in the area and will certainly lead to further research and fruitful application. We trust the field will benefit from their work and hope it will similarly profit from our commentary and our tetrahedral model of performance.

REFERENCES

Burke, J. L. (2006). *RSVP: An investigation of the effects of remote shared visual presence on team process and performance in urban search and rescue teams.* Doctoral dissertation, University of South Florida, Tampa, FL.

Clark, H. H., & Marshall, C. E. (1981). Definite reference and mutual knowledge. In: A. K. Joshi, B. L. Webber & I. A. Sag (Eds), Elements of discourse understanding (pp. 10–63). Cambridge, UK: Cambridge University Press.

Coovert, M. D., & Burke, J. L. (2005). Leadership and decision making. In: Y. Amichai-Hamburger (Ed.), *The social net: Human behavior in cyberspace* (pp. 219–246). New York: Oxford University Press.

Cramton, C. D. (2001). The mutual knowledge problem and its consequences for dispersed collaboration. *Organization Science, 12*(3), 346.

Endsley, M. R. (1995). Toward a theory of situation awareness in dynamic systems. *Human Factors, 37*(1), 32–64.

Fiore, S. M., & Schooler, J. W. (2004). Process mapping and shared cognition: Teamwork and the development of shared problem models. In: E. Salas & S. M. Fiore (Eds), *Team cognition: Understanding the factors that drive process and performance* (pp. 133–152). Washington, DC: American Psychological Association.

Friedman, T. (2005). *The world is flat: A brief history of the twenty-first century.* New York: Farrar, Strauss and Giroux.

Hall, A., Bawden, T., & Butler, S. (2006). Wal-Mart pulls out of Germany at cost of $1bn. *The Times Online,* July 29. Retrieved August 20, 2006, from http://business.timesonline.co.uk/article/0,,13129-2290398,00.html

Hinds, P. J., & Bailey, D. E. (2003). Out of sight, out of sync: Understanding conflict in distributed teams. *Organization Science, 14*(6), 615–632.

Kelloway, E., Barling, J., Kelley, E., Comtois, J., & Gatien, B. (2003). Remote transformational
    leadership. *Leadership and Organizational Development Journal, 24*, 162–171.
Klimoski, R., & Mohammed, S. (1994). Team mental model: Construct or metaphor? *Journal of
    Management, 20*(2), 403–437.
Krauss, R. M., & Fussell, S. R. (1990). Mutual knowledge and communicative effectiveness. In:
    J. Galegher & R. E. Kraut (Eds), *Intellectual teamwork: Social and technological foun-
    dations of cooperative work* (pp. 111–145). Mahweh, NJ: Lawrence Erlbaum Associates.
Lewis, W., Agarwal, R., & Sambamurthy, V. (2003). Sources of influence on beliefs about
    information technology use: An empirical study of knowledge workers. *MIS Quarterly,
    27*(4), 657–768.
Stagl, K., Salas, E., Rosen, M., Priest, H., Burke, C., Goodwin, G., & Johnston, J. (this
    volume). Distributed team performance: A multi-level review of distribution, demog-
    raphy, and decision making. In: F. Dansereau & F. J. Yammarino (Eds), *Multi-level
    issues in organizations and time* (Vol. 6). Oxford: Elsevier.
Thompson, L. F., & Coovert, M. D. (2003). Teamwork online: The effects of computer con-
    ferencing on perceived confusion, satisfaction and postdiscussion accuracy. *Group
    Dynamics, 7*(2), 135–151.

DISTRIBUTED TEAM PERFORMANCE: CONTINUING THE DIALOGUE

Kevin C. Stagl, Eduardo Salas, Michael A. Rosen, Heather A. Priest, C. Shawn Burke, Gerald F. Goodwin and Joan H. Johnston

ABSTRACT

Stagl, Salas, Rosen, Priest, Burke, Goodwin, and Johnston (this volume) conducted a review of distributed team performance and discussed some of the implications of distributed, multicultural operations for individual, team, and organizational decision making. Expanding upon Stagl and colleagues' discussion, Alutto (this volume), and Coovert and Burke (this volume) provided thought-provoking commentary on these issues. The current note briefly responds to some of the questions posed and comments made by Alutto, Coovert, and Burke and concludes by calling for a continued dialogue by all stakeholders concerned with fostering effective distributed teams.

Multi-Level Issues in Organizations and Time
Research in Multi-Level Issues, Volume 6, 83–91
Copyright © 2007 by Elsevier Ltd.
All rights of reproduction in any form reserved
ISSN: 1475-9144/doi:10.1016/S1475-9144(07)06004-3

INTRODUCTION

Distributed team performance arrangements are increasingly prevalent in private and public sector organizations, making the management of their members, performance, and productivity mission critical priorities. The spread of distributed teams is fueled in part by the fact that when they are effectively instituted and supported, their implementation can result in a sizable return on investment. Monetary concerns aside, there are many other benefits that can accrue from effective distributed team performance to stakeholders directly and indirectly vested in distributed teams (Stagl et al., this volume).

Most distributed teams, however, fall somewhat short of their promise. In an effort to help stakeholders cultivate distributed team effectiveness and to incrementally contribute to the science of distributed teams, Stagl and colleagues (this volume) conducted a multi-level review of distributed team performance. Stagl et al. sought to illuminate some of the positive and negative factors associated with the use of distributed performance arrangements to organize teamwork. To this end, Stagl and colleagues' review emphasized some of the structural and cultural features of distributed teams that can affect individual, team, and organizational decision-making; advancing several propositions to summarize these issues.

As part of Stagl and colleagues' (this volume) review of distributed team performance, distinguished researchers were asked to provide commentary and constructive criticism to further the conversation about distributed teams. In response to this request, Alutto (this volume), and Coovert and Burke (this volume) provided thought-provoking commentary on the issues raised by Stagl et al. The commentary advanced by Alutto, Coovert, and Burke also posed intriguing new questions and provided fresh insight into effective distributed team performance. Undoubtedly, the science and practice of distributed teams have benefited from their efforts, and we thank them for their valuable contribution in shaping our thinking on these matters.

The current note responds to some of the issues discussed by Alutto (this volume) and Coovert and Burke (this volume). The new directions and perspectives advanced by these researchers are also discussed. The current chapter concludes with a call for increased commentary and research on distributed team performance. It is only through a continued dialogue and the persistent efforts by all parties that the goal of strengthening the science and practice of distributed teams can be achieved. And, it is only by the achievement of this goal that organizations can tap into, harness, and capitalize upon the true power of distributed teams.

A BRIEF RECAP

In their review, Stagl et al. (this volume) noted that when distributed performance arrangements are effectively used, they offer attractive humanitarian and utilitarian benefits that can be reaped by team members, their employers, and society in general. For example, distributed performance arrangements allow teams and their members increased versatility in scheduling and executing their assignments. Distributed performance arrangements, when coupled with related practices such as telecommuting and video conferencing, can also reduce the number of days, or even weeks, per year team members lose to commuting and time consuming travel. These aspects of distributed work directly benefit team members.

The benefits of distributed performance arrangements are also reaped by employers. Organizations that institute distributed performance arrangements are better positioned to increase their adaptive capacity and build their social capital (Zaccaro & Bader, 2003). This is because distributed teams can be purposively staffed to capitalize on a wider range of member experiences, talents, and localized social networks. Organizations can also reduce the role overload, job-induced stress, and the strain experienced by their employees by leveraging distributed teams. Curtailing workplace stressors, the perception of stress, and the proximal and distal effects of strain can translate into a healthy and productive workforce. Moreover, benefits result from reducing medical and insurance costs and ultimately absenteeism and turnover.

There are also a number of other compelling rationales for instituting distributed team structures. For example, distribution in space-time can reduce the initial and ongoing organizational costs associated with securing and maintaining commercial properties. For example, distributed teams offer a viable means of substantially reducing the mounting costs associated with infrastructure expansion, especially in major metropolitan areas. All of these issues can impact the bottom line of organizations, and together with the personal benefits mentioned above, make a compelling case for the use of distributed performance arrangements.

Unfortunately, however, distributed teams are no panacea. Team scholars have long noted that teams of experts often fail to evolve into expert teams (Salas, Cannon-Bowers, & Johnston, 1997), and distributed teams face a particularly difficult path to effectiveness. It is certainly no surprise to anyone who has ever been a team member that all teams are subject to the process losses inherent to coordination. Distributed teams are also susceptible to performance decrements, but distribution in space time results in challenges that are somewhat differentially important in comparison to those that characterize collocated interactions. For example, mutual performance monitoring, a core process of teamwork, can become exceptionally difficult and sometimes even impossible when team members are separated by geographic distances.

In order to better understand some of the challenges distributed teams must navigate, Stagl and colleagues (this volume) conducted a review of the scientific literature to examine the implications of distributed team performance in multicultural contexts for individual, team, and organizational decision making. To help organize the issues addressed in Stagl et al.'s review, the authors advanced a multi-level heuristic figure of distribution, demography, and decision-making. The purpose of this framework was not to present a comprehensive multi-level theory, or even a preliminary testable model of distributed team performance. Rather, the simplistic framework advanced by Stagl et al. was presented merely as a convenient and quick means of summarizing the main issues discussed throughout their chapter. Multi-level models of distributed team performance that specify how the individual-level performance of distributed team members compile to emerge as distributed team performance would be beneficial.

Stagl and colleagues (this volume) advanced several propositions that addressed some of the implications of distributed team performance for decision making at multiple levels in the conceptual space. The propositions provided by Stagl et al. were based on the simple premise that distributed team members who are dispersed in different geographical and temporal locations must cope with an increased level of ambiguity or opacity (see Fiore, Salas, Cuevas, & Bowers, 2003). This additional amount of abstraction serves as an obstacle when team members send, receive, and interpret information, and ultimately how and what decisions are made based on available information. To help organizations minimize the performance decrements that result from team opacity, Stagl and colleagues discussed several practices that can be implemented by organizational stakeholders to improve the decision making of distributed teams and thereby the effectiveness of distributed teams.

COMPELLING COMMENTARY

In response to Stagl and colleagues' (this volume) review of the implications of distributed team performance for team member, team, and organizational decision making, Alutto (this volume), and Coovert and Burke (this volume) were asked to contribute their reactions and thoughts on distributed team performance. This section outlines and responds to some of their commentary and the next section discusses some of the new directions and insight advanced by these researchers.

The first response to Stagl et al. (this volume) was provided by Alutto (this volume). The prevailing theme of Alutto's response spoke of his concern with the focus and form of the propositions advanced by Stagl and colleagues (this volume). Alutto notes some reservations about the clarity of Stagl et al.'s propositions concerning the implications of distributed, multicultural operations for individual, team, and organizational decision making. Specifically, Alutto stated his concerns about whether the propositions advanced by Stagl and colleagues were sufficiently detailed enough as to be directly tested in empirical research efforts. A similar concern was voiced about the lack of discussion devoted to the interactive effects of distribution, organizational factors, and cultural variables for distributed team performance.

In regard to the amount of detail provided by Stagl and colleagues (this volume), we wholeheartedly agree that additional specificity is warranted, particularly in terms of advancing testable interactions that can guide forthcoming empirical research conducted to illuminate the nature of distributed team performance. We eagerly anticipate such propositions emanating from Alutto and others. In the meantime, we hope that the propositions in the form advanced by Stagl and colleagues (this volume) will help in some small way to shape the articulation of more specific and testable hypotheses.

In relation to the lack of emphasis placed on organizational-level issues, we do not believe that some of the propositions of the type suggested by Alutto (this volume) are consistent with the type of analysis we conducted. Our propositions were focused on the performance processes engaged in during decision making at multiple levels; therefore, propositions concerning the more logistic issues of distribution versus co-location do not fit the intent of this chapter, which was undertaken to examine the affects of distribution on decision-making processes. For example, "the cost of operation for distributed work teams is lower than that for co-located teams working on identical or similar problems" is an extremely valuable proposition in need of systematic empirical investigation, but it does not speak of the processes of distributed team performance. The operating cost may be lower, but what about the quality of outcomes generated by distributed teams? How are those outcomes maximized? What are the qualitative shifts in performance processes resulting in technological mediation? These are the types of issues we focused on in our treatment of the subject.

We also agree to a certain extent that our work has focused primarily on the intra and inter individual-level at the expense of a more exhaustive treatment of organizational-level phenomenon. There are several reasons for this. First, our focal level of analysis was the team and our primary process of interest was decision making. In agreement with many in the Organizational Decision-Making camp, we take the position that organizations do not make decisions, people do (e.g., March, 1988; Beach, 1998). Given limited space constraints, we opted for more in-depth coverage of micro- and meso-level phenomena, with the idea that ultimately these are the levels most directly involved in decision-making processes. However, we do agree that, in the spirit of bracketing a phenomenon of interest (Hackman, 2003), a more in-depth coverage of both organizational-level influences on distributed team performance, as well as the implications of distribution in teams on organizational processes and outcomes is warranted.

The second response to Stagl et al.'s (this volume) review of distributed team performance was provided by Coovert and Burke (this volume). Coovert and Burke began their commentary by noting the need for increased attention to multi-level theory building and research. We concur, it is only via a multi-level perspective that emergent phenomenon nested within constraining hierarchical systems can truly be understood. Coovert and Burke continued their discussion by reinforcing a point noted by Stagl and colleagues that most studies examining distributed teams have rarely considered teams that are a mix of both distributed and collocated members. This is clearly an inherent limitation to most distributed team research conducted to date. We strongly encourage researchers to consider teams which have a blend of distributed and collocated members in their efforts. Coovert and Burke also astutely point out the various connotations that the meaning of distributed carries. It is no doubt important to specify whether the term distributed is used to refer to a specific job, team members dispersed in different locales, or distributed members operating at different times. All of these issues require closer scrutiny as researchers and practitioners strive to understand and facilitate distributed team performance.

FRESH PERSPECTIVES

In addition to commenting on some of the issues raised by Stagl and colleagues (this volume), Alutto (this volume), and Coovert and Burke (this volume) also provided intriguing new directions and offered interesting new insight into effective distributed team performance. The discussion presented in this section briefly details some of the fresh perspectives advanced by Alutto, Coovert, and Burke in their chapters.

One important issue raised by Alutto (this volume) is concerned with the effects of distributed work for organizational structures. Specifically, Alutto asks whether the typical organizational structure would become more or less hierarchically structured in order to effectively support distributed teams. For our part, we suggest that one of the key advantages of teams is their capacity to take control of responsibilities typically relegated to management such as process planning, execution, and regulation. Thus, it seems reasonable, that distributed teams are a means to flattening hierarchical organizational structures. Whether or not flattened structures are ultimately a better conduit for facilitating effective distributed teamwork is a question to be answered by a programmatic line of empirical research.

Alutto (this volume) also raised an important issue regarding the need for trust in distributed teams. Alutto questioned whether the level of trust required in distributed teams fluctuates with the importance of the challenges a team faces, with the nature of the means via which a team makes its decisions, and/or by the types of members comprising a team. Each of these issues presents an interesting direction for research. We suggest that while the level of trust in distributed teams may vary with situational and organizational contingencies, there exists some baseline level of trust, which must exist for distributed teams to be effective. Additionally, we posit that the level of trust becomes more critical with increasing levels of interdependence and distribution among team members.

In addition to the meaningful insight provided by Alutto (this volume), Coovert and Burke (this volume) also provided fresh perspectives on distributed team performance. Among many insightful comments, Coovert and Burke raised an interesting point concerning the role of technology in distribution. As treated in our analysis, technology served only (or primarily) in the capacity of mediating team processes. That is, the communication necessary for a team to reach its goals was transmitted in varying degrees through different types of information technologies. Coovert and Burke allude to technology playing a more active role in team processes, one that amounts to having "artificial" team members wherein technology automates some of the teamwork processes necessary for coordination. This is undoubtedly an important topic that raises important issues and concerns (Klein, Woods, Bradshaw, Hoffman, & Fletovich, 2004) that we do not address in our chapter. Just as there is a continuum in the distribution of teamwork, there is likely a continuum in the degree to which technology plays a role in team processes, anchored on one end by pure mediation of team processes and on the other by fully artificial team members. These issues must be addressed by researchers in order to maximize the value of distributed teams.

Additionally, Coovert and Burke (this volume) provide a high level model of the relationships between three dimensions of distribution (geospatial, temporal, and technology), culture, and individual, team, and organizational capacity (the T-MoP Model). Capacity is the central construct of the T-MoP and though it is defined differently for each level (individual, team, and organizational), it generally can be understood as a "readiness" for effective performance. The capacity of any one level is related to capacities at other levels, as well as the influence of culture and characteristics of distribution. In general, the T-MoP summarizes a large amount of the empirical and theoretical literature on teams and distributed performance in a parsimonious manner. This approach and focus on performance capacities is promising and further efforts to tightly define relationships between capacities at different levels and subsequently the effects of movement along the continuums of distribution may yield valuable insight into how to engineer effective distributed teams and organizations.

A CONTINUED DIALOGUE

The importance of research conducted to understand distributed teams can not be understated – as underscored by the increasing prevalence of distributed teams in both private sector organizations (e.g., global mergers, strategy implementations) and public sector institutions (e.g., network-centric warfare). It seems organizations of all types are increasingly relying on distributed performance arrangements to adapt to the transformational changes that characterize modern operations. While distributed teams can offer important benefits to their members and employers when they are effectively instituted and managed, much remains to be learned about how best to facilitate their performance. We trust that Stagl and colleagues' (this volume) review of distributed team performance and the commentary and insights offered by Alutto (this volume) and Coovert and Burke (this volume) will shed some light on these issues.

REFERENCES

Alutto, J. A. (this volume). Issues in distributed team performance. In: F. Dansereau & F. Yammarino (Eds), *Research in multi-level issues* (Vol. 6). Amsterdam: Elsevier.

Beach, L. R. (Ed.) (1998). *Image theory: Theoretical and empirical foundations.* Mahwah, NJ: Erlbaum.

Coovert, M. D., & Burke, J. L. (this volume). T-MoP: A tetrahedral model of performance. In: F. Dansereau & F. Yammarino (Eds), *Research in multi-level issues* (Vol. 6). Amsterdam: Elsevier.

Fiore, S. M., Salas, E., Cuevas, H. M., & Bowers, C. A. (2003). Distributed coordination space: Toward a theory of distributed team process and performance. *Theoretical Issues in Ergonomics, 4,* 340–364.

Hackman, J. R. (2003). Learning more by crossing levels: Evidence from airplanes, hospitals, and orchestras. *Journal of Organizational Behavior, 24,* 905–922.

Klein, G., Woods, D. D., Bradshaw, J. M., Hoffman, R. R., & Fletovich, P. J. (2004). Ten challenges for making automation a "Team Player" in joint human-agent activity. *IEEE Intelligent Systems, 19*(6), 91–95.

March, J. G. (Ed.) (1988). *Decisions and organizations.* Oxford, UK: Basil Blackwell.

Salas, E., Cannon-Bowers, J. A., & Johnston, J. H. (1997). How can you turn a team of experts into an expert team? Emerging training strategies. In: C. E. Zsambok & G. Klein (Eds), *Naturalistic decision making* (pp. 359–370). Mahwah, NJ: Lawrence Erlbaum Associates.

Stagl, K. C., Salas, E., Rosen, M. A., Priest, H. A., Burke, C. S., Goodwin, G. F., & Johnston, J. H. (this volume). Distributed team performance: A multi-level review of distribution, demography, and decision-making. In: F. Dansereau & F. Yammarino (Eds), *Research in multi-level issues* (Vol 6). Amsterdam: Elsevier.

Zaccaro, S. J., & Bader, P. (2003). E-Leadership and the challenges of leading E-teams: Minimizing the bad and maximizing the good. *Organizational Dynamics, 31,* 377–387.

PART II:
MENTAL MODELS IN TEAMS

MENTAL MODEL CONVERGENCE: THE SHIFT FROM BEING AN INDIVIDUAL TO BEING A TEAM MEMBER

Sara A. McComb

ABSTRACT

Mental model convergence occurs as team members interact. By collecting information and observing behaviors through their interactions, team members' individual mental models evolve into shared mental models. This process requires a cognitive shift in an individual's focal level. Specifically, the individual assigned to the team must shift his or her focus from thinking about the team domain using an individual perspective to thinking about it from a team perspective. Thus, mental model convergence may be the key to understanding how individuals are transformed into team members. This chapter presents a framework describing the mental model convergence process that draws on the extant research on group development and information processing. It also examines temporal aspects of mental model convergence, the role of mental model contents on the convergence process, and the relationship between converged mental models and team functioning. Preliminary evidence supporting the framework and the important role that converged mental models play in high-performing teams is provided. The chapter concludes with a

Multi-Level Issues in Organizations and Time
Research in Multi-Level Issues, Volume 6, 95–147
ISSN: 1475-9144/doi:10.1016/S1475-9144(07)06005-5

discussion of the implications of this mental model convergence frame-
work for research and practice.

INTRODUCTION

Individuals assembled into project teams are considered team members even
from the team's inception. They join the team as representatives of different
functional units (Cohen & Bailey, 1997). The functional perspectives they
bring to the team are internalized and drive their interactions. Indeed, even
when instructed to act in the team's best interest, these team members may
demonstrate bias toward the interests of their functions (Dearborn &
Simon, 1958). In this way, they act as individuals rather than team members.
As a result, organizations hoping to tap the specialized, unique knowledge
of these team members to the advantage of the team may not achieve their
anticipated results due to these internalized functional perspectives of the
individuals assigned to the team. The challenge is to turn individuals focused
on their own goals and the goals of their functional units into team members
working toward the collective good. As described in this chapter mental
model convergence may represent a means to accomplish this transition.

Examining the transition from individual to cross-functional project team
member provides an interesting opportunity to examine multi-level team
behavior. The level shift of interest occurs within the minds of individuals as
their focus shifts from the individual level to the team level through interaction with their teammates. Thus, the level issue being investigated is the
individual's shift in focal level. The resultant team perspective, while originating at the individual level, can also be studied as a team-level collective
construct that guides team behavior. Explicating how the focal shift transpires at the individual level, however, is the primary interest in this chapter.

The focal shift occurs during the initial stages of development when team
members process information regarding their assignment, the team members
assembled to complete it, and the collaborative processes that may be used
to accomplish it. By processing this team-relevant information, they become
familiar with their team circumstances. Cognitively, however, they have not
become team members until they achieve some degree of cognitive unifi-
cation with their teammates. Shared mental models are a useful means of
assessing such a cognitive shift in perspectives (Salas, Dickinson, Converse,
& Tannenbaum, 1992).

Research on team cognition, in general, and shared mental models, in
particular, is maturing (Fiore & Salas, 2004). Advances have been made in

our understanding of the role that shared mental models play in improving team performance (e.g., Baba, Gluesing, Ratner, & Wagner, 2004; Marks, Zaccaro, & Mathieu, 2000; Marks, Sabella, Burke, & Zaccaro, 2002; Mathieu, Heffner, Goodwin, Salas, & Cannon-Bowers, 2000; Mathieu, Heffner, Goodwin, Cannon-Bowers, & Salas, 2005; Smith-Jentsch, Mathieu, & Kraiger, 2005; Webber, Chen, Payne, Marsh, & Zaccaro, 2000) and in devising effective ways to measure shared mental models (e.g., Cooke, Salas, Kiekel, & Bell, 2004; Mohammed, Klimoski, & Rentsch, 2000). Despite this large body of literature, the way in which mental model content converges over time to become shared mental models has not been fully explicated. This chapter remedies that omission by presenting a framework describing the mental model convergence process. To accomplish this purpose, it focuses on the general convergence process of mental model content for project teams.

Other types of teams may follow the same process, but project teams face unique challenges when trying to establish shared mental models because they are made up of cross-functional representatives and their assignments are both time-limited and nonrepetitive (Cohen & Bailey, 1997). Through her investigation of product development teams, Dougherty (1992) found that when team members view information strictly from their respective functional perspectives, they might overlook, or ignore, information critical to the completion of the project. Furthermore, team members who have this proclivity for viewing their environment through their own particular specialized paradigms are inclined to limit the amount of interaction that occurs among members. Approaching a project in this manner hinders a team's ability to collaborate, thereby diminishing its ability to generate an innovative solution. Time limitations set for project teams and the nonrepetitiveness of the team's task may further aggravate these circumstances. If team members feel time pressure to complete their tasks, they may be unable or unwilling to spend time gathering information from teammates. Protocols and lessons learned from previous projects may be minimally useful given the nonrepetitive nature of project work. As a consequence, the establishment of shared mental models may prove particularly challenging for project teams, while at the same time being necessary for high-quality performance. This chapter focuses on project teams both to limit the scope of the discussion and to provide a context for examples.

The chapter begins with a brief review of the mental models and shared mental models literature that is relevant to this work. It then examines the process of creating one mental model by introducing a framework describing mental model convergence. In later sections of the chapter, the convergence process is expanded to multiple mental models, the role of mental model content in the convergence process is explicated, and the mental model convergence process is embedded in team functioning. Preliminary evidence is provided that represents a first step toward validating the mental model convergence framework and identifying the relationship between converged mental model content and team performance. The chapter concludes with a discussion of the implications of this research for academicians and practitioners.

REVIEW OF THE SHARED MENTAL MODELS LITERATURE

Mental Models and Shared Mental Models Defined

Humans create representations of their worlds that are simpler than the entities they represent (Johnson-Laird, 1983). These representations, also known as *mental models*, are cognitive structures that include specific knowledge that humans use to describe, explain, and predict their surroundings (Rouse & Morris, 1986). Mental models reduce uncertainty in the lives of the individuals possessing them in at least two ways (Klimoski & Mohammed, 1994). First, individuals devise heuristics to classify and retrieve the most salient pieces of information about situations, objects, and environments from their mental models (Cannon-Bowers, Salas, & Converse, 1993). This process allows them to develop an understanding of their current situation based on extant knowledge related to it, thereby reducing uncertainty associated with the current situation. Second, information contained in mental models can be used to identify potential outcomes in a manner similar to a computer simulation. Specifically, humans can "run" possible scenarios based on the information that is categorically sorted and stored within their minds and the complex situation in which they find themselves to identify potential outcomes (Cannon-Bowers et al., 1993). This process of identifying potential outcomes also reduces uncertainty.

A collection of individuals working together as a team also create mental representations, or shared mental models, that reduce uncertainty relating to team activities. Shared mental models are "knowledge structures held by members of a team that enable them to form accurate explanations and expectations for the task, and in turn, to coordinate their actions and adapt their behavior to demands of [their unique domain]" (Cannon-Bowers et al., 1993, p. 228). As the definition indicates, these structures are not held collectively at the team level, but rather are held at the individual level (Hill & Levenhagen, 1995; Rentsch & Woehr, 2004). As members of the team begin to interact, the individual mental models evolve as the team undergoes a complex, iterative process (Donnellon, Gray, & Bougon, 1986; Hill & Levenhagen, 1995) until they converge to a point that allows the team to function as a collective. Once converged, shared mental models are expected to influence the way in which individuals cognitively process new team-relevant information. Specifically, they will influence both the content of what is processed and the speed with which it is processed (Walsh, 1995). Thus, by shifting their focus from the individual level to the team level, team members are better able to complete the project in a manner that is globally optimal for themselves, their teammates, and their organization.

Mental Model Content and Structure

Both the content and the structure of the shared mental models may be of interest. Content refers to knowledge about "tasks, situations, response patterns, working relationships" as well as "internalized beliefs, assumptions, and perceptions" that individual team members hold regarding their team circumstances (Klimoski & Mohammed, 1994, p. 426). The structure of mental models references how this content is organized and stored. The way in which the content is structured "may derive from presumed cause and effect linkages or ... merely may reflect learned patterns ..., in all likelihood, such knowledge is organized semantically" (Klimoski & Mohammed, 1994, p. 426). Although the critical distinction between content and structure has been made in the mental model literature (e.g., Klimoski & Mohammed, 1994; Mohammed et al., 2000; Rentsch & Woehr, 2004), the interplay between content and structure has not yet been fully elucidated. Rentsch and Woehr (2004) speculate that the congruence in content, in structure, or in both may be of interest. Research is needed to clarify the relative importance of content and structure with respect to shared mental models.

Owing to the lack of empirical evidence, it is necessary to use logic to demonstrate the progression of sharing across content and structure that may occur as teams interact. At the beginning of team activity, individuals join the team possessing mental model content. This content may be unique or overlapping. Also, it may be organized in unique or overlapping structures. Indeed, team members may share common knowledge structures based on their experiences that have been common or shared (Bar-Tal, 1990). Through collective activity their content may become shared across members, but the content may be stored differently by different individuals (Mohammed et al., 2000). To reorganize the shared content so that the structure is also shared may be possible, but extensive training – such as that provided to military teams – would be required.

In their review of mental model measurement techniques, Mohammed and colleagues (2000) imply that mental models are relevant only if structure is considered. This perspective seems justified when situations demand immediate, predictable action from team members functioning in an uncertain environment, such as the actions of military teams conducting an operation in the field. When team members' lives depend on one another's actions, those actions should be predictable even as the dynamic situation in which they are functioning unfolds. Shared mental model structure facilitates this predictability by ensuring that the connections between pieces of information are the same across team members, so the application of mental model content should happen in the same manner across team members. In this sense, the commonality of structure across these team members' mental models is critical because it may guide a member's behavior in a manner that is anticipated by his or her teammates. Military teams and the like are provided extensive training through which shared mental model content *and* shared mental model structure emerge.

In non-life-threatening situations where team members have an opportunity to communicate before decisions are made, developing common mental model structure may not be as important. For instance, under normal circumstances, project teams (e.g., new-product development teams) have time to discuss issues and reflect on courses of action. Under these conditions, the actions of fellow team members need not be as immediately predictable as those of military team members. Therefore, the structure of their mental models, which dictates their information retrieval process, need not be similar. As long as team members are able to reach similar conclusions through their common mental model content, regardless of the cognitive path each individual follows to get there, the project team has the potential to function effectively.

The distinct roles of content and structure have not been clearly articulated in the shared mental model empirical research conducted to date. For instance, research results with respect to convergence have been mixed. Mathieu and colleagues (2000, 2005) did not find convergence, whereas Eden, Jones, Sims, and Smithin (1981) did. The manner in which mental model content was identified in this research may help to explain the different results with respect to convergence.

Mathieu and colleagues (2000, 2005) did not find convergence of mental model structure using a network-analysis program (i.e., UNICET) that calculates an index of convergence. This index calculates the similarity between team member mental model matrices. The matrices consisted of the team members' assessments of the relationship between mental model attributes (e.g., amount of information and quality of information) that had been identified by the researchers prior to the experiment. In short, this approach focuses on patterns among attributes provided to the team by the researchers. These patterns are used to represent the mental model structure associated with these attributes.

Eden and colleagues (1981) discuss how convergence has been observed through the use of causal maps consisting of "concepts and language used by members of a team" (Eden et al., 1981, p. 41). The authors explain how they have successfully used causal maps with individuals and groups to facilitate the process of achieving mutual understanding. Through their process, they have been able to observe how individual and group maps mutually influence one another as team members iteratively create individual and group maps over time. Thus, this approach focuses on patterns among attributes identified by the team members. This limited evidence suggests that content elicited from individuals may play a significant role in our ability to capture mental model convergence, including structural convergence.

Shared Mental Models and Team Performance

The framework presented in this chapter will not link mental models to team performance directly. Recent empirical advances demonstrating the role that shared mental models play in effective team functioning, however, provide motivation for examining the mental model convergence process. Specifically, evidence indicates that the existence of shared mental models is useful in developing greater understanding among team members regarding one another's needs and information requirements (Stout, Cannon-Bowers, Salas, & Milanovich, 1999) and in minimizing the need for explicit communication and coordination in high-stress situations (Entin & Serfaty, 1999). Shared mental models have also been shown to improve team processing (Hong, Doll, Nahm, & Li, 2004; Marks et al., 2000; Mathieu et al., 2000, 2005) and team performance (Baba et al., 2004; Marks et al., 2000, 2002; Mathieu et al., 2000, 2005; Smith-Jentsch et al., 2005; Webber et al., 2000). More specifically, those teams relating higher-quality mental models appear to exhibit better team processes and higher performance (Mathieu et al., 2005). Finally, shared mental models can be enhanced through training (Marks et al., 2000, 2002; Smith-Jentsch, Campbell, Milanovich, & Reynolds, 2001). Together, these results demonstrate an overwhelming need to better understand how a collection of individuals interact to create shared mental models.

A MENTAL MODEL CONVERGENCE FRAMEWORK

Mental model convergence is a bottom-up (emergent) process (Klimoski & Mohammed, 1994; Kozlowski & Klein, 2000). This process begins at the onset of team activity when each individual team member has a unique, independent view of the team domain, including the individual team members, the team, the organization, and the environment (Kraiger & Wenzel, 1997). Through teammates' interactions, the contents of team members' mental models converge to become similar to the content of other members' mental models. Over time, as new information becomes available (e.g., a new team member joins the team, team goals are revised), the mental models may be revisited, and correspondingly revised, to incorporate the new information. Thus, the mental model convergence process is continuous throughout the team's existence, and it occurs at the individual level because mental models are held by individuals (Hill & Levenhagen, 1995; Rentsch & Woehr, 2004).

Although the cognitive processing required to create mental models occurs at the individual level, the focal level of the mental model content shifts from the individual to the team. Stated another way, individuals assigned to the team must shift their focus away from themselves as individual functional representatives assigned to a team and to their roles as team members working toward the collective good. The cognitive processes that facilitate this shift in focal level are a primary focus of this research. To identify these cognitive processes, one can draw upon group development and information processing research. The result is the framework of mental model convergence depicted in Fig. 1.

As previously discussed in the review of the shared mental model literature, content and structure are the two aspects of mental models that require clear articulation by researchers. As the logic laid out earlier suggests, converged content may be a precursor to converged structure. For this reason, both this chapter and the framework itself emphasize the convergence of mental model content. The way in which mental model structural

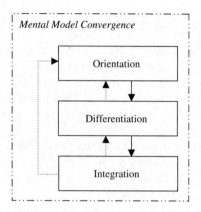

Fig. 1. The Mental Model Convergence Process.

convergence proceeds may follow the same process that mental model content follows. Achieving structural convergence, however, may require a longer period of time and more focused attention. The task of articulating any specific differences between the mental model convergence process of content and structure is left to future researchers. The rest of this section is devoted to explaining the mental model convergence framework, beginning with a brief review of the literatures on group development and information processing as they relate to the framework.

Research on group development has evolved into at least three distinct approaches. First, early research focused on a socially driven process – most notably, Tuckman's (1965) forming, storming, and norming model. Other variations are found in the literature, but the generalized process is basically the same (Tuckman & Jensen, 1977). Second, Gersick (1988, 1989) introduced a pace-driven team development process that uses punctuated equilibrium to explain how team activity is divided into two periods of equilibrium during which team member behavior does not substantively change. A mid-point transition occurs between the two periods. During this transition, significant changes in team behavior are implemented to enable the team to function effectively throughout the second equilibrium period. Third, Kozlowski, Gully, Nason, and Smith (1999) devised a task-driven, multi-level approach to team development that focuses on those team processes required at different stages of development and the corresponding way in which the focal level shifts from the individual to dyads to the team. These three approaches may all be valid. Indeed, evidence suggests that during the periods of equilibrium identified in Gersick's (1988) pace-driven approach, both socially driven and task-driven group development may be occurring (Chang, Bordia, & Duck, 2003).

All three approaches relate to the mental model convergence framework presented in this chapter. Specifically, the stages of the socially driven process inform the level shift that occurs during the phases of mental model convergence. The task-driven approach is used to demonstrate when multiple mental models may develop over the course of a team's life. Finally, the pace-driven approach helps to identify when mental models may need maintenance. The roles of the task- and pace-driven approaches in the mental model convergence process will be examined in later sections of this chapter. The role of socially driven group development processes in mental model convergence is described next.

The mental model convergence process is a cognitive process in which the focal level of interest begins at the individual level and evolves to the team level. Socially driven group development research provides guidance for explaining the shift from an individual to a team member. Specifically, members (1) form – orient themselves to the team domain; (2) storm – view the team from their individual perspectives, which may cause conflict among team members; and (3) transform – allow their individual perspectives to evolve into team norms. In the process described here, the shift to the team level happens in the third stage of development.

While group development research is useful for explaining the level shift in the mental model convergence process, information processing research helps to describe the cognitive aspects of the framework. The information processing required to integrate new information with existing information follows a three-phase process. In particular, information processing occurs when (1) information captures an individual's attention (Hinsz, Tindale, & Vollrath, 1997); (2) the information is encoded, stored (Hinsz et al., 1997), and differentiated (Driver & Streufert, 1969; Schroder, Driver, & Streufert, 1967); and (3) the differences are reconciled, or integrated, in such a way that the information becomes useful for making a response (Driver & Streufert, 1969; Hinsz et al., 1997; Schroder et al., 1967).

Overlapping the socially driven team development and information processing perspectives results in a three-phase framework for examining the cognitive processing that team members undertake to shift their focus from themselves as individuals to themselves as functioning team members (see Fig. 1). The first phase requires an *orientation* to the team domain through the capture of team-relevant information. This information is *differentiated* as it is encoded and stored in a manner that provides individual team members with a view of the team that may (or may not) be similar to their fellow team members' views in the second phase of mental model convergence. In the final phase, these disparate views are *integrated* into a team view that can be used to guide team behavior. This three-phase framework can be summarized in the following proposition:

Proposition 1. Mental model convergence is a three-phase process whereby individuals (1) orient themselves to the team domain, (2) differentiate the disparate perspectives of the team members, and (3) integrate these views into a team perspective.

The following paragraphs provide detailed descriptions of the three phases of mental model convergence and offer subpropositions relating to each phase. This section ends by examining temporal aspects of the mental model convergence process.

Orientation

The orientation phase of mental model convergence occurs at the individual level through team-level interaction. As team members provide and collect information among themselves, individual team members amass team-relevant information that they did not previously possess. In this manner, the team members are functioning as a team-level memory retrieval system. Specifically, they exchange team-relevant information among themselves in a manner analogous to an individual retrieving relevant information from memory (Larson & Christensen, 1993). The collected information is then used to inform the team members' mental models about the team. This initial phase of mental model convergence can be described as a collective induction process, in which information – in the form of ideas, knowledge, and strategy – is disseminated among all members (McNeese, 2000).

The dissemination process through which information is acquired and exchanged may transpire through a number of modes. The most obvious and critical mode is verbal articulation (Hill & Levenhagen, 1995). Verbal articulation facilitates the pooling of unshared information, which is the motivation for assembling teams (Wittenbaum & Stasser, 1996). Yet, individuals have a proclivity for discussing only knowledge that is commonly held by all members of the team (Stasser, Stewart, & Wittenbaum, 1995; Stasser, Taylor, & Hanna, 1989). One reason for this practice may be that those members who hold common information are more inclined to participate in the conversation (Larson, Sargis, & Bauman, 2004). If only shared knowledge is discussed, however, the proclaimed benefits of cross-functionality will not be realized (Mohammed & Dumville, 2001; Wittenbaum & Stasser, 1996).

Perceived experts (i.e., those members whose task-relevant expertise is acknowledged by their teammates) can help realize these benefits as they emphasize both shared knowledge and others' unique knowledge (Thomas-Hunt, Ogden, & Neale, 2003). In this way, perceived experts play a critical role in the collective induction process that transpires during orientation. They can facilitate discussions that increase the amount of commonly held information and establish the credibility of the other team members. By establishing individual expertise and credibility through facilitated discussions, the team creates an atmosphere in which information sharing among all team members can thrive throughout the team's life (Wittenbaum & Stasser, 1996), because individuals seek information from those they deem to possess relevant, valuable information (Borgatti & Cross, 2003).

More than just an exchange of words, however, may be necessary. Indeed, the information acquisition process among individuals who are unfamiliar with one another occurs via observation, experimentation, *and* inquiry (Ostroff & Kozlowski, 1992). More specifically, it may occur through surveillance (i.e., broad, routine scans of the team domain) or motivated search (i.e., intense focus on a specific area to gain specific information) (Corner, Kinicki, & Keats, 1994). Regardless of the acquisition method employed, team members need more than a series of facts. They must also appreciate the differences among themselves (Mitchell, 1986). Gaining this appreciation requires that team members gather information during the orientation phase regarding the way in which their teammates interpret the words (Dougherty, 1992) and the significance that other team members attach to the discovered differences among themselves (Smircich & Chesser, 1981).

Even if the orientation phase is facilitated, some information may be missing from mental models. The goal of the orientation phase is to use the techniques described to create a comprehensive understanding of the team situation. This comprehensive understanding represents the foundation upon which the remaining convergence process rests and facilitates the emergence of the most complete mental models possible. This leads to the following proposition:

Proposition 1a. Orientation is the phase of mental model convergence, where team members collect new information and pool unshared information about the team domain and their fellow team members through observation, experimentation, and inquiry.

Differentiation

Differentiation is the mental model convergence phase that occurs when the information collected about each team member is cognitively organized and merged with existing knowledge to form individuals' mental models governing their behavior. The mental models will contain information about the team, but the focal level remains the individual because the content is the team members' perspectives, which may or may not be shared across team members at this point in the convergence process. This phase is critical because many pieces of information collected during orientation must be consolidated and organized. This consolidation and organization step is necessary so that each individual member can recognize the different perspectives regarding the information collected that are held by his or her teammates (Bartunek, Gordon, & Weathersby, 1983; Gruenfeld & Hollingshead, 1993) in preparation for integrating these perspectives in the next phase.

The process of differentiation described here is analogous to creating a transactive memory system, which is a cooperative memory system for encoding, storing, and retrieving information (Wegner, 1987, 1995). In a transactive memory system, individuals hold their own unique knowledge about a particular situation and a directory of the knowledge held by their teammates about the same situation. In this manner, members of the team share the storage responsibilities of critical information among themselves, thereby creating meta-knowledge of who knows what on the team (Yoo & Kanawattanachai, 2001). A married couple provides a simple example of a dyadic transactive memory system: For instance, the husband does not have to learn how to program the DVR because he knows that his wife possesses the knowledge necessary to complete the task for him.

To date, inquiry in this area has explored only expertise as the type of knowledge stored in a transactive memory system (e.g., Levine & Moreland, 1999; Lewis, Kinnett, & Gillis, 2001). Austin's (2003) work is a notable exception. In addition to testing for expertise transactive memory, he examined relationship transactive memory. The concept of the transactive memory system may be generalized to include any type of knowledge structure, particularly those relevant to the team domain. For example, team members may create an indexing system of how other members interpret the team's goals or what they believe about the way in which the organization supports the team. Thus, the transactive memory system provides a means of encoding and storing information relevant to the mental models under development. This understanding leads to the following proposition:

Proposition 1b. Differentiation is the phase of mental model convergence where team members sort, consolidate, organize, and store the information collected in the orientation phase to create a transactive memory system that can easily be accessed when the information must be retrieved.

Integration

Integration represents the final phase of the mental model convergence process. During this phase, the team must reconcile the diversity among their individual perspectives (Gruenfeld & Hollingshead, 1993). As part of this reconciliation process, the focal unit of interest shifts from the individual level to the team level. To accomplish this shift in focal unit, team members interact and negotiate with one another about the differences in their mental model content that were identified during the differentiation phase of mental model convergence. Thus, integration is a transformational process (Dansereau, Yammarino, & Kohles, 1999) through which individuals modify their own mental models. As the mental model content converges across team members, the information contained in the mental models becomes shared and shared mental models emerge. In sum, the result of integration is a reconciliation of the various team members' individual mental models into shared mental models that will allow team members to collaborate effectively as they complete their assignment.

While this process sounds straightforward, it is not. The remainder of this section examines two issues that influence the success of the integration effort – namely, defining the term "sharing" and achieving optimal integration.

Definitions of Sharing
One criticism of shared mental models research is that it does not offer adequate explanation regarding the way in which knowledge must be shared to successfully approach and accomplish assigned projects (Cannon-Bowers & Salas, 2001; Rentsch & Woehr, 2004). The definition of "shared" could indicate that knowledge structures are held in common (e.g., sharing a religious belief) or are divided (e.g., sharing a candy bar) among team members (Cannon-Bowers & Salas, 2001; Cooke, Salas, Cannon-Bowers, & Stout, 2000; Klimoski & Mohammed, 1994; Mohammed & Dumville, 2001).

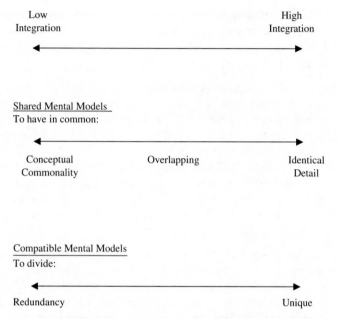

Fig. 2. The Relationship between Integration and Sharing.

These two definitions can also represent the way in which integration will be manifested as team members reconcile the diversity among their perspectives. The shared content resulting from integration may be held commonly by team members (e.g., sharing a perspective regarding the team's goal), while other content may be divided among team members (e.g., sharing responsibility for attaining the goal).

These definitions do not represent two static states. Rather, each definition represents a continuum along which degrees of sharing may emerge (Mohammed et al., 2000). Fig. 2 depicts how integration corresponds to the two definitions of sharing and how the degree of integration and the corresponding degree of sharing range along a continuum. The appropriate definition of sharing to be applied is determined by the mental model contents, as will be discussed later in this chapter.

If knowledge structures are held "in common," the degree of integration is determined by examining the level of detail commonly held among team members. Commonality could range from conceptual commonality (i.e., very little detail is shared across team members) to identical (i.e., complete detail is shared across team members), as shown in Fig. 2. For example, one benefit of a cross-functional project team is that all relevant functional perspectives are represented on the team and each perspective has its own functional requirements that must be met. The integration of the different functional requirements could occur in one of three ways:

- The team could work with conceptually common mental models by understanding that each member has different functional requirements that he or she will ensure are met by the end product.
- The team may create identical mental models so that each team member is aware of all functional requirements.
- The amount of detail held commonly would be overlapping somewhere between conceptual commonality and identical detail, where everyone understands that various functional requirements exist and they possess some detail about the other functional requirements most relevant to their own.

When the "to divide" definition of sharing is applied, knowledge is distributed among the team members. Distribution implies that the team's knowledge is stored in dispersed locations (i.e., with various team members) and that the team's collective memory comprises the memory of the individuals and the processes of communication that occur among the team members (Wegner, 1987, 1995). This type of mental model is applicable to content that represents individual responsibilities, such as work allocation and expertise. Applying this definition, the transformation from the individual level to the team level occurs when team members find their niche on the team and understand how their roles relate to the roles of other members. As depicted in Fig. 2, highly integrated teams include members who have unique knowledge that is not held in common with any other member. When knowledge redundancy exists on the team, the degree of integration is lower.

Both definitions rely on the amount of detail shared by team members. If the amount of detail shared by team members is high, however, the degree of integration is the opposite for each definition. That is, when the "in common" definition is applied and a high amount of detail is shared, the mental models are highly integrated and approach the identical end of the continuum shown in Fig. 2. Conversely, if information is divided among team members, then sharing a high amount of detail indicates redundancy or low integration.

Selecting the appropriate definition depends on the mental model content. In many cases, common sense drives the definition applied. For instance, the team's goal is held in common while expertise is divided among the members of a cross-functional project team. A more rigorous approach to ascertain which definition is most appropriate may be useful, such as an economic cost-benefit analysis. For example, Postrel (2002) developed a production function in which optimal levels of specialization and mutual understanding are determined by two criteria: the relative learning costs and the marginal payoff to overall capability. The conclusion he draws, based on his results, is that too much emphasis has been placed on the role of trans-specialists (versus specialists) when these trans-specialists could be replaced with competent specialists for less-learning costs. Overlaying Postrel's research on the two definitions of sharing allows us to look at trans-specialists as those individuals who hold information in common and specialists as those individuals who divide information. Thus, where the costs of learning information are low (e.g., general understanding of individual competencies), the knowledge can be held in common. Where the learning costs are high (e.g., becoming a specialist in a given area), the team may be better served if the knowledge is divided among team members.

Degrees of Integration
The final phase of the mental model convergence process is complete when the team has achieved a degree of integration that allows it to successfully conduct its requisite taskwork. Identifying the precise degree of integration is a very important consideration because the ability of the team to perform may be hindered when the optimal degree of integration is not obtained. Put succinctly, team performance may suffer if too much or too little integration transpires. If information is highly integrated among team members when less integration is optimal, performance may suffer in at least two ways. First, the team may consider only a limited scope of information (Corner et al., 1994; Walsh, 1995), thereby reducing its capacity to be innovative (Gersick & Hackman, 1990). Second, the team may misinterpret situations by misreading a novel circumstance or failing to see a change (Gersick & Hackman, 1990). Alternatively, if information is not adequately integrated, the team may not achieve the process and performance improvements shown to result from the presence of shared mental models. Or worse, they may suffer from no focus and competing efforts.

The precise degree of integration may depend on the scope and nature of the team's assignment, the team's unique cognitive style, and the content of its mental model. The discussion here briefly highlights why the team's assignment and its cognitive style are relevant; a later section of this chapter addresses, in general terms, the role of mental model content. Detailed investigations of these important topics are left to future researchers.

If the team's assignment is relatively simple and small in scope, the team may choose to be highly integrated with respect to commonly held information and, at the same time, possess redundancy in its distributed knowledge about the required tasks. In this way, everyone on the team understands the requirements, and those requirements could be fulfilled by several team members. Alternatively, a large, complex assignment would make mental models consisting of identical content and large amounts of redundant knowledge inefficient. Under these circumstances, careful consideration of what information should be held in common is needed.

The nature of the assignment might also influence integration. Specifically, Gruenfeld and Hollingshead (1993) found that high integration was useful for tasks that required members to identify trade-offs and joint solutions cooperatively. In contrast, tasks requiring members to act independently to protect their own individual interests were best accomplished with low levels of integration.

Team-level cognitive style describes differences in the way in which cognitive structures and cognitive processing evolve in different teams (Schneider & Angelmar, 1993). Various ways in which cognitive style may become manifest are presented by Leonard, Beauvais, and Scholl (2005). They apply a Jungian framework of individual cognitive style to the team level. In particular, they advocate that teams may have cognitive approaches along four pairs of dimensions:

- Introverted (discuss among group members) versus extroverted (discuss with individuals outside group).
- Sensing (gather detailed, specific information to frame problems in operational terms) versus intuitive (gather abstract information that focuses on possibilities to frame problems in strategic terms).
- Thinking (use logic and facts to evaluate information) versus feeling (use relative weights and merits to evaluate information).
- Perceptive (focus on gathering – versus evaluating – information) versus judging (seek closure based on information available for evaluation).

When attempting to specify the precise degree of integration, these dimensions of cognitive style may influence the way in which integration transpires for teams. The following proposition summarizes this discussion about integration:

Proposition 1c. Integration is the phase of mental model convergence in which team members reconcile the differences in their individual perspectives so as to shift their focal unit of interest to the team level by: (i) holding information in common or dividing it among the team members, depending on the type of information being shared, and (ii) achieving an optimal degree of integration.

Temporal Aspects of Mental Model Convergence Process

Individuals and teams will pass through the three-phase mental model convergence process to shift their individual-level perspectives to the team level. This process transpires over time at different speeds for different teams and for different mental model content. At the individual level, Schroder and colleagues (1967) identified two factors that will affect the speed at which integration can be completed: the amount of information processing required and the speed with which individuals can process information. Generalizing to the team level, these two factors may also determine the pace at which shared mental models will emerge. To begin the discussion, I offer the basic proposition:

Proposition 2. Mental model convergence will follow the three-phase framework regardless of the pace of information processing.

Amount of Information Processing

The amount of information processing required may be dependent, primarily, on the amount of shared information that is imported (Gersick & Hackman, 1990). The most prevalent way in which shared information is imported is through team member familiarity. If the team members have worked together on prior occasions, then the amount of information processing required may be minimal because the members are already familiar with one another and may have established protocols for working together. The main focus of their mental model convergence process will pertain to unique information about their new assignment. At the opposite end of the spectrum, a team composed of individuals who have never worked together will require a significant amount of information processing to achieve mental model convergence. Many teams will fall between these two extremes because they include some members who have worked together before and others who are new to one another. Under these conditions, mental model convergence occurs with limited information processing for those team members familiar with one another and may require significant information processing for those unfamiliar with one another. In addition to team member familiarity, shared information could be imported in the form of a strong team leader or other team member who dictates many of the protocols, thereby limiting the amount of information processing required. Hence:

Proposition 2a. The amount of information processing required to converge mental models will depend on the amount of imported information that is already shared among team members.

Speed of Information Processing
With respect to speed of information processing, mental model convergence may range from quick convergence at the first team encounter to an evolutionary process that transpires over time (Gersick & Hackman, 1990).

Quick development may be due to the perceptions that team members bring to the team, such as "expectations about task, each other, and the context and their repertoires of behavioral routines and performance strategies" (Gersick, 1988, p. 33). Such quick development may imply that the process is done implicitly (Gersick, 1988). Even when mental models converge implicitly, the mental model convergence process presented is still relevant because each individual processes information to develop a mental model of the team circumstances. Such quick, implicit information processing may speed the convergence process. The resultant mental models, however, may be more inconsistent across team members, as they have not shared as much information. Further, the accuracy and comprehensiveness of the resultant mental models may be questionable.

At the other end of the spectrum, information processing speed may unfold as an evolutionary process based on team activity. For example, information gathering may occur over several meetings. Under these circumstances, mental model convergence may be iterative. Team members may process information gathered at one encounter and use it to create preliminary mental models. These mental models may then be altered at the next encounter, when additional information becomes available. This evolutionary process may occur throughout the life of the team. Indeed, team members may become more able, or more motivated, to identify diverse perspectives among members over time (Gruenfeld & Hollingshead, 1993), thereby prolonging the mental model convergence process as the mental models are further refined.

Information processing speed may also depend on the direction of movement through the mental model convergence phases (i.e., orientation, differentiation, and integration). Movement between phases may be triggered when the equilibrium in one phase is upset (Gibson, 2001). In other words, when further processing in a given phase is no longer possible, a shift out of that phase becomes necessary. As the arrows between phases in Fig. 1 indicate, shifts to different phases may be either forward (solid-line arrows) or back to a previous phase (dotted-line arrows). Logic suggests that constant forward movement will result in quicker mental model convergence than a process that shifts back to previous phases for further clarification. For instance, as an individual consolidates data regarding the motivations and abilities of team members, he or she may have incomplete information about one or more teammates. Under such circumstances, team members may be required to follow a recursive loop back into the orientation phase to give the individual with incomplete information an opportunity to collect the missing pieces of information. Alternatively, if the missing information is deemed ancillary to the team assignment, the individual may proceed directly into the integration phase, where differences among team members' transactive memory systems can be reconciled. In sum:

Proposition 2b. The speed of information processing will depend on whether the convergence process occurs implicitly, explicitly, and/or iteratively.

THE SIMULTANEOUS EXISTENCE OF MULTIPLE MENTAL MODELS

Recent evidence suggests that multiple mental models exist simultaneously. In particular, they can be invoked concurrently and influence team performance uniquely. Studies have found that teamwork and taskwork mental models function at the same time (e.g., Mathieu et al., 2000; Smith-Jentsch et al., 2005). Teamwork references the many collaborative processes required to maintain the team, such as cooperation, communication, and interpersonal relationships (McIntyre & Salas, 1995). Taskwork describes the functional job behaviors required to accomplish the assignment (McIntyre & Salas, 1995). Mathieu and colleagues (2000) examined teamwork and taskwork mental models held by undergraduates who collaborated in a simulated military exercise. They found partial support for a positive relationship between shared mental models and performance. Specifically, the teamwork shared mental model had a direct influence on performance. Both the teamwork and the taskwork shared mental models, when mediated by team processes, had positive relationships with performance.

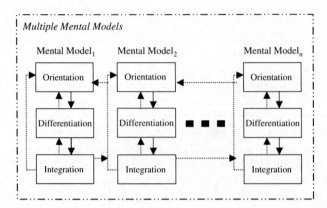

Fig. 3.   The Mental Model Convergence Process for Multiple Mental Models.

Smith-Jentsch and colleagues (2005) moved beyond generic teamwork and taskwork mental model assessment by focusing on domain-specific mental models – namely, positional–goal interdependence (teamwork) and cue–strategy associations (taskwork). The consistency (i.e., "the extent to which respondents have the same relative priority of perceptions – but not whether those perceptions are identical" (Smith-Jentsch et al., 2005, p. 526)) of these mental models across team members interacted to influence per-formance. These findings support the notion of multiple mental models existing simultaneously.

Fig. 3 expands the mental model convergence process to include multiple mental models based on the evidence presented. While the existence of multiple mental models might occur simultaneously, the convergence may not. The convergence process could potentially occur at different speeds for each mental model. The speed may depend, in part, on the amount of previously held knowledge team members possess that is applicable to the current situation. For example, if a majority of team members have worked together on previous projects, logic suggests that much less time may be required for mental model convergence than when a set of individuals have no previous experience working together.

In addition to the speed to convergence difference, the point in a team's life when various shared mental models emerge may be different because the convergence process is entwined in the team development process. Indeed, mental model convergence may occur, to various degrees, across all stages of development. Kozlowski and colleagues (1999) present a multi-level task-driven model of team development that can be used to demonstrate the content of various mental models and indicate when the corresponding convergence processes may be initiated. Their four-stage process begins at the individual level, with the team formation and task compilation stages. The team members then shift their focus to the dyad in the role compilation stage and then to the team in the team compilation stage. The following discussion describes the purpose of each stage put forth by Kozlowski and colleagues and examines how shared mental models may emerge at each stage. To correspond with this discussion, Fig. 4 maps the multiple mental model convergence processes that may emerge onto the team development stages. The purpose of this exercise is to demonstrate how multiple mental models may emerge and how information processed for one mental model (or set of mental models) may influence the emergence of other mental models.

Team formation is the first phase of team development. During this phase, team members make sense of the uncertainty under which they find themselves working, particularly the social uncertainty. Through this stage, they must gain interpersonal knowledge of their teammates and orient themselves to the goal set before the team. At the end of the team formation stage, team members will have worked their way through the three phases of mental model convergence and developed a preliminary set of shared mental models about interpersonal behavior and any associated expectations. They will also have collected and organized the information needed for establishing mental models concerning the team's goals. A preliminary set of shared mental models based on this content is anticipated.

The second stage of team development proposed by Kozlowski et al. (1999) is the task compilation stage, wherein team members begin to focus on their individual roles within the team as those roles relate to the task assigned. Through this stage, individuals will gain a better understanding of the task goals as they determine how their own expertise fits with the task facing the team and develop self-regulatory skills that will help them apply their expertise appropriately throughout the team's existence. As the team members begin to think about the task, their goal mental models will become integrated. They will also begin to think about the types of expertise required and how they, as individuals, fill those requirements. Logically, they will also want to understand how the remaining expertise needs will be met. Therefore, this task-related expertise exploration may be expanded to include gathering information about the expertise of other team members. Team members do not begin to ascertain linkages with these other team-mates at this point, but rather simply engage in data gathering and organizing activities. Thus, from the mental model convergence perspective, the

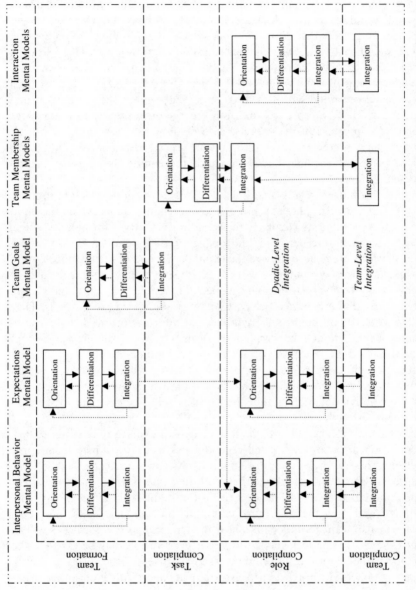

Fig. 4. Sample Mental Models Corresponding to Kozlowski et al.'s (1999) Stages of Team Development.

team members would complete the integration phase of their goal mental models and the orientation and differentiation phases of team membership models. When they possess all the information relating to their respective expertise and have it organized, they are ready to move into the integration stage, when these team membership mental models will converge. As they make this transition into the team developmental stage of role compilation, the team members will, therefore, have mental models about interpersonal behavior, associated expectations pertaining to that behavior, team goals, and differentiated information pertaining to team membership.

Role compilation represents a shift in focus from the individual level to the dyadic level, particularly with respect to team membership. At this stage, team members begin to think about their roles as they pertain to the roles of other members of the team. As a consequence, mental models regarding team membership can be expected to converge – that is, pass through the integration phase of mental model convergence – during role compilation. Also, task interdependencies begin to drive the mental model convergence process at this developmental stage. As such, shared mental models regarding team interaction within the dyadic relationships may be developed. This developmental stage may also prompt the emergence of a feedback loop in the mental model convergence process, particularly for those mental models developed in the team formation stage – namely, interpersonal behavior and expectations mental models. As personality characteristics come into play during role routinization, the social interpersonal knowledge of other team members may have to be reconciled with task-based interpersonal knowledge gathered in this stage. The dotted arrows in Fig. 3 between different mental models allow for this iterative process to occur.

In the team compilation stage, teams reach the point at which they can start to connect their task-based dyadic links into team-level networks. At this point, the dyadic shared mental models developed in the role compilation stage may need to be revisited to better represent the network of interdependence at the team level. As the team-level shared mental models emerge from the dyadic-level shared mental models established in the role compilation stage, the team becomes ready to transition into taskwork with the mental models guiding their behavior. They can work under the guidance of these mental models until a situation requiring adaptation arises that requires revisiting mental model content and re-converging the changing mental models.

Mapping Kozlowski and colleagues' (1999) team development model over the mental model convergence framework presented in this chapter provides a glimpse at the number of mental models that may be simultaneously functioning. While research to date has largely focused on multiple mental models, two mental models (teamwork and taskwork) have been examined. Smith-Jentsch et al.'s (2005) move to domain-specific versions of these two models was a good next step. Further advances are now needed to determine a more comprehensive set of mental models that govern team behavior. Nevertheless, the following proposition can be forwarded:

> **Proposition 3.** Multiple mental models will simultaneously exist, but the convergence process for each will progress at different speeds.

THE ROLE OF MENTAL MODEL CONTENTS IN THE CONVERGENCE PROCESS

Mental model content will influence the way in which mental models converge, both in the definition of sharing applied (i.e., the content held in common or divided among team members) and the degree of integration realized (i.e., the detail shared by team members). Marks and colleagues (2002) provide further support for this premise. While they found that a common understanding of the coordination processes to be used is important, they speculate that explicit detail regarding other aspects of teamwork, such as expertise, may not improve team effectiveness. For this reason, they imply, the integration processes of a coordination mental model and of an expertise mental model conclude differently, where highly integrated "in common" coordination mental models and highly integrated "to divide" expertise mental models may represent the optimal levels of integration.

Before one can determine mental model content, the domain of interest must first be identified. This identification is critical because different domains have unique requirements for what to include as mental model content (Mohammed et al., 2000; Rouse & Morris, 1986). When studying mental models held by team members, the type of team being studied represents the domain of interest and, therefore, dictates specific mental model content. In general, individuals need to have cognitive structures regarding individual team members, the team, the organization, and the environment (Kraiger & Wenzel, 1997).

Cannon-Bowers and associates (1993) have delineated four mental models that teams need during tactical decision-making exercises in the military: the equipment model, the task model, the team interaction model, and the team model. Each model provides a unique aspect of the military team domain that is necessary for soldiers to function effectively in complex situations. Likewise, a project team may need a task model, a team interaction model, and a team model. The equipment model, however, may or may not make sense for a project team. By contrast, an organizational model that contains an understanding of matters such as the power structure of the team members and their respective functions and the upper management support for the team may be useful.

In sum, the mental model contents necessary for optimal performance may differ for various types of team. Thus:

Proposition 4. Mental model content will depend on the type of team.

Identifying specific mental model contents that may prove useful for team processes and performance is beyond the scope of this chapter. Nevertheless, it is helpful to illustrate how three mental models related to the membership of a cross-functional project team could emerge. These mental models would be held simultaneously by the team members and have different sharing definitions and different degrees of integration. By definition, cross-functional project teams are composed of individuals who represent a number of different functional areas, because effectiveness can be enhanced when teams are staffed with individuals possessing diverse knowledge and skills (Eisenhardt & Tabrizi, 1995). To realize the potential benefits of assembling cross-functional teams, "individuals must have mutually recognized and complementary domains of expertise" (Mohammed & Dumville, 2001, p. 93). Furthermore, the right complement of individuals is imperative (Larson & LaFasto, 1989). The process of creating the team membership mental models, therefore, requires that team members recognize the specialized qualifications their fellow team members can contribute to taskwork and the cooperative team environment. The identification of this expertise does not require a detailed understanding of all knowledge each individual possesses relevant to the task assigned – if too many details are shared, the team may arrive at incorrect decisions that will go unchallenged (Cannon-Bowers et al., 1993). Instead, team members need general knowledge of the qualifications (e.g., technical and/or team expertise) and relevant personality characteristics (e.g., dependability) of each individual team member. Additionally, they must understand how their own qualifications and characteristics fit within the team.

As team members begin to collaborate, they will orient themselves to the various expertise represented on the team. The information they collect is sorted and organized through the differentiation phase of mental model convergence and then integrated through further dialogue into at least three mental models:

- A member adequacy mental model that considers the team as a whole to ascertain whether the requisite complement of functional expertise is available to complete the team's assignment.
- An expertise mental model matching specific members with requisite functional expertise.
- An individual contribution mental model that indicates how the individual's expertise relates to, complements, and/or overlaps with the expertise of the other members.

Up to this point in the chapter, the discussion has emphasized the focal shift from individual to team member at the individual level. In addition to these individually held mental models, a collective-level construct emerges that guides team behavior (Morgeson & Hofmann, 1999). Specifically, this collective construct emerges through the integration phase of mental model convergence. The three potential team membership mental models may be used to demonstrate how the individually held mental models also can be considered collective constructs. In addition, this example illustrates how mental models can be specified for use in research projects. In particular, specification across the following three dimensions is given: (1) the sharing definition and corresponding way in which emergence unfolds, (2) the view of the construct, and (3) the degree of integration. In the following paragraphs, these three dimensions are discussed and corresponding propositions offered.

First, the definition of sharing guides the way in which content is integrated and the emergence process unfolds. Emergence unfolds through either composition or compilation. When the phenomenon of interest is essentially the same at two hierarchical levels, composition models can be used to explain this emergence. When mental models are held "in common," they will have shared unit properties across levels because the characteristics will be shared among team members (Kozlowski & Klein, 2000). Thus, they will emerge as composition models. Alternatively, compilation models of emergence may be appropriate when the phenomena are complex combinations of lower-level contributions. "To divide" mental models exemplify compilation models at the team level. They have configural unit properties because they "capture the array of [team members'] differential contributions to the [team]" (Kozlowski & Klein, 2000, p. 31).

Kozlowsi and Klein (2000) recommend calling compilation models "compatible mental models" to distinguish them from shared mental models that emerge through composition. This chapter retains the moniker "shared mental models" to describe both simply because it is the more familiar term. As research on shared mental models, in general, continues to grow and more compatible mental models are explored, the distinction may become useful.

Kozlowski and Klein (2000) can be consulted for a comprehensive explanation of composition and compilation models of emergence. In sum, explicating the link between mental model content, sharing definition, and integration describes how shared mental models emerge:

> **Proposition 5.** The mental model convergence process will unfold either through composition or compilation depending on whether the information is held "in common" or "divided," respectively.

Second, the view of the construct refers to where the differences within and between teams can be found (Dansereau et al., 1999; Klein, Dansereau, & Hall, 1994). Homogeneity (i.e., differences between units), independence (i.e., differences between units independent of groups), and heterogeneity (i.e., differences within groups) are used to depict the view of the team. For complete discussions of views (also known as levels of theory or levels of constructs), see Dansereau, Alutto, and Yammarino (1984), Dansereau et al. (1999), and Klein et al. (1994). With respect to mental models, "in common" composition models will be homogeneous at both the individual and the team levels. "To divide" compilation models will be independent at the individual level and heterogeneous at the team level. These distinctions are further explored in the example discussed below and summarized in the next proposition:

> **Proposition 6.** The view of the mental model construct depends on the way in which the mental model emerges, where "in common" composition models will be homogeneous at both the individual and team levels and "to divide" compilation models will be independent at the individual level and heterogeneous at the team level.

Third, the degree of integration was previously discussed and is represented in Fig. 2. If the "in common" definition of sharing is applied, the amount of detail commonly held by team members defines the degree of integration. It may range from conceptual commonality to identical detail. Alternatively, the degree of integration of "to divide" mental models will range from redundant to unique. The way in which the degree of integration

Table 1.   Sample Mental Models Relating to Team Membership.

		Individual-Level Construct	Team-Level Construct
Member adequacy mental model	View	Homogeneity	Homogeneity
	Integration	Commonality/identical	Commonality/ identical
Expertise mental model	View	Homogeneity	Homogeneity
	Integration	Commonality/overlap	Commonality/ overlap
Individual contribution mental model	View	Independence	Heterogeneity
	Integration	Division	Division

may be specified is highlighted in the following example. The relevant proposition follows:

Proposition 7.   The degree of integration depends on the way in which the mental model emerges, where "in common" composition models will range from conceptual commonality to identical detail and "to divide" compilation models will range from redundant to unique.

Shifting back to the three potential team membership mental models (member adequacy, expertise, and individual contribution), it is illuminating to consider how they might develop among team members and specify them across the dimensions just described. These specifications are summarized in Table 1. To aid the discussion, consider two electrical engineers who are assigned to a team: a junior engineer who has expertise in hardware design and a more senior engineer who has expertise in software design and some experience with hardware design. The junior engineer views himself as the hardware design expert and the senior engineer as the software design expert. The senior engineer views herself as the expert in both software and hardware design and views the junior engineer as someone who can assist her with the hardware design.

Together these two engineers may see that, with respect to the electrical engineering requirements of the project, the team has adequate membership. In other words, no other electrical engineers are required. These two engineers develop individual-level member adequacy mental models that view the group as a whole (i.e., the mental models are homogeneous across individuals) and the degree of information integration is identical. The individual-level expertise mental models may also comprise homogeneous content because the two electrical engineers view the team as a whole. Their degree of integration, however, may overlap only because of the way in which they view expertise respectively. Thus, at the individual level, the expertise mental model is a homogeneous mental model that overlaps across members.

In both cases at the individual level, our interest is in the similarity across team members because it allows us to ascertain the amount of mental model content held in common across team members. Aggregate scores representing this commonalty, such as r_{wg}, provide meaningful information about the team-level shared mental models. These aggregate scores can be used to compare how different amounts of variability among team member mental models affect team performance. In this case, the differences of interest are between units at both levels. At the individual level, our interest is between team members. At the team level, our interest is between teams. Thus, the member adequacy and expertise mental models, as described in the example, are similar in that they are homogeneous composition models (i.e., shared mental models).

The difference between the member adequacy and expertise mental models lies in the way in which the content is integrated across team members. The member adequacy content is identical across team members, whereas the expertise content is overlapping. Therefore, more variability among team members' contents exists in the expertise shared mental model than in the member adequacy shared mental model. Even though variability exists among team members, the shared mental models are homogeneous because, as previously stated, the differences between units (team members at the individual level and teams at the team level) are of interest.

The individual contribution mental model provides an example of a mental model that follows the "to divide" definition of sharing and in which the team is viewed as consisting of parts. Each individual creates an independent mental model of how his or her expertise complements or overlaps with the expertise of other team members. In the case of the two electrical engineers, the junior engineer views his individual contribution as complementary expertise, while the senior engineer sees overlapping expertise. Thus, the amount of variability among the independent mental models is of interest. At the team level, the independent mental models are heterogeneous compilation models (i.e., compatible mental models). In other words, the variability of interest is between the team members. The way in which content is aggregated depends on the purpose of the research being undertaken. Cooke and colleagues (2000) and Rentsch and Woehr (2004) discuss appropriate aggregation techniques for distributed data.

This example results in the following proposition regarding the specification of these three example mental models. This proposition can also be viewed as a set of rigorously specified mental model hypotheses that could be tested.

Proposition 8. Three team membership mental models will exist simultaneously – namely, member adequacy, expertise, and individual contribution mental models.

Proposition 8a. The member adequacy mental model (i) emerges through composition, (ii) is homogeneous at both the individual and team levels, and (iii) is integrated identically.

Proposition 8b. The expertise mental model (i) emerges through composition, (ii) is homogeneous at both the individual and team levels, and (iii) with respect to integration, overlaps across members.

Proposition 8c. The individual contribution mental model (i) emerges through compilation, (ii) is independent at the individual level and heterogeneous at the team level, and (iii) with respect to integration, is unique across members.

MENTAL MODEL CONVERGENCE AND TEAM FUNCTIONING

Project teams are not assembled so that they can spend all of their time creating shared mental models. Instead, the mental model convergence process must be embedded in team functioning. In particular, the relationship between mental model convergence and the taskwork for which the team is assembled is of interest. Fig. 5 depicts this relationship. Upon convergence of their mental models, team members will use them to guide their taskwork. The cognitive shift to taskwork will occur automatically as the team members' familiarity with the mental model content increases (Dutton, 1993; Yoo & Kanawattanachai, 2001). The team will work on its taskwork until such that when one or more mental models need revision to accommodate changes in the circumstances surrounding the team (Smircich, 1983). In other words, periodic mental model maintenance may be necessary. When maintenance is needed, the individual team members may shift to an individual focal level, where they can orient themselves to the new information available and re-differentiate the information they have (including the new information just attained) before reintegrating the information back to the team focal level.

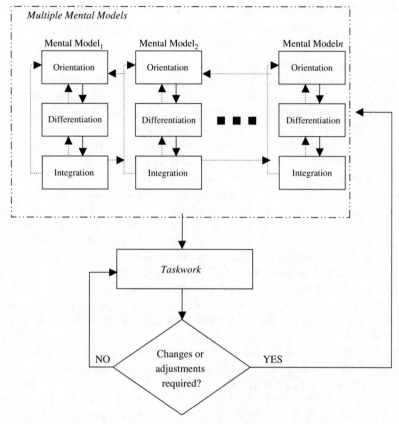

Fig. 5. The Mental Model Convergence Process Embedded in Team Functioning.

Such maintenance requires that team members actively think about mental model content. Research suggests six situations when switching from automatic to conscious cognitive mode may be beneficial:

1. *Novel* circumstances arise (Gersick & Hackman, 1990; Louis & Sutton, 1991).
2. *Discrepancies* between expectations and reality arise (Louis & Sutton, 1991), particularly when the discrepancy results in failure (Gersick & Hackman, 1990).
3. *Deliberate initiatives* are requested (Louis & Sutton, 1991).
4. *Milestones* are achieved (Gersick & Hackman, 1990).

5. An *intervention* is performed (Gersick & Hackman, 1990).
6. A *structural change* occurs (Gersick & Hackman, 1990).

Additionally, Gersick's (1988) pace-driven approach to group development suggests that teams go through a major transition at the halfway point of their existence. During this transition stage, team members establish new protocols for governing the remaining team functioning. In other words, they conduct maintenance on their mental models.

Mental model maintenance requires that team members (1) recognize the need for modifying their mental models and, correspondingly, shift to active thinking and (2) use a feedback loop (shown in Fig. 5) to revisit the three phases of mental model convergence. Progressing through all of the phases may be necessary, although the time required for their traversal is expected to be reduced significantly because the mental models are being modified (rather than new mental models being created). The shift to active thinking does not occur effortlessly, because individuals do not always perceive the need to shift to conscious thought (Beyer, Chattopadhyay, George, Glick, & Pugliese, 1997). Moreover, individuals often lapse into automatic mode in stressful situations (i.e., feeling time pressure or experiencing a high-information load) (Dutton, 1993) or when they experience failure (Gersick & Hackman, 1990). These types of situations are precisely the times when a team benefits the most from mental model maintenance and a corresponding shift to active thinking, because active thinking may help to overcome any "cognitive inertia" that often befalls individuals (Reger & Palmer, 1996), improve the overall accuracy of the mental models (Blickensderfer, Cannon-Bowers, & Salas, 1997), and facilitate better performance than if the team continues functioning automatically (Waller, 1999). Leader briefings and interaction training may be useful in helping teams identify when they must shift to conscious thought and adapt their mental models (Marks et al., 2000).

The following propositions summarize this discussion:

Proposition 9. Converged mental models will guide taskwork until such time when newly available information contradicts the existing mental model content and mental model maintenance is required.

Proposition 10. Mental model maintenance will be more successful if team members shift to actively thinking about mental model content and progress through the three phases of mental model convergence.

PRELIMINARY EVIDENCE

A research study was undertaken to provide preliminary evidence for mental model convergence as it has been described in this chapter. Based on the framework presented here and the extant literature on shared mental models, four hypotheses are put forth for testing.

First, the primary purpose of the mental model convergence framework is to delineate how individuals' mental models evolve over time. Indeed, the framework details how the mental models shift in focus from the individual level to the team level through the explicated convergence process. Thus, to test for convergence, the first hypothesis is as follows:

Hypothesis 1. Mental model content converges over time.

The description of how the mental model convergence framework was embedded in team functioning highlighted several occasions when mental model maintenance may be necessary (e.g., novel circumstances, discrepancies between expectations and reality). Through mental model maintenance, team members change the content of their mental models by revisiting the three phases of mental model convergence (i.e., orientation, differentiation, and integration). To test whether content changes occur, the second hypothesis is as follows:

Hypothesis 2. Mental model content changes over time.

Empirically, teamwork and taskwork mental models have been found working simultaneously in teams (e.g., Mathieu et al., 2000; Smith-Jentsch et al., 2005). To extend this line of inquiry beyond teamwork and taskwork models, the current study was designed to capture mental models that may be relevant across project teams, regardless of task. Following the guidance of Cannon-Bowers and colleagues (1993), four potential mental models were identified, related to the team's task (the goal mental model), team interaction (the team interaction mental model), the team (the organization structure mental model), and equipment (the communication medium mental model). The third hypothesis seeks to test whether these shared mental models exist simultaneously:

Hypothesis 3. The goal, team interaction, organization structure, and communication medium mental models will function simultaneously.

Finally, empirical evidence suggests that shared mental models positively influence team performance (e.g., Baba et al., 2004; Marks et al., 2000, 2002; Mathieu et al., 2000, 2005; Smith-Jentsch et al., 2005; Webber et al., 2000).

While the relationship between shared mental models and team performance is not included explicitly in the mental model convergence framework, investigating these relationships is critical because, if they are indeed positive, they provide the motivation for studying mental model convergence. This leads to the fourth hypothesis:

Hypothesis 4. Converged mental models are positively related to team performance.

To test these hypotheses, the appropriate methodological approach had to be identified. In an effort to focus the process of identifying the appropriate approach, the investigation was limited in two ways. First, it examined only shared mental models (versus compilation mental models) because focusing on one type of mental model convergence is a reasonable first step toward validating the framework and shared mental models are the most abundant type discussed in the shared mental model literature. Second, following the advice of Kozlowski and Klein (2000), who recommend viewing phenomena at a single level when exploring new avenues, the study was narrowed to focus on the team-level collective construct. This construct represents the commonality among individual team members' mental models and allowed the study to capture increases in commonality over time that occurred as the individuals' mental models shifted from having an individual focus to having a team focus. Selecting this approach did not mean that team-level data had to be collected. Rather, individual-level data were required because data collection must match the level of origin for composition processes (Kozlowski & Klein, 2000). Therefore, a measurement approach was identified that allowed for the collection of individual data that could be aggregated to represent team-level shared mental models.

Several mental model measurement techniques exist from which to choose. Mohammed and colleagues (2000) provide a review and set of recommendations for the best approaches available with which to assess mental model content and structure. Cooke and colleagues (2004) outline gaps in the current state-of-the art in team cognition measurement and suggest the analysis of communication data as a viable methodology to bridge those gaps. The logic behind this suggestion is that team communication is analogous to the think-aloud verbal protocols that are routinely used to assess individual-level cognition.

For this project, the goal was to find elicitation methods that would uncover mental model content held by individuals and permit content to be tracked over time. The most commonly used techniques reported for content elicitation are similarity indices of questionnaire items (see Mohammed et al., 2000, for a list of studies using this technique) and transcript analysis (see Cooke et al., 2004). These methods, however, did not seem appropriate for assessing mental model convergence. Calculating the similarity indices of questionnaire items would provide a measure of convergence, but the depth of information provided through questionnaires would not be rich enough to ensure which content was being tapped. This approach seems to be more appropriate for use after convergence has been established using other, more rigorous methods. Analysis of communication via team transcripts would provide team-level data. As individual mental model content was of interest, this process was not viable. It may, however, be useful after convergence has been proven. Thus, an alternative method was needed.

In the search for a suitable method, the literature on information processing provided fertile ground. The intent in reviewing this literature was to find a method that would elicit the information contained in an individual's mental models through questionnaires. Questionnaires can be used to collect data because, in circumstances where mental models can be manipulated explicitly (i.e., subjects are aware that they must manipulate their mental models to complete their assigned tasks), they can be appropriately described via verbalization methods such as questionnaires (Rouse & Morris, 1986). Questionnaires, however, may elicit information about espoused theories (what respondents think the researcher wants to find) rather than theories-in-use (what actually drives respondent behavior) if the questionnaire items are not carefully crafted.

To overcome the inherent difficulties in tapping theories-in-use, Argyris and Schön's (1974) seminal research in this area recommends asking respondents questions requiring answers that focus on directly observable behaviors rather than generalizations drawn from espoused theory. For example, respondents have to establish what was actually said, how individuals actually behaved, how others actually responded, and so forth.

Schroder and colleagues (1967) devised a sentence completion test and scoring protocol to determine the integrative complexity of which an individual was capable as he or she integrated multiple pieces of information into a coherent response. This approach meets the Argyris and Schön recommendation because the sentence stems focus the respondents on describing – rather than evaluating – the information they possess. For the current study, the sentence completion test was modified to elicit information contained in individuals' mental models. Additionally, a scoring protocol was devised to determine the degree of integration among team members' mental

Table 2.   Sentence Completion Test and Scoring Protocol.

Score	Degree of Integration	Description
1	No similarity	The whole team has completely different responses. No common ideas or topics are reported
2	Half the team reports same topics, different formulations	Half of the team has very similar responses in that they contain the same topic but are formulated differently
3	Majority of team reports same topics, different formulations	The majority of team members have similar responses and the formulations are different
4	All team members report same topics, different formulations	All team members have similar responses that are formulated differently. The responses must show that all the team members possess similar ideas with respect to the mental model being scored
5	All team members report same topics, half use same formulation	All team members have similar responses, and half of the team formulates the response in the same way
6	All team members report same topics, majority use same formulations	All team members have similar responses, and the majority of the team formulates the response in the same way
7	All team members report same topics and use same formulations	All team members have responses that are formulated in the same way

models (see Table 2) that is analogous to the 7-point Integration Index devised by Schroder and colleagues (1967). Using this approach, the study was able to achieve four goals:

- Assess mental model convergence by scoring commonality across individual-level responses.
- Identify content changes by examining the information provided.
- Test for multiple mental models existing concurrently by examining convergence patterns of the entire sample of teams and of high- versus low-performing teams.
- Compare team-level convergence to team-level performance.

In short, the sentence completion test, as modified, proved to be a useful method for assessing mental model convergence and supported testing of all the hypotheses forwarded.

Sample and Procedures

The study designed to address the research questions had 102 participants, all of whom were undergraduate business students. These students were divided into 25 teams containing 3–5 members each. They were enrolled in one of two classes that required the completion of a team semester-long project. The projects were complex in that students were required to complete interdependent tasks to accomplish the project goals. The final output ranged from a substantial report to conducting an event. In both classes, students were allowed to self-select their projects.

At four points during the semester, the team members completed a questionnaire. Time 1 was immediately after the semester project was introduced, and Time 2 was one week later. The Time 3 and Time 4 questionnaires were administered at the mid-semester and at the end of the semester, respectively. Team members earned extra credit for participating in the study if they completed all questionnaires throughout the semester. If all team members from the team completed all questionnaires, then the team was entered in a random drawing where they had an opportunity to win $50 per member. The odds of winning the prize money were 1:5.

To assess knowledge similarity of the team member mental model content, questionnaire items were written based on the sentence completion test as previously described (Schroder et al., 1967). Respondents were asked to complete sentence stems related to the mental models of interest – namely, the goal, team interaction, organization structure, and communication medium mental models. Consequently, sentence stems were written to identify individual perceptions regarding the project goals ("The goals of our project are ..."), team interaction ("Our team has discussed coordinating work flow among team members in the following manner ..."), team organization structure ("Our project team is organized (i.e., who is the leader, etc.) in the following manner ..."), and team communication media ("Our team has discussed using the following modes of communication to exchange information ..."). These sentence stems required respondents to focus on directly observable behaviors rather than generalizations drawn from espoused theory, following Argyris and Schön's (1974) methodology.

The team members' responses were content-analyzed using the aforementioned scoring protocol developed for this project (see Table 2). Independently, a doctoral candidate and the author assessed each team member's response for a given team to determine a score that represented the degree of integration across team members. In other words, the score represented the amount of overlap in team members' shared mental models.

Inter-rater reliability was 73%. When our ratings did not agree, we discussed our respective scores and came to an agreement on the appropriate score for the team's mental model under consideration.

Team performance was assessed as the team's grade on the semester-long project. To identify high- and low-performing teams, the sample was split into two subsamples based on the team's grades. The 13 teams with the highest-team grades were identified as high-performing teams; the remaining 12 teams were identified as low-performing teams.

Preliminary Results

Figs. 6 and 7 show the results of the study. Fig. 6 plots the rater's scores for the entire sample's mental models, highlighting the significant shifts in level of agreement. Fig. 7 depicts the convergence patterns of high- and low-performing teams for comparison; in the figure, significant differences are highlighted. The $p < 0.1$ cutoff is reported when assessing performance for two reasons: (1) when the sample is split into two, n becomes quite small and (2) the pattern of results has been consistent over several semesters and across classes. Together, these results provide preliminary support for the four hypotheses driving this study.

The first hypothesis was aimed at determining whether individually held mental models converge over time. The results in Fig. 6 can be used to explore convergence over time. For team processes, team organization, and team communication, the shift in mental model content converges significantly from the initial questionnaire to the second questionnaire, which was completed one week later. The shift was not significant for the team goals mental model. One plausible reason for this lack of significance may be that the project goals in both classes were explained thoroughly just prior to when the team members completed the first questionnaire. Therefore, the initial understanding of the team's purpose was well established and commonly understood. Together, these results provide preliminary support for Hypothesis 1.

The second hypothesis asks if we can expect to see shifts in the mental model content over time. As new information became available to the team, the mental model content shifted and the level of convergence remained high. For example, as the semester progressed, team members' goal mental models shifted from containing information about the overarching goal to more detailed information about the task-oriented goals required to complete the project. Similarly, the team organization structure mental

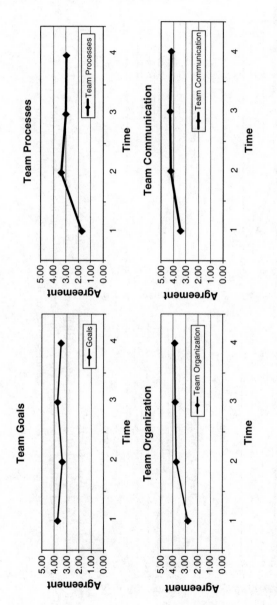

Fig. 6. Mental Model Convergence over Time. The Shift from Time 1 to Time 2 in Agreement is Significant for Team Processes, Team Organization, and Team Communication at $p < 0.05$.

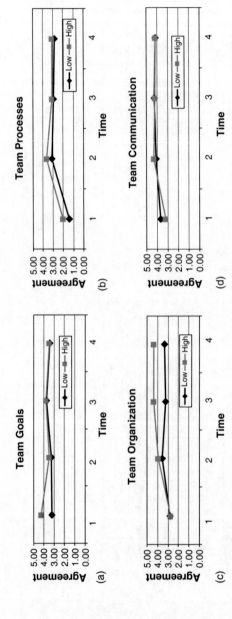

Fig. 7. Mental Model Convergence–Performance Relationship. (a) Difference between High- and Low-Performing Teams is Significant at Time 1 ($p = 0.06$), (b) Difference between High- and Low-Performing Teams is Significant at Time 1 ($p = 0.10$) and Time 2 ($p = 0.08$), (c) Difference between High- and Low-Performing Teams is Significant at Time 3 ($p = 0.06$) and Time 4 ($p = 0.08$), and (d) No Significant Difference between High- and Low-Performing Teams over Time.

model went from a high-level description of the structure to a detailed description of who was doing which tasks needed to complete the project. Although the re-convergence process was not captured due to the time between data-collection points, these results provide preliminary support for Hypothesis 2.

The existence of multiple mental models working simultaneously within a team was put forth as the third hypothesis, and the fourth hypothesis sought a positive relationship between shared mental models and team performance. The results in Fig. 7 show the amount of agreement found for high- and low-performing teams for each mental model studied. Significant differences between high- and low-performing teams were found as follows, where high-performing teams had more convergent mental model content: goal mental model Time 1, team processes mental model Time 1 and Time 2, team organization mental model Time 3 and Time 4. The variation across mental model types provides evidence that multiple mental models function simultaneously in support of the third hypothesis. Additionally, these results suggest that teams who understand what their goals are, how they are going to interact at the onset of the team's life cycle, and how responsibilities are divided at the end of their life cycle will perform better, supporting the fourth hypothesis.

Taken together, the results of this study provide preliminary validation of the mental model convergence framework presented in this chapter. More extensive research on this topic is justified based on these results.

DISCUSSION AND IMPLICATIONS

The aim of this research was to better understand the way in which individuals assigned to a team are transformed from individuals into team members. This chapter attempted to address this phenomenon by describing the mental model convergence process that shifts team members' thinking from the individual level to the team level. This undertaking contributes to the literature on shared mental models in at least two distinct ways. First, the mental model convergence process has not been explicated previously, particularly in the level of detail specified here. The current effort has been informed by a wide range of previous research, including research on project teams, information processing, group development, and information sharing, as well as by many research streams associated with understanding collective cognition (e.g., shared cognition, shared/team mental models, sociocognition, transactive memory). Using such a diverse base of extant

knowledge allowed for a more complete view of the mental model convergence process.

The second contribution to the literature on shared mental models relates
to the definition of sharing. While numerous researchers have defined
"shared" in the context of shared cognition/shared mental models (e.g.,
Cannon-Bowers & Salas, 2001; Cooke et al., 2000; Mohammed & Dumville,
2001), no other research appears to extend this line of thought beyond the
definition. This chapter linked sharing to the degree of integration that
results from the mental model convergence process and posited that the
appropriate degree of sharing/integration will depend on mental model
contents. Awareness of this intersection is critical, because it identifies two
distinct ways in which team members can distribute information among
themselves and provides a basis for examining how the distributed information is shared across members.

This chapter also addressed issues related to theory testing in three ways:
(1) by advancing the discussion of the unique and combined roles of mental
model content and structure; (2) by introducing a measurement technique;
and (3) by providing preliminary empirical evidence as a first step toward
validating my mental model convergence framework.

First, understanding the relative roles of mental model content and structure has received some attention in the shared mental models literature (e.g.,
Mohammed et al., 2000; Rentsch & Woehr, 2004). Continued discussion,
and empirical research supporting that discussion, is needed to determine
the unique and combined roles of content and structure to different team
types. This chapter adds to this much-needed dialogue by focusing on mental model content in a project team domain.

Second, the sentence completion test has not been used in the past to
measure shared mental models. This approach, as modified for the current
study, is a viable addition to the set of measurement techniques available.
Indeed, the preliminary results obtained using this method verify that multiple mental models simultaneously converge, are revised over time, and
affect team performance in positive ways.

Finally, using a sample of undergraduate student teams was a manageable
first step in the process of validating this measurement technique and, more
importantly, validating the mental model convergence framework (Lam &
Schaubroeck, 2000). The teams worked on small projects of similar scope.
These projects represent a reasonable middle ground between the controlled
tasks used in laboratory research and the complex tasks found in the field.
Thus, these results indicate that further research is warranted.

In addition to advancing our current understanding of shared mental models by explicating the mental model convergence process and providing preliminary evidence of its validity, the research presented in this chapter lays a foundation for future inquiry in at least three ways.

First, the preliminary results presented need to be replicated, and extended to include compilation mental models and more complex tasks, to further validate the framework. Moreover, in-depth methods or combinations of methods are needed to test the phases of mental model convergence and the transitions among phases. For example, Austin's (2003) method for assessing transactive memory systems or the social relations model (described in Rentsch & Woehr, 2004) might prove useful for studying differentiation and integration of compatible mental models.

Second, approaches for identifying mental model content and specifying the appropriate definition of sharing and degree of integration for each mental model are needed. Smith-Jentsch and colleagues (2005) advanced this research stream by moving beyond generic teamwork and taskwork mental models and testing domain-specific mental models. Further research is needed to identify mental models that are relevant across teams and to devise approaches for identifying task-specific mental model content. After delineating the appropriate mental model content, the definition of sharing for each mental model must be decided. Methods for systematically selecting the definition, such as Postrel's (2002) economic approach, are needed. Finally, the optimal degree to which information is integrated must be determined. A combination of laboratory experimentation, field research, and mathematical modeling will be necessary to fully understand the level of integration among various mental models required to realize optimal team performance.

The third area for future research relates to the relationship between shared mental models and team performance. The evidence to date, including the preliminary evidence provided in this chapter, suggests that shared mental models positively influence team performance (e.g., Baba et al., 2004; Marks et al., 2000, 2002; Mathieu et al., 2000, 2005; Smith-Jentsch et al., 2005; Webber et al., 2000). The majority of these studies, however, have focused on very specific applications and measured domain-specific shared mental models. Therefore, they need to be replicated and extended across a variety of teams working under differing circumstances. In particular, field research is needed to ascertain whether the results obtained in the laboratory can be generalized to teams in the field. Additionally, non-domain-specific means of measuring shared mental models, such as the sentence completion test described in this chapter, need to be developed and applied. These non-domain-specific measures will allow for better comparisons across studies. Finally, the role of mental model accuracy/quality in team performance needs further investigation. To date, only limited research incorporating mental model accuracy has been conducted (e.g., Mathieu et al., 2005; Rentsch & Woehr, 2004; Smith-Jentsch et al., 2001). The evidence so far indicates that accuracy may be related to team performance (Rentsch & Woehr, 2004) and that individuals with more experience are better able to create accurate mental models (Smith-Jentsch et al., 2001). Methods for assessing accuracy, particularly in the field, and further examination of this construct are needed.

Researchers may also find the mental model convergence framework described in this chapter useful when studying other types of teams. Consider self-managed work teams, which – like project teams – are frequently used by organizations. Case study research has found that self-managed work teams are more productive and make better decisions than workers in a more traditional setting (Yeatts & Hyten, 1998). As with project teams, however, quantitative evidence on this topic is mixed (Cohen, Ledford, & Spreitzer, 1996). For example, data on the impact of self-managed work teams on behavioral outcomes (e.g., absenteeism), attitudinal outcomes (e.g., quality of work life), and performance outcomes (e.g., productivity) have been inconsistent across studies (Cohen & Bailey, 1997). These differences may be due to how the team members view their team and whether these views are shared. Hence, shared mental models may offer some useful guidance for future research.

The mental model convergence process described in this chapter can be expected to remain the same regardless of team domain. The domain change, however, requires revisiting the mental model content requirements. Following the research of Kraiger and Wenzel (1997), one can identify a sample of the necessary mental models relating to the individual team members, the team, the organization, and the environment for successful self-managed work team functioning. As with project teams, a complete understanding of the individual team members – and particularly their skill levels – is necessary. Whereas the focus of a project team would be on the technical expertise of the team member, in the self-managed work teams domain, interpersonal, management, and decision-making skills may be more relevant (Yeatts & Hyten, 1998). With respect to the team, a detailed understanding of the work content, structure, and allocation are necessary (Yeatts & Hyten, 1998), because team members may be called upon to fill in for or help each other at various times. The level of empowerment

(Cohen et al., 1996) and the adequacy of training (Cohen et al., 1996; Yeatts & Hyten, 1998) are both organizational elements about which teams may share beliefs. Finally, the role of the environment external to the organization may be relevant. For example, the demand for the product or service, the team provides may influence the number of hours self-managed work teams work. If the team members do not share a belief about the need to work the scheduled hours, absenteeism and turnover may rise, causing a hardship for the remaining team members and limiting their ability to perform effectively (Cohen & Bailey, 1997). These content requirements exemplify the mental models that may prove useful when researching in the self-managed work teams domain.

In addition to making its own contribution to the literature, this research clearly extends several current theoretical streams. To demonstrate these extensions, consider two examples of the complementary nature of this research.

Beginning with sense making, Weick's (1995) research highlights processes that individuals and organizations use to make sense of their worlds. Mental models can aid the sense-making process by acting as a lens through which individuals can view situations that require sense making. When conduct is dependent upon the conduct of others, for example, sense-making processes must often be invoked. Such interdependent conduct lies at the heart of cross-functional project team activity. If the team has progressed through the mental model convergence process as described in this chapter, the act of sense making may be enhanced. For instance, shared mental models may help team members identify cues necessary for making sense. Furthermore, as members enact sensible environments in anticipation of future activities, they can use their shared mental models to frame their enactment. In this manner, future activity relating to the team may be constrained by the enacted realities that are based on the shared understanding inherent in shared mental models. Other sense-making processes (e.g., those driven by plausibility rather than accuracy) may be enhanced through the exploitation of shared mental models in a similar manner.

A second theoretical stream that may benefit from the current line of research is process consultation. Schein (1999) describes the difficulty associated with process consultation as a situation where "both parties must learn about each other while at the same time creating a safe environment for the client to tell his or her story" (Schein, 1999, p. 40). As with project teams, these conditions require the development of mutual acceptance so that participants can give and receive help. A shared understanding regarding client/consultant collaboration, such as relevant expertise, the problem, interaction protocols, the organization culture, and the environmental context, are also needed. The mental model convergence process described here may provide insight into the cognitive structures necessary for this process consultation. Specifically, the orientation and differentiation phases represent the time required to exchange information and to create cognitive structures of this information, respectively. These structures then become useful as the client and the consultant develop a common understanding of what the problem is and how it can best be solved. In other words, their respective structures are integrated and shared mental models emerge. Without this integration phase, the client/consultant exchange will result in another shelved consultant's report because the recommendations provided by the consultant may not work within the organization. In other words, consultation – rather than process consultation – will have occurred.

The practitioner community may find a number of useful strategies in the mental model framework presented in this chapter. In particular, managers in organizations using teams may find that an understanding of the mental model convergence process will benefit team effectiveness in at least three ways. First, the emergence of mental models across team members can be expedited, as opposed to allowing mental models to evolve naturally over time, by facilitating the team's progression through the convergence process. Second, the content of the mental models can be manipulated through focused attention on the elements necessary for successful team performance. Third, explicit conversations regarding mental model content may improve consistency across team members. Together, shared and compatible mental models created under these conditions will provide a solid foundation upon which taskwork can be done more effectively. For all these reasons, leaders may want to encourage team members to spend time – albeit a small percentage of their collective time – on discussing mental model content to expedite the convergence process, manipulate mental model content, and improve mental model consistency across team members. Also, trainers focused on improving team processes and performance may want to incorporate the mental model convergence process into new training programs to realize similar benefits.

In conclusion, researchers and practitioners interested in learning more about how teams can function more effectively may find value in this research. Regardless of the type of team, exploring the cognitive aspects of team activity, through mental model convergence, may provide insight into how team members can make the necessary shift in their perspectives from the individual to the team.

ACKNOWLEDGMENTS

This research is supported in part by the Innovations in Organizations program of the National Science Foundation, Grant no. 0092805, and the Collaboration and Knowledge Interoperability program of the Office of Naval Research, Grant no. N000140210535. The author would like to thank Sam Jelinek, Linda Smircich, Ralitza Vozdolska, and Melissa Woodard for their help in preparing this manuscript. Ralitza Vozdolska also helped with the data analysis presented as preliminary evidence.

REFERENCES

Argyris, C., & Schön, D. A. (1974). *Theory in practice: Increasing professional effectiveness*. San Francisco, CA: Jossey-Bass.

Austin, J. R. (2003). Transactive memory in organizational groups: The effects of content, consensus, specialization, and accuracy on group performance. *Journal of Applied Psychology, 88*, 866–878.

Baba, M., Gluesing, J., Ratner, H., & Wagner, K. H. (2004). The contexts of knowing: Natural history of a globally distributed team. *Journal of Organizational Behavior, 25*, 547–587.

Bar-Tal, D. (1990). *Group beliefs: A conception for analyzing group structure, processes, and behavior*. New York: Springer-Verlag.

Bartunek, J. M., Gordon, J., & Weathersby, R. P. (1983). Developing "complicated" understanding in administrators. *Academy of Management Review, 8*, 273–284.

Beyer, J., Chattopadhyay, P., George, E., Glick, W. H., & Pugliese, D. (1997). The selective perception of managers revisited. *Academy of Management Journal, 40*, 716–737.

Blickensderfer, E. L., Cannon-Bowers, J. A., & Salas, E. (1997). Theoretical bases for team self-correction: Fostering shared mental models. In: M. M. Beyerlein, D. A. Johnson & S. T. Beyerlein (Eds), *Advances in interdisciplinary studies of work teams* (pp. 249–279). Greenwich, CT: JAI Press.

Borgatti, S. P., & Cross, R. (2003). A relational view of information seeking and learning in social networks. *Management Science, 49*, 432–445.

Cannon-Bowers, J. A., & Salas, E. (2001). Reflections on shared cognition. *Journal of Organizational Behavior, 22*, 195–202.

Cannon-Bowers, J. A., Salas, E., & Converse, S. A. (1993). Shared mental models in expert team decision making. In: N. J. Castellan Jr. (Ed.), *Individual and group decision making: Current issues* (pp. 221–246). Hillsdale, NJ: Lawrence Erlbaum Associates.

Chang, A., Bordia, P., & Duck, J. (2003). Punctuated equilibrium and linear progression: Toward a new understanding of group development. *Academy of Management Journal, 46*, 106–117.

Cohen, S. G., & Bailey, D. E. (1997). What makes teams work: Group effectiveness research from the shop floor to the executive suite. *Journal of Management, 23*, 239–290.

Cohen, S. G., Ledford, G. E., Jr., & Spreitzer, G. M. (1996). A predictive model of self-managing work team effectiveness. *Human Relations, 49*, 643–676.

144   SARA A. McCOMB

Cooke, N. J., Salas, E., Cannon-Bowers, J. A., & Stout, R. J. (2000). Measuring team knowledge. *Human Factors, 42*, 151–173.
Cooke, N. J., Salas, E., Kiekel, P. A., & Bell, B. (2004). Advances in measuring team cognition.
In: E. Salas & S. M. Fiore (Eds), *Team cognition: Understanding the factors that drive
process and performance* (pp. 83–106). Washington, DC: American Psychological Association.
Corner, P. D., Kinicki, A. J., & Keats, B. W. (1994). Integrating organizational and individual
information processing perspectives on choice. *Organization Science, 5*, 294–308.
Dansereau, F., Alutto, J. A., & Yammarino, F. J. (1984). *Theory testing in organizational
behavior: The varient approach.* Englewood Cliffs, NJ: Prentice-Hall.
Dansereau, F., Yammarino, F. J., & Kohles, J. C. (1999). Multiple levels of analysis from a
longitudinal perspective: Some implications for theory building. *Academy of Manage-
ment Review, 24*, 346–357.
Dearborn, D. C., & Simon, H. A. (1958). Selective perception: A note on the departmental
identifications of executives. *Sociometry, 21*, 140–144.
Donnellon, A., Gray, B., & Bougon, M. (1986). Communication, meaning, and organized
action. *Administrative Science Quarterly, 31*, 43–55.
Dougherty, D. (1992). Interpretive barriers to successful product innovation in large firms.
Organization Science, 3, 179–202.
Driver, M. J., & Streufert, S. (1969). Integrative complexity: An approach to individuals
and groups as information-processing systems. *Administrative Science Quarterly, 14*,
272–285.
Dutton, J. E. (1993). Interpretations on automatic: A different view of strategic issue diagnosis.
Journal of Management Studies, 30, 339–357.
Eden, C., Jones, S., Sims, D., & Smithin, T. (1981). The intersubjectivity of issues and issues of
intersubjectivity. *Journal of Management Studies, 18*, 35–47.
Eisenhardt, K. M., & Tabrizi, B. N. (1995). Accelerating adaptive processes: Product inno-
vation in the global computer industry. *Administrative Science Quarterly, 40*, 84.
Entin, E. E., & Serfaty, D. (1999). Adaptive team coordination. *Human Factors, 41*, 312.
Fiore, S. M., & Salas, E. (2004). Why we need team cognition. In: E. Salas & S. M. Fiore (Eds),
Team cognition: Understanding the factors that drive process and performance (pp. 235–
248). Washington, DC: American Psychological Association.
Gersick, C. J. G. (1988). Time and transition in work teams: Toward a new model of group
development. *Academy of Management Journal, 31*, 9–41.
Gersick, C. J. G. (1989). Marking time: Predictable transitions in task groups. *Academy of
Management Journal, 32*, 274–309.
Gersick, C. J. G., & Hackman, J. R. (1990). Habitual routines in task-performing groups.
Organizational Behavior and Human Decision Processes, 47, 65–97.
Gibson, C. (2001). From knowledge accumulation to accommodation: Cycles of collective
cognition in work groups. *Journal of Organizational Behavior, 22*, 121–134.
Gruenfeld, D. H., & Hollingshead, A. B. (1993). Sociocognition in work groups: The evolution
of group integrative complexity and its relation to task performance. *Small Group
Research, 24*, 383–405.
Hill, R. C., & Levenhagen, M. (1995). Metaphors and mental models: Sensemaking and sense-
giving in innovative and entrepreneurial activities. *Journal of Management, 21*, 1057.
Hinsz, V. B., Tindale, R. S., & Vollrath, D. A. (1997). The emerging conceptualization of
groups as information processors. *Psychological Bulletin, 121*, 43–64.

Hong, P., Doll, W. J., Nahm, A. Y., & Li, X. (2004). Knowledge sharing in integrated product development. *European Journal of Innovation Management, 7*, 102–112.

Johnson-Laird, P. N. (1983). *Mental models: Towards a cognitive science of language, inference, and consciousness.* Cambridge, MA: Harvard University Press.

Klein, K. J., Dansereau, F., & Hall, R. J. (1994). Levels issues in theory development, data collection, and analysis. *Academy of Management Review, 19*, 195–229.

Klimoski, R., & Mohammed, S. (1994). Team mental model: Construct or metaphor?. *Journal of Management, 20*, 403–437.

Kozlowski, S. W. J., & Klein, K. J. (2000). A multilevel approach to theory and research in organizations. In: K. J. Klein & S. W. J. Kozlowski (Eds), *Multi-level theory, research, and methods in organizations: Foundations, extensions, and new directions* (pp. 3–90). San Francisco, CA: Jossey-Bass.

Kozlowski, S. W. J., Gully, S. M., Nason, E. R., & Smith, E. M. (1999). Developing adaptive teams: A theory of compilation and performance across levels and time. In: D. R. Ilgen & E. D. Pulakos (Eds), *The changing nature of performance: Implications for staffing, motivation, and development* (pp. 240–292). San Francisco, CA: Jossey-Bass.

Kraiger, K., & Wenzel, L. H. (1997). Conceptual development and empirical evaluation of measures of shared mental models as indicators of team effectiveness. In: M. T. Brannick, E. Salas & C. Prince (Eds), *Team performance assessment and measurement: Theory, methods, and applications* (pp. 63–84). Mahwah, NJ: Lawrence Erlbaum Associates.

Lam, S., & Schaubroeck, J. (2000). Improving group decisions by better pooling information: A comparative advantage of group decision support systems. *Journal of Applied Psychology, 85*, 565–573.

Larson, C. E., & LaFasto, F. M. J. (1989). *Teamwork: What must go right, what can go wrong.* Newbury Park, CA: Sage.

Larson, J. R., Jr., & Christensen, C. (1993). Groups as problem-solving units: Toward a new meaning of social cognition. *British Journal of Social Psychology, 32*, 5–30.

Larson, J. R., Jr., Sargis, E. G., & Bauman, C. W. (2004). Shared knowledge and subgroup influence during decision-making discussions. *Journal of Behavioral Decision Making, 17*, 245–262.

Leonard, N. H., Beauvais, L. L., & Scholl, R. W. (2005). A multi-level model of group cognitive style in strategic decision making. *Journal of Managerial Issues, 17*, 119–138.

Levine, J. M., & Moreland, R. L. (1999). Knowledge transmission in work groups: Helping newcomers to succeed. In: L. L. Thompson, J. M. Levine & D. M. Messick (Eds), *Shared cognition in organizations* (pp. 267–296). Mahwah, NJ: Lawrence Erlbaum Associates.

Lewis, K., Kinnett, J., & Gillis, L. (2001). Examining group knowledge and long-term performance: Does transactive memory "last" over time and task? Paper presented at the annual meeting of the academy of management, Washington, DC.

Louis, M. R., & Sutton, R. I. (1991). Switching cognitive gears: From habits of mind to active thinking. *Human Relations, 44*, 55–76.

Marks, M., Sabella, M. J., Burke, C. B., & Zaccaro, S. J. (2002). The impact of cross-training on team effectiveness. *Journal of Applied Psychology, 87*, 3–13.

Marks, M., Zaccaro, S. J., & Mathieu, J. E. (2000). Performance implications of leader briefings and team-interaction training for team adaptation to novel environments. *Journal of Applied Psychology, 85*, 971–986.

Mathieu, J. E., Heffner, T. S., Goodwin, G. F., Cannon-Bowers, J. A., & Salas, E. (2005). Scaling the quality of teammates' mental models: Equifinality and normative comparisons. *Journal of Organizational Behavior, 26*, 37–56.

Mathieu, J. E., Heffner, T. S., Goodwin, G. F., Salas, E., & Cannon-Bowers, J. A. (2000). The influence of shared mental models on team process and performance. *Journal of Applied Psychology, 85*, 273–283.

McIntyre, R. M., & Salas, E. (1995). Measuring and managing for team performance: Emerging principles from complex environments. In: R. A. Guzzo, E. Salas & Associates (Eds), *Team effectiveness and decision making in organizations* (pp. 9–45). San Francisco, CA: Jossey-Bass.

McNeese, M. D. (2000). Socio-cognitive factors in the acquisition and transfer of knowledge. *Cognition, Technology, and Work, 2*, 164–177.

Mitchell, R. (1986). Team building by disclosure of internal frames of reference. *Journal of Applied Behavioral Science, 22*, 15–28.

Mohammed, S., & Dumville, B. C. (2001). Team mental models in a team knowledge framework: Expanding theory and measurement across disciplinary boundaries. *Journal of Organizational Behavior, 22*, 89–106.

Mohammed, S., Klimoski, R., & Rentsch, J. R. (2000). The measurement of team mental models: We have no shared schema. *Organizational Research Methods, 3*, 123–165.

Morgeson, F. P., & Hofmann, D. A. (1999). The structure and function of collective constructs: Implications for multi-level research and theory development. *Academy of Management Review, 24*, 249–265.

Ostroff, C., & Kozlowski, S. W. J. (1992). Organization socialization as a learning process: The role of information acquisition. *Personnel Psychology, 45*, 849–874.

Postrel, S. (2002). Islands of shared knowledge: Specialization and mutual understanding in problem solving teams. *Organization Science, 13*, 303–320.

Reger, R. K., & Palmer, T. B. (1996). Managerial categorization of competitors: Using old maps to navigate new environments. *Organization Science, 7*, 22–39.

Rentsch, J. R., & Woehr, D. J. (2004). Quantifying congruence in cognition: Social relations modeling and team member schema similarity. In: E. Salas & S. M. Fiore (Eds), *Team cognition: Understanding the factors that drive process and performance* (pp. 11–31). Washington, DC: American Psychological Association.

Rouse, W. B., & Morris, N. M. (1986). On looking into the black box: Prospects and limits in the search for mental models. *Psychological Bulletin, 100*, 349–363.

Salas, E., Dickinson, T. D., Converse, S. A., & Tannenbaum, S. I. (1992). Toward an understanding of team performance and training. In: R. W. Swezey & E. Salas (Eds), *Teams: Their training and performance* (pp. 3–30). Norwood, NJ: Ablex.

Schein, E. H. (1999). *Process consultation revisited: Building the helping relationship*. Reading, MA: Addison-Wesley Longman.

Schneider, S. C., & Angelmar, R. (1993). Cognition in organizational analysis: Who's minding the store?. *Organization Studies, 14*, 347.

Schroder, H. M., Driver, M. J., & Streufert, S. (1967). *Human information processing*. New York: Holt, Rinehart and Winston.

Smircich, L. (1983). Implications for management theory. In: L. L. Putnam & M. E. Pacanowsky (Eds), *Communication and organizations: An interpretive approach* (pp. 221–241). Beverly Hills, CA: Sage.

Smircich, L., & Chesser, R. J. (1981). Superiors' and subordinates' perceptions of performance: Beyond disagreement. *Academy of Management Journal, 24,* 198–205.

Smith-Jentsch, K. A., Campbell, G. E., Milanovich, D. M., & Reynolds, A. M. (2001). Measuring teamwork mental models to support training needs assessment, development, and evaluation: Two empirical studies. *Journal of Organizational Behavior, 22,* 179–194.

Smith-Jentsch, K. A., Mathieu, J. E., & Kraiger, K. (2005). Investigating linear and interactive effects of shared mental models on safety and efficiency in a field setting. *Journal of Applied Psychology, 90,* 523–535.

Stasser, G., Stewart, D. D., & Wittenbaum, G. M. (1995). Expert roles and information exchange during discussion: The importance of knowing who knows what. *Journal of Experimental Social Psychology, 31,* 244–265.

Stasser, G., Taylor, L. A., & Hanna, C. (1989). Information sampling of structured and unstructured discussions of three- and six-person groups. *Journal of Personality and Social Psychology, 57,* 67–78.

Stout, R. J., Cannon-Bowers, J. A., Salas, E., & Milanovich, D. M. (1999). Planning, shared mental models, and coordinated performance: An empirical link is established. *Human Factors, 41,* 61.

Thomas-Hunt, M. C., Ogden, T. Y., & Neale, M. A. (2003). Who's really sharing? Effects of social and expert status on knowledge exchange within groups. *Management Science, 49,* 464–477.

Tuckman, B. W. (1965). Developmental sequence in small groups. *Psychological Bulletin, 63,* 384–399.

Tuckman, B. W., & Jensen, M. (1977). Stages of small-group development revisited. *Group and Organization Studies, 2,* 419–427.

Waller, M. J. (1999). The timing of adaptive group responses to nonroutine events. *Academy of Management Journal, 42,* 127–137.

Walsh, J. P. (1995). Managerial and organizational cognition: Notes from a trip down memory lane. *Organization Science, 6,* 280–321.

Webber, S. S., Chen, G., Payne, S. C., Marsh, S. M., & Zaccaro, S. J. (2000). Enhancing team mental model measurement with performance appraisal practices. *Organizational Research Methods, 3,* 307–322.

Wegner, D. M. (1987). Transactive memory: A contemporary analysis of the group mind. In: B. Mullen & G. R. Goethals (Eds), *Theories of group behavior* (pp. 185–208). New York: Springer-Verlag.

Wegner, D. M. (1995). A computer network model of human transactive memory. *Social Cognition, 13,* 319–339.

Weick, K. E. (1995). *Sensemaking in organizations.* Thousand Oaks, CA: Sage.

Wittenbaum, G. M., & Stasser, G. (1996). Management of information in small groups. In: J. L. Nye & A. M. Brower (Eds), *What's social about social cognition?* (pp. 3–363). Thousand Oaks, CA: Sage.

Yeatts, D. E., & Hyten, C. (1998). *High-performing self-managed work teams.* Thousand Oaks, CA: Sage.

Yoo, Y., & Kanawattanachai, P. (2001). Developments of transactive memory and collective mind in virtual teams. Paper presented at the annual meeting of the academy of management, Washington, DC.

FOSTERING MENTAL MODEL CONVERGENCE THROUGH TRAINING

Jan Cannon-Bowers

ABSTRACT

The construct of shared mental models has garnered interest among team researchers as a means to explain how teams develop into highly coordinated units. McComb (this volume) contributes to this body of work by synthesizing a host of empirical findings and theoretical assertions into a model of mental model convergence. This advancement is significant, because it begins to shed light on how shared mental models may develop in teams. The present commentary takes McComb's work a step further by combining it with findings from the area of team training. The result is a set of propositions describing when various training interventions may be most beneficial to the team and the mental model convergence process, and why. These propositions are intended to stimulate further efforts to empirically validate team-training strategies as a means to foster development of shared mental models.

Multi-Level Issues in Organizations and Time
Research in Multi-Level Issues, Volume 6, 149–157
Copyright © 2007 by Elsevier Ltd.
ISSN: 1475-9144/doi:10.1016/S1475-9144(07)06006-7

INTRODUCTION

I read with great interest the piece by Sara McComb (this volume) on shared mental models. These models have been an interest of mine for more than 15 years, and it was most gratifying to see how much excellent work has been done on this construct. McComb's summary is masterful. Most impressive, perhaps, is the extent of integration she offers, by pulling together research from disparate areas (and filling in with logical deductions where no research exists), as a basis for specifying a model of how mental model convergence may actually occur. Because further empirical work is necessary to establish the validity of this model, I will not comment on it directly. Instead, this commentary focuses on an issue that has been a driving force in our desire to understand shared mental models and their role in teamwork–namely, training.

THE ROLE OF TRAINING IN MENTAL MODEL CONVERGENCE

To initiate the discussion, I begin with a consideration of several (related) issues that McComb (this volume) did not address in much detail–consciousness (of the convergence process), volition, and motivation. Specifically, it is not clear whether McComb views the convergence process as being one that the team members are aware is happening or, moreover, whether this convergence process is volitional. At times, she seems to suggest that this process is under the conscious control of team members; at other times, its status seems less certain.

My belief is that convergence probably is not a naturally conscious process (i.e., team members are typically not consciously aware that it is happening, nor do they exert control over the process). Having said that, some team members–either because of individual differences or experience–likely have a better "sense" that they need to share information with their teammates and may be more inclined to do so. I suspect that this tendency is common or consistent enough to conclude that *most* team members (especially novice ones) have knowledge or control over the shared mental model convergence process. The point is that the convergence process *can* be conscious and volitional, but it probably isn't in many cases. So the question becomes, *How can we make team members aware of the convergence process and induce them to exert control over it?*

Given that there is awareness of the convergence process and that team members can have conscious control over it, the next issue is motivation—namely, which factors may motivate team members to converge their knowledge with teammates' knowledge? Actually, this is probably too big a question to address here, as a host of individual and situational factors likely affect motivation in a team setting. For the present purposes, this commentary focuses on the extent to which team members are motivated to perform successfully as a team and strategies to enhance this source of motivation. Put another way, *How can we motivate team members to effectively and efficiently converge their mental models?*

These two questions combine to generate a third question: *Which competencies (knowledge, skills, or attitudes) do team members need to optimize the convergence process?* If it is not already obvious at this point, my answer to all of these questions is "training." In fact, several training strategies that were initially tested with military teams (Cannon-Bowers & Salas, 1998) have since been generalized to other high-performance situations (see Sims, Salas, & Burke, 2005). While this body of work shows promise, it has not been organized in a way that makes it clear at which point in the team's development cycle a particular training intervention may be (most) useful. McComb's framework may help to generate specific hypotheses about which training interventions are most likely to have an impact based on the phase of convergence that the team is experiencing.

The goal in this commentary, therefore, is to organize and expand past findings related to team training using the convergence model developed by McComb. The remainder of this commentary is organized around the three phases of convergence in the McComb model: orientation, differentiation, and integration. It also addresses continuous learning as a mechanism of shared mental model maintenance.

TRAINING STRATEGIES IN THE ORIENTATION PHASE

According to McComb, the first phase of mental model convergence is orientation. In this phase, team members gather information about the team and its members. The goal of this phase is to create a comprehensive understanding of the team situation, to pool unshared information, and to discover similarities and differences among members. As noted, team members–especially novice ones–probably do not enter team settings with a preexisting understanding of what this orientation phase (or the mental model convergence process in general) is or why it is important.

Perhaps an analogy to metacognition at the individual level is in order here. Metacognition (i.e., being aware of one's own thought process) is a tendency that appears to be more common in experts (see Bransford, Brown, & Cocking, 1999) than in novices, and one that can be trained. In fact, some evidence suggests that helping decision makers become aware of their metacognition process can help them to make better decisions (Cohen, Freeman, & Thompson, 1997).

Related to this, evidence from early experiences in Cockpit Resource Management (essentially, teaching teamwork in aviation crews) indicated that team members did not have positive attitudes toward teamwork or an appreciation for how essential effective teamwork was to their task success (Helmreich, Foushee, Benson, & Russini, 1986). Hence, several efforts were made to improve attitudes toward teamwork (Helmreich, Wilhelm, Gregorich, & Chidester, 1990). In fact, attitudes toward teamwork have been implicated as a crucial teamwork competency (Cannon-Bowers, Tannenbaum, Salas, & Volpe, 1995). Given these assertions, I offer the following propositions:

Proposition 1. Early in the orientation phase, team members should be instructed about the importance of shared mental models in teams and of the convergence process in general.

Proposition 2. Early in the orientation phase, attempts should be made to ensure that team members have an appreciation of, and positive attitudes toward, teamwork and shared knowledge.

As the orientation phase proceeds, it may also be of value to provide specific information to teammates about their role in the team and the unique contributions that they have to offer. This sort of role clarification training can increase interpositional knowledge and establish a basis for knowledge sharing. As McComb (this volume) argues, it is crucial that team members in the orientation phase build a foundation of knowledge about the team, especially in cross-functional teams. This understanding leads to the following proposition:

Proposition 3. Later in the orientation phase, team members should receive training that clarifies their roles and illuminates how each contributes to the team task.

In this regard, we have successfully tested cross-training as a means to provide team members with a detailed understanding of the specific needs and contributions of each member (Cannon-Bowers, Salas, Blickensderfer, & Bowers, 1998). In fact, cross training may be an excellent strategy for helping team members to appreciate the challenges confronted by their teammates in accomplishing certain tasks, thereby fostering greater tolerance and patience. Hence, I offer the following proposition:

Proposition 4. Later in the orientation phase, team members should be cross-trained (in as realistic a manner as possible) so that they can gain detailed team-level knowledge.

TRAINING STRATEGIES IN THE DIFFERENTIATION PHASE

According to McComb (this volume), the differentiation phase of mental model convergence involves the organization, consolidation, and merging of team-level knowledge. In this phase, team members begin to build a transactive memory that essentially acts as a shared repository of knowledge across the team. This process may be viewed as an iteration of the orientation phase, in which team members begin to make sense of what they are learning about the team and form deeper understandings of how the team will work together.

While not explicitly stated by McComb, this team-level knowledge likely begins as a general understanding of the role in the orientation phase (e.g., someone from Engineering will generally have this type of knowledge and skill) and proceeds during differentiation to become more specific to the actual team member who represents that role. The actual division–and hence sharing of knowledge–will depend on the particular strengths, weaknesses, preferences, desires, and other facets of the individual filling any given role on the team (i.e., not all teammates from Engineering are created equal). This type of team-specific knowledge (see Cannon-Bowers et al., 1995) is essential for team members so that they can adjust their behavior to coordinate with specific teammates.

Building teammate-specific knowledge is obviously a natural process that occurs over the life of the team as members gain more experience with one another across a variety of situations. One way to accelerate this process is to provide realistic simulations of the task so that members can gather specific knowledge about how teammates will respond under various conditions. Such simulations may be sophisticated, computer-driven mock-ups of the task, or they may be simpler attempts (e.g., paper-based descriptions of problems or cases the team must discuss) to engage team members in the appropriate thought process. What is crucial is that the simulated environment represents the important cues in the task that trigger specific responses. In this way, team members can build up a repertoire of cases or instances of team performance that can help them organize and consolidate their knowledge of the team and its processes. This leads to the next proposition:

Proposition 5. During the differentiation phase, simulations representing the important cues in the team task environment should be provided to team members so that they can gain experience in working with specific teammates and build team-level knowledge.

TRAINING STRATEGIES IN THE INTEGRATION PHASE

According to McComb (this volume), the integration phase of the mental model convergence process involves reconciliation of the diversity of members and a shift in focus from the individual to the team level. This process finally results in shared mental models that allow the team to coordinate their efforts effectively in accomplishing their task. McComb discusses two issues that affect the integration process: the definition of sharing (i.e., overlapping versus distributed knowledge) and the degree of integration of knowledge needed to support performance. Both issues are complex and depend on the nature of the team and its task, so this commentary will not address them in detail. Nevertheless, regardless of the potential differences in the nature of sharing and degree of integration, this final phase of mental model convergence depends heavily on the team members' experiences with one another. In other words, by the time the team reaches the integration phase, team members gain actual experience with one another, and use this experience as a basis for reconciling and integrating their mental models.

Given this assumption—that actual experience with one another helps to drive the integration process—efforts to use experience as a learning opportunity should enhance shared mental model formation. In this regard, an intervention called guided team self-correction (see Smith-Jentsch, Zeisig, Acton, & McPherson, 1998) appears promising. This intervention seeks to teach team members to observe one another's performance and provide constructive feedback at the conclusion of an exercise or episode of performance. Originally developed for use with simulated exercises, this technique can also be used in actual performance settings by training team members in self-correction principles and instructing them to employ these concepts after important episodes of performance. Hence, team members can be trained to pay attention to the behavior of teammates, to provide explanations for their own behavior that help teammates better understand their rationale, and to provide feedback to teammates about how they can better coordinate. For these reasons, I offer the following proposition:

Proposition 6. Guided team self-correction techniques should be taught to team members so that they can make better use of actual episodes of performance to help integrate and consolidate their mental models.

TRAINING STRATEGIES DURING MAINTENANCE

Once shared mental models are formed, McComb (this volume) contends that a maintenance process must ensue to ensure that mental model convergence remains current. She delineates several cognitive processes that describe how team members might recognize that mental model adjustment is necessary. My contention is that the guided team self-correction techniques described previously, if applied correctly, can provide the basis for a continuous improvement model within the team. To accomplish this goal, the requirement that team members learn to accurately monitor their teammates' behavior and recognize when adjustment is necessary must be emphasized. Moreover, team members must be made aware that continual monitoring, intra-team feedback, and adjustment are necessary parts of effective team functioning. This leads to the final proposition:

Proposition 7. Team members must be taught the importance of continuous improvement and instructed in how guided team self-correction techniques–with emphasis on intra-team performance monitoring and feedback–can be applied over the life of the team to ensure that shared mental models are accurate and up-to-date.

CONCLUSION

This commentary has attempted to build on the excellent work of McComb (this volume) by focusing on training to foster mental model convergence in teams. From a theoretical standpoint, I would welcome attempts to empirically verify the propositions offered here. In fact, combing the McComb framework with the training perspective described in this commentary may help future researchers to more precisely specify hypotheses regarding training interventions based on the phase of mental model convergence that the team is experiencing.

From a practical standpoint, I hope that the propositions I have offered are useful to managers and team leaders who desire to enhance shared knowledge as a means to improve performance. Certainly, many teams are able to experience the convergence process successfully and perform effectively without external intervention. Nevertheless, well-designed training interventions that are applied at the appropriate phase should both accelerate the convergence process and increase the likelihood that it will be successful. Moreover, the scarcity of resources in most organizations dictates that training dollars be allocated wisely so that outcomes are optimized. The propositions offered here suggest that training interventions may be best applied in accordance with the team's developmental phase. If empirically verified, such guidelines can be useful in determining when a team is likely to realize the maximum benefit from a particular intervention.

When the notion of shared mental models began to gain traction a few years ago, critics of this line of thinking contended that it was an unnecessary construct that could not be measured with any confidence. I am delighted (and gratified) that so much excellent work has been conducted in this area and that the construct has turned out to be useful in describing how teams develop "from a team of experts into an expert team." Efforts to integrate what we have learned into testable models–that describe not only what shared mental models are, but also the process by which they develop– are evidence that the notion of shared mental models has evolved into a viable and useful team construct. McComb's work is an excellent example of such evolution.

REFERENCES

Bransford, J. D., Brown, A. L., & Cocking, R. R. (Eds). (1999). *How people learn: Brain, mind, experience, and school.* Washington, DC: National Academy Press.

Cannon-Bowers, J. A., & Salas, E. (Eds). (1998). *Making decisions under stress: Implications for individual and team training.* Washington, DC: American Psychological Association.

Cannon-Bowers, J., Salas, E., Blickensderfer, E., & Bowers, C. (1998). The impact of cross-training and workload on team functioning: A replication and extension of initial findings. *Human Factors, 40*(1), 92–101.

Cannon-Bowers, J. A., Tannenbaum, S. I., Salas, E., & Volpe, C. (1995). Defining competencies and establishing team training requirements. In: R. A. Guzzo & E. Salas (Eds), *Team effectiveness and decision-making in organizations* (pp. 333–380). San Francisco: Jossey-Bass.

Cohen, M., Freeman, J., & Thompson, B. (1997). Training the naturalistic decision maker. In: C. Zsambok (Ed.), *Naturalistic decision making* (pp. 257–268). Mahwah, NJ: Lawrence Erlbaum Associates.

Helmreich, R., Foushee, H., Benson, R., & Russini, W. (1986). Cockpit resource management: Exploring the attitude–performance linkage. *Aviation, Space, and Environmental Medicine, 57*(12), 1198–1200.

Helmreich, R., Wilhelm, J., Gregorich, S., & Chidester, T. (1990). Preliminary results from the evaluation of cockpit resource management training: Performance ratings of flightcrews. *Aviation, Space, and Environmental Medicine, 61*(6), 576–579.

McComb, S. (this volume). Mental model convergence: The shift from being an individual to being a team member. In: F. Dansereau & F. Yammarino (Eds), *Research in multi-level issues* (Vol. 6). Amsterdam: Elsevier.

Sims, D. E., Salas, E., & Burke, C. S. (2005). Promoting effective team performance through team training. In: S. A. Wheelan (Ed.), *The handbook of group research and practice* (pp. 407–425). Thousand Oaks, CA: Sage.

Smith-Jentsch, K., Zeisig, R., Acton, B., & McPherson, J. (1998). Team dimensional training: A strategy for guided team self-correction. In: J. A. Cannon-Bowers & E. Salas (Eds), *Making decisions under stress: Implications for individual and team training* (pp. 271–297). Washington, DC: American Psychological Association.

UNDERSTANDING TEAM COGNITION: THE SHIFT TO COGNITIVE SIMILARITY CONFIGURATIONS

Joan R. Rentsch and Erika E. Small

ABSTRACT

This commentary focuses on S. A. McComb's chapter on the process of mental model convergence and provides guidance for advancing this research stream. McComb's chapter highlights many of the theoretical and methodological challenges that have plagued the study of cognition in teams. This commentary addresses those challenges and offers suggestions for the next steps in this field. Specifically, it considers the complex and abstract nature of team cognition and offers an elaborated model for understanding cognitive similarity that includes cognitive similarity configurations.

INTRODUCTION

Cognition in teams emerged in the 1990s as an important research area, and it remains highly relevant in understanding team processes and team performance (e.g., Cannon-Bowers, Salas, & Converse, 1993; Fiore & Salas,

Multi-Level Issues in Organizations and Time
Research in Multi-Level Issues, Volume 6, 159–174
Copyright © 2007 by Elsevier Ltd.
All rights of reproduction in any form reserved
ISSN: 1475-9144/doi:10.1016/S1475-9144(07)06007-9

2004; Klimoski & Mohammed, 1994; Mohammed & Dumville, 2001; Rentsch & Hall, 1994; Rentsch & Zelno, 2003). A substantial body of empirical evidence supports the continuation of research in this area (e.g., Levesque, Wilson, & Wholey, 2001; Lim & Klein, 2006; Mathieu, Heffner, Goodwin, Cannon-Bowers, & Salas, 2005; Mathieu, Heffner, Goodwin, Salas, & Cannon-Bowers, 2000; Rentsch & Klimoski, 2001). However, at this point, there exists a need for sophisticated theory related to the formation of cognition in teams. Theoretical development may be advanced by related work in socialization and organizational meanings that addresses processes relevant to how team members develop common interpretations of ambiguous team-related events (e.g., Levine & Moreland, 1991; Louis, 1980; Schneider & Reichers, 1983; Moreland & Levine, 1989; Rentsch, 1990).

Properly, socialized team members contribute to a team's performance partly because they develop cognitive similarity with respect to their team-mates. Cognitive similarity is achieved, in turn, from the social construction process that occurs through direct or indirect interaction among unit members (e.g., Berger & Luckmann, 1966; Levine & Moreland, 1991; Schein, 1985; Schneider & Reichers, 1983; Walsh, Henderson, & Deighton, 1988). Team members draw on their past personal experiences and on their interactions with one another to develop similar cognitive structures for understanding and attributing meaning to team-related events and factors including one another, the task, and the team's context (Rentsch, Small, & Hanges, in press).

Thus, cognitive similarity transpires in teams not simply because of a newcomer's adaptation to existing members, but also through negotiation among team members and through external interpretative influences such as strong leaders and training. Furthermore, similarity in interpretations of events among team members may increase or decrease team effectiveness, although most theoretical perspectives emphasize the positive effects. Implicit in these perspectives are two assumptions: that the cognitive content is functional and that the degree and form of the similarity are beneficial and exist at optimal levels. Under these assumptions, teams in which members interpret events similarly are hypothesized to gain from smooth interactions and high performance.

McComb (this volume) drew from much of this type of thinking and attempted to address the need for additional theoretical work aimed directly at the formation of cognition in teams. She took on this major challenge by presenting a model of mental model convergence and conducting an empirical study, which she argued provided a preliminary test of her model. One outcome of her work was that it highlighted pervasive and important issues in the study of cognition in teams.

This commentary addresses these issues and offers suggestions for the next steps in the study of team cognition. The specific focus here is on the complex and abstract nature of team cognition. First, a model of configurations of cognitive similarity is presented. Next, measurement and methodological issues are addressed, followed by a discussion of the need for researchers to articulate their assumptions.

CONFIGURATIONS OF COGNITIVE SIMILARITY

McComb focuses on mental model convergence, particularly with respect to the shared content of mental models (e.g., team members, the team, the task, the organization, the environment; Cannon-Bowers et al., 1993; Kraiger & Wenzel, 1997). This conceptualization of cognition in teams has proved worthy of continued study. McComb acknowledges that multiple mental models may occur simultaneously, and she describes some complex relationships that may exist. We agree that cognition in teams is complex, and we propose that researchers broaden their approaches to the study of cognition in teams in an effort to develop comprehensive models of team cognition. Rentsch et al. (in press) addressed this issue, referring to configurations of cognitive similarity.

Rentsch et al. (in press) defined cognitive similarity as "forms of related meanings or understandings attributed to and utilized to make sense of and interpret internal and external events including affect, behavior, and thoughts of self and others that exist amongst individuals." They chose to emphasize similar rather than shared cognition so as to accentuate that the probability of individuals developing identical interpretations (as is implied by "shared") is exceedingly small. Rather, individuals will develop cognitive *similarity*. Clearly, although individuals may develop cognitive similarity, cognition is assumed to reside exclusively within the individual.

Cognitive similarity is a general term that incorporates multiple *types* that are defined by the intersection of three features: (1) the form of the cognition, (2) the form of similarity, and (3) the cognitive content domain. Types of cognitive similarity (e.g., Cognitive Form A with Similarity Form B with Content Domain C) in combination produce *configurations of cognitive similarity*. To illustrate, Cognitive Similarity Type X (consisting of Cognitive Form A, Similarity Form B, and Content Domain C) may occur simultaneously with Cognitive Similarity Type Y (consisting of Cognitive Form E, Similarity Form F, and Content Domain G). The complexity of cognition in teams might be better understood and be more predictive of team processes and outcomes when *configurations of cognitive similarity* are incorporated in team theory. Therefore, we present a description of the three key features that form the foundation for types of cognitive similarity and, ultimately, for configurations of cognitive similarity.

Forms of Cognition

Researchers who study teams, individuals, and organizations have conceptualized and examined many forms of cognition. Typically, within team research, cognition has been conceptualized as structured or organized knowledge. Mental models, strategic consensus, and team member schema similarity represent three basic approaches to defining the similarity of structured cognition. Much of the work from this perspective is based on the assumption that cognition is organized in the form of a knowledge structure that aids a person in interpreting and responding to events (Klimoski & Mohammed, 1994).

To the extent that the team members' individually held mental models about team-related events are consistent with one another, the team is said to have a shared mental model or team mental model (Mohammed & Dumville, 2001; Mathieu et al., 2005). Similarly, team members can create shared strategic consensus as a result of debating strategic decisions until their strategic mental models overlap (Ensley & Pearce, 2001). The concept of schema (Rumelhart, 1980) also represents the organized knowledge perspective, and team-related schemata aid in the interpretation and understanding of team events. Team member schema similarity exists when team members have comparable, complementary, or accurate schemas for organizing team-related information (Rentsch et al., in press; Rentsch & Klimoski, 2001; Rentsch & Woehr, 2004).

These forms of cognition within the organized knowledge conceptualization – that is, shared mental models, shared strategic consensus, and team member schema similarity – are the primary sources that team cognition researchers rely upon, and it is this research base that is the backbone of McComb's model. However, other forms of cognition are also relevant to the study of cognition in teams.

The perceptual conceptualization of team cognition is based on psychological climate research in which cognitive similarity is determined to comprise congruence among team members' perceptions of the team or work environment (Glisson & James, 2002; Schneider, 1975; Schneider & Reichers, 1983). From this perspective, individual team members observe behavioral patterns in the environment and develop perceptions of it that become shared (i.e., overlapping, similar) through interactions with one another and social construction processes (e.g., Naumann & Bennett, 2000). In this way, a socially constructed understanding of the environment emerges through group interaction. Likewise, team members may come to share beliefs and expectations. For example, team members may develop congruent beliefs about the way in which the team should respond to failure (Cannon & Edmondson, 2001) or about the team's ability to perform the task (Gibson, 2001, 2003) as team members interact over time. Furthermore, team members may come to share expectations for team behavior (e.g., expectations that define appropriate attendance behavior; Xie & Johns, 2000). Forms of cognition from the perceptual conceptualization include team climate, team culture, shared beliefs, shared expectations, and shared attitudes. (Although "shared" is the term used in the literature, some of these researchers acknowledge lack of identical agreement.)

Another conceptualization of team cognition is interpretive and involves sense making, interpretive systems, and collective learning. For example, sense-making research asserts that team members collaboratively and retroactively make sense of their past experiences and their environment (Greenberg, 1995; Weick, 1993). Likewise, interpretive convergence refers to the process by which team members negotiate an understanding of their experiences through discussion and information sharing (Baba, Gluesing, Ratner, & Wagner, 2004; Gioia & Thomas, 1996). Thus, the construction and negotiation of meaning is itself a shared process among team members. The relevant cognitive forms here are sense-making processes, interpretive systems, and cognitive convergence.

As stated earlier, team members may develop similarity with respect to each form of cognition. Just as the cognition may take different forms, so, too, may similarity.

Forms of Similarity

McComb distinguishes between two types of cognitive convergence: complementary or compatible (i.e., "to divide") and shared or similar (i.e., "to have in common"). Although she does mention mental model accuracy, she does not include it in her model. Nevertheless, we commend her for considering multiple forms of similarity, and we suggest that cognitive similarity may take a variety of forms, including congruent, accurate, complementary, and forms derived from the social relations model (e.g., team meta-accuracy; Rentsch & Woehr, 2004). Furthermore, each form of similarity may be described in terms of the level, variability, and stability of the similarity

among team members and, when examining multiple types of cognitive
similarity, in terms of profile shape (Rentsch, Delise, & Hutchison, in press).

Thus, although McComb includes two forms of similarity that are critical
in defining and describing the convergence process, other forms of cognitive
similarity also require consideration. Again, there is complexity associated
with team cognition in terms of forms of similarity. For example, various
forms of cognitive similarity (e.g., team-assumed reciprocity and accuracy)
with respect to different cognitive contents are likely to occur simultaneously. At this point, researchers are merely beginning to tap the surface of
the possibilities.

Cognitive Content Domain

The cognitive content may be defined with reference to anything that is
being understood (knowledge about individuals, groups, organizations; appropriate responses to systems and the environment; the team's purpose;
team members' actions and roles, and so on; Marks, Sabella, Burke, &
Zaccaro, 2002). McComb ultimately chose to focus on shared cognitive
content rather than shared structure, arguing that developing shared content
is a precursor to developing shared structure, which requires time and extensive training. She suggests that shared structure is not necessary for teams
in which time for communication is abundant. In addition, she discusses
mental model structure and content at length.

We agree that structure and content are two defining features of types of
cognitive similarity, and that specifying the focus of one's research question
is important. For example, structured cognition is one of many possible
forms of cognition. In the case of structured cognition, cognitive similarity
(regardless of the form of similarity of interest) may be assessed with respect
to the structure of the cognition and/or with respect to the cognitive domain
(i.e., content). In other words, team members may have similar structural
features of cognition, including complexity, integration, and coherence.
Likewise, team members may attain similarity in the content of cognition,
which may include information from any domain.

One caveat in the discussion of forms of cognition, forms of similarity,
and content domains must be acknowledged. When considering cognitive
features, one must bear in mind that the purpose of any cognition –
including team cognition – is to create understanding and to interpret and
give meaning to stimuli. For example, the interrelationships between content
nodes and the interconnections across cognitive structures somehow, by
some unarticulated and unknown process, produce thoughts, insights,

meaning, and understanding. By differentiating cognitive structure and content as critical aspects of this process, researchers have been able to develop theoretical propositions and measurement tools that have proved remarkably successful in capturing some aspect of the factors involved in the process of interpretation and understanding. (Evidence exists in the predictive validity of a variety of measures.)

That said, structure and content are two features that are inextricably intertwined in the process of understanding, and their separation is a matter of theoretical and methodological convenience. Perhaps, cognitive content domain more accurately refers to a dense, well-organized, or, for lack of better phrasing, "more solidly constructed" portion of the cognitive structure that contains concentrated knowledge or interpretive information related to a given content domain. Although it may be referred to as cognitive content, any portion of the organized knowledge is always connected to other portions of an individual's cognitive structure. In other words, the portion of the cognitive structure representing the cognitive content domain will not stand alone, unconnected from the rest of the cognitive structure. Therefore, examining any cognitive content domain places a perhaps arbitrary boundary on organized knowledge. As researchers, we apply arbitrary boundaries to be able to measure something that is potentially unlimited. However, we must recognize these constraints.

Clearly, the complexity and abstract nature of the phenomenon under study results in difficulties in defining and measuring it. Consequently, much of the recent research on team cognition has focused on measurement issues and techniques (e.g., Langan-Fox, Code, & Langfield, 2000; Mohammed, Klimoski, & Rentsch, 2000).

MEASUREMENT AND METHODOLOGICAL ISSUES

McComb collected empirical data from a small study that she argues tested hypotheses related to her model. Her effort illustrates the many difficulties inherent in conducting empirical work on team cognition and the types of problems that tend to limit the inferences that can be drawn. For example, it is often difficult to obtain a sample size that affords substantial statistical power. In addition, the measurement of cognition is difficult. When this endeavor involves coding and interpreting qualitative data, typically researchers seem to believe that they will better understand participants' responses if they are involved in the data coding. (As curious researchers, we would have enjoyed seeing sample responses from McComb's data collection.) Unfortunately, this results in at least one coder who is not blind to the hypotheses. This section describes four alternative measurement approaches that researchers studying team cognitions have applied: aggregated scale scores, collective consensus, structured assessments, and qualitative methods. All of these methods tend to be associated with assessments of specific forms of cognition. All of the methods described here have relative strengths and weaknesses, and each is susceptible to researcher influence at various points.

Aggregated scale scores and collective consensus methods tend to be associated with the perceptual forms of cognition. These methods require researchers to provide stimuli that participants then rate. Aggregated responses to questionnaire items highlight the content of the team cognition by making the specific content domain of interest be the referent in the items.

Collective consensus is a measurement technique that requires a group to respond as a unit to each item on a questionnaire. This method does not provide information regarding the degree of agreement among team members' understandings.

When researchers conceptualize team cognition as structured cognition, they tend to assess it using structural assessments that capture the structure of the cognition and the degree to which team members' structured cognitions are similar. Structured assessments are more informative regarding cognitive structure than aggregated scale scores and collective consensus. The analysis of paired comparison ratings (ratings provided by individual team members in response to researcher-supplied items) using UCINET, multidimensional scaling, or Pathfinder is a common means to assess structured cognition. Likewise, concept-mapping techniques (maps provided by individual team members or by the entire team) are used to assess structured cognition (Mohammed et al., 2000).

Team cognition in the form of interpretive convergence is typically assessed using such qualitative data sources as case studies, observations, interviews, essays, e-mails, and teleconferences. These data are usually transformed into descriptions of interpretive convergence content and of the processes yielding the convergence. Several researchers have applied coding schemes to the qualitative data (e.g., Fiol, 1994). We would contend that these types of qualitative data, although they can be very useful, are at high risk of researcher influence.

McComb explicitly states that cognition resides in the individual. Furthermore, she is insightful in her recognition that it is useful to elicit participants' cognitive content. We agree with both stances. Meaning resides in the individual, and actions are dependent upon an individual's subjective understandings (Burrell & Morgan, 1979). In addition, it cannot be denied that individuals have partially different interpretations of stimuli such as a teammate's behavior and other team-related events. Thus, researchers cannot take for granted that their own cognitive structures and contents are the same as those of their subjects.

McComb selected as her measurement technique a sentence completion method in an attempt to measure mental models accurately and without imposing content on respondents. We commend this effort, because minimizing researcher influence in the measurement of cognitive similarity is extremely difficult. An anecdote provides an example of how researchers may misinterpret data even though they conscientiously apply accepted research practices.

One researcher's initial study of team cognition was designed to assess individuals' schemas of teamwork (Rentsch & Duffy, 1991). This work was based on the previously mentioned assumption – that each individual thinks differently (i.e., possesses a unique schema for understanding, in this case, teamwork), but that there is likely to be some similarity in how people understand teamwork. In an effort to keep her own cognitive content and structure out of the data collection process, the researcher refused to build a questionnaire or to present specific stimuli to subjects. Instead, data were collected using a version of Kelly's Repertory Grid (Kelly, 1955), which required participants to generate idiosyncratic teamwork descriptors and a list of teams with which they were familiar. Then, they rated each team on each descriptor. Essentially, the participants generated their own assessments, thereby minimizing researcher influence and revealing idiosyncratic differences in understandings of teamwork.

At this point, the rating data were factor analyzed for each participant, and the researcher and a graduate student attempted to use the results to detect cognitive similarity among the participants. The researchers, intrigued by the results, attempted to interpret the descriptors participants had generated, such as "divided" and "salient." This was difficult, but validated the assumption that each individual had a unique schema of teamwork. The researchers discussed commonly used descriptors such as "friendly" and "task-focused"; again, it became clear that many possible interpretations could be applied to each descriptor.

Although deciphering the various interpretations was difficult, the researchers' persistence appeared to pay off as they began to detect convergence among the participants' responses. Then one day, in the middle of debating the meaning of a descriptor, it finally dawned on them that they were doing exactly what the conscientious researcher was so determined *not* to do: They were diligently and scrupulously examining their *own* understandings of teamwork rather than the participants' understandings.

By meticulously searching for common understandings among the participants, they were actually discovering their own schemas for teamwork. Furthermore, they were engaged in a process of gaining cognitive convergence between themselves!

The solution was to conduct interviews with the participants to learn how they interpreted their own data. During the interviews, the statistical results surprised the novice participants, who contended that they did not accurately represent their understanding of teamwork. In many cases, these individuals could not define the descriptors that they themselves had generated. In these cases, the researchers could not have possibly extracted accurate interpretations of the provided data (although, before their "insight," they thought they had). During the interviews, it also became apparent that participants who were team experts (i.e., reported having been members of a high number of teams) could articulate their understanding of teamwork with ease. The factor analysis results made sense to them, and the expert participants commented that the statistical results accurately captured their understandings of teamwork.

The repertory grid technique was quite effective in extracting individuals' teamwork schemas. Nevertheless, in many cases, the participants' interpretations clearly did not match those that the researchers had conjured up for them. The researchers had applied their own interpretations to the descriptors and to the quantitative results.

The moral of this story: Qualitative data are simply fascinating and quite informative, but the researcher will interfere with them at some point. This interference must be acknowledged when drawing inferences from the data. The challenge is to compare qualitative information using quantitative methods. One approach is to use property fitting combined with multidimensional scaling analysis to approximate quantitatively evaluating qualitative data.

For example, using paired comparisons analyzed using multidimensional scaling, and interpreting the multidimensional scaling results using adjective ratings and property fitting, Rentsch (1990) found that members of organizational interaction groups tended to interpret organizational events similarly, but that between-group differences in interpretation existed. Although there was some agreement between groups in terms of the interpretation of organizational events (e.g., most groups interpreted the organizational events as ranging along the scales of nonprofessional–professional, unfair–fair, and care about employees–neglect employees), there were distinct differences in the adjectives used to describe and interpret events, demonstrating more complex interpretations. For example, some groups interpreted working more than 40 hours per week as "professional," others interpreted it as "caring about employees," still others interpreted it as "stressful," and so on. In other words, different groups interpreted the same events not only by using different bipolar scales, but also by using opposite ends of the same bipolar scales. Although some overlap and agreement in meaning between some groups existed, these rather strikingly different interpretations of events suggested that different interaction groups do interpret organizational events qualitatively differently.

The methodology enabled the researcher to assess these qualitative differences using quantitative analyses. However, the organizational events and the adjectives that provided these data were presented to the participants; the participants did not generate their own assessments. Although these stimuli were extracted from interviews with a sample of the participants, the researcher ultimately selected the limited set of stimuli to be rated. As a consequence, the most relevant descriptors for some groups may not have been available for rating.

Researcher influence will inevitably enter the data, most likely when generating stimuli (items) or when coding qualitative data. Knowledge structures have been represented using such methodologies as verbal protocols, observations, audiotapes, videotapes, or interviews (e.g., Hillerbrand & Claiborn, 1990). The obtained information is coded to represent participants' schemas. Typically, the researchers themselves complete these coding tasks (e.g., Borko & Livingston, 1989), which leave these methods vulnerable to researcher influence. We encourage researchers to select methods that minimize researcher influence on the data, or to use multiple methods to converge on the participants' schemas.

Rentsch, Heffner, and Duffy (1994) employed multiple methods when they used paired comparison ratings analyzed via multidimensional scaling (MDS) and compared the results to free-hand concept maps. Blind coders rated the degree of similarity of the spatial representations of schemas extracted from the MDS analyses with the concept maps drawn by the participants. This choice of methodology was based on the assumption that each individual may have unique knowledge structures. Although stimuli extracted from a sample of team members were presented to participants in this study, the methods chosen permitted each individual to represent the structure of his or her teamwork knowledge. As predicted, the measurement results converged more for team experts than for team novices. Although these researchers were most interested in within-person consistency, raters could compare results produced by different participants to determine cognitive congruence (i.e., the form of similarity) with respect to cognitive structure (i.e., the form of cognition).

As this discussion suggests, we believe McComb is on target by examining different contents of cognition. The challenges are to capture the qualitative differences while minimizing researcher influence *and* to use a method that enables quantitative evaluation of similarities among the qualitative differences. Techniques such as MDS, Pathfinder, network analysis, and concept mapping aid in this effort. McComb's use of the modified Streufert sentence completion method was effective in eliciting qualitative differences in cognition. However, because the responses were made to fixed stems, the challenge is to determine whether the stems probed or elicited the relevant cognitive contents of the participants or whether they limited the extraction of relevant cognitive content. Another challenge for the researcher using this method is to minimize researcher influence on the interpretations, particularly when the researcher, who is coding responses, also generated the hypotheses being tested.

When examining how mental models converge over time, researchers will invariably inherit the added challenge of measuring process variables. Not only will we continue to strive for the most effective and efficient way to elicit mental model content and structure, and to measure the amount of convergence, but we will also continue to be challenged to examine how these factors change over time as a function of the team's developmental stage. Clearly, measurement issues have been, and will remain, the primary obstacle to team cognition research. McComb has attempted to address some of these measurement difficulties in her chapter, and we have attempted to highlight several specific examples here.

ASSUMPTIONS AND CONSTRAINTS

McComb's work reminds us to articulate assumptions. As mentioned previously, she articulated many of her assumptions, but it is not always feasible to expect all researchers to articulate all of their assumptions. Nevertheless, researchers might increase their efforts to state their important implicit assumptions, because many variables moderate predictions about team cognition.

For example, team type is likely to play a significant role in many theories of cognition convergence. McComb was unambiguous about the team type of interest, focusing solely on project teams. The cross-functional, short-term nature of these teams, she argued, made cognitive convergence especially difficult to achieve. Therefore, by limiting the scope of her research to only teams with these unique characteristics, McComb was able to limit the scope of her chapter while also providing a conservative examination of the convergence process. In addition, she increased the generalizability of the results to a specific team type. Team member experience and expertise is another important variable, as described earlier.

Team researchers tend not to address their assumptions about other potentially key variables, particularly those related to team dynamics, individual differences (e.g., dominant personality) among team members, and team member motivation. Examples of such variables include the degree to which team members are motivated to work together as a team, are invested and motivated to integrate their views into a view that can guide functional team behavior, value their interactions with one another, value one another's input, or desire to reconcile their cognitive differences.

CONCLUSION

McComb's chapter covered much ground, and our commentary has focused on only a small portion of the implications of her work. Nevertheless, the intention of this focused commentary is to encourage researchers of team cognition to continue to accept the difficult challenges posed by these phenomena and to draw broadly from available research. The notion of cognitive similarity configurations represents one approach to advance the exploration of these phenomena. Although conceptualization of cognition in teams is complex and the measurement issues are challenging, efforts in one area should not limit the other. McComb's work contributes to this field by illustrating some of the challenges.

ACKNOWLEDGMENTS

The contribution of the first author was funded in part by the Office of Naval Research Award Number: N00014-05-1-0624. The authors thank Debra Steele-Johnson and Lisa Delise for their comments on an earlier draft of this paper.

REFERENCES

Baba, M. L., Gluesing, J., Ratner, H., & Wagner, K. H. (2004). The contexts of knowing: Natural history of a globally distributed team. *Journal of Organizational Behavior, 25,* 547–587.

Berger, P. L., & Luckmann, T. (1966). *The social construction of reality*. New York: Doubleday.

Borko, H., & Livingston, C. (1989). Cognition and improvisation: Differences in mathematics instruction by expert and novice teachers. *American Educational Research Journal, 26*, 473–498.

Burrell, G., & Morgan, G. (1979). *Sociological paradigms and organizational analysis*. London: Heinman Educational Books.

Cannon, M. D., & Edmondson, A. C. (2001). Confronting failure: Antecedents and consequences of shared beliefs about failure in organizational work groups. *Journal of Organizational Behavior, 22*, 161–177.

Cannon-Bowers, J. A., Salas, E., & Converse, S. A. (1993). Shared mental models in expert team decision making. In: N. J. Castellan Jr. (Ed.), *Individual and group decision making: Current issues* (pp. 221–246). Hillsdale, NJ: Lawrence Erlbaum Associates.

Ensley, M. D., & Pearce, C. L. (2001). Shared cognition in top management teams: Implications for new venture performance. *Journal of Organizational Behavior, 22*, 145–160.

Fiol, C. M. (1994). Consensus, diversity, and learning in organizations. *Organizational Science, 5*, 403–420.

Fiore, S. M., & Salas, E. (2004). Why we need team cognition. In: E. Salas & S. M. Fiore (Eds), *Team cognition: Understanding the factors that drive process and performance* (pp. 235–248). Washington, DC: American Psychological Association.

Gibson, C. B. (2001). Me and us: Differential relationships among goal-setting training, efficacy and effectiveness at the individual and team level. *Journal of Organizational Behavior, 22*, 789–808.

Gibson, C. B. (2003). The efficacy advantage: Factors related to the formation of group efficacy. *Journal of Applied Social Psychology, 33*, 2153–2186.

Gioia, D. A., & Thomas, J. B. (1996). Institutional identity, image, and issue interpretation: Sensemaking during strategic change in academia. *Administrative Science Quarterly, 41*, 370–403.

Glisson, C., & James, L. R. (2002). The cross-level effects of culture and climate in human service teams. *Journal of Organizational Behavior, 23*, 767–794.

Greenberg, D. N. (1995). Blue versus gray: A metaphor constraining sensemaking around a restructuring. *Group and Organization Management, 20*, 183–209.

Hillerbrand, E. T., & Claiborn, C. D. (1990). Examining reasoning skill differences between expert and novice counselors. *Journal of Counseling and Development, 68*(6), 684–691.

Kelly, G.A. (1955). *The psychology of personal constructs* (Vol. 1). New York: Norton.

Klimoski, R., & Mohammed, S. (1994). Team mental model: Construct or metaphor?. *Journal of Management, 20*, 403–437.

Kraiger, K., & Wenzel, L. H. (1997). Conceptual development and empirical evaluation of measures of shared mental models as indicators of team effectiveness. In: M. T. Brannick, E. Salas & C. Prince (Eds), *Team performance assessment and measurement: Theory, methods, and applications* (pp. 63–84) Mahwah, NJ: Lawrence Erlbaum Associates.

Langan-Fox, J., Code, S., & Langfield, K. (2000). Team mental models: Techniques, methods, and analytic approaches. *Human Factors, 42*, 242–271.

Levesque, L. L., Wilson, J. M., & Wholey, D. R. (2001). Cognitive divergence and shared mental models in software development project teams. *Journal of Organizational Behavior, 22*, 135–144.

Levine, J. M., & Moreland, R. L. (1991). Culture and socialization in work groups. In: L. B. Resnick, J. M. Levine & S. D. Teasley (Eds), *Perspectives on socially shared cognition*. Washington, DC: American Psychological Association.

Lim, B., & Klein, K. J. (2006). Team mental models and team performance: A field study of the effects of team mental model similarity and accuracy. *Journal of Organizational Behavior, 27,* 403–418.

Louis, M. R. (1980). Surprise and sense making: What newcomers experience in unfamiliar organizational settings. *Administrative Science Quarterly, 25,* 226–251.

Marks, M. A., Sabella, M. J., Burke, C. S., & Zaccaro, S. J. (2002). The impact of cross-training on team effectiveness. *Journal of Applied Psychology, 87,* 3–13.

Mathieu, J. E., Heffner, T. S., Goodwin, G. F., Salas, E., & Cannon-Bowers, J. A. (2000). The influence of shared mental models on team process and performance. *Journal of Applied Psychology, 85,* 273–283.

Mathieu, J. E., Heffner, T. S., Goodwin, G. F., Cannon-Bowers, J. A., & Salas, E. (2005). Scaling the quality of teammates' mental models: Equifinality and normative comparisons. *Journal of Organizational Behavior, 26,* 37–56.

McComb, S. (this volume). Mental model convergence: The shift from being an individual to being a team member. In F. Dansereau & F. J. Yammarino (Eds), *Research in multi-level issues* (Vol. 6). Amsterdam: Elsevier.

Mohammed, S., & Dumville, B. C. (2001). Team mental models in a team knowledge framework: Expanding theory and measurement across disciplinary boundaries. *Journal of Organizational Behavior, 22,* 89–106.

Mohammed, S., Klimoski, R., & Rentsch, J. R. (2000). The measurement of team mental models: We have no shared schema. *Organizational Research Methods, 3,* 123–165.

Moreland, R. L., & Levine, J. M. (1989). Newcomers and oldtimers in small groups. In: P.B. Paulus (Ed.), *Psychology of group influence* (2nd ed., pp. 143–186). Hillsdale, NJ: Lawrence Erlbaum Associates.

Naumann, S. E., & Bennett, N. (2000). A case for procedural justice climate: Development and test of a multi-level model. *Academy of Management Journal, 43,* 881–889.

Rentsch, J. R. (1990). Climate and culture: Interaction and qualitative differences in organizational meanings. *Journal of Applied Psychology, 75,* 668–681.

Rentsch, J. R., Delise, L. A., & Hutchison, S. (in press). Cognitive similarity configurations in teams: In search of the Team MindMeld™. In: E. Salas, G. F. Goodwin & S. Burke (Eds), *Team effectiveness in complex organizations: Cross-disciplinary perspectives and approaches*. Mahway, NJ: Lawrence Erlbaum.

Rentsch, J. R., & Duffy, L. T. (1991). Assessing meanings of teamwork. In: M. Citeria (Chair), *Teamwork: Cognitive representations, accountability, and team decision making*. Symposium conducted at the meeting of the American Psychological Association, San Francisco, CA.

Rentsch, J. R., & Hall, R. J. (1994). Members of great teams think alike: A model of team effectiveness and schema similarity among team members. In: M. M. Beyerlein, D. A. Johnson & S.T. Beyerlein (Eds.), *Advances in interdisciplinary studies of work teams: Theories of self-managing work teams* (Vol. 1, pp. 223–261). Greenwich, CT: JAI Press.

Rentsch, J. R., Heffner, T. S., & Duffy, L. T. (1994). What you know is what you get from experience: Team experience related to teamwork schemas. *Group and Organization Management, 19*(4), 450–474.

Rentsch, J. R., & Klimoski, R. J. (2001). Why do "great minds" think alike? Antecedents of team member schema agreement. *Journal of Organizational Behavior, 22*, 107–120.

Rentsch, J. R., Small, E. E., & Hanges, P. J. (in press). Cognitions in organizations and teams: What is the meaning of cognitive similarity. In: B. Smith & B. Schneider (Eds), *The people make the place*. Mahwah, NJ: Lawrence Erlbaum Associates.

Rentsch, J. R., & Woehr, D. J. (2004). Quantifying congruence in cognition: Social relations modeling and team member schema similarity. In: E. Salas & S. M. Fiore (Eds), *Team cognition: Understanding the factors that drive process and performance* (pp. 11–31). Washington, DC: American Psychological Association.

Rentsch, J. R., Zelno, J. A. (2003). The role of cognition in managing conflict to maximize team effectiveness. In: M. A. West, D. Tjosvold & K. G. Smith (Eds), *International handbook of organizational teamwork and cooperative working* (pp. 131–150). New York: Wiley.

Rumelhart, D. E. (1980). On evaluating story grammars. *Cognitive Science, 4*, 313–316.

Schein, E. (1985). *Organizational culture and leadership: A dynamic view*. San Francisco, CA: Jossey-Bass.

Schneider, B. (1975). Organizational climates: An essay. *Personnel Psychology, 28*, 447–479.

Schneider, B., & Reichers, A. E. (1983). On the etiology of climates. *Personnel Psychology, 36*, 19–39.

Walsh, J. P., Henderson, C. M., & Deighton, J. (1988). Negotiated belief structures and decision performance: An empirical investigation. *Organizational Behavior and Human Decision Processes, 42*, 194–216.

Weick, K. E. (1993). The collapse of sensemaking in organizations: The Mann Gulch disaster. *Administrative Science Quarterly, 38*, 628–652.

Xie, J. L., & Johns, G. (2000). Interactive effects of absence culture salience and group cohesiveness: A multi-level and cross-level analysis of work absenteeism in the Chinese context. *Journal of Occupational and Organizational Psychology, 73*, 31–52.

CONVERGING MENTAL MODELS ABOUT MENTAL MODEL CONVERGENCE

Sara A. McComb

ABSTRACT

The three preceding articles highlight the ongoing research designed to better understand shared mental models and their role in team functioning. In some respects, research scholars have achieved an integrated view (a.k.a. shared mental models) about the field (e.g., the growing body of empirical research results underscores the important role of the shared mental model construct in effective team functioning). In other respects, our mental models have not converged. Thus, we still need additional conceptual and empirical research to advance the field (e.g., many dimensions of mental models have been identified, but no agreement exists about their validity or the completeness of the list). In this response, I use the similar, divergent, and complementary views presented in the trio of articles by myself, Cannon-Bowers (this volume), and Rentsch and Small (this volume) to demonstrate how the process of scholarship is analogous to the mental model convergence process.

Multi-Level Issues in Organizations and Time
Research in Multi-Level Issues, Volume 6, 175–184
Copyright © 2007 by Elsevier Ltd.
All rights of reproduction in any form reserved
ISSN: 1475-9144/doi:10.1016/S1475-9144(07)06008-0

INTRODUCTION

As I read the articles prepared by Cannon-Bowers (this volume) and by Rentsch and Small (this volume), I could not help but think that we, in conjunction with the other scholars studying shared cognition, are analogous to team members attempting to achieve mental model convergence. Through the research process, scholars extend, test, and confirm existing research as they contribute to a growing body of knowledge on a particular subject. The result is a theoretical foundation upon which further research can be grounded. One way to characterize this process is to consider the mental model shift that occurs when the individual scholars' mental models about the field begin to converge as the field coalesces.

The result of this mental model shift will be shared mental models about various aspects of the field. I do not anticipate a situation, however, where all scholars will have a set of identical mental models about any aspect of a given field, particularly in the social sciences. We are all far too attached to our own points of view in many cases. For example, Tuckman's (1965) long-standing socially driven view of group development has been called into question by Gersick's (1988, 1989) pace-driven approach and Kozlowski, Gully, Nason, and Smith's (1999) task-driven, multi-level approach. Yet, the Tuckman approach is still regularly included in organizational behavior textbooks. The authors of these textbooks may be unwilling or may think it is inappropriate to revise their mental models about group development. Even if identical mental models among scholars were not an impracticality, they would be detrimental because, under these conditions, scholars may become complacent and no longer work to better understand social phenomena.

In this response, I demonstrate how my mental model convergence framework can be applied to research scholarship. Examining mental models in the team domain is a relatively new field of research that is gaining momentum. As such, it offers excellent examples of how a field progresses through the three phases of mental model convergence. Therefore, I provide examples of the convergence process in action from my chapter and the articles prepared by Cannon-Bowers (this volume) and by Rentsch and Small (this volume). To begin my examination, I start from the integration phase and move to the differentiation phase and finally to the orientation phase. While this ordering is the opposite of the mental model convergence process, it represents the way in which most scholarship transpires. Indeed, scholars begin with commonly held knowledge (i.e., integrated knowledge), extend it by incorporating research findings and logic to support their new ideas (i.e., differentiate by organizing extant knowledge), and test it by collecting data (i.e., orient by collecting new information). An iterative loop between differentiation and orientation will continue until a point where the scholars in the field agree that enough results have been attained, and confirmed, to constitute commonly held knowledge.

INTEGRATION

The integration phase represents the point where the focal level of interest shifts from the individual to the collective through a reconciliation of diverse perspectives. When considering the mental model convergence process attributable to a set of scholars, the integration phase results in knowledge that is broadly accepted by scholars who study the field. In the case of shared mental models, the majority of scholars will agree that the field is (1) worthy of study and (2) that capturing cognition is very difficult. The field's worth is demonstrated by the growing body of empirical research demonstrating the positive relationship between shared mental models and team performance, the increasing number of scholars focusing on shared mental models, and the array of funded research projects being conducted (e.g., the Office of Naval Research's Collaboration and Knowledge Interoperability program focuses exclusively on team cognition). The difficulty in extracting individuals' cognitive contents and structures has given rise to a number of scholars addressing methodological issues associated with this field of study. As Rentsch and Small (this volume) point out, the most prevalent issue is the inability of the researcher to collect data without interfering in the process at some point, thereby influencing either the information solicited from study subjects or the interpretation of that information. Together this integrated knowledge describes the inherent value in studying shared mental models and underscores the need for research, particularly methodological research, in this area.

Convergent knowledge may also comprise a more detailed summary of the field's progress. Two examples demonstrate this type of convergence in the shared mental model literature. First, the majority of scholars operationalize mental models as cognitive structures that are held by individuals and evolve over time. The result of this evolutionary process in a team domain is similar mental models across team members. This convergent view of mental models provides information about where to look for mental models and their dynamic nature. It does not, however, include information about the content of these mental models, the specific architecture in which the information is stored (i.e., the mental models' structures), or the process by which mental models evolve. Moreover, as Cannon-Bowers (this volume) points out, we do not know if the process is conscious and/or volitional. These elements await future research.

Second, researchers appear to have reached convergence that multiple mental models do exist simultaneously. This notion was introduced in the shared mental model literature by Cannon-Bowers, Salas, and Converse (1993) when they suggested that individuals will hold mental models about the team's task, team interaction, the team, and equipment. Since that time, several scholars have tested the existence of multiple mental models by assessing teamwork and taskwork mental models within the same study (e.g., Mathieu, Heffner, Goodwin, Salas, & Cannon-Bowers, 2000). Advancing this distinction further, Smith-Jentsch, Mathieu, and Kraiger (2005) examined the effects of domain-specific teamwork and taskwork mental models, namely, positional-goal interdependence (teamwork) and cue-strategy associations (taskwork). Finally, my preliminary evidence using the sentence stem completion test and additional evidence using agreement scores on questionnaire items (McComb & Vozdolska, 2007) have demonstrated that multiple teamwork mental models co-exist and impact performance differently. Rentsch and Small (this volume) identified perceptions of the team environment and constructed meanings as additional content that is worthy of investigation. Thus, adequate evidence has surfaced indicating a convergent view of the simultaneous existence of multiple mental models that guide team behavior. Additional research is necessary to identify exactly what contents are necessary under varying circumstances.

These examples establish that a group of scholars can achieve convergence. At the same time, they demonstrate that, with respect to research, converged mental models among scholars often result in more questions than answers. Thus, progressing through the differentiation phase becomes necessary.

DIFFERENTIATION

During the differentiation phase, extant information is cognitively organized and merged with an individual's existing knowledge. The majority of scholarship involves differentiation because much of what we do requires us to (1) identify gaps in the literature, (2) develop hypotheses, and (3) discuss how empirical results augment extant knowledge.

Identifying Gaps and Developing Hypotheses

To identify gaps in the literature and develop hypotheses, we must begin by examining the literature that is currently available in the area of interest and in complementary areas. We then cognitively organize this new information and merge it with what we already know, so that we can apply it to our research. The framework I developed describing the mental model convergence process is an example of this differentiation process. Specifically, I determined that the mental model convergence process was not part of the extant literature on shared mental models. I then organized the shared mental model literature and augmented it with complementary knowledge from other literatures (e.g., information processing and group development) in such a manner that allowed me to put forward a theoretically grounded framework describing the mental model convergence process.

In a scholarly domain, the result of the differentiation phase typically requires a shift back to the orientation phase because a new concept is introduced that requires testing (i.e., gathering of new information). For instance, my mental model convergence framework can now be tested to determine its validity. My chapter and the two articles highlight three additional aspects of the shared mental model research that have been differentiated and require further information gathering: (1) the dimensionality of the mental model construct, (2) the semantics of convergence, and (3) the role of training in the mental model convergence process.

Dimensionality of the Mental Model Construct

The dimensionality of the mental model construct refers to the various ways that mental models can be assessed (versus the multiple mental models that may simultaneously exist that I described in the Integration section). As Rentsch and Small (this volume) so accurately point out, this nascent field has only begun to discover the various dimensions that will help us to describe shared cognition among team members. Thus, dimensionality is a gap in the literature that needs to be addressed. Both my article and the Rentsch and Small (this volume) article present dimensions of mental models. Through this discussion, I highlight the process through which these dimensions may emerge during the differentiation phase.

In my chapter, I discussed four possible dimensions: content, structure, development stage, and degree of integration. These dimensions demonstrate two paths that can lead to differentiated knowledge. First, content and structure have been tested, but the distinction between these two dimensions has not been clearly articulated in much of the extant research. Thus, examining the shared mental model empirical results, as I progressed through the differentiation phase, allowed me to identify this opportunity for further clarity in our research specification that may not have been identifiable before a reasonable number of studies had been completed. Second, the developmental stage and the degree of integration are two dimensions resulting from the construction of my mental model convergence framework. These dimensions have not yet been tested explicitly. Based on our current understanding in the field, however, they represent amalgamated knowledge that extends our thinking about these constructs.

Rentsch and Small (this volume) present a categorization scheme for examining the many dimensions of mental models and the like. Their dimensions are: (1) forms of cognition, (2) forms of similarity, and (3) cognitive content domain. The first dimension can be used to introduce a third path that can lead to differentiated knowledge. Specifically, this dimension arose from successfully testing various cognitive forms including structured or organized knowledge, perceptions of the team environment, and construction of meaning. The results reveal the importance of these forms, thereby validating the inclusion of cognitive forms as a dimension worthy of further consideration. Forms of similarity and cognitive content domain parallel to the differentiation process of the dimensions were presented in my article. For instance, the forms of similarity described by Rentsch and Small (this volume) have not been completely specified, nor have some of them been tested. The extant research results, however, have begun to highlight their existence. This dimension, therefore, presents an opportunity for further clarity in the way we specify forms of similarity. This path toward differentiated knowledge is analogous to the aforementioned need for further clarity in the distinction between mental model content and structure. Finally, the dimension cognitive content domain is similar to the developmental stage and the degree of integration in the sense that it has not received much, if any, empirical attention. Yet, examining the literature through the differentiation process has led Rentsch and Small (this volume) to suggest that it is an important dimension that has the potential to extend our current understanding.

Our approaches are very different in some respects. For instance, Rentsch and Small (this volume) view content and structure as inseparable constructs, whereas I view them as unique dimensions of mental models that need to be understood independently. In other respects, our approaches overlap. For example, degrees of integration may be a critical form of similarity to investigate. For the purposes of this response, the similarities and differences in our two views are not the focal point. Rather, these two views demonstrate (1) how two views can emerge from the same body of literature and (2) that many more iterations between the differentiation and orientation phases are necessary before scholars attain an integrated view of mental model dimensionality.

Semantics of Convergence
The second example of knowledge in need of differentiation is semantics. Semantics is an issue throughout the scholarly literature. Groups of scholars often study similar concepts under different names. The examination of mental models in a team domain is no exception. For instance, Rentsch and Small (this volume) advocate examining mental model similarity, while Cannon-Bowers (this volume) and I describe shared mental models. Additionally, I introduce the concept of converged mental models as a more generic term derived from the process required to achieve shared or similar understandings. We can also extend beyond these three constructs and examine additional terms such as strategic consensus, team member schema similarity, common ground, intersubjectivity, and shared cognition. By differentiating these perspectives and organizing what we know about each term, we can ascertain where overlaps in meaning exist. I leave the differentiation among these terms to future researchers. The point to be made here is that we may never convince sets of scholars to change their semantics. We may be able to better understand their similarities and differences, however, by examining them through the differentiation process. Such an examination will increase the precision with which we apply the findings derived in the related research streams.

The Role of Training in the Mental Model Convergence Process
Cannon-Bowers (this volume) provides a third example of how differentiation activities can lead to data collection opportunities. She identified a gap in the current body of shared mental model research. Specifically, she questioned how practitioners could expedite the mental model convergence process. She addressed this question by overlaying results from training research on my mental model convergence framework to propose training interventions most appropriate for the various stages of convergence. Moreover, she applied both the mental model and training literatures to devise propositions that are testable.

Discussing Empirical Results

As mentioned in the beginning of this section, three activities require scholars to work through the differentiation process to organize the knowledge currently available in a manner that will help them to advance the field. The previous discussion presented several ways in which the differentiation process can be used to identify gaps and develop testable hypotheses, which are the first two activities that I introduced. The third scholarly activity that requires differentiation is discussing how empirical results augment our current understanding of the field. My preliminary results demonstrate that mental models converge over time, mental model content changes over time, multiple mental models function simultaneously, and converged mental models positively impact team performance. Through differentiation, we can see that the first two results are, to my knowledge, new contributions to the field and the second two results confirm the results of other scholars. The onus of explicating how these results enhance our current understanding was on me. In this case, the enhancement comes in the form of preliminary validation of my mental model convergence framework and justification for further research in this area.

ORIENTATION

The orientation phase of the mental model convergence process represents the information collection activities of the team. When applying this concept to scholarly research, orientation represents the data collection efforts of researchers. In my article and the article prepared by Rentsch and Small (this volume), several methods for collecting data about shared mental models and the like are described. I, therefore, will not reiterate them here. Whether data are collected via observation, structured experimentation, questionnaires, archive retrieval, or some other method, the results represent new pieces of information that must be differentiated. For example, in the previous section, I demonstrated how differentiation was used to examine the way in which my preliminary results fit into the extant research on shared mental models. I also demonstrated how data collection needs may arise. Specifically, I discussed how the differentiation process resulted in (1) my mental model convergence framework, (2) the identification of multiple dimensions of the mental model construct, and (3) propositions based on the complementary aspects of the training and mental model literatures. Each of these results prepares us for more data collection.

In sum, when applying my mental model convergence framework to scholarship, orientation (i.e., data gathering) is regularly the consequence of the differentiation phase.

CONCLUSION

Scholars spend most of their research lives in a cycle between differentiation and orientation. Even after certain aspects of the field have evolved to a point of integration, opportunities to advance our understanding based on this integrated knowledge exist. Herein, I demonstrated this mental model convergence process by using examples from the three articles presented in this volume. I have, therefore, only scratched the surface because many other scholars are examining shared mental models and the like. By not including their contributions I do not mean to imply that they are not critical for the advancement of this field. Indeed, these additional perspectives are imperative as we continue to work toward converged mental models about mental model convergence.

ACKNOWLEDGMENT

This research was supported in part by the Innovations in Organizations program of the National Science Foundation, Grant no. 0092805 and the Collaboration and Knowledge Interoperability program of the Office of Naval Research, Grant no. N000140210535. The author would like to thank Ralitza Vozdolska for her help in preparing this manuscript.

REFERENCES

Cannon-Bowers, J. A. (this volume). Fostering mental model convergence through training. In: F. Dansereau & F. J. Yammarino (Eds), *Research in multi-level issues* (Vol. 6). Amsterdam: Elsevier.

Cannon-Bowers, J. A., Salas, E., & Converse, S. A. (1993). Shared mental models in expert team decision making. In: N. J. Castellan, Jr. (Ed.), *Individual and group decision making: Current issues* (pp. 221–246). Hillsdale, NJ: Lawrence Erlbaum Associates, Inc.

Gersick, C. J. G. (1988). Time and transition in work teams: Toward a new model of group development. *Academy of Management Journal, 31*, 9–41.

Gersick, C. J. G. (1989). Marking time: Predictable transitions in task groups. *Academy of Management Journal, 32*, 274–309.

Kozlowski, S. W. J., Gully, S. M., Nason, E. R., & Smith, E. M. (1999). Developing adaptive teams: A theory of compilation and performance across levels and time. In: D. R. Ilgen & E. D. Pulakos (Eds), *The changing nature of performance: Implications for staffing, motivation, and development* (pp. 240–292). San Francisco, CA: Jossey-Bass.

Mathieu, J. E., Heffner, T. S., Goodwin, G. F., Salas, E., & Cannon-Bowers, J. A. (2000). The influence of shared mental models on team process and performance. *Journal of Applied Psychology, 85*, 273–283.

McComb, S. A., & Vozdolska, R. P. (2007). Capturing the convergence of multiple mental models and their impact on team performance. Paper presented at the annual meeting of the Southwestern Academy of Management, San Diego, CA.

Rentsch, J. R., & Small, E. E. (this volume). Understanding team cognition: The shift to cognitive similarity configurations. In: F. Dansereau & F. J. Yammarino (Eds), *Research in multi-level issues* (Vol. 6). Amsterdam: Elsevier.

Smith-Jentsch, K. A., Mathieu, J. E., & Kraiger, K. (2005). Investigating linear and interactive effects of shared mental models on safety and efficiency in a field setting. *Journal of Applied Psychology, 90*, 523–535.

Tuckman, B. W. (1965). Developmental sequence in small groups. *Psychological Bulletin, 63*, 384–399.

PART III:
DIMENSIONS OF TIME

ORGANIZATIONALLY RELEVANT DIMENSIONS OF TIME ACROSS LEVELS OF ANALYSIS

Allen C. Bluedorn and Kimberly S. Jaussi

ABSTRACT

As part of the developing attention being paid to time in organization science, this chapter discusses two temporal dimensions – polychronicity and speed – and develops propositions relating these two temporal dimensions to other organization science variables. The propositions are specified according to levels of analysis, at least three of which are considered in propositions presented for each dimension. Two other temporal dimensions – punctuality and temporal depth – are also described, albeit not as extensively as polychronicity and speed. A fifth temporal phenomenon, entrainment, provides insights into organizational processes as well as the four temporal dimensions. The chapter concludes by outlining some reasons for caution for both theory and practice.

INTRODUCTION

A French manager was employed by a German firm and reported directly to a German boss. Unfortunately, the boss and the subordinate were having

Multi-Level Issues in Organizations and Time
Research in Multi-Level Issues, Volume 6, 187–223
ISSN: 1475-9144/doi:10.1016/S1475-9144(07)06009-2

a difficult time getting along together. Indeed, their working relationship was nearly intolerable until it was explained to them that they had very different approaches to life and work. The boss had grown up in Germany, which has a culture emphasizing a monochronic (deal with one thing at a time) approach to life and work, whereas the manager who reported to him had been reared in more polychronic (deal with several things simultaneously) France. Each misinterpreted these differences in the other and tended to treat them as personal affronts. Once they understood the nature of these differences as manifestations of two different cultures, however, the tone of the relationship changed considerably (Bluedorn, 1998, pp. 112–113).

This vignette illustrates a case in which temporal differences between a leader and a follower had a major effect on their relationship and their ability to work together. In this scenario, the temporal differences involved the temporal dimension of polychronicity: the extent to which people prefer to be engaged in multiple tasks simultaneously. In reality, leaders and followers can differ or be similar on several temporal dimensions, including polychronicity, speed, punctuality, and temporal depth. And just as with the polychronicity differences between the French and German managers, we would expect differences on these other dimensions to affect the relationships between colleagues in ways such as their attitudes and beliefs about each other, the quality of their collaborations, and the duration of their relationship.

In truth, the issue is more complex than whether two colleagues are similar or different on a specific temporal characteristic. As we have noted, there are several temporal characteristics on which individuals can differ, not just one. Beyond this source of complexity is the issue of the context in which individual differences occur. Returning to our example of the German boss and the French subordinate, what difference might it make if the company for which the two worked tended to value and practice relatively polychronic behavior? What if the department in which the two worked tended to value and practice monochronic behavior even though the culture of the organization tended to emphasize more polychronic behaviors? Would these contextual factors influence the frame in which the French and German managers would have seen their differences? Within these contexts, would the nature of their working relationship have mattered? That is, would it make a difference if the two worked independently and made individual contributions to the group effort (pooled interdependence) rather than if what the French subordinate produced was something the German boss then used as an input for further processing (sequential interdependence; see Thompson, 1967)? As these questions illustrate, the effects of temporal differences and similarities among colleagues are likely to be contingent on a variety of factors, including the level of task interdependence and the context in which those relationships occur.

To explore these issues and possibilities, this chapter examines four temporal dimensions – polychronicity, speed, punctuality, and temporal depth – along which individuals and collectivities may differ. In considering these differences, we will assess the context in which they occur by examining how these dimensions are embedded in contexts involving multiple levels of analysis. Moreover, to demonstrate that temporal dimensions are multilevel phenomena, theory and propositions will be presented regarding the differences between them at several levels of analysis. We will then examine the theoretical and applied implications of our theoretical discussions and findings.

DIMENSIONS OF TIME AND LEVELS OF ANALYSIS

Polychronicity

Polychronicity may be the most fundamental yet least recognized of the four temporal dimensions. It was first described by anthropologist Edward Hall (1981, 1983). Bluedorn (2002, p. 48) has described it as "a fundamental strategy for engaging life." As a fundamental strategy, polychronicity involves the consistent choice – either conscious or unconscious – about how to engage tasks and events. It is formally defined as "the extent to which people (1) prefer to be engaged in two or more tasks or events simultaneously and are actually so engaged (the preference strongly implying the behavior, and vice versa), and (2) believe their preference is the best way to do things" (Bluedorn, 2002, p. 51).

Several important points help clarify the concept. First, polychronicity is a continuum of behaviors ranging from the extremely high-end, where people prefer to engage in a multitude of tasks at the same time, to the low-end (sometimes called the monochronic end), where people prefer to engage in only a single task or event at a time and will resist moving on to a second task until the first task is completed.

The second point is the meaning of *simultaneously* or *at the same time*. This can be literally so, such as when one reads the newspaper while eating breakfast. More often, however, polychronicity refers to engaging in several tasks during a given time period. For example, during the morning, instead of dealing with tasks sequentially, an individual may prefer dealing with them in a back-and-forth manner. For example, the person might spend

30 minutes working on task A, then shift to task B for 15 minutes, then shift back to working on task A again, and so forth.

A third point is that the highly polychronic end of the continuum is *not* about getting more done during a given time period. It is simply a preference for how to deal with two or more activities or events – that is, to engage in them at the same time, often meaning moving back-and-forth among them until one or more of the tasks is completed.

Individual Level

As the preceding discussion indicates, individuals vary in their polychronicity, generally in a trait-like manner (Slocombe & Bluedorn, 1999). Cotte and Ratneshwar (1999), however, found that some people had the ability to shift their behaviors along the polychronicity continuum to meet the demands of their circumstances, something Hall described as a "high adaptive factor" (Bluedorn, 1998).

In a work context, the job will limit and often determine the extent to which people conduct themselves in a polychronic manner. A key characteristic of jobs is their skill variety, which concerns the variety of activities and skills that an individual must perform and use when undertaking a task (Hackman & Oldham, 1976, p. 257). Because a task requiring high-skill variety would involve many different activities likely involving qualitatively different skills, a behavior pattern characterized by a relatively high level of polychronicity would seem better suited to this type of task. A high level of polychronicity would seem better suited because several skills would be employed as well as many activities performed while working on a single task. Thus, we offer this proposition:

> **Proposition 1.** The more polychronic a person, the better the person's performance will be on tasks characterized by high skill variety.

Continuing this line of thought, because tasks involving high levels of skill variety are more compatible with a polychronic pattern of engagement, more polychronic individuals are likely to be more comfortable in performing them because they are likely to be more successful in doing so (Proposition 1) and the task requirements require a method of engagement consistent with their preferred pattern of highly polychronic behavior. Hence, we offer this proposition:

> **Proposition 2.** An individual's level of polychronicity will be positively correlated with job satisfaction when tasks are characterized by high levels of skill variety.

A similar proposition was actually supported by a recent study in which individual preferences for performing work polychronically were compared to the opportunities they had to actually do work in a way consistent with their preferences for polychronicity (Hecht & Allen, 2005). Given this finding, we present the following proposition:

Proposition 3. The greater the extent to which individuals have the opportunity to perform work in a manner consistent with their preferences for how polychronically they prefer to work, the greater their job satisfaction will be.

Hecht and Allen (2005) found two other important variables related to the similarity of preferences for polychronic work and the opportunity to do work in a manner consistent with the individual's preferences. That is, when individuals have an opportunity to perform work in a manner consistent with their preferences for how polychronically they prefer to work, they had greater self-efficacy and lower levels of psychological strain. Bluedorn (2002, p. 282) examined the relationships among three of these variables – polychronicity, stress (similar to psychological strain), and job satisfaction – and found that stress mediated the relationship between polychronicity and job satisfaction in the sample of dentists he examined.

Polychronicity is positively correlated with tolerance for ambiguity (Bluedorn, 2000a; Haase, Lee, & Banks, 1979). Many tasks are sufficiently unstructured that the means to accomplish them is open to multiple interpretations and strategies; hence how to proceed will be ambiguous. Given polychronicity's relationship with tolerance for ambiguity, we put forth this proposition:

Proposition 4. The greater an individual's polychronicity, the more job satisfaction the person will experience when performing unstructured tasks.

Polychronicity has also been positively correlated with creative personality traits (Bluedorn, 2000a) and creative behavior itself (Hecht, 2003). However, the relationship between polychronicity and creativity may be moderated by the nature of the task. Madjar and Oldham (in press) found that when individuals had to deal with tasks sequentially, polychronicity was negatively related to creativity; in contrast, when individuals had to deal with overlapping tasks, polychronicity was positively correlated with creativity. Given this finding, it is likely that autonomy provided by the job will moderate the relationship between polychronicity and creativity because high levels of autonomy ("the degree to which the job provides substantial freedom, independence, and discretion to the individual in scheduling the work and in determining the procedures to be used in carrying it out", Hackman & Oldham, 1976, p. 258), will make it more possible for individuals to perform their work with the level of polychronicity they prefer. Thus, each worker will be able to more closely align his or her performance of a set of tasks in a way that is most associated with the individual's work patterns and results in creativity.

Proposition 5. The level of autonomy on the job will moderate the relationship between polychronicity and creativity such that when autonomy is high, polychronicity will be positively correlated with creativity, but when autonomy is low, polychronicity will either be less strongly correlated with creativity or not correlated with it at all.

Workgroup Level
Groups develop values and norms, which then guide the groups' resultant work processes. For this reason, we will examine one factor that might lead workgroups to greater levels of polychronicity – namely, the number of organizational units represented in the workgroup.

Cross-functional teams are usually created for a combination of instrumental and political reasons. The instrumental reason is straightforward: to bring the necessary expertise to the group so that it can perform its tasks. The political reason is also straightforward: to avoid the appearance of favoring some units over others through the differential representation of units in the group. The instrumental reasons, in particular, lead us to suggest that cross-functional workgroups are likely to engage in more projects and take on more responsibilities simultaneously than other workgroups. Such groups can create a division of labor in which subgroups or individuals can work on different tasks simultaneously. This outcome is particularly likely to happen in cross-functional teams because the skills and expertise brought by individuals from differing functional backgrounds probably would not be equally useful for the same portion of a project or a task. Thus, to the extent that the parts of a project can be addressed independently, cross-functional teams will tend to engage in multiple parts of a single project simultaneously and may even engage in multiple projects simultaneously. We state this expectation in the form of the following propositions:

Proposition 6. Cross-functional workgroups will display more group-level polychronicity (i.e., the group will engage in more projects and tasks simultaneously) than single-function groups.

Proposition 7. Cross-functional workgroups will be more likely than single-function groups to develop norms and values indicating that the *group* should take on multiple projects and tasks simultaneously.

Organizational Level
Organizational culture and structure are two different, yet closely related phenomena. Because polychronicity is a dimension of culture, we should anticipate it being related to attributes of an organization's structure. To see how, we will use the standard theoretical understanding of organizational growth: As organizations develop, they typically become more bureaucratic and formalized (Donaldson, 2001, pp. 61–68). In the early days of an organization, it is small; this small size is accompanied by less differentiation (Blau, 1970; Donaldson, 2001). Less differentiation means that the organization's members must perform multiple jobs and assignments rather than focusing on just a single job or assignment. The organization's small size also means that its members will tend to interact more and deal with one another in a face-to-face manner, lessening the need for formalization. Thus, it is not surprising that Schein (1992, p. 108) has described a relationship between organizational size and polychronicity ("polychronic time is therefore more suitable ... for smaller systems") – a relationship that we will summarize in the form of a proposition:

Proposition 8. The larger the organization, the less polychronic its culture will be.

Because greater organizational size is related to the tendency for an organization to develop a more organic structure, we suspect that the degree to which an organization's structure is organic will be related to how polychronic its culture is as well. Thus, we propose:

Proposition 9. The more organic an organization's structure, the more polychronic its culture will be.

Speed

Speed refers to the "frequency (number) of activities in some unit of social time" (Bluedorn, 2002, p. 104). The desire for speed lends itself naturally to a level-of-analysis discussion because it is driven by different mechanisms at different levels. At the individual level, it is associated with several personality traits. At the group level, it is driven by group dynamics and the task environment. At the organizational level, it is driven by structures associated with a focus on efficiency and/or mass production, and by social psychological mechanisms.

Individual Level

At the individual level, speed has been associated with the personality trait of impulsivity (Ortet, Ibanez, Llerena, & Torrubia, 2002), Type A personality (Baron, 1989; Friedman & Rosenman, 1974), time urgency (Conte, Mathieu, & Landy, 1998), and sensation seeking and risk taking (Zuckerman, 1979; Westaby & Lowe, 2005). As such, at the individual level, it is a temporal dimension rooted in one's genetic makeup and developmental history.

Results are mixed about whether these personality-trait driven preferences for speed affect performance. For example, the link between speed and effectiveness has been supported by research examining top executives and their strategic decision-making times (e.g., Eisenhardt, 1989). However, because of its relationship to impulsiveness, an individual's preference for speed may lead to lower effectiveness in a variety of areas. For example, when faced with a complex task or decision, an individual's preference for speed might lead to lower effectiveness because adequate time will not be devoted to searching seemingly unrelated domains for additional perspectives. In fact, research suggests that speed in problem solving can prohibit creativity and performance on complex tasks (Knorr & Neubaur, 1996). Thus, while problem-solving speed is associated with high levels of performance on routine tasks, speed is not as desirable with complex tasks that require a search for alternative perspectives.

The potential pitfalls of individual preferences for speed may be mitigated by specific decision-making techniques. Jaussi, Randel, and Dionne (in press) provide empirical support for the role of a particular problem-solving skill in facilitating creative thought. They found when individuals purposefully applied lessons learned in nonwork situations to solve work-related problems, they were able to be more creative at work. Their findings suggest further support for Root-Bernstein, Bernstein, and Garnier's (1995) findings on the creative process of elite scientists. Using interview transcripts and notes, Root-Bernstein et al. found that scientists were far more successful when they saw their hobbies as something to help generate creative insights for their scientific work than when they viewed their hobbies differently.

We argue that speed in and of itself does not have to lead to poor-quality problem solving. Rather, if the speed is accompanied by an effective problem-solving strategy such as the cross-application from nonwork to work described above, its effects will be less negative.

Proposition 10. The relationship between an individual's preference for speed and performance on a complex task will be moderated by his or her ability to cross-apply situations for problem solving. Specifically, the relationship will be less negative when the individual has a strong ability to cross-apply situations for problem solving than when he or she has a low level of ability to cross-apply situations for problem solving.

Group Level

Ancona, Okhuysen, and Perlow (2001) urge scholars and practitioners to consider "zones" within organizations and the corresponding temporal perspectives that can differ by "zone." They describe the task environment as well as the norms that develop within each zone as producing a shared view of time. Speed preferences are one dimension that can differ by zone. Similarly, a workgroup can be a zone and develop shared perceptions of a preferable speed at which to work.

Increasingly, research suggests that groups can share temporal perspectives (Ancona et al., 2001). Through a process of social influence and negotiation, groups develop a shared temporal schema unique to each group (Labianca, Moon, & Watt, 2005). That unique schema will then influence a team's preference for speed as well as the use of temporal pacers, thereby differentiating it from other teams. The shared temporal schema and team-negotiated preference for speed will decrease the group's process loss associated with conflict and coordination costs. By negotiating a shared schema, groups can avoid the pitfalls – for example, poor performance – associated with a lack of group orientation toward speed and temporal norms (Montoya-Weiss, Massey, & Song, 2001).

A group's preference for speed can change depending on the presence of a pacer such as a deadline (Gersick, 1989). For example, a group's speed generally increases as task deadlines approach (Lim & Murnighan, 1994). Likewise, other factors may alter a group's preference for speed. For example, a large body of research suggests that groups are influenced by levels of perceived deep-level diversity, or diversity based on differing values and attitudes (Harrison, Price, Gavin, & Florey, 2002). Harrison et al. (2002) found that perceived deep-level diversity was negatively related to social integration. Decreased social integration will decrease the likelihood of shared mental models developing. Given that a group preference for speed requires a shared mental model among group members, we would expect the degree of perceived deep-level diversity to be negatively related to the likelihood of the presence of a group-level preference for speed.

Chatman and Flynn (2001) note that group collaborative norms can develop over time even among demographically diverse groups as a result of increased contact. Once norms regarding collaboration are in place, a group with high levels of perceived deep-level diversity will, as part of members' efforts to collaborate, adopt a slower pace in an attempt to allocate enough time to benefit from the vast differences in the group. When groups who recognize their deep-level diversity have collaborative norms, a shared cognition will exist about how those differences affect the way in which collaboration can occur most effectively. That shared cognition will drive a shared perspective that speed should be slower so as to include all group members' perspectives in the collaborative processes.

Proposition 11. The relationship between a group's perceived deep-level diversity and preference for speed will be moderated by the group's cooperative norms. Specifically, a more negative relationship will be present when group cooperative norms are strong than when group cooperative norms are low.

Organizational, Strategic Group, and Industry Level
The organizational level is perhaps the level of analysis at which speed has been most widely studied by organizational scholars. Because organizations are nested within industries, the competitive environment is often deemed responsible for the speed orientation of the organization. Ancona et al. (2001) note that organizational speed norms will develop as a result of the culture, the task/product environment, and the competitive environment associated with the industry. As such, organizational speed may actually be a phenomenon at the level of the strategic group or even at the level of the industry, nested within a national culture (as are all temporal variables).

Bluedorn (2002) outlines two organizationally relevant orientations regarding speed: (1) a scientific management orientation, whereby efficiency results in speed, which then leads to effectiveness and (2) a time-based competitive orientation, where speed leads to efficiency, which then leads to effectiveness. Yet, it may be that industry or strategic-group norms drive firm preferences for speed. Institutional theory suggests that firms should behave in accordance with their size group norms in efforts to perform optimally (DiMaggio & Powell, 1983). Chen and Hambrick (1995) support this perspective; they found that small and large airlines that followed the speed norms of their size group performed better than those that deviated from the group norms. Organizations in industries or strategic groups focusing on mass production (Orlikowsk & Yates, 2002) will also have a focus on speed.

Perlow, Okhuysen, and Repenning (2002) describe how organizations become "speedier," potentially to the point of being *too* speedy. Their work suggests that depending on the competitive environment, organizations may make fast decisions in an effort to grow through realizing a "first mover" advantage. By doing so, they may force the environment to become even more dynamic, which then increases the pressure on them to make even faster decisions. Eventually, those faster decisions become "too fast," and mistakes are made through inaccurate analyses. As a result of this process, organizations may fall victim to the "speed trap."

The size of organizations can also influence the differences between strategic groups. Chen and Hambrick's (1995) research on the airline industry suggests that smaller organizations as a group are prone to taking action in marketplaces more quickly than larger firms do, but are slower than larger firms in responding to competitive attacks.

Thus, while the competitive environment can influence the speed requirements and preferences of the organizations operating within similar strategic groups (thereby suggesting a higher level of analysis than the organization), Perlow et al. (2002) point to within-organization variables that can create differences between organizations in a given industry or strategic group. Included in these variables are the degree of decision content search, the presence or absence of temporal pacers such as budget deadlines and reporting requirements, and the management of the organization's customer expectations (Perlow et al., 2002).

We argue that two approaches can be used to think of organizational-level speed. The first approach involves a structural perspective. Organizations will have a unique speed at which internal processes such as production and decision making occur that will both directly reflect and be strongly influenced by their structures. This first type of organizational speed will be evident in the execution of standardized processes, such as production. The second perspective involves a social/psychological perspective. Using this lens, organizational speed may be considered with respect to the shared schemata of all organizational members regarding preferable levels of speed. This second approach will be generated from attraction–similarity–attrition processes (ASA) (Schneider, 1987) and the organization's leadership. As such, it will be evident in the consistent preferences of organizational members for speed.

Structural Mechanisms. One organization differs from another organization because of its size and structure, and both factors will be related to the organization's preference for speed. As noted earlier, increased size brings increased bureaucracy, which creates structural complexity and inflexibility at the organizational level. Speed will be built into the structure through evolving formalization, routinization, and standardization. Because individuals have formalized procedures to follow, they will complete their work more quickly. In these situations, the routinized and standardized procedures will substitute for individual-level personality preferences for speed, and will create a consistent speed of execution within the organization. However, this speed will be a product of the structure. Because it does not involve an internal commitment from individuals to creating that speed, it will not be internalized by organizational members. Consequently, a shared cognitive schema for speed will not exist at the organizational level. In addition, organizations with an efficiency or cost-cutting strategy will have a focus on speed (Orlikowsk & Yates, 2002), as those strategies require speed in execution.

Another structural variable that can influence organizational speed is the organizational reward system. Peterson and Luthans (2006) found that organizational speed was related to the incentive systems used within the organization. When either financial or nonfinancial rewards were implemented at the unit level (whereby unit performance was measured and the reward was delivered equally to all members of the unit), execution speed (drive-through times) was increased. Peterson and Luthans' study raises another question, however: What is the role of intrinsic motivation generated by shared responsibility for the assignment of a reward at the organizational level? Their findings, particularly those regarding the effectiveness of the unit-level nonfinancial rewards, suggests that in addition to the structural influences of organizational speed, social psychological mechanisms are at work.

Social-Psychological Mechanisms. While the structural variables will induce a speed orientation for execution of processes associated with routinization and standardization, the presence of shared mental models within the organization existing in agreement throughout the organization will result in an organizational-level preference for speed or attitude about speed. This type of organizational speed will result from social psychological mechanisms and processes stemming from processes that underlie the organizational culture, as well as from its leadership. ASA processes suggest that individuals will self-select their entry into different organizations depending on their own values and interests. Through ASA processes, individuals with a preference for speed will seek out employment in organizations with a similar speed preference. Those individuals who match the speed preferences of the organization will be selected; once selected, they will remain with the organization only if the two entities' speed preferences continue to be similar. Through this process, an organization can maintain a very unified perspective on speed that is shared by the members of the organization and yet differs from the perspective adopted by other organizations.

Research on contagion (Totterdell, 2000) and social information processing (Zalesny & Ford, 1990) argues that attitudes can be "caught" by others
in the organization. Therefore, by virtue of being present with the same
individuals in the same organization, a shared perspective on speed can
result. Similar to Hall's (1981) suggestion that individuals from a given
culture possess a shared perspective unique to individuals from that culture,
individuals from an organization with a particular focus on speed will adopt
a shared perspective on speed that will reflect the organization's preference.

Organizations that pursue a first-mover strategy will also have a focus on
speed, as they try to modify their competitive environment to their advantage (Perlow et al., 2002). In this case, the strategy will create a culture for
speed, which will result in an organization-level shared schema for speed.

An organization's preference for speed can also be strongly influenced by
its leader, thereby making it unique to that organization. Organizational
leaders set the tone for the expected pace of the organization (Lee, Lee, Lee,
& Choi, 2005). Research suggests that the top-level leader's or top management team's perceptions of time are often considered representative of
the organization's perceptions (Ancona et al., 2001). Because leaders
strongly influence their organizations, organizational-level effects are
assumed to be present, as is agreement within the organization. Generally,
these types of assumptions do not address the types of leaders who are more
likely to create this organizational-level agreement; such agreement will
result differentially depending on the processes underlying the way in which
leaders influence followers within their organizations.

Because of their ability to motivate members of entire organizations
toward movement, the presence of charismatic leaders lends itself well to
a discussion of organizational effects of leadership. The ability of these
leaders to mobilize organizational members as a whole to take action occurs
through a variety of mechanisms. Because of their propensity for speed and
taking action, charismatic leaders are differentiated from other leaders and
are noted for their effectiveness in organizational change efforts. Followers
relate to charismatic leaders through identification processes (Kets de Vries,
1988) and through the social learning mechanisms associated with their role
model of risk-taking behavior (Conger & Kanungo, 1998). By their unique
and effective use of symbols and articulation of a vision, these leaders can
successfully create a mental model that organizational members can easily
adopt and from which they can easily operate. Because of these processes,
individuals in organizations are moved to take actions they would otherwise
not take. While other types of leaders may be able to make swift decisions
on behalf of their organizations (Eisenhardt, 1989), the processes underlying

a charismatic leader's influence suggest that such a leader may be influential in creating a shared mental model of speed within the organization.

Proposition 12. The degree to which a shared schema for speed exists at the organizational level will be positively related to level of charismatic leadership present in the top management team.

The Combination of Speed and Polychronicity

If you speak to a group about polychronicity, regardless of whether it is a formal class or a general audience, invariably at least one person will ask the same question: Is polychronicity the same thing as multitasking? For many years, one of the authors has been answering this question with a firm "no" and then explaining that polychronicity is simply a preference for the way one engages in tasks – it has nothing to do with how fast one performs the tasks. Polychronicity does not suggest a desire to get more done in a day. More recently, we have reconsidered this question and now believe the answer should be changed to a response incorporating both polychronicity and speed.

The new answer involves thinking about polychronicity and multitasking, and realizing that both phenomena refer to the behavior of dealing with multiple tasks simultaneously. This characteristic is what prompts most people to ask if they are synonymous. If one considers the original answer, that the two concepts are not synonymous, the rationale underlying this answer can be stated as follows: The types of behaviors labeled *multitasking* are characterized by a sense of haste and are driven by a desire to get more done in less time, whereas polychronicity by itself (actually the higher parts of the polychronicity continuum) is simply a preference for dealing with multiple tasks simultaneously. Multitasking involves the behavior of engaging in several tasks simultaneously, not necessarily because one prefers to do so, but because one wants to get more done in the same amount of time. Thus, the speed at which work is completed seems to be combined with – perhaps even drives – the number of tasks a person handles in a given time period.

Both speed and polychronicity are continua – the first ranging from slow to fast, and the second ranging from a preference for engaging in a single task at a time to a preference for engaging in many tasks at the same time. Thus two variables, conceptually orthogonal, are involved in this issue. A way to work with them is to dichotomize and combine them, as shown in Fig. 1.

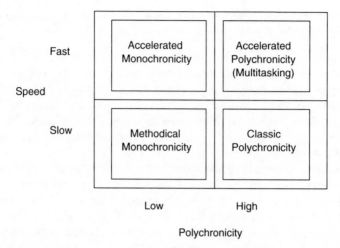

Fig. 1. Four Task Engagement Strategies.

We have cross-classified the two continua, not in an attempt to reduce the two variables to binary form for methodological reasons, but rather for heuristic purposes. Psychometric measures exist for both variables (Bluedorn, Kalliath, Strube, & Martin, 1999; Schriber & Gutek, 1987), and there are sound analytical reasons for not converting continua to dichotomies. We chose this approach because the four categories in Fig. 1 emphasize the extremes of both variables and, thereby, make them easier to understand – even if several levels of analysis will eventually be involved.

By dichotomizing the two variables, two forms of polychronic behavior become apparent: classic and accelerated. Classic polychronicity is likely the original form and is associated with a relatively slow pace of life or work. It can be observed in the relatively polychronic cultures of the world, such as many in Latin America (Hall, 1983), which are also characterized by a slower pace of life (Levine, 1997). Conversely, accelerated polychronicity is the polychronic pattern of task engagement associated with a faster pace of work or life, which we argue is what most people have in mind when they think of multitasking. Thus, the typical illustration of a multitasker is of an individual who is juggling many tasks simultaneously and who bears a stressed look, often with sweat falling from the face. As good a description of the multitasker as any yet crafted was written by Ray Bradbury:

> And what was that man who spun plates, globes, stars, torches, his elbows twirling hoops, his nose balancing a blue feather, sweating everything at once! What, I ask

myself, but the commuter husband, lover, worker, the quick lunchers, juggling hour, Benzedrine, Nembutal, bank balances, and budgets? (Bradbury, 1996, p. 126)

So, the proper answer to the question posed earlier is that there are two forms of polychronicity, classic and accelerated, and only one of them is the same thing as multitasking. As Fig. 1 also indicates, two forms of monochronicity (low polychronicity) exist: methodical and accelerated. The methodical form is the one-thing-at-a-time approach performed at a slow, measured pace, whereas the accelerated form involves a laser-beam-like focus on a single task performed at a fast pace.

Given these conceptual distinctions, we can ask whether some combinations are more likely than others. For example, is an orientation toward doing things fast more likely to be associated with a preference for being engaged with several tasks simultaneously, or is an orientation toward high speed just as likely to be associated with a focus on handling just one or only a few tasks at a time? Fig. 1 does not address this question, nor does it indicate whether the answer will vary across different levels of analysis. Fortunately, empirical data provide some preliminary answers that will help us develop propositions.

Individual Level
In a sample of 191 Missouri-based entrepreneurs, Bluedorn and Richtermeyer (2005) found a statistically significant positive correlation ($r = 0.33, p \leq 0.001$) between the entrepreneurs' levels of polychronicity and their preferences for working fast. This finding allows us to propose the following relationship:

Proposition 13. The higher an individual's polychronicity, the greater the individual's preference for speed.

Organizational Level
Onken (1999) studied polychronicity and speed in 20 companies from the telecommunications and publishing industries. Through a within-and-between analysis (WABA), she was able to demonstrate that both speed and polychronicity orientations were attributes of the companies' cultures. She found a substantial ($r = 0.44$) and statistically significant ($p < 0.05$) positive correlation between speed and polychronicity orientations in these 20 companies' cultures. This finding leads us to the following proposition:

Proposition 14. The more polychronic an organization's culture, the more doing things fast will be emphasized in the organization's culture.

OTHER TEMPORAL DIMENSIONS

Although our discussion so far has emphasized the temporal dimensions of polychronicity and speed, and we have explored them in combination as well, we do not wish to suggest these two parameters are the only important temporal dimensions for organizational research nor suggest they are the only ones that can be investigated at multiple levels of analysis. Consequently, we will briefly consider two other temporal dimensions – punctuality and temporal depth – while being mindful that many other temporal dimensions (e.g., Schriber & Gutek, 1987) are also potentially relevant to organizational analysis.

Punctuality

Punctuality is about being on time, but the very notion of what punctuality – or being "on time" – means, is relative to a variety of individual and contextual factors; these factors may vary from person to person, from culture to culture (Bluedorn, 2002), and even by event within cultures (Levine, West, & Reis, 1980). While being "on time" is thought by many to be an "objective" construct that may be concretely determined by a clock and a corresponding assigned starting time, it also has a strong element of social construction. From country to country, being "on time" can vary from being early to consistently being five or ten minutes late. These differences can stem from the fact that the degree to which time is kept accurately and consistently within countries technologically can vary. For example, in their sampling of bank clocks across different countries, Levine and colleagues found that more accurate clocks tended to be in colder climates and more individualistic cultures (Levine & Norenzayan, 1999).

Individual Level
Punctuality is often related to speed, for it involves getting to the starting point on time at any cost. At the individual, organizational, and country levels, there is support for a relationship between these two variables. Bluedorn and Richtermeyer (2005) found a statistically significant positive correlation between preferences for punctuality and speed in their sample of entrepreneurs. Hence, at the individual level, we propose the following:

Proposition 15. The more an individual emphasizes punctuality, the more the individual will emphasize speed.

As for punctuality and polychronicity, Conte and Jacobs (2003) found statistically significant positive correlations between the polychronicity levels of 181 train operators and both their levels of absenteeism and lateness: The more polychronic the train operator, the more likely the operator was to be absent and late. These relationships persisted in multiple regression analyses after several control variables were added to the analysis. Because lateness is a direct behavioral indicator of punctuality, and absence behavior can be interpreted as a larger version of the same, we propose the following:

Proposition 16. The more polychronic an individual, the more likely the individual is to be late for work and absent from work.

Punctuality usually involves a deadline. After all, to be on time, there must be something to be on time for. Deadlines directly involve the requirement of being on time and can serve as a zeitgeber, a signal to act. As Bluedorn (2002, p. 102) notes, "A true deadline is really a very precise appointment, and when appointments become deadlines, those appointments have a strong structuring effect on human behavior." As an anchor for the task at hand, deadlines create the endpoint from which to work backward and assess progress toward an objective. Gersick (1988, 1989) outlines how task groups in organizations readjust their processes and schedules, thereby increasing productivity, midway between the beginning of the project and the deadline.

Also using the logic of a clear and final endpoint that underlies deadlines and explains why they are motivating, goal-setting theory (e.g., Locke, Shaw, Saari, & Latham, 1981) describes the need for a goal to serve as a clear and specific deadline and target. With both deadlines and goals, the mechanism of having something specific against which your progress can be monitored serves as an internal stimulus; both allow self-generated feedback about one's progress on the task, which has been shown to create intrinsic motivation in individuals (Hackman & Oldham, 1976).

At the individual level of analysis, preferences for punctuality may well be linked to preferences for schedules and deadlines (Bluedorn, 2002). In that they can serve as a structure-inducing, ambiguity-reducing strategy (Lewis & Weigart, 1985), preferences for schedules and deadlines might also be associated with tolerance for ambiguity, a personality dimension. Thus, we add two more propositions:

Proposition 17. The greater an individual's preference for punctuality, the greater the individual's emphasis on schedules and deadlines.

Proposition 18. The greater an individual's preference for punctuality, the lower the individual's tolerance for ambiguity.

Organizational Level

Punctuality also exists at the organizational level, as organizations can have clear norms and standards for starting times and deadlines. As with individuals, we expect this organizational orientation toward punctuality to be coupled with an emphasis on speed. A study of publicly traded U.S. companies reported a statistically significant positive correlation between the extent to which a company's culture emphasized both speed and punctuality (Bluedorn, 2002, p. 285). Hence, at an organizational level, we expect the following proposition to hold:

> **Proposition 19.** There will be a positive correlation between the percentage of organizational events starting and finishing in a punctual fashion and the organization's focus on speed.

National (Country) Level

At the country level, Levine and Norenzayan (1999) created a pace (speed)-of-life index for a country by combining two objective measures of task speed (walking speed and the amount of time it takes postal workers to process a request for stamps) with the accuracy of bank clocks in the country. Bank-clock accuracy is not a direct measure of speed and would seem to be just as plausibly regarded as an indicator of punctuality. To wit: The more important it is to be on time, the more important it is that clocks be accurate. Consistent with this interpretation, walking speed and postal clerk speed were more highly correlated with each other than either was with the accuracy of bank clocks. Nevertheless, both walking speed and postal clerk speed were significantly positively correlated with bank clock accuracy (Levine & Norenzayan, 1999, p. 189). This leads us to propose the following:

> **Proposition 20.** The more a country's culture emphasizes speed, the more the country's culture will emphasize punctuality.

Temporal Depth

Temporal depth was originally defined as the temporal distances into the past and future that an individual typically considers when contemplating events that have happened, may have happened, or may happen (Bluedorn, 2000b, p. 124). It was later extended to the cultural level (Bluedorn, 2002, p. 114; Bluedorn & Ferris, 2004). Temporal depth is distinguished from temporal focus, as the latter deals with general orientations to the past or future rather than the distances into the past or present that individuals typically consider (Bluedorn, 2000b). Temporal depth includes the combined distances into both the past and the future (total temporal depth); however, it is also permissible to speak of "future temporal depth" or "past temporal depth," if one of these temporal realms is the principal topic of interest. As with other temporal variables, past and future temporal depths have been found to be significantly correlated at both the individual and organizational levels of analysis.

Individual Level
Bluedorn (2002, pp. 265–272) reported results from four large samples of University of Missouri students, all of which revealed statistically significant positive correlations between individuals' past and future temporal depths. El Sawy (1983) found the same relationship in data from the sample of Silicon Valley executives he studied. Likewise, Bluedorn and Richtermeyer (2005) found a statistically significant positive correlation between past and future temporal depths in a sample of Missouri-based entrepreneurs. Such consistency across six samples indicates the farther into the past a person typically thinks about things, the farther into the future he or she typically thinks about things as well. The past depth seems to be the cause of this relationship between the two components of temporal depth. Indeed, El Sawy's (1983) experimental research with the executives revealed that varying the length of past depths led to increases in the executives' future depths, but not the reverse. The results from all six samples indicate that the longer an individual's past temporal depth, the longer his or her future temporal depth will be.

Also at the individual level, Bluedorn and Richtermeyer (2005) found a statistically significant negative correlation between the length of individual entrepreneurs' future temporal depths and the amounts of life stress they were experiencing. This relationship persisted after hierarchical regression analysis introduced statistical control variables.

Organizational Level
The same correlation between past and future temporal depths found at the individual level has been found at the organizational level. Bluedorn and Ferris (2004) reported a statistically significant positive correlation between past and future temporal depths in the cultures of the organizations they studied – a positive relationship that persisted in hierarchical regression analysis after several other variables were taken into account.

Also at the organizational level, Bluedorn and Ferris (2004) discovered statistically significant positive correlations between total temporal depth (the length of the combined distances into the past and future) emphasized in the cultures of the organizations they studied and four measures of organizational financial performance: return on assets (ROA), return on equity (ROE), return on sales (ROS), and earnings per share (EPS). However, after examining these four relationships in hierarchical regression analysis, only one of the positive relationships – that between total temporal depth and EPS – remained statistically significant.

In addition to higher financial performance, we would expect an organization's total temporal depth to be related to the way in which the organization values its employees. With a long temporal depth, an organization will recognize the substantial costs of replacing and retraining employees. It will therefore focus on employee retention policies and practices. Thus, we propose the following:

Proposition 21. The longer the total temporal depth emphasized in an organization's culture, the lower the organization's turnover rate.

The relationship between temporal depth and an organization's financial performance may actually prove to be more complex. For example, Judge and Spitzfaden (1995) found that executives work with a portfolio of time horizons (future temporal depths – Judge and Spitzfaden's analysis focused solely on future horizons) rather than with a single unchanging horizon. Furthermore, Judge and Spitzfaden found variance in the future temporal depths of the executives they studied to be positively related to organizational performance: The greater the variances in future temporal depths, the better the organizations' financial performance. Consequently, we suggest the following relationship holds:

Proposition 22. The greater the variance in the future temporal depths of an organization's executives, the better the organization's financial performance.

Taking Judge and Spitzfaden's findings in combination with Bluedorn and Ferris's work, we also make this proposition:

Proposition 23. The greater the variance in the total temporal depths of an organization's executives, the better the organization's financial performance.

We should note that the references to an organization's executives in these two propositions might technically be references to the top management team. Given that the temporal depths of top executives will certainly be reflected in the temporal depths of the plans and strategies they develop for their organizations (see Das, 1986, 1987), however, such plans and strategies are clearly organization-level properties. As such, these propositions are organization-level propositions.

Propositions 22 and 23, though important in their own right, suggest yet more questions: Which depths would be more dominant – those about the past or those about the future? Or would they be equally important? As most contemporary readers would tend to respond, those answers would likely depend on a host of factors, including the national and organizational cultures in which the organizations are embedded. Another contextual factor likely to play a role is environmental dynamism, the extent to which the organization's environment changes unpredictably (Dess & Beard, 1984, p. 56); Bluedorn and Ferris (2004) found this factor to be negatively related to an organization's total temporal depth. Thus, organizational temporal depth is nested within larger levels of analysis.

One other relationship is especially noteworthy because it differs by level of analysis. As a consequence, it not only informs our understanding of temporal depth, but also demonstrates the importance of distinguishing levels of analysis and not simply assuming that relationships are isomorphic across levels. This relationship is between age and temporal depth, which differs across the organizational and individual levels of analysis. At the organizational level, Bluedorn and Ferris (2004, p. 127) found a statistically significant positive correlation between total temporal depth and organizational age ($r = 0.46$, $p \leq 0.001$) that persisted, largely unaffected, in hierarchical regression analysis; it was also basically the same finding for each component – past and future – of total temporal depth. As an explanation for this relationship, these authors suggest that the existence of a socially constructed event such as a collectivity's agreement about when an organization was started will establish a temporal benchmark when thinking about the past concerning organizational matters. They combined this thinking with El Sawy's (1983) finding about the causal impact of past temporal depth on future temporal depth to complete the explanation of why age is positively correlated with total temporal depth and its two components (Bluedorn & Ferris, 2004, pp. 119–120).

However, there is at best a partial analogue of this proposition at the individual level. Although humans seem to increase both their past and future temporal depths (and hence their total temporal depths) from birth through their late teens, this trend does not continue in a simple linear fashion after that point in life (Fraisse, 1963, pp. 177–182; see also

Doob, 1971, pp. 267–268). This appraisal is reinforced by Bluedorn and Richtermeyer's (2005) results, which revealed no statistically significant correlations between the ages of entrepreneurs and the lengths of either their past or future temporal depths. Consequently, we recognize the difference in the relationship between age and temporal depth at the organizational level of analysis and the individual level, and believe it reveals how important it is to avoid assuming relationships are isomorphic across analytical levels without having an empirical basis for drawing that conclusion.

A Meta-Dimension: Entrainment

To this point we have discussed four temporal dimensions – polychronicity, speed, punctuality, and temporal depth – across multiple levels of analysis. In doing so, we have demonstrated the relevance of these dimensions and their importance for organizational scientists to consider and include in their work. This discussion should encourage organizational scientists to investigate other temporal dimensions as well. We believe one such dimension is not only important in its own right, but may also help us understand other temporal dimensions, including the four we have presented so far in this chapter. This dimension is entrainment. In this section, we first define entrainment and specify the various types of entrainment. We then briefly discuss the levels-of-analysis implications inherently associated with entrainment. Finally, we present level-specific propositions regarding entrainment and the temporal dimensions described earlier in this chapter.

Entrainment is about rhythms and their relationships with one another. Although the concept of a rhythm may not come to mind initially when thinking of a dimension such as a time horizon (temporal depth) or pace of work, all four of the temporal dimensions demonstrate the key attribute of a rhythm – namely, periodicity. In other words, all four dimensions reveal temporal patterns that recur regularly.

Entrainment is formally defined as "the adjustment of the pace or cycle of an activity to match or synchronize with that of another activity" (Ancona & Chong, 1996, p. 253). Bluedorn (2002, p. 148) has noted that this definition does not mean the patterns of the rhythms overlap exactly; instead, it means the rhythmic patterns maintain a consistent relationship with one another. As such, the phases of one rhythm might actually precede the corresponding phase in another rhythm, but entrainment would still occur so long as this relationship between the rhythms remains constant.

When entrainment is conceptualized as the *consistent* relationship of one rhythmic activity with another, three possible forms of entrainment can occur: synchronous, leading, and lagging (Bluedorn, 2002, pp. 148–150). Of the three forms, synchronous entrainment is probably the easiest to envision. In this form of entrainment, the corresponding phases of the two rhythms occur at the same time. An example would be the players in an orchestra (followers) all being in rhythm with one another and with the conductor as far as the piece of music they are playing is concerned. Ideally, no player would get ahead or fall behind the rhythm intended by the conductor.

To understand the lagging and leading forms, we need to introduce another term: power. When entrainment occurs, often one of the rhythms is the more powerful and is said to play an entraining role because it "captures" the other (entrained) rhythm. In lagging entrainment, the phases of the entrained rhythm follow the corresponding phases of the more powerful entraining rhythm. In leading entrainment, the phases of the entrained (less powerful) rhythm occur before the corresponding phases of the entraining (more powerful) rhythm. An example of leading entrainment would be the employee (follower) who arrives five minutes early for an appointment with the boss (leader).

This understanding extends the principle that with greater power comes greater temporal discretion. Because the employee will generally have less power than the boss, the employee must take greater care to avoid being late for the appointment lest offense be given. This cautionary behavior on the part of the employee demonstrates the premise that the more powerful person in a relationship can keep the less powerful waiting (Levine, 1997). It is an example of leading entrainment because the employee arrives before the boss arrives, and arrival time is the corresponding phase in each person's rhythm. Normally the boss – who is generally the more powerful member of the dyad – and the boss' schedule and preferences would be the entraining rhythm that leads the employee to arrive earlier than the boss. Hence the employee's rhythm, as marked by its arrival time phase, precedes the phases of the boss's rhythm. In short, there is leading entrainment.

Just the opposite occurs in the case of lagging entrainment, where the phases of the entrained rhythm follow the corresponding phases of the entraining rhythm. An example here can be taken from the daily routines of the New York Stock Exchange (NYSE). The NYSE "opens with the bell" at 9:00 A.M. Eastern Time, which signals the beginning of the day's buying and selling that occurs on the trading floor. The officials who manage the exchange have a rhythm to their daily rounds, one phase of which is the sounding of the bell to begin the day's trading. Similarly, the traders on the exchange floor display regular patterns in their daily activities, one of which is to begin trading tasks once they are authorized to do so by the sound of the bell. In terms of leaders and followers, the NYSE managers are the leaders and the traders are the followers. Hence, the rhythms of the NYSE managers are the entraining rhythms – at least as far as the beginning and ending of trading is concerned. Furthermore, trading begins after the bell is rung – not before or during its ringing. Thus, the ringing of the bell manifests a phase of the managers' rhythms, and the initiation of trading by the traders a millisecond or so after it rings is a phase in the traders' daily cycles. Even if the interval is brief in terms of human perception, the key is that the bell rings and then trading begins; the phase from the entraining rhythm occurs followed by a corresponding phase from the entrained rhythm.

Underlying all three forms of entrainment – synchronous, leading, and lagging – is the principle that the relationships between corresponding phases in the rhythms are consistent. Yet, entrainment includes one more element: the zeitgeber (Whitrow, 1980). In the most technical sense, a zeitgeber is a signal that reveals the phases of a rhythm and as such serves as a tangible synchronizer or pacing agent (Ancona & Chong, 1996, p. 253), making it a marker for an entraining rhythm. The zeitgeber is not technically the agent displaying the rhythm, but rather a *signal that marks the rhythm*. However, as noted by Bluedorn (2002, p. 150), this distinction often leads to infelicitous prose, forcing the writer to continuously distinguish the agent from the signal that expresses the agency. (This last phrase should provide an example of the infelicity we are trying to avoid.) Following Bluedorn's example, we will avoid pedantic priggishness and use the term *zeitgeber* to refer to both the signal and the signaler, while recognizing that formally the two are distinct – a distinction that may be useful at points in some analyses.

Zeitgebers are important because, without them, it is very difficult for entraining entities and their rhythms to entrain others. Similarly, many entities often want to become entrained, something likely true of the followers in many leader–follower dyads. They, too, have a much harder time entraining to a dominant rhythm if the phases of that rhythm are not manifested tangibly. This point is well illustrated by the example given earlier from the NYSE and its starting bell. If the NYSE managers did not ring the bell daily (the daily zeitgeber) to tangibly mark this phase of the day (the authorization for the traders to begin trading), the traders could not as precisely align their rhythms (from not trading to trading) with the rhythms of the managers – and by extension with other traders, because one trader might believe it was time to begin trading while another might not be sure. Thus a function of the zeitgeber – the bell in this case – not only aligns the rhythms of the entraining entity (the managers) and the entrained (the traders), but also helps align the rhythms of the traders with one another.

In this example, we see an illustration of how fundamental a process entrainment is and how powerfully it affects human behavior as an organizing force. As our description implies, entrainment may involve multiple levels of analysis simultaneously. An individual could be entrained with another individual (dyadic), while at the same time be entrained with a workgroup, an organization, a neighborhood, a city, a religion, and a national culture. While the zeitgeber can be an inanimate object (e.g., a church bell), collective entities can also be entrained to the zeitgeber (e.g., a neighborhood). By contrast, a single individual could be entrained with an inanimate object (e.g., a train), thereby making it an individual-level phenomenon. Research investigating relationships that occur across levels of analysis regarding entrainment is necessary, as an individual could be entrained to a collectivity (an organization's temporal context), which will have individual-level outcomes. We now depict one such case, and then turn to a more detailed discussion of the nested nature of entrainment.

Entrainment and Polychronicity, Speed, Punctuality, and Temporal Depth
The polychronicity continuum reveals a wide array of behaviors, extending from a preference for focusing on a single task to a somewhat open upper bound where the preference is to engage many tasks simultaneously. Therefore, each position along the continuum possesses a distinct rhythm of work. Given polychronicity's status as a universal attribute of human behavior, individually as well as in collectivities, when an analysis or investigation moves beyond simply the characteristics within a single entity at one unit of analysis and addresses polychronicity, by definition it is dealing with entrainment. For example, because individuals deal with one another, with task demands, and with other aspects of their work context, people tend to prefer similarities (jobs, coworkers, bosses, and so forth) to their own polychronicity orientation (e.g., Hecht & Allen, 2005; Slocombe & Bluedorn, 1999). Because the similarity involved includes the actual manifestation of polychronicity, which is a rhythm, the preference for similar rhythms likely amounts to a preference for the entrainment of these two rhythms. Similarly, entrainment involves pace or speed, and we assume people will prefer work contexts that present them with task demands and coworkers who prefer to work at the same speed that they prefer to work.

Likewise, this logic should apply to punctuality and temporal depth. Thus, we make the following assertion:

> **Proposition 24.** The greater the entrainment between an individual and the characteristics of the individual's work and organizational context along the temporal dimensions of polychronicity, speed, punctuality, and temporal depth, the greater the individual's job satisfaction.

Nested Entrainment

Entrainment does not just involve elements in the same system at the same level of analysis (e.g., individuals in the same workgroup or departments in the same organization). Instead, it often occurs in a nested hierarchy. For example, an individual is nested in a department, which is nested in an organization, which is nested in a national culture. To further complicate matters, the individuals and collectivities may be part of several nested hierarchies that may, at times, exert conflicting entrainment demands on the individual, department, and so on. An example of such conflicting demands would be a manager who has a full-time day job and who is also a student in either an executive or evening MBA program. The rhythms of the manager's work, especially as he or she is entrained to the rhythms of the employing department and organization, may not be isomorphic with the rhythms of the MBA program, which are in turn tightly entrained to the rhythms of the college or university of which it is a part.

Another example would be individuals and departments that play boundary-spanning roles. To successfully play such roles, the rhythms and speeds of both the parent organization and organizations in its environment must be accommodated and managed (see Standifer & Bluedorn, 2006). Such balancing is likely revealed in the differing future temporal depths that Lawrence and Lorsch (1967) reported for different types of departments in their classic study of organizations and environments.

Nesting structures indicate that entrainment is a complicated matter and likely represents a balance among competing zeitgebers and other forces that would lead a person or collectivity to come into alignment with the rhythms or speeds of other people or collectivities. For these reasons, we propose the following:

> **Proposition 25.** In a context of multiple zeitgebers, rhythms, and speeds, individuals and collectivities will entrain their speeds and rhythms so as to balance the demands of the multiple zeitgebers, rhythms, and speeds, even if one zeitgeber, speed, or rhythm is dominant in the context.

Clearly, entrainment occurs across adjacent levels in nested hierarchies and, by extension, across the several levels of the hierarchy. The question is, How does this entrainment arise? We believe a critical factor for cross-level entrainment is the collectivity's manager/leader. (We realize that these roles are not always filled by the same person, but the manager is normally considered to be a collectivity's formal leader. For purposes of this discussion, therefore, we will regard the collectivity's leader and manager as the same person and use the labels interchangeably.)

The group's leader is critical, we believe, because entrainment is one of the linking pin (Likert, 1967) functions a group's leader performs for the group. The leader deals directly with the next higher level in the nested hierarchy and, to meet its rhythmic and speed demands, helps the group come into at least adequate alignment with those demands. But there will likely be a continuing tension between alignment with these demands and demands from other sources, including those from inside the group itself, which may prefer a different speed and set of rhythms. Because of these conflicting demands, we believe individuals who hope to be successful in these linking pin roles need to be flexible in their abilities to deal with differing rhythms and speeds. As we noted in our discussion of polychronicity, Cotte and Ratneshwar's (1999) research revealed that individuals can adjust their levels of polychronicity to match the demands of different contexts (e.g., work versus home), but that individuals seem to vary in their ability to do so. Extending these findings to temporal difference in general, we develop two propositions:

Proposition 26. The greater an individual's flexibility in regard to temporal differences, the more effective the individual will be in the entrainment functions of the linking pin role.

Proposition 27. The more temporally flexible the individual who plays a group's linking pin role with the next higher level in a nested hierarchy, the more effectively the group will be entrained to the temporal demands of the higher level.

CAVEATS FOR THEORY AND APPLICATION

There is often a tendency to assume that similarity leads to positive outcomes for individuals and collectivities. This is likely an overly simplistic view of things, regardless of whether we are dealing with issues of theory or application. For that reason, we offer some caveats concerning both application and theory. We will first consider theory and then focus on polychronicity to illustrate a more general point.

Theoretical Caution

It would be easy to assume that the more similar two individuals or groups are in terms of polychronicity, the easier it would be to entrain them, given that polychronicity is a rhythmic pattern of behavior. In reality, ease of entrainment does not mean the results of the entrainment will be optimal. As we shall see, ease of entrainment and optimal consequences are two different matters.

As discussed earlier in this chapter, polychronicity is a fundamental aspect of most human relationships. In the case of leaders and subordinates, it may be especially critical. We can cite the example given at the beginning of the chapter, the leader–follower dyad of a German manager with a French subordinate who had a difficult time working together, and whose leader–follower relationship was strained, to say the least. The reason given was differences in polychronicity, with the German manager tending toward the lower (monochronic) end of the continuum and the French subordinate tending toward the higher (polychronic) end of the continuum. And as Hall (1983, pp. 45–46) has noted, like water and oil, these differences do not combine well. Or maybe they can.

Perspectives such as ASA theory (Schneider, 1987) would lead us to anticipate that managers would select as subordinates individuals with temporal characteristics similar to their own. Thus, highly polychronic managers would be anticipated to search for highly polychronic subordinates. Conversely, and consistent with such a perspective, subordinates would be expected to prefer managers whose polychronicity was similar to their own. In support of this expectation are the results of experimental research that found respondents rated organizations as more attractive workplaces when the level of polychronicity displayed by its managers was similar to that of the respondents' (Bluedorn, 2000a). Consistent with this finding, Slocombe and Bluedorn (1999) found organizational commitment increased as the similarity increased between individuals' polychronicity and their perception of the polychronicity norms in their work units. But how similar? Would identical levels of polychronicity be optimal for the quality of the leader–follower relationship or other outcomes? We argue that it would not – that some degree of difference might well be preferable.

For example, Bluedorn, Kaufman, and Lane (1992) have proposed that highly polychronic people may have difficulty focusing on tasks, which may impede their ability to complete them. Thus, if both leader and follower were highly polychronic, tasks might not get completed. Conversely, low-polychronicity (monochronic) people may stick to a task so single-mindedly that they fail to exhibit the requisite flexibility to exploit opportunities by switching to them when they arise. That scenario would also result in less than ideal results from the leader–follower dyad. Further, combining a leader and a follower whose polychronicity levels fall at the two ends of the polychronicity continuum may be too extreme of a difference for either party to cope with well. In contrast, a leader and a follower whose polychronicity levels differ by a quarter, or even half, of the continuum range may be a workable degree of similarity. They may be similar enough to yield reasonable relationship levels, while the difference in their polychronicity levels may help each other compensate for the weaknesses characteristic of the different styles. Thus, rather than maximum similarity, moderate diversity in the dyad may actually be the optimal combination of leader and follower.

But which is the easier combination: a polychronic leader and a monochronic follower, or a monochronic leader with a polychronic follower? In the context of formal organizations, most managerial work tends to be relatively polychronic (Bluedorn, 2002, pp. 49–51). This suggests that a relatively polychronic individual might adjust to managerial work more readily because the interface between the work context and the manager would be more similar. Being more similar would facilitate their entrainment because the manager already tends to work polychronically, and fewer adjustments would be required in the manager's work style than would be the case with a monochronic individual. In terms of dyadic effectiveness, the less-polychronic subordinate could provide a positive force on the more polychronic manager's behavior by providing greater focus and insisting that things get done.

But the follower is in a more difficult position than the leader in this regard because the leader, almost by definition, has more power over the follower than the follower has over the leader. It is no great insight and is well known that those in subordinate positions are not powerless vis-à-vis the leader (Mechanic, 1962). Nevertheless, on average, the leader has greater power and, at least in organizations, usually has a strong influence on organizational rewards, such as pay, that the follower receives. This imbalance puts the follower at risk.

Persing (1992) conducted an experiment in which she found that the temporal patterns people were believed to have employed to produce a tangible outcome had a strong effect on their perception of the outcome's quality, even though the quality of the outcomes was objectively identical.

Hence we would anticipate that leaders who observe subordinates performing their tasks with substantially greater or lower polychronicity than the leader's own level of polychronicity would be more likely to believe the follower's work was of lower quality than the work of a follower who is believed to perform their tasks in a manner closer to the leader's level of polychronicity, regardless of the objective quality of the follower's work. Interestingly, and consistent with this expectation, Slocombe and Bluedorn (1999) found that the less similar members of work units believed they were to the polychronicity norms and values of the work unit, the less fairly they believed their work was evaluated. Although coworkers certainly form opinions about the quality of one another's skills and quality of work, the key evaluation is the one that leads to tangible rewards such as pay. Such a finding is consistent with the impact of leader–follower similarity we believe was occurring in the work units studied and was manifested in the beliefs about unfair work evaluation.

This reasoning supports our contention that although leaders and followers with differing levels of polychronicity complement each other by addressing the blind spots in each other's styles, the differences cannot be too great, lest the follower's work be assessed unfairly enough to lead to conflict, dismissal, or voluntary turnover. In terms of entrainment, it suggests that moderate entrainment, by bringing together the rhythms of relatively similar but not identical levels of polychronicity, may be the optimal balance for the leader and the follower as well as for the organization.

Proposition 28. Moderate levels of polychronicity entrainment between a leader and a follower will result in greater dyad productivity and effectiveness than either extremely high or extremely low levels of polychronicity entrainment.

Caveats Concerning a Naive Implementation

We are concerned that the uncritical implementation of these ideas in a selection context may be unwise, regardless of whether a manager is hiring a new employee or a company is looking to acquire another firm. Logistical concerns aside (and they may be formidable in their own right), our concerns follow from Edward Hall's work with people who had trouble getting along due to their differences in polychronicity. In addition to describing the French and German managers with which we began this chapter, Hall described a husband and wife who had a difficult time with their relationship. After working with them he noted that like the French and German managers, the husband and wife had major differences in polychronicity. After he explained to them what this difference was – that is, a preferred way of engaging life rather than a tactic for annoying the other partner – their relationship improved considerably. Simply understanding what was involved, which allowed the husband and wife to reframe the situation and hence their interpretations of it, made a major difference (Bluedorn, 1998).

Might not the same effect hold true between leaders and followers, workers and coworkers, and acquirers and acquired companies: They could come to understand that the other's pace of work was not slow to try to sabotage the work flow, that the other was not scatterbrained because of involvement with a bewildering number of tasks, that the lack of interest in the future of the company a decade from now does not imply a lack of interest in the well-being of the company, and that expectations of firm compliance with deadlines does not a martinet make. El Sawy's (1983) research showed that individuals' temporal depths can be deliberately changed through specific interventions. Even without interventions being involved, Cotte and Ratneshwar (1999) found that some people seem to have a natural and relatively stress-free ability to shift back and forth over major distances along the polychronicity continuum as the context requires. This finding inspires us to emphasize Hall's accounts (Bluedorn, 1998) of how just making people aware of such differences and their legitimacy can go a long way toward reducing conflict and improving relationships. Defaulting to similarity-based selection strategies would reduce the possibilities for such learning and understanding as well as the other advantages that might stem from moderate degrees of difference. All of this suggests that there are many ways to accommodate differences along the temporal dimensions other than differential selection strategies. Indeed, in a world where the virtues of diversity have become a contemporary mantra, it seems almost anachronistic to contemplate selection based on these temporal characteristics in an attempt to homogenize these traits within dyads and larger collectivities. Thus, we feel it is only responsible to present this caveat against a naive conversion of these ideas to selection practices. It also leads us to a final premise, which we present in our conclusion.

CONCLUSION

Over the span of this chapter, we have presented five temporal dimensions – polychronicity, speed, punctuality, temporal depth, and entrainment – and explained them and their relationships to other important variables. In doing so, we sometimes proposed similar relationships between commensurate manifestations of the same dimensions and other variables across levels of analysis. In other cases, however, we proposed differing relationships. We believe we have demonstrated the importance of these five temporal dimensions and, by extension, the general importance of time and temporal variables for organizational analysis. We have done so by relating the five temporal dimensions to other important variables in organization science. We have also demonstrated the importance of specifying the levels of analysis involved when considering relationships between the temporal dimensions and other variables because, at least in some cases, the form of the relationship differs by level of analysis.

But as important as these demonstrations may be, we believe that our most important contribution is our ideas' potential to enhance the temporal imaginations of scientists and those who would use the resulting science in their work and everyday life. The temporal imagination is, fundamentally, the ability to recognize and understand one's own temporal behaviors within the temporal contexts in which one lives and works (Bluedorn & Standifer, in press). Thus, to truly possess a robust temporal imagination, one must recognize and understand not just one's own temporal behaviors, but those manifested in the larger context in which one exists.

The success Hall found by simply getting the German and French managers and the husband and wife to recognize and understand a key temporal feature of their relationships (polychronicity) illustrates a mature and insightful temporal imagination. It also suggests the profound implications of the effects that can be achieved through the skillful use of such an imagination. Understanding the concepts we have presented and recognizing them when they are present (and they are always present) may be the most important contribution to theory and practice that our analysis can make. In the tradition of Lewin's (1951, p. 169) legendary belief that "there is nothing so practical as a good theory," we believe the theoretical base of organization science is incomplete without good temporal theory considered, specified, and applied at the appropriate level of analysis. And as Hall demonstrated, even a good fragment of temporal theory can have profound practical effects.

REFERENCES

Ancona, D., & Chong, C.-L. (1996). Entrainment: Pace, cycle, and rhythm in organizational behavior. *Research in Organizational Behavior, 18*, 251–284.

Ancona, D. G., Okhuysen, G. A., & Perlow, L. A. (2001). Taking time to integrate temporal research. *Academy of Management Review, 26*, 512–529.

Baron, R. A. (1989). Personality and organizational conflict: Effects of the type A behavior pattern and self-monitoring. *Organizational Behavior and Human Decision Processes, 44*, 281–296.

Blau, P. M. (1970). A formal theory of differentiation in organizations. *American Sociological Review, 35*, 201–218.

Bluedorn, A. C. (1998). An interview with anthropologist Edward T. Hall. *Journal of Management Inquiry, 7*, 109–115.

Bluedorn, A. C. (2000a). Polychronicity, change orientation, and organizational attractiveness. Paper presented at the annual meeting of the society for industrial and organizational psychology, New Orleans, LA, April 14–16.

Bluedorn, A. C. (2000b). Time and organizational culture. In: N. M. Ashkanasy, C. P. M. Wilderom & M. F. Peterson (Eds), *Handbook of organizational culture and climate* (pp. 117–128). Thousand Oaks, CA: Sage.

Bluedorn, A. C. (2002). *The human organization of time: Temporal realities and experience.* Stanford, CA: Stanford University Press.

Bluedorn, A. C., & Ferris, S. P. (2004). Temporal depth, age, and organizational performance. In: C. F. Epstein & A. L. Kalleberg (Eds), *Fighting for time: Shifting boundaries of work and social life* (pp. 113–149). New York: Russell Sage Foundation.

Bluedorn, A. C., Kalliath, T. J., Strube, M. J., & Martin, G. D. (1999). Polychronicity and the inventory of polychronic values (IPV): The development of an instrument to measure of fundamental dimension of organizational culture. *Journal of Managerial Psychology, 14*, 205–230.

Bluedorn, A. C., Kaufman, C. F., & Lane, P. M. (1992). How many things do you like to do at once? An introduction to monochronic and polychronic time. *Academy of Management Executive, 6*(4), 17–26.

Bluedorn, A. C., & Richtermeyer, G. (2005). The time frames of entrepreneurs. Paper presented at the annual meeting of the academy of management, Honolulu, HI, August 5–10.

Bluedorn, A. C., & Standifer, R. L. (in press). Time and the temporal imagination. *Academy of Management Learning and Education.*

Bradbury, R. (1996). *Quicker than the eye.* New York: Avon Books.

Chatman, J. A., & Flynn, F. J. (2001). The influence of demographic heterogeneity on the emergence and consequences of cooperative norms in work teams. *Academy of Management Journal, 44*, 956–974.

Chen, M., & Hambrick, D. (1995). Speed, stealth, and selective attack: How small firms differ from large firms in competitive behavior. *Academy of Management Journal, 38*, 453–482.

Conger, J. A., & Kanungo, R. N. (1998). *Charismatic leadership in organizations.* Thousand Oaks, CA: Sage.

Conte, J. M., & Jacobs, R. R. (2003). Validity evidence linking polychronicity and big five personality dimensions to absence. Lateness, and supervisory performance ratings. *Human Performance, 16*, 107–130.

Conte, J. M., Mathieu, J. E., & Landy, F. J. (1998). The nomological and predictive validity of time urgency. *Journal of Organizational Behavior, 19*, 1–13.

Cotte, J., & Ratneshwar, S. (1999). Juggling and hopping: What does it mean to work polychronically? *Journal of Managerial Psychology, 14*, 184–204.

Das, T. K. (1986). *The subjective side of strategy making: Future orientations and perceptions of executives.* New York: Praeger.

Das, T. K. (1987). Strategic planning and individual temporal orientation. *Strategic Management Journal, 8*, 203–209.

Dess, G. G., & Beard, D. W. (1984). Dimensions of organizational task environments. *Administrative Science Quarterly, 29*, 52–73.

DiMaggio, P. J., & Powell, W. W. (1983). The iron cage revisited: Institutional isomorphism and collective nationality in organizational fields. *American Sociological Review, 48*, 147–160.

Donaldson, L. (2001). *The contingency theory of organizations.* Thousand Oaks, CA: Sage.

Doob, L. W. (1971). *Patterning of time.* New Haven, CT: Yale University Press.

Eisenhardt, K. M. (1989). Making fast strategic decisions in high-velocity environments. *Academy of Management Journal, 32*, 543–576.

El Sawy, O. A. (1983). Temporal perspective and managerial attention: A study of chief executive strategic behavior. (Doctoral dissertation, Stanford University, 1983). *Dissertation Abstracts International, 44*(05A), 1556–1557.

Fraisse, P. (1963). *The psychology of time.* New York: Harper & Row.

Friedman, M., & Rosenman, R. H. (1974). *Type A behavior and your heart.* New York: Knopf.

Gersick, C. J. G. (1988). Time and transition in work teams: Toward a new model of group development. *Academy of Management Journal, 31*, 9–41.

Gersick, C. J. G. (1989). Marking time: Predictable transitions in task groups. *Academy of Management Journal, 32*, 274–309.

Haase, R. F., Lee, D. Y., & Banks, D. L. (1979). Cognitive correlates of polychronicity. *Perceptual and Motor Skills, 49*, 271–282.

Hackman, J. R., & Oldham, G. R. (1976). Motivation through the design of work: Test of a theory. *Organizational Behavior and Human Performance, 16*, 250–279.

Hall, E. T. (1981). *The silent language.* New York: Anchor Books (Original work published in 1959).

Hall, E. T. (1983). *The dance of life: The other dimension of time.* Garden City, NY: Anchor Press.

Harrison, D. A., Price, K. H., Gavin, J. H., & Florey, A. T. (2002). Time, teams and task performance: Changing effects of surface- and deep-level diversity on group functioning. *Academy of Management Journal, 45*, 1029–1045.

Hecht, T. D. (2003). Person–job fit on the dimension of polychronicity: An examination of links with well-being and performance. (Doctoral dissertation, University of Western Ontario, 2002). *Dissertation Abstracts International, 65*(11B), 6079.

Hecht, T. D., & Allen, N. J. (2005). Exploring links between polychronicity and well-being from the perspective of person–job fit: Does it matter if you prefer to do only one thing at a time? *Organizational Behavior and Human Decision Processes, 95*, 155–178.

Jaussi, K. S., Randel, A. E., & Dionne, S. D. (in press). I am, I think I can, and I do: The role of personal identity, self-efficacy, and cross-application of experiences in creativity at work. *Journal of Creativity Research.*

Judge, W. Q., & Spitzfaden, M. (1995). The management of strategic time horizons within biotechnology firms: The impact of cognitive complexity on time horizon diversity. *Journal of Management Inquiry, 4*, 179–196.

Kets de Vries, M. (1988). Origins of charisma: Ties that bind the leader and the lead. In: J. A. Conger & R. N. Kanungo (Eds), *Charismatic leadership: The elusive factor in organizational effectiveness* (pp. 237–252). San Francisco: Jossey-Bass.

Knorr, E., & Neubaur, A. C. (1996). Speed of information-processing in an inductive reasoning task and its relationship to psychometric intelligence. *Personality and Individual Differences, 20*, 653–660.

Labianca, G., Moon, H., & Watt, I. (2005). When is an hour not 60 minutes? Deadlines, temporal schemata, and individual and task group performance. *Academy of Management Journal, 48,* 677–694.

Lawrence, P. R., & Lorsch, J. W. (1967). *Organization and environment: Managing differentiation and integration.* Boston: Harvard University, Graduate School of Business Administration.

Lee, H., Lee, J.-H., Lee, J., & Choi, C. (2005). Time to change, time for change: How was time used to change a global company. Academy of Management Best Conference Paper, Honolulu, Hawai, *Academy of Management Proceedings,* F1–F5.

Levine, R. (1997). *A geography of time: The temporal misadventures of a social psychologist, or how every culture keeps time just a little bit differently.* New York: Basic Books.

Levine, R. V., & Norenzayan, A. (1999). The pace of life in 31 countries. *Journal of Cross-Cultural Psychology, 30,* 178–205.

Levine, R. V., West, L. J., & Reis, H. T. (1980). Perceptions of time and punctuality in the United States and Brazil. *Journal of Personality and Social Psychology, 38,* 541–550.

Lewin, K. (1951). *Field theory in social science: Selected theoretical papers.* New York: Harper & Brothers.

Lewis, J. D., & Weigart, A. (1985). Trust as a social reality. *Social Forces, 63,* 967–985.

Likert, R. (1967). *The human organization: Its management and value.* New York: McGraw-Hill.

Lim, S. G.-S., & Murnighan, J. K. (1994). Phases, deadlines, and the bargaining process. *Organizational Behavior and Human Decision Processes, 58,* 153–171.

Locke, E. A., Shaw, K. N., Saari, L. M., & Latham, G. P. (1981). Goal setting and task performance. *Psychological Bulletin* (January), *90,* 125–152.

Madjar, N., & Oldham, G. R. (in press). Task rotation and polychronicity: Effects on individuals' creativity. *Human Performance.*

Mechanic, D. (1962). Sources of power of lower participants in complex organizations. *Administrative Science Quarterly, 7,* 349–364.

Montoya-Weiss, M. M., Massey, A. P., & Song, M. (2001). Getting it together: Temporal coordination and conflict management in global virtual teams. *Academy of Management Journal, 44,* 1251–1262.

Onken, M. H. (1999). Temporal elements of organizational culture and impact on firm performance. *Journal of Managerial Psychology, 14,* 231–243.

Orlikowsk, W. J., & Yates, J. (2002). It's about time: Temporal structuring in organizations. *Organization Science, 13,* 684–700.

Ortet, G., Ibanez, M. I., Llerena, A., & Torrubia, R. (2002). The underlying traits of the Karolinska scales of personality. *European Journal of Psychological Assessment, 18,* 139–148.

Perlow, L. A., Okhuysen, G. A., & Repenning, N. P. (2002). The speed trap: Exploring the relationship between decision-making and temporal context. *Academy of Management Journal, 45,* 931–955.

Persing, D. L. (1992). The effect of effort allocation information on perceptions of intellectual workers and evaluations of their products. (Doctoral dissertation, University of Oregon, 1991). *Dissertation Abstracts International, 52*(09A), 3350–3351.

Peterson, S. J., & Luthans, F. (2006). The impact of financial and nonfinancial incentives on business-unit outcomes over time. *Journal of Applied Psychology, 91,* 156–165.

Root-Bernstein, R. S., Bernstein, M., & Garnier, H. (1995). Correlations between avocations, scientific style, work habits, and professional impact of scientists. *Creativity Research Journal, 8,* 115–137.

Schein, E. H. (1992). *Organizational culture and leadership* (2nd ed.). San Francisco: Jossey-Bass.

Schneider, B. (1987). The people make the place. *Personnel Psychology, 40,* 437–453.

Schriber, J. B., & Gutek, B. A. (1987). Some time dimensions of work: Measurement of an underlying aspect of organization culture. *Journal of Applied Psychology, 72,* 642–650.

Slocombe, T. E., & Bluedorn, A. C. (1999). Organizational behavior implications of the congruence between preferred polychronicity and experienced work-unit polychronicity. *Journal of Organizational Behavior, 20,* 75–99.

Standifer, R. L., & Bluedorn, A. C. (2006). *Alliance management teams and entrainment: Sharing temporal mental models.* Manuscript submitted for publication.

Thompson, J. D. (1967). *Organizations in action.* New York: McGraw-Hill.

Totterdell, P. (2000). Catching moods and hitting runs: Mood linkage and subjective performance in professional sports teams. *Journal of Applied Psychology, 85,* 848–859.

Westaby, J. D., & Lowe, J. K. (2005). Risk-taking orientation and injury among youth workers: Examining the social influences of supervisors, coworkers, and parents. *Journal of Applied Psychology, 90,* 1027–1035.

Whitrow, G. J. (1980). *The natural philosophy of time* (2nd ed.). Oxford: Oxford University Press.

Zalesny, M. D., & Ford, J. K. (1990). Extending the social information processing perspective: New links to attitudes, behaviors, and perceptions. *Organizational Behavior and Human Decision Processes, 46,* 205–246.

Zuckerman, M. (1979). *Sensation seeking: Beyond the optimal level of arousal.* Hillsdale, NJ: Earlbaum.

MEASURING TEMPORAL CONSTRUCTS ACROSS MULTIPLE LEVELS OF ANALYSIS

Jeffrey M. Conte

ABSTRACT

This commentary focuses on the measurement of temporal dimensions at different levels of analysis. In particular, it examines the measures that are available for various levels of analysis for four temporal dimensions: polychronicity, speed, punctuality, and temporal depth. The discussion is meant to spur additional research using reliable and valid temporal measures at multiple levels of analysis.

INTRODUCTION

Bluedorn and Jaussi's chapter (this volume) does an excellent job of introducing and describing organizationally relevant dimensions of time across levels of analysis. Although these authors address some measurement issues related to temporal constructs, their work principally focuses on developing theoretical relationships and corresponding propositions. The current commentary addresses the measurement of temporal dimensions at different levels of analysis. In particular, it examines measures that are available for the levels of analysis described for the four temporal dimensions

Multi-Level Issues in Organizations and Time
Research in Multi-Level Issues, Volume 6, 225–237
Copyright © 2007 by Elsevier Ltd.
All rights of reproduction in any form reserved
ISSN: 1475-9144/doi:10.1016/S1475-9144(07)06010-9

—polychronicity, speed, punctuality, and temporal depth—discussed in Bluedorn and Jaussi's chapter.

POLYCHRONICITY

Individual-Level Polychronicity

The individual-level scale is typically adapted from the 10-item, team-level polychronicity scale developed by Bluedorn, Kalliath, Strube, and Martin (1999). These authors reported that they had collected a sizable amount of unpublished individual-level data that indicated that the team-level scale could be easily modified to provide an equally reliable and valid measure of individual-level polychronicity. The adaptation simply involves changing "We" to "I" in each item shown in Table 1 of Bluedorn et al. (1999).

In two recent studies (Conte & Gintoft, 2005; Conte & Jacobs, 2003), individual-level polychronicity was assessed with a 6-item scale modified in such a manner. Both studies reported adequate internal consistency reliability (the two studies reported reliability greater than 0.77). Nevertheless, it is generally recommended that researchers begin with the 10-item individual-level scale that is adapted from Bluedorn et al.'s (1999) team-level scale. In terms of stability over time, Conte and Jacobs (2003) found that the individual-level polychronicity scale had a test–retest reliability of 0.95 over a one-hour interval and a test–retest reliability coefficient of 0.78 over a two-month interval.

Conte, Rizzuto, and Steiner (1999) provided convergent and discriminant validity evidence for individual-level polychronicity. They demonstrated that different raters were able to agree on the level of an individual's polychronicity. They also found that individual-level polychronicity had low, but significant correlations with achievement strivings ($r = 0.18$), impatience/irritability ($r = 0.18$), and the general hurry time-urgency dimension ($r = 0.16$), all of which are subcomponents of the Type A behavior pattern (Landy, Rastegary, Thayer, & Colvin, 1991; Spence, Helmreich, & Pred, 1987). Conte and Jacobs (2003) found that individual-level polychronicity did not overlap substantially with traditional measures of cognitive ability (i.e., the Wonderlic Personnel Test or the Scholastic Aptitude Test).

Conte and Gintoft (2005) noted that the results of their factor analyses of the individual-level polychronicity items indicated the existence of a 2D factor structure. However, the dimensionality of the polychronicity items had been investigated extensively in the earlier scale development study conducted by Bluedorn et al. (1999), who found that the two factors were simply an artifact of the positive or negative wording of the items, rather than reflecting any substantive differences in the items. Several other studies have found that negatively worded items can produce artifactual factors, resulting in a two-factor solution when a single-factor solution is actually more appropriate (Cordery & Sevastos, 1993; Greenberger, Chen, Dmitrieva, & Farruggia, 2003; Kelloway, Catano, & Southwell, 1992; Spector, Van Katwyk, Brannick, & Chen, 1997).

Slocombe (1999) analyzed polychronicity at the cultural level, then compared that analysis with an analysis of polychronicity at the level of the individual member of the culture. He suggested that a more detailed examination of an individual's polychronicity is appropriate, including assessment of the individual's beliefs, attitudes, and behaviors. Separate consideration of beliefs, attitudes, and behaviors is common in the behavioral sciences (Fishbein & Ajzen, 1975), and this approach might be fruitfully pursued for individual-level polychronicity given that the construct is still in early stages of its development.

Palmer and Schoorman (1999) have argued that three distinct dimensions are typically associated with the construct of polychronicity—time-use preference, context, and time tangibility—and they developed measures of each. Bluedorn's Index of Polychronic Values (IPV) was used as the measure of time use preference. The context measure focused on the multifaceted form of communication that polychronics often employ. In particular, the context was measured using an 8-item scale based on the work of Gudykunst et al. (1996). Time tangibility derives from the notion that some individuals and cultures view time as something that can be bought, sold, wasted, or spent, whereas other cultures and individuals view time as intangible and serving only as a backdrop against which events unfold (Palmer & Schoorman, 1999). Time tangibility was measured with a 14-item scale that included items from several previous studies on time (e.g., Calabresi & Cohen, 1968; Palmer, 1997; Schriber & Gutek, 1987; Usunier, 1991). Palmer and Schoorman found that the three dimensions of polychronicity had low correlations, suggesting that the dimensions are independent. Although few studies have followed up on this approach, like the Slocombe (1999) article, it does provide alternative opportunities to conceptualize and measure individual-level polychronicity.

Group-Level Polychronicity

As mentioned earlier, Bluedorn et al. (1999) originally developed the IPV for measurement at the group level or higher. The items on the IPV focused on asking members about the polychronicity of the group or culture to which they belonged. Bluedorn and colleagues used data from 11 samples to demonstrate the internal consistency, test–retest reliability, content adequacy, construct validity, and nomological validity of the IPV.

The latest research on polychronicity has used this scale or a slight modification of it to measure a different level of analysis. For example, Slocombe and Bluedorn (1999) assessed experienced work-unit polychronicity (the polychronic behaviors and preferences of the supervisor and coworkers) via self-report measures and compared that result to preferred polychronicity, also a self-report measure. Thus, their team-level polychronicity measure was derived from individual perceptions of the work unit's or team's preference for multitasking. Waller, Giambatista, and Zellmer-Bruhn (1999) used the IPV to examine the effects of individual time urgency on team polychronicity, essentially studying cross-level relationships of temporal variables. They measured polychronicity at the team level in a lab setting by examining group-level polychronic behavior—that is, the group's performance of multiple tasks simultaneously. Note that this team-level variable was measured in different ways in these two studies (Slocombe & Bluedorn, 1999; Waller et al., 1999). Each measure focused on slightly different assessments of group-level polychronicity, allowing for different inferences depending on which assessment was used.

Organizational-Level Polychronicity

Few studies have explicitly investigated polychronicity at the organizational level. One exception is a study by Onken (1999), which examined two temporal elements of organizational culture (polychronicity and speed values) and their effects on organizational performance. The effects of these temporal elements were examined both individually and within the context of hypercompetitive industries. The polychronicity measure used was adapted from Bluedorn et al.'s (1999) IPV measure. The sample consisted of 90 respondents from 20 different firms. The polychronicity dimension was measured by "aggregating individual responses from each firm, [and] a within- and between-analysis (WABA) correlation procedure was performed to simultaneously examine individual and group-level effects in order to justify the aggregation procedure" (Onken, 1999, p. 237). The results of the WABA procedure indicated that the between-group correlations were larger than the within-group correlations, supporting the notion that aggregation of the individual-level responses from each firm is justified and that polychronicity can be considered a dimension of organizational culture. Onken found that polychronic cultures lead to higher firm performance, particularly in non-hypercompetitive industries. This study demonstrates the challenge of measuring polychronicity at the organizational level—in particular, the challenge of justifying aggregation when collecting data from individual representatives of various organizations.

SPEED

Individual-Level Speed

The time-urgency construct and measures, which were developed by Landy et al. (1991), can be used to assess individual-level speed on a variety of dimensions. Individuals characterized by time urgency are concerned with the passage of time and the way in which they can most efficiently fill that time with productive activity (Price, 1982). For example, the "general hurry" time urgency dimension is defined as the extent to which individuals rush when performing activities.

Landy et al. developed time urgency measures using both Likert-type scales and Behaviorally Anchored Rating Scales (BARS). The dimensions assessed by the Likert scales include Competitiveness, Eating Behavior, General Hurry, Task-Related Hurry, and Speech Patterns. The dimensions assessed by the BARS include Awareness of Time, Eating Behavior, Nervous Energy, List Making, Scheduling, Speech Patterns, and Deadline Control. Alternate forms of six of the time urgency BARS exist. Deadline Control does not have an alternate form, however, because not enough behavior survived the retranslation process in the study conducted by Landy et al. (1991). As a consequence, test–retest reliability is used for the Deadline Control dimension by including the same scale twice in the survey, and the alternate forms of the other dimensions provide one kind of reliability evidence for the other six time-urgency dimensions assessed by the BARS.

The study by Landy et al. (1991) emphasized the multidimensionality of the time-urgency construct and found support for multiple dimensions, each of which may produce relationships with other variables. Nevertheless, some investigators have explored the factor structure of the seven-dimension BARS. In several studies, a two-factor structure resulted from a factor analysis of the BARS dimensions (Conte, Mathieu, & Landy, 1998; Kohler, 1991; Menon, Narayanan, & Spector, 1996). For the Likert-type time-urgency items, Table 1 in Landy et al. (1991) shows which items mapped to which dimensions in the original study. A later validity study (Conte, Ringenbach, Moran, & Landy, 2001) showed a similar (but not identical) item–dimension mapping in a large sample of travel agents. In most studies, only a subset of the time urgency BARS and Likert measures is used—those measures that are meaningfully linked to other variables of interest. This preference explains why one might use the BARS in one study and the Likert scales in another study.

Conte, Schwenneker, Dew, and Romano (2001) provided additional validity evidence for the time-urgency measures by linking them to observable behaviors and health outcomes. Their study indicated that better prediction of behavioral and health criteria can be obtained by using more specific TABP (Type A Behavior Pattern) subcomponents rather than a global Type A measure.

Menon et al. (1996) examined the relation of time urgency to occupational stress, job attitudes, and health outcomes. They found that time-urgency dimensions were related to health problems in two samples of health care professionals.

As described earlier, to date these time urgency measures have been used in a limited number of student and field studies. Additional reliability and validity data are needed as well as tests of theoretical propositions for the time-urgency measures. Notably, Waller, Conte, Gibson, and Carpenter (2001) have presented propositions that describe how time urgency influences individuals' deadline perceptions and subsequent deadline-oriented behaviors, and how different deadline perceptions and behaviors among team members affect the ability of teams to meet deadlines. These propositions provide a variety of ideas that need to be tested using time urgency and other temporal measures.

Group-Level Speed

Schriber and Gutek (1987) emphasized that understanding and adapting to group norms relating to time can spell the difference between an employee's success or failure within an organization. These authors developed measures of 14 temporal variables focused on the group level. Schriber and Gutek's Time Dimensions Scales include 56 five-point Likert-type items that focus on the following dimensions: Schedules and Deadlines, Punctuality, Future Orientation, Speed Versus Quality, Allocation of Time, Time Boundaries Between Work and Nonwork, Awareness of Time Use, Work Pace, Autonomy of Time Use, Synchronization and Coordination of Work with Others Through Time, Routine Versus Variety, Intraorganizational Time Boundaries, Time Buffer in Workday, and Sequencing of Tasks Through Time. Respondents indicate their level of agreement, ranging from "strongly disagree" (1) to "strongly agree" (5), with each statement based on their perceptions of what is most typical within their work unit (or organization). As reported by the authors, three of the scales (Schedules and Deadlines, Punctuality, and Future Orientation) had very good levels of reliability (in the 0.70 and 0.80 ranges). The other seven scales (Time Boundaries Between Work and Nonwork, Speed Versus Quality, Synchronization and Coordination of Work with Others Through Time, Awareness of Time Use, Work Pace, Allocation of Time, and Sequencing of Tasks Through Time) showed moderate reliabilities (ranging from the high 0.50 s to the high 0.60 s). Marginal reliabilities (in the mid-0.50 range) were obtained for the Autonomy of Time Use, Intraorganizational Time Boundaries, and Routine Versus Variety scales.

Schriber and Gutek (1987) suggest that it may be beneficial to match individual and organizational time orientations. The idea is that a good fit is likely to lead to increased satisfaction and commitment and may have performance implications. Conversely, a mismatch between individual and organizational time orientations may lead to negative outcomes such as worker stress and alienation. For example, an employee whose views of the importance of schedules and deadlines differ from those of his/her colleagues might exhibit withdrawal behaviors, such as low satisfaction, absenteeism, and turnover (Conte, Landy, & Mathieu, 1995). Viewing time from such an interactionist perspective provides several additional avenues for research on multi-level issues related to time.

Organization-, Strategic-, and Industry-Level Speed

As noted in the Bluedorn and Jaussi article, several researchers have examined or speculated about speed at the organizational, strategic, or industry level, but the different measures of speed at this level have varied widely, and many papers focused on this level have been conceptual or theoretical. For example, Eisenhardt (1989) assessed the overall speed of organizational decision making from interview and story data. She corroborated these qualitative assessments with measurement of the duration of each strategic decision studied. Perlow, Okhuysen, and Repenning (2002) also used qualitative data to assess decision-making speed in a 19-month ethnographic study of an Internet start-up company.

In contrast, Chen and Hambrick (1995) assessed speed norms of airlines by measuring different types of speed. First, they assessed action execution speed, response announcement speed, and response execution speed. The particular measurement strategies used are complex and described in detail in their article. The measures used in their study were all indirect and based on industry press and public information; because of this constraint, the measures and their corresponding labels may not have fully captured the phenomena they intended to investigate. For instance, the authors noted that (1) their measures of action and response execution speed might not correspond perfectly to the ideas that they intended to study, because they lacked internal information and company cooperation and (2) with their data, they could not gauge the actual amount of time firms took to execute actions and responses, although they believed their measures to be generally accurate surrogates. Clearly, measurement of speed at this high level is quite varied and quite challenging.

PUNCTUALITY

Individual-Level Punctuality

Individual-level punctuality refers to the degree of rigidity to which schedules or deadlines are adhered; it has often been measured via lateness measures at work. An example study was conducted by Conte and Jacobs (2003), who investigated polychronicity and Big Five personality dimensions as predictors of absence and lateness. In terms of lateness measures, researchers typically assess the frequency and duration of lateness on the part of individuals in jobs in which punctuality is important. For example, Conte and Jacobs investigated a sample of subway drivers, for whom it is extremely important to arrive on time to work to keep the subway schedule on track.

The literature on measuring lateness in general is quite large. The reader is referred to Blau (1994) for further reading about lateness and punctuality measures.

Organizational-Level Punctuality

Schriber and Gutek (1987) measured punctuality as one dimension of their group-level temporal norms, and this dimension can be applied to the organizational level of analysis. For example, Benabou (1999) examined organizational, temporal culture variables adapted from Schriber and Gutek's scales. He asked participants: "Suppose you were able to choose the company in which you would like to work ... Indicate to what extent you would agree to work in an organization described by the following statements, including 'People get upset when you are late for work' and 'If people arrive an hour late for work, they will feel rushed all day' for punctuality." In a sample of 301 graduating management students, this punctuality scale demonstrated good reliability and showed a negative relationship with polychronicity, indicating that polychronic individuals would prefer not to avoid organizations in which punctuality is emphasized. Alternative designs and approaches to assessing organizational punctuality would do well to start with Schriber and Gutek's items and perhaps include additional items or samples.

National/Cultural Punctuality

Punctuality at the national or country level is challenging to measure. Nevertheless, a notable set of studies by Levine and colleagues has used some unique measures of punctuality to examine cultural differences in punctuality and other temporal indicators.

Levine, West, and Reis (1980) conducted three cross-national experiments to investigate whether Americans and Brazilians differed in punctuality. The results of their first experiment revealed that public clocks were less accurate in Brazil than in the United States. Their second experiment demonstrated that watches were less accurate in Brazil, that Brazilians who did not wear watches were less accurate than Americans who did not wear watches in estimating the time of day, and that Brazilians were less exact than Americans in reporting the time on their watches. Their third experiment, which used a questionnaire about punctuality, found that Brazilians reported that they were more often late for appointments and social gatherings, were more flexible in their definitions of "early" and "late," and expressed less regret over being late than Americans.

In a follow-up study, Levine and Bartlett (1984) examined pace of life, punctuality, and coronary heart disease in six countries. They found that cultures with a faster work pace and an emphasis on punctuality had a higher incidence of heart disease. This set of studies provided some rather unique measures of punctuality and demonstrated that punctuality and other temporal variables can be assessed at these higher levels of analysis.

TEMPORAL DEPTH

Individual-Level Temporal Depth

The temporal-depth construct is defined as the combined distance into the past and future that individuals and organizations consider when contemplating events that have happened, may have happened, or may happen (Bluedorn, 2000). The temporal-depth inventory (TDI) measures an individual's future, past, and total temporal depths (Bluedorn, 2002). The measure includes six items—three items each for future temporal depth and for past temporal depth. The scores for the future- and past temporal-depth scales can be added together to obtain the total temporal-depth scale.

Bluedorn developed both convergent and discriminant validity evidence for the TDI, which also demonstrated adequate internal consistency reliability. Notably, Bluedorn showed that the temporal-depth measure does not overlap the potentially related construct of temporal focus, which is the degree of emphasis on the past, present, and future (Bluedorn, 2000).

Using the TDI, Bluedorn and Richtermeyer (in press) examined the time frames of entrepreneurs. They provided further reliability and validity evidence for the TDI in a random stratified sample of 191 entrepreneurs in Missouri. The TDI is still in its early stages of development, but this promising psychometric evidence suggests that this measure is an excellent starting point for researchers interested in assessing temporal depth at the individual level and further developing the nomological network surrounding the temporal-depth construct.

Organizational-Level Temporal Depth

Bluedorn and Ferris (2004) investigated relationships among temporal depth, age, and organizational performance. They measured temporal depth via a sample of CEO and other top executives. The TDI and other questionnaires asked for responses about how things were done and seen in the company as a whole and thereby provided information about an organization's temporal depth. Notably, Bluedorn and Ferris (2004) found that the positive correlation between past and future temporal depths that had been observed at the individual level in several studies was also found at the organizational level, suggesting a consistency in relationships across levels of analysis. Examining this and other temporal variables at the organizational level and linking them to financial outcomes seems a fruitful endeavor that management researchers and those in related fields should continue to pursue.

CONCLUSION

This commentary examined the measures that are available for the various levels of analysis described for the four temporal dimensions discussed in

Bluedorn and Jaussi's chapter—namely, polychronicity, speed, punctuality, and temporal depth. Specifically, this commentary discussed the measurement options for temporal measures that are available in the research literature. This examination was illustrative rather than exhaustive, as additional temporal measures are likely to exist, including those found in literatures outside of psychology and management. Nevertheless, a variety of ways to measure temporal dimensions at and across multiple levels of analysis are available for further investigation. Ideally, this commentary, in conjunction with Bluedorn and Jaussi's work, will help spur additional research on temporal constructs using reliable and valid measures at multiple levels of analysis.

REFERENCES

Benabou, C. (1999). Polychronicity and temporal dimensions of work in learning organizations. *Journal of Managerial Psychology, 14*, 257–268.

Blau, G. (1994). Developing and testing a taxonomy of lateness behavior. *Journal of Applied Psychology, 79*, 959–970.

Bluedorn, A. C. (2000). Time and organizational culture. In: N. M. Ashkanasy, C. Wilderom & M. Peterson (Eds), *Handbook of organizational culture and climate* (pp. 117–128). Thousand Oaks, CA: Sage.

Bluedorn, A. C. (2002). *The human organization of time: Temporal realities and experience.* Stanford, CA: Stanford University Press.

Bluedorn, A. C., & Ferris, S. P. (2004). Temporal depth, age, and organizational performance. In: C. F. Epstein & A. L. Kalleberg (Eds), *Shifting boundaries of work and social life.* New York: Russell Sage Foundation.

Bluedorn, A., & Jaussi, K. (this volume). Organizationally relevant dimensions of time across levels of analysis. In: F. Dansereau & F.J. Yammarino (Eds), *Multi-level issues in organizations and time* (Vol. 6). Oxford: Elsevier.

Bluedorn, A. C., Kalliath, T. J., Strube, M. J., & Martin, G. D. (1999). Polychronicity and the inventory of polychronic values (IPV): The development of an instrument to measure a fundamental dimension of organizational culture. *Journal of Managerial Psychology, 14*, 205–230.

Bluedorn, A. C., & Richtermeyer, G. (in press). The time frames of entrepreneurs. *Journal of Business Venturing.*

Calabresi, R., & Cohen, J. (1968). Personality and time attitudes. *Journal of Abnormal Psychology, 73*, 431–439.

Chen, M., & Hambrick, D. C. (1995). Speed, stealth, and selective attack: How small firms differ from large firms in competitive behavior. *Academy of Management Journal, 38*, 453–482.

Conte, J. M., & Gintoft, J. N. (2005). Polychronicity, Big Five personality dimensions, and sales performance. *Human Performance, 18*, 427–444.

Conte, J. M., & Jacobs, R. R. (2003). Validity evidence linking polychronicity and Big 5 personality dimensions to absence, lateness, and supervisory ratings of performance. *Human Performance, 16*, 107–129.

Conte, J. M., Landy, F. J., & Mathieu, J. E. (1995). Time urgency: Conceptual and construct development. *Journal of Applied Psychology, 80*, 178–185.

Conte, J. M., Mathieu, J. E., & Landy, F. J. (1998). The nomological and predictive validity of time urgency. *Journal of Organizational Behavior, 19*, 1–13.

Conte, J. M., Ringenbach, K. L., Moran, S. K., & Landy, F. L. (2001). Criterion–validity evidence for time urgency: Associations with burnout, organizational commitment, and job involvement in travel agents. *Applied Human Resource Management Research, 6*, 129–134.

Conte, J. M., Rizzuto, T. E., & Steiner, D. D. (1999). A construct-oriented analysis of individual-level polychronicity. *Journal of Managerial Psychology, 14*, 269–287.

Conte, J. M., Schwenneker, H. H., Dew, A. F., & Romano, D. M. (2001). The incremental validity of time urgency and other Type A subcomponents in predicting behavioral and health criteria. *Journal of Applied Social Psychology, 31*, 1727–1748.

Cordery, J. L., & Sevastos, P. P. (1993). Responses to the original and revised Job Diagnostic Survey: Is education a factor in responses to negatively worded items?. *Journal of Applied Psychology, 78*, 141–143.

Eisenhardt, K. M. (1989). Making fast strategic decisions in high-velocity environments. *Academy of Management Journal, 32*, 543–576.

Fishbein, M., & Ajzen, I. (1975). *Belief, attitude, intention, and behavior: An introduction to theory and research.* Reading, MA: Addison-Wesley.

Greenberger, E., Chen, C., Dmitrieva, J., & Farruggia, S. P. (2003). Item-wording and the dimensionality of the Rosenberg Self-Esteem Scale: Do they matter?. *Personality and Individual Differences, 35*, 1241–1254.

Gudykunst, W. B., Matsumoto, Y., Ting-Toomey, S., Nishida, T., Kim, K., & Heyman, S. (1996). The influence of cultural individualism–collectivism, self-construals, and individual values on communication styles across cultures. *Human Communication Research, 22*, 510–543.

Kelloway, E. K., Catano, V. M., & Southwell, R. R. (1992). The construct validity of union commitment: Development and dimensionality of a shorter scale. *Journal of Occupational and Organizational Psychology, 65*, 197–211.

Kohler, S. S. (1991). *Time urgency: Psychophysiological correlates.* Unpublished doctoral dissertation, Pennsylvania State University, University Park, PA.

Landy, F. J., Rastegary, H., Thayer, J., & Colvin, C. (1991). Time urgency: The construct and its measurement. *Journal of Applied Psychology, 76*, 644–657.

Levine, R. V., & Bartlett, K. (1984). Pace of life, punctuality, and coronary heart disease in six countries. *Journal of Cross-Cultural Psychology, 15*, 223–255.

Levine, R. V., West, L. J., & Reis, H. T. (1980). Perceptions of time and punctuality in the United States and Brazil. *Journal of Personality and Social Psychology, 38*, 541–550.

Menon, S., Narayanan, L., & Spector, P. E. (1996). The relation of time urgency to occupational stress and health outcomes for health care professionals. In: C. D. Spielberger, I. G. Sarason, Associates (Eds), *Stress and emotion: Anxiety, anger, and curiosity* (Vol. 16, pp. 127–142). London: Taylor & Francis.

Onken, M. H. (1999). Temporal elements of organizational culture and impact on firm performance. *Journal of Managerial Psychology, 14*, 231–243.

Palmer, D. K. (1997). *Harmonic temporality: An investigation of the dimensionality of polychronicity and its implications for individuals and organizations.* Unpublished doctoral dissertation, Purdue University, West Lafayette, IN.

Palmer, D. K., & Schoorman, F. D. (1999). Unpacking the multiple aspects of time in polychronicity. *Journal of Managerial Psychology, 14,* 323–344.

Perlow, L., Okhuysen, G., & Repenning, N. (2002). The speed trap: Exploring the relationship between decision making and temporal context. *Academy of Management Journal, 45,* 931–955.

Price, V. A. (1982). *Type A behavior pattern: A model for research and practice.* New York: Academic Press.

Schriber, J. B., & Gutek, B. A. (1987). Some time dimensions of work: Measurement of an underlying aspect of organization culture. *Journal of Applied Psychology, 72,* 642–650.

Slocombe, T. E. (1999). Applying the theory of reasoned action to the analysis of an individual's polychronicity. *Journal of Managerial Psychology, 14,* 313–324.

Slocombe, T. E., & Bluedorn, A. C. (1999). Organizational behavior implications of the congruence between preferred polychronicity and experienced work-unit polychronicity. *Journal of Organizational Behavior, 20,* 75–99.

Spector, P. E., Van Katwyk, P. T., Brannick, M. T., & Chen, P. Y. (1997). When two factors don't reflect two constructs: How item characteristics can produce artifactual factors. *Journal of Management, 23,* 659–677.

Spence, J. T., Helmreich, R. L., & Pred, R. S. (1987). Impatience versus achievement strivings on the Type A pattern: Differential effects on students' health and academic achievement. *Journal of Applied Psychology, 72,* 522–528.

Usunier, J. G. (1991). Business time perceptions and national cultures: A comparative survey. *Management International Review, 31,* 197–217.

Waller, M. J., Conte, J. M., Gibson, C., & Carpenter, M. (2001). The impact of individual time perception on team performance under deadline conditions. *Academy of Management Review, 26,* 586–600.

Waller, M. J., Giambatista, R. C., & Zellmer-Bruhn, M. (1999). The effects of individual time urgency on team polychronicity. *Journal of Managerial Psychology, 14,* 244–256.

PREFERENCES, BEHAVIORS, AND STRATEGIES IN MULTIPLE-TASK PERFORMANCE

Mary J. Waller

ABSTRACT

Given the environmental turbulence surrounding organizations today, polychronicity – the preference to attend to more than one task simultaneously – may be an increasingly important characteristic of individuals, groups, and organizations. Polychronicity and its behavioral counterpart, multitasking, are inextricably linked, but high levels of polychronicity may not lead to productive multitasking behavior, as multitasking can vary tremendously in its implementation and effectiveness. This commentary offers further clarification of the differences between polychronicity and multitasking, and it explores the role of task performance strategies in multitasking behavior.

INTRODUCTION

This commentary examines two issues discussed by Allen Bluedorn and Kimberly Jaussi (this volume): polychronicity and multitasking. After introducing this focus, it discusses Bluedorn and Jaussi's suggestion of a

Multi-Level Issues in Organizations and Time
Research in Multi-Level Issues, Volume 6, 239–247
Copyright © 2007 by Elsevier Ltd.
All rights of reproduction in any form reserved
ISSN: 1475-9144/doi:10.1016/S1475-9144(07)06011-0

"speed requirement" for the definition of multitasking behavior, and then suggests some fundamental questions regarding the identification of simultaneity in multiple-task performance. After presenting a discussion of multitasking strategies – strategies that may influence overall performance of individuals and teams – the commentary closes by echoing Bluedorn and Jaussi's caveats for practitioners.

Bluedorn and Jaussi's work provides a solid and comprehensive multi-level overview of organizationally relevant temporal constructs. Perhaps the most important concepts they discuss are the preference of polychronicity and the behavior of multitasking, and the distinction between the two. This notion of importance is based on three points. First, good treatments of polychronicity have appeared in the organizational behavior literature over the past several years, providing the groundwork necessary for understanding the concept in organizational contexts. Second, as Bluedorn and Jaussi discuss, there is some evidence of volition associated with the behavioral manifestation of polychronicity, or multitasking. Some individuals may be better able than others to multitask when the need arises, which potentially transforms polychronicity from an interesting individual difference into a lever of adaptablity in organizations (Cotte & Ratneshwar, 1999). Third, polychronicity can be (and has been) studied at the individual, group, organizational, and national culture levels of analysis, setting the stage for a rich cross-level sharing of ideas, metaphors, and evidence regarding polychronicity and the behavior it motivates.

These three characteristics – existing work, adaptability, and multi-level relevance – help make polychronicity and multitasking worthy targets of inquiry. Additionally, given that the environments surrounding and within organizations are becoming increasingly turbulent and unpredictable, the ability of individuals, groups, and organizations to switch focus among tasks, projects, and programs adaptively – that is, to multitask – will continue to play an important role in determining their effectiveness at each level. The extent to which polychronicity, as a preference, motivates multitasking at and across each level of analysis also makes the preference a potentially potent organizational asset.

Of course, all multitasking behavior is not the same. *Good* multitasking resembles ballet, with near-seamless transitions among tasks. *Bad* multitasking resembles uncoordinated, unfocused flailing – what has been described on the team level as "losing the music" (Hackman, 1993, p. 48). Wide variations in actual multitasking behavior suggest possible differences in the task performance strategies underlying multiple-task performance. High polychronicity, even keeping all contextual factors equal, does not always lead to multitasking behavior; for example, perceptions of tasks and time may also act as a trigger for the need or desire to multitask, even for highly polychronic individuals (as discussed later in this commentary). Furthermore, when polychronicity does motivate multitasking, it may not always lead to the same quality of multitasking behavior.

Exploring such statements necessitates (1) commenting and building on Bluedorn and Jaussi's conceptualizations of polychronicity and multitasking, (2) considering the nature of simultaneity and tasks, and (3) examining various task performance strategies that underlie multiple-task performance. These are the three points of this commentary.

POLYCHRONICITY VERSUS MULTITASKING

Drawing from Bluedorn (2002, p. 51), Bluedorn and Jaussi (this volume) define polychronicity as "the extent to which people (1) prefer to be engaged in two or more tasks or events simultaneously and are actually so engaged (the preference strongly implying the behavior, and vice versa) and (2) believe their preference is the best way to do things." This definition suggests that polychronicity is at the same time a preference, a behavior, and a belief. However, the authors later suggest that "polychronicity by itself ... is just a preference for dealing with multiple tasks simultaneously."

Most of the recent work on polychronicity is aligned with the latter definition of polychronicity as a preference. For example, in their study of time congruity in organizations, Francis-Smythe and Robertson (2003, p. 308) define polychronicity as "a preference for doing more than one thing at a time." Similarly, Hecht and Allen (2005, p. 155) refer to polychronicity as a "preference for working on many things simultaneously as opposed to one at a time." Drawing from Hall (1983), Waller, Giambatista, and Zellmer-Bruhn (1999, p. 245), in their study of group-level multitasking, remark that "people with a polychronic orientation prefer to be involved with several tasks simultaneously." It seems relatively clear that polychronicity is generally regarded as a preference, and not as a behavior or belief.

What, then, is the relationship between polychronicity and multitasking? Polychronicity and multitasking behavior are most likely highly correlated, but not perfectly so, as Bluedorn and Jaussi point out, given that contextual determinates may influence opportunities or mandates for multitasking behavior. According to Bluedorn and Jaussi's argument, polychronicity is the preference for multitasking, and multitasking is the actual resultant behavior motivated by both the preference *and* a need for speedy task performance.

The assumption here is that multitasking behavior is "characterized by a sense of haste and (is) driven by a desire to get more done in less time." The authors, using a figure, go on to juxtapose speed and polychronicity to illustrate their combined influence, with only the condition of high polychronicity and high-speed requirements culminating in multitasking behavior.

The speed requirement in the authors' definition of multitasking becomes an important point when comparing their conceptualization with other work on multitasking behavior. Other research on multitasking does *not* include the requirement for speed or getting more done in less time as an integral part of the behavior. Instead, in this literature, multitasking is regarded simply as what the word describes: simultaneous performance of multiple tasks. Multitasking has been cited as a means for creating more task variety and decreasing boredom for workers (Lindbeck & Snower, 2000) and as an information retrieval strategy used by individuals searching (without haste) for information on the Internet (Spink, Park, Jansen, & Pedersen, 2006).

In organizational contexts, though, why would an individual engage in multitasking if such behavior was not mandated by a speed requirement? Without time constraints, would workers simply plod sequentially through one task at a time, even though they might be highly polychronic and have a *preference* to perform multiple tasks simultaneously? In such a situation, might not individuals engage in multitasking simply to alleviate boredom, combining easy tasks and languishing more time on interesting ones?

These questions underscore the practical reality of polychronicity's influence on behavior. Polychronicity may be a relatively stable individual difference, but its translation into enacted multitasking is highly dependent on an individual's perception of the tasks and context – for example, perceptions of boring work and other, more interesting task alternatives. This dependence does *not necessarily* include a perceived speed requirement. In organizational contexts, a speed requirement, like polychronicity, may be highly correlated with the incidence of multitasking behavior, but neither a speed requirement nor polychronicity (classic or accelerated) is absolutely necessary for multitasking behavior to occur. As a consequence, the definition of multitasking behavior should not include rapid task completion as a necessary component.

SIMULTANEITY

The definition of multitasking also requires a determination of simultaneity and a clear definition of tasks. Within what period of time must multiple tasks be performed for this activity to be deemed multitasking? What length of time serves as the denominator in the multitasking equation? Early studies of dichotic listening skills (e.g., Broadbent, 1958) focused on the ability of individuals to listen and attend to two sources of information simultaneously, with one source being fed into a speaker for the left ear and another source simultaneously being fed into a speaker for the right ear. Even under these conditions, researchers found that individuals could attend to one or the other source of information, but not truly attend to both simultaneously, although individuals could switch back and forth among information and tasks quite rapidly (Huey & Wickens, 1993, p. 217).

Thus, within what time period do we consider an individual, group, or organization to have multitasked? As Bluedorn and Jaussi rightly point out, polychronicity motivates "engaging in several tasks *during a given time period*" (this volume, my emphasis). But how should this time period be defined? Even the most monochronic of individuals can be described as multitasking if the time period is long enough or if the activities defined as tasks are minute enough. For example, a project may have core tasks with subtasks that have sub-subtasks. If an individual is juggling several subtasks each workday, yet making progress on only one task, should the behavior be classified as monotasking or multitasking?

Some researchers suggest that an observation period for data collection should be at least as long as the average length needed for one iteration of the behavior of interest to be completed (Weick, 1968). Although this rule of thumb does not address the definition of a task versus a subtask, perhaps it provides a starting point in defining the length of time needed to determine simultaneity. The definition of tasks, however, is most likely best left to the domain of the organizational participants themselves, whose experience of engagement and closure is probably the best indication of where work can be segmented into particular tasks and whose real experience of multitasking is, after all, idiosyncratic and perceptual. Given the same time and the same tasks, one person's experienced multitasking may be another person's experienced monotasking.

However, individuals perceive and segment work into tasks; tasks are not equivalent to skills, as Bluedorn and Jaussi (this volume) seem to suggest. Likewise, the usage of multiple skills within a given time is fundamentally different from the performance of multiple tasks. One task may require several different skills to complete – a situation that lends no support to the authors' suggestion that polychronic individuals will be more satisfied if tasks involve multiple skills. Theoretically, switching among skills may provide a sense of efficacy, but it does not provide a switch in terms of psychological task engagement.

MULTITASKING STRATEGIES

Beyond specifying differences between polychronicity and multitasking, there remains the fact that all multitasking is not equal. One can imagine an inverted U-shaped relationship between multitasking and effectiveness, where the right side of the curve represents the unfocused, frenetic-but-not-necessarily-faster, inefficient activity mentioned earlier. But the point made by Bluedorn and Jaussi, and reinforced by research findings, is that polychronic individuals derive a certain satisfying, energizing motivation from multitasking, representing the left side of that inverted U-shaped relationship. Thus one reason we see good and bad examples of multitasking in organizations may be due to individual polychronic preferences and their resultant effects on satisfaction and motivation, assuming that satisfaction and motivation have positive effects on multitasking ability.

Other evidence suggests that task performance strategies may influence multitasking effectiveness, above and beyond the influence of polychronicity. Multitasking involves frequent starting and stopping and starting again of multiple tasks within a certain defined length of time. Each such re-engagement of a task imposes a "cognitive overhead" during which one must "get back into" the task at hand. This suggests that the more frequently tasks are switched, the higher the cognitive overhead paid in terms of cognitive resources available for task performance. Polychronic individuals who switch among tasks too often may, therefore, pay a cognitive price in terms of overall effectiveness.

Similarly, assuming the absence of an imposed task performance sequence, good multitaskers may be those individuals who excel at "chunking" tasks together based on their similarity on some dimensions, similar to the chunking strategy detailed in cognitive science problem-solving studies (see Koch, Philipp, & Gade, 2006, for an example). For example, an individual may choose to perform verbal tasks during one segment of time and writing tasks during the next segment and so on, versus attempting to switch rapidly among tasks that require very different skill sets. This strategy may help avoid cognitive overhead in terms of disengaging and re-engaging different skills, accessing different information stores, or switching among other cognitive or physical resources needed for task performance.

Conversely, research by Wickens and Carswell (1995) suggests that task performance strategies that overload one cognitive resource, such as auditory resources, with multiple-task inputs result in inefficient task performance. A task performance strategy that spreads multiple tasks over visual, auditory, and motor resources over time may result in better overall performance. Given a certain context and task characteristics, whether a chunking strategy or a strategy that distributes the workload across task dimensions is more effective is ultimately an empirical question.

Another strategy for dealing with multiple simultaneous tasks, also described by Wickens, is to interleave time sharing with time swapping (Wickens, 1991). Time sharing is the truly simultaneous performance of multiple tasks (e.g., talking and writing simultaneously), whereas time swapping is the sequential performance (but not necessarily completion) of tasks. Sharing and swapping strategies have also been used to describe multitasking at the group level of analysis (Waller, 1997). Engaging in time swapping when resources begin to become overloaded and then returning to time sharing when resources are adequate may be an adaptive and efficient task performance strategy employed by adroit multitaskers at all levels of analysis.

A final multitasking strategy has been suggested both by the work of Waller (1999) and in research by Ishizaka, Marshall, and Conte (2001). Waller found that higher-performing flight crews were significantly more likely than other crews to weigh and reprioritize tasks after unexpected nonroutine events. Similarly, Ishizaka and colleagues reported that individuals who were high in some components of the Type A behavior pattern were more likely than other participants to devote more time to completing tasks assigned a high priority in a multitasking situation. Thus assigning accurate priorities to tasks and expending time and effort based on that task prioritization would seem to be an effective multitasking strategy.

CONCLUSION

Today more than ever, individuals, groups, and organizations must attend to multiple tasks simultaneously. The likely motivation of multitasking behavior by polychronicity now seems clear – so clear, in fact, that we run the risk of embedding the definition of multitasking either within polychronicity itself or within elements of the contexts in which multitasking behavior is most often witnessed. This, I believe, would be a mistake, even though I have also referred to group-level multitasking in the past as a group's "polychronic behavior" (Waller et al., 1999, p. 245). We know that contextual characteristics such as time pressure are filtered through layers of perception and shared cognition and that such filtering can lead to very different interpretations of temporal factors (Waller, Conte, Gibson, & Carpenter, 2001). It is, indeed, highly likely that perceived time pressure is a catalyst for multitasking behavior at multiple levels. Until that likelihood reaches 1.0, however, the relationships among polychronicity, time pressure, and multitasking behavior should continue to be described as "typically highly correlated."

Why make such an issue of this definitional separation? New research concerning person–job fit provides compelling evidence regarding the possible benefits of placing polychronic individuals in time-pressured multitasking job environments. This is information that organizations could potentially act upon immediately, particularly due to its congruence with managers' own observations and experience. However, and following Bluedorn and Jaussi's well-formulated caveats, unless managers are made aware (1) that polychronicity may not always lead to multitasking behavior and (2) why all multitasking behavior is not necessarily effective, what could be a potentially effective practice is likely to result in frustrating, equivocal results. Indeed, preliminary results from new field research suggest that in some multiple-task contexts in organizations, monochronicity – not polychronicity – is more closely associated with team effectiveness (Kaplan, 2006), underscoring the need for more and careful context-based research in this area.

REFERENCES

Bluedorn, A. C. (2002). *The human organization of time: Temporal realities and experience.* Stanford, CA: Stanford University Press.

Bluedorn, A. C., & Jaussi, K. S. (this volume). Organizationally relevant dimensions of time across levels of analysis. In: F. Dansereau & F. J. Yammarino (Eds), *Multi-level issues in organizations and time* (Vol. 6). Oxford: Elsevier.

Broadbent, D. (1958). *Perception and communication.* Oxford, UK: Pergamon.

Cotte, J., & Ratneshwar, S. (1999). Juggling and hopping: What does it mean to work polychronically?. *Journal of Managerial Psychology, 14,* 184–204.

Francis-Smythe, J. A., & Robertson, I. T. (2003). The importance of time congruity in the organization. *Applied Psychology: An International Review, 52*(2), 298–321.

Hackman, J. R. (1993). Teams, leaders, and organizations: New directions for crew-oriented flight training. In: E. L. Wiener, B. G. Kanki & R. L. Helmreich (Eds), *Cockpit resource management* (pp. 47–69). Orlando, FL: Academic Press.

Hall, E. T. (1983). *The dance of life: The other dimension of time.* Garden City, NY: Anchor Press.

Hecht, T. D., & Allen, N. J. (2005). Exploring links between polychronicity and well-being from the perspective of person–job fit: Does it matter if you prefer to do only one thing at a time?. *Organizational Behavior and Human Decision Processes, 98,* 155–178.

Huey, B. M., & Wickens, C. P. (1993). *Workload transition: Implications for individual and team performance.* Washington, DC: National Academy Press.

Ishizaka, K., Marshall, S. P., & Conte, J. M. (2001). Individual differences in attentional strategies in multitasking situations. *Human Performance, 14*(4), 339–358.

Kaplan, S. (2006). *The affective bases of team performance during nonroutine events: The case of nuclear power plant control room crews.* Unpublished doctoral dissertation.

Koch, I., Philipp, A. M., & Gade, M. (2006). Chunking in task sequences modulates task inhibition. *Psychological Science, 17*(4), 346–350.

Lindbeck, A., & Snower, D. J. (2000). Multitask learning and the reorganization of work: From tayloristic to holistic organization. *Journal of Labor Economics, 18*(3), 353–376.

Spink, A., Park, M., Jansen, B. J., & Pedersen, J. (2006). Multitasking during web search sessions. *Information Processing and Management, 42*, 264–275.

Waller, M. J. (1997). Keeping the pins in the air: How work groups juggle multiple tasks. In: M. Beyerlein, D. Johnson & S. Beyerlein (Eds), *Advances in interdisciplinary studies of work teams* (Vol. 4, pp. 217–247). Greenwich, CT: JAI Press.

Waller, M. J. (1999). The timing of adaptive group responses to nonroutine events. *Academy of Management Journal, 42*, 127–137.

Waller, M. J., Conte, J. M., Gibson, C. G., & Carpenter, M. A. (2001). The impact of individual time perception on team performance under deadline conditions. *Academy of Management Review, 26*, 586–600.

Waller, M. J., Giambatista, R. C., & Zellmer-Bruhn, M. E. (1999). The effects of individual time urgency on group polychronicity. *Journal of Managerial Psychology, 14*(3/4), 244–256.

Weick, K. E. (1968). Systematic observational methods. In: G. Lindzey & E. Aronson (Eds), *Handbook of social psychology* (pp. 357–451). Reading, MA: Addison-Wesley.

Wickens, C. D. (1991). Processing resources and attention. In: D. Damos (Ed.), *Multiple-task performance* (pp. 3–34). London: Taylor & Francis.

Wickens, C. D., & Carswell, C. M. (1995). The proximity compatibility principle: Its psychological foundation and relevance to display design. *Human Factors, 37*, 473–494.

TIME AND THE CHALLENGE OF TEMPORAL CONCEPTS

Allen C. Bluedorn and Kimberly S. Jaussi

ABSTRACT

Addressing the challenges of temporal concepts in organizations involves precise measurement and clear definitions. In this essay, we propose a number of future research ideas generated by Waller and Conte's (this volume) thought-provoking essays. Our hope in presenting these ideas is that future studies consider them in efforts to further close the definitional and measurement gaps in current research on temporal variables in organizations. In particular, we invite scholars to consider the implications of the dimensionality of polychronicity, of context on temporal variables, and of temporal variables interacting together.

INTRODUCTION

Considering temporal constructs in organizational settings presents challenges not unlike other types of organizational research. Questions of how to measure constructs are omnipresent, and thus Conte's (this volume) review of extant temporally related measurement scales across multiple levels of analysis is and will continue to be a valuable resource for scholars interested in examining temporal constructs and their influence in

Multi-Level Issues in Organizations and Time
Research in Multi-Level Issues, Volume 6, 249–255
Copyright © 2007 by Elsevier Ltd.
ISSN: 1475-9144/doi:10.1016/S1475-9144(07)06012-2

organizations. Because of the breadth of variables across different levels discussed by Conte (this volume), scholarly investigations of these constructs will be more accessible for future study. Waller's (this volume) efforts are also aimed at furthering the study of temporal variables, and she provides a detailed discussion of two specific temporal variables: polychronicity and multitasking. Scholars looking for a rich research agenda have great opportunities to follow up on both Waller's (this volume) and Conte's (this volume) comments; we agree strongly with them that further empirical research is needed in a variety of temporally related domains at a variety of levels of analyses.

POLYCHRONICITY

Waller (this volume) and Conte (this volume) both raise questions about the field's conceptualization of polychronicity and its components. As they both discuss, research has measured polychronicity in a variety of ways; some scholars have examined individual preferences for polychronicity, while others have considered it as polychronic behavior. To these points, Conte (this volume) also described how polychronicity has been considered, not just as one or the other, but rather as comprising three parts: preferences as well as context and time tangibility.

Given these inconsistencies, Conte's (this volume) point about the need for future research need to explore the dimensionality of polychronicity is an excellent one, and we agree that more empirical research is necessary to determine if polychronicity is a higher-order factor consisting of several different dimensions. In tackling this question, researchers will have to decide what the dimensions might be – for example, is it captured by a traditional framework of beliefs, attitudes, and behaviors, as Conte (this volume) notes that Slocombe (1999) suggested more research explore? Where do the preferences, context, and time tangibility fall in with respect to those dimensions? Indeed, extensive future empirical work is necessary to build on these questions and attempt to address these recurring thoughts about the underlying dimensionality of polychronicity at the individual level. From there, questions about whether that structure of polychronicity holds at higher levels of analysis can be considered.

Our personal beliefs are that polychronicity is much as it was first recognized and conceptualized by Hall (1981, 1983), as both a preference and a behavior. Hall's emphasis on observation as a technique for study reinforces the point that actual behavior is a critical element of polychronicity. From its formal introduction under the label of "monochronism" (Hall, 1981, p. 153), through what may be his final published statement on the topic (Bluedorn, 1998, p. 110), Hall has included and emphasized actual behavior in the polychronicity concept. Consequently, we believe any future work on polychronicity must trace its roots back to Hall's original conceptualization, and not stray from it without first theoretically developing a superior framework.

Our belief that polychronicity includes both preferences and behaviors is supported empirically by psychometric data about the Index of Polychronic Values (IPV) (Bluedorn, Kalliath, Strube, & Martin, 1999), which, when modified and shortened versions are included in the count, may be the most frequently used psychometric instrument to measure polychronicity in organizational research (e.g., Bluedorn, 2002, in press; Bluedorn & Martin, in press; Carraher, Cuthbert, & Carraher, 2004; Conte & Gintoft, 2005; Conte & Jacobs, 2003; Conte, Rizutto, & Steiner, 1999; Hecht & Allen, 2005; Nonis, Teng, & Ford, 2005; Onken, 1999; Palmer & Schoorman, 1999). (As Conte (this volume), notes, both individual and group versions of the IPV were developed.) While this scale includes measures of both dimensions (as noted by both Conte (this volume) and Waller (this volume)), some scholars have chosen to examine just the preference aspect of polychronicity without providing any rationale for why they strayed from Hall's original conception.

In following our prompts (and those of Conte (this volume) and Waller (this volume)) to further investigate the dimensionality of polychronicity, future research may want to consider the extant empirical support for polychronicity as one construct consisting of both preferences and behavior. For example, one of the items in the full 10-item version of the IPV is as follows: "When I work by myself, I usually work on one project at a time" (Bluedorn et al., 1999, p. 227; for the group version, "we" is substituted for "I" and "ourselves" is substituted for "myself"). As a simple description of behavior (and not an expression of a preference), in factor analyses it loads very well with the other nine items that express either a preference or a belief. According to Bluedorn et al.'s (1999) original report on this scale's psychometric development, in three separate samples confirmatory factor analysis of the scale revealed factor loadings for this item that were neither the highest nor the lowest in each sample, thereby indicating that the item loads solidly on the underlying factor. Similarly, Carraher, Cuthbert III, and Carraher (2004) performed principal components analyses on each of eight samples (one sample of American college students with the remaining seven samples being drawn from Chinese small business owners and small business owners in the United States, Ukraine, Poland, Hungary, Bulgaria, and Mexico). Strong single-factor solutions were obtained in each sample, with the factor loadings of the "When I work by myself" item again being neither the highest nor the lowest in each sample, but loading solidly in the factor solution for each sample. These factor analysis results strongly support the construct as *both* a preference *and* a behavior. Additionally, the IPV has produced alpha coefficients that range from the high 0.70 s to the mid 0.90 s (see Bluedorn et al., 1999; Carraher et al., 2004), even when reduced to six items but retaining the "When I work by myself" item (see Conte & Gintoft, 2005; Conte & Jacobs, 2003).

Although the aforementioned research suggests a single polychronicity factor, perhaps the addition of more behaviorally oriented items to the scale – currently but one item out of the scale's 10 items describes actual behavior rather than a preference or a belief – will help answer the question of whether polychronicity is a unidimensional or multidimensional higher-order construct. And, if polychronicity is multidimensional, how many dimensions are there? One plausible model might have two, preferences and behavior, while another plausible model might include three: preferences, behaviors, and beliefs. Another plausible model is Palmer and Schoorman's (1999) model as Conte (this volume) describes it, with context and time tangibility. Future research will have to untangle which of these models might best represent the construct, and also how the different models may or may not be related to one another. Finally, we wonder if socialization and basic life skills in the modern world may have added other components as well. As such, we would welcome future empirical studies that explore these kinds of possibilities.

OTHER RESEARCH AREAS

For us, Waller's (this volume) and Conte's (this volume) comments sparked another agenda for researchers interested in conducting group and organizational level research, and that is *the process by which* temporal variables become norms. As Conte (this volume) notes, research on groups suggests that punctuality norms occur at these higher levels, and thus we wonder about the process by which these preferences and behaviors, for all the temporal variables discussed in our chapter, become norms in groups and organizations. In order to investigate this further, research will have to adopt a process approach toward the consideration of these variables, thereby providing all of us interested in these temporal variables with some understanding of the mechanisms that do or do not morph these variables into cognate higher-level phenomena.

Additionally, Conte (this volume) notes the need for more research to be conducted on urgency, and we strongly second his point. We also urge future research to consider the relationship between speed/urgency and the underlying dimensions of polychronicity, which would thereby help address the concern Waller (this volume) raises about the relationship between polychronicity and multitasking. Waller's (this volume) point that multitasking could be caused by factors other than speed (e.g., boredom) prompted us to consider the possibility of "substitutes" for speed. We wondered if boredom might be a substitute for speed in the two by two model that we presented in Fig. 1 in our original chapter (Bluedorn & Jaussi, this volume). We also were intrigued by the prospect of multiple causes of multitasking, as well as by the possibility of boredom (and likely other variables) working in an interactive fashion with speed and polychronicity. We did, however, keep circling back to the fact that we cannot imagine monochronic individuals multitasking more than their preference levels would suggest unless other factors led them to do so, which leads us to urge future research to investigate these possibilities empirically.

One very interesting agenda for future research to explore is how the different dimensions of urgency, Conte (this volume) refers to, relate to the underlying dimensions of polychronicity (should underlying dimensions be found). As Conte (this volume) describes, the different dimensions of urgency have been found to relate differently with other variables. Future research might continue to determine if these differential relationships also hold with respect to interacting relationships with the other temporal variables, and if so, at which levels of analysis those relationships do hold.

Waller's (this volume) work also prompts us to urge researchers to consider additional questions in future explorations in this area, questions that focus on the impact of *contexts*, which allow for the full expression of temporal preferences and behaviors at different levels of analysis. Specifically, are the contexts or tasks that allow for the full expression of temporal preferences and behaviors the most effective and/or efficient? Under what conditions are contexts and tasks preferable if they are characterized by temporal patterns opposing the focal entity's preferences and behaviors? Underlying both these questions is the fundamental question of, "By which processes do contexts and tasks with their corresponding temporal characteristics impact individuals and groups, given such individuals' and groups' respective preferences for temporal behaviors?"

CONCLUSION

We wish to thank both Mary Waller (this volume) and Jeff Conte (this volume) for their engaging discussions of the conceptualization and measurement of temporal constructs. We found them both to be stimulating and we are confident that their comments have raised many questions for future empirical research to resolve. We hope that through the integration of their thoughts we have also raised questions for future studies to address. We are certain that through the thoughtful consideration of their comments, we have pushed our own thinking about these issues forward.

Our goal in this essay was to clarify our conceptualization of polychronicity as one that follows the construct's historical roots, and to thoughtfully describe why we feel multitasking is indeed one aspect of polychronicity. Another goal of ours was to encourage future research to build on Waller's (this volume) important point that matching individuals and work contexts based on the similarity of their respective polychronicities may not always produce the optimal outcomes (however the outcomes are defined). One final goal we had was to encourage researchers to use Conte's (this volume) work as a guide for measuring the effects of time as likely *combinations* of temporal variables. To investigate such combinations, these temporal variables need to be measured in some manner, and Conte (this volume) provides the interested scientist with a cogent primer about such measures. Future research is needed to identify the processes by which the combinations of these temporal variables have their effects. We strongly encourage such research, and we hope that polychronicity and other temporal variables will be the subject of many such future investigations.

REFERENCES

Bluedorn, A. C. (1998). An interview with anthropologist Edward T. Hall. *Journal of Managerial Inquiry, 7*, 109–115.

Bluedorn, A. C. (2002). *The human organization of time.* Stanford, CA: Stanford University Press.

Bluedorn, A. C. (in press). Polychronicity, individuals, and organizations. *Research in the sociology of organizations.*

Bluedorn, A., & Jaussi, K. (this volume). Organizationally relevant dimensions of time across levels of analysis. In: F. Dansereau & F. J. Yammarino (Eds), *Multi-level issues in organizatins and time* (Vol.6). Oxford: Elsevier.

Bluedorn, A. C., Kalliath, T. J., Strube, M. J., & Martin, G. D. (1999). Polychornicity and the inventory of polychronic values (IPV): The development of an instrument to measure a fundamental dimension of organizational culture. *Journal of Managerial Psychology*, *14*, 205–230.

Bluedorn, A. C., & Martin, G. (in press). The time frames of entrepreneurs. *Journal of Business Venturing*.

Carraher, S. M., Cuthbert III, S., & Carraher, S. C. (2004). A comparison of polychronicity levels among small business owners and non-business owners in the U.S., China, Ukraine, Poland, Hungary, Bulgaria, and Mexico. *International Journal of Family Business*, *1*, 97–101.

Conte, J. M. (this volume). Measuring temporal constructs across multiple levels of analysis. In: F. Dansereau, & F. Yammarino (Eds). *Research in multi-level issues* (Vol. 6). Amsterdam: Elsevier.

Conte, J. M., & Gintoft, J. N. (2005). Polychronicity, big five personality dimensions, and sales performance. *Human Performance*, *18*, 427–444.

Conte, J. M., & Jacobs, R. R. (2003). Validity evidence linking polychronicity and big five personality dimensions to absence, lateness, and supervisory performance ratings. *Human Performance*, *16*, 107–130.

Conte, J. M., Rizzuto, T. E., & Steiner, D. D. (1999). A construct-oriented analysis of individual-level polychronicity. *Journal of Managerial Psychology*, *14*, 269–287.

Hall, E. T. (1981). *The silent language*. New York: Anchor Books (Original work published in 1959.).

Hall, E. T. (1983). *The dance of life: The other dimension of time*. Garden City, NY: Anchor Press.

Hecht, T. D., & Allen, N. J. (2005). Exploring links between polychronicity and well-being from the perspective of person-job-fit: Does it matter if you prefer to do only one thing at a time?. *Organizational Behavior and Human Decision Processes*, *98*, 155–178.

Nonis, S. A., Teng, J. K., & Ford, C. W. (2005). A cross-cultural investigation of time management practices and job outcomes. *International Journal of Intercultural Relations*, *29*, 409–428.

Onken, M. H. (1999). Temporal elements of organizational culture and impact on firm performance. *Journal of Managerial Psychology*, *14*, 231–243.

Palmer, D. K., & Schoorman, F. D. (1999). Unpackaging the multiple aspects of time in polychronicity. *Journal of Managerial Psychology*, *14*, 323–344.

Slocombe, T. E. (1999). Applying the theory of reasoned action to the analysis of an individual's polychronicity. *Journal of Managerial Psychology*, *14*, 313–322.

Waller, M. J. (this volume). Preferences, behaviors, and strategies in multiple task performance. In: F. Dansereau, & F. Yalmmarino (Eds). *Research in multi-level issues* (Vol. 6). Amsterdam: Elsevier.

PART IV:
TIMESCAPES

TIMESCAPES: A MULTI-LEVEL APPROACH FOR UNDERSTANDING TIME USE IN COMPLEX ORGANIZATIONS

Richard Reeves-Ellington

ABSTRACT

Organizational studies of time tend to be done by academic researchers rather than practitioners. This chapter builds on academic research to provide a practitioner perspective by reviewing time situated in theory and constructing two phenotypes: timescapes of business and social time. These timescapes are defined by six dimensions, each with a social and business time parameter. Organizational business and social timescapes have different functions and applications. Timescapes, with their concomitant dimensions and sets of parameters, are used differently by senior managers, middle managers, and entry-level managers. Three multi-level approaches (self, dyadic, and social relationships), composition theory, and compilation theory confirm these three managerial timescape usages. After a review of the theoretical bases of the timescape constructs and a brief discussion of the grounded, anthropological, research methodology used in the study, this chapter applies timescape theory and models to an extended time case study of the Procter & Gamble Company that frames the company's timescape understanding and use from a practitioner's view.

Multi-Level Issues in Organizations and Time
Research in Multi-Level Issues, Volume 6, 259–316
Copyright © 2007 by Elsevier Ltd.
All rights of reproduction in any form reserved
ISSN: 1475-9144/doi:10.1016/S1475-9144(07)06013-4

INTRODUCTION

Although researchers have developed multiple time theories in organizational studies (Blount & Janicik, 2001; Boden, 1997; George & Jones, 2000; Reeves-Ellington, 1997), a coherent and integrated theory of organizational time is lacking (Abbott, 2001; Adam, 1995, 1998; Albert, 1995; Bluedorn & Denhardt, 1988; Clark, 1985; Anon, 2002; George & Jones, 2000; Mainemelis, 2001; "P&G's Focus," 2002). Goodman (2000) set a goal of "understanding time in organizations, with a focus on spanning individual, group, organizational and inter-organizational units of analysis." Clark (2000), George and Jones (2000), and Goodman, Lawrence, Ancona, and Tushman (2002) have all argued that the study of organizations must include the element of time. Ancona, Okhuysen, and Perlow (2001) and Mitchell and James (2001) offered methodologies and theories that further the understanding of time in organizations. These and other studies of time focus on the theory (Abbott, 2001; Adam, 1995, 1998; Albert, 1995; Clark, 1985; George & Jones, 2000; Mitchell & James, 2001) and illuminate the ways in which time affects organizations (Bluedorn & Denhardt, 1988; Mainemelis, 2001) and people, both individually and as groups in organizations (Blount & Janicik, 2001; Boden, 1997; Covey, 1989; Reeves-Ellington, 1999b). Such studies tend to examine time from an outsider research perspective.

While these viewpoints offer insights and structures for studying organizational time, understanding of specific time usage comes from insider and practitioner information. By examining time through the eyes of organizational actors, both researchers and practitioners can make organizational rhythms of time transparent and use them to promote successful organizational activities (Adam, 1995). While the results reflect organizational idiosyncrasies, they also support Adam's (1995) contention that a theoretical model for examining time in organizations is feasible.

This chapter has two objectives

1. To create a model of time.
2. To demonstrate the model's viability to examine insider information and views through a case study.

To satisfy the first objective, using the assumption that every organization uses time for both business and social organization, a model is proposed that is based on two organizational time phenotypes: business timescape and social timescape. This model expands the timescapes through inclusion of multiple dimensions and polar-opposite parameters for each dimension. The chapter then analyzes the model using three multi-level approaches.

Specifically, each timescape and its accompanying dimensions are viewed as being under the leadership of senior, mid-level, or entry-level managers, who are empowered by organizational structure to determine when a specific timescape and accompanying dimension and parameters will rely primarily on self, dyadic, or social relationships. Composition and compilation theory, applied longitudinally, confirms that timescape usage contributes to organizational integration or organizational dysfunction.

To accomplish the second objective, the time model and multi-level applications are explicated in an extended Procter & Gamble (P&G) case, using grounded and anthropological research methods.

TIMESCAPES

Proposition 1. Two complex time constructs interact within organizations.

The systematic study of organizational timescapes requires a model. Fig. 1 shows the proposed model for this chapter. This model reflects the business and social timescape phenotypes, along with their six dimensions: type, movement, use, action, management, and work habits. Each of these dimensions has a bipolar set that informs the understanding of the time dimensions of business and social timescapes.

Understanding the importance of timescapes requires a detailed examination of organizational time. Bluedorn and Denhardt (1988) postulate two timescapes (fungible and epochal time), set boundaries for organizational tensions, and provide utilitarian dimensions (Adam, 1995, 1998; Bluedorn, 2002). Fungible and epochal time are complex constructs: they exist in all organizations, and they cover the ways that organizations experience time (Flanherty, 1999; Kern, 1983). The interplay of the tensions determines how organizations approach their activities and relationships in creating and sustaining successful commerce. According to Hatch (1997), while an organization and its members might only consciously acknowledge one type of timescape, they cannot live without the other. The two timescapes are inescapably intertwined, and both are required for an organization to function.

Based on the author's field discussions with organizational practitioners, these time constructs may be labeled as *business timescape* (fungible), which references the chartered outcomes of the organization (what they do), and *social timescape* (epochal), which celebrates human activities and interchanges (how they do what they do). These restatements of time provide greater ease of understanding to practitioners.

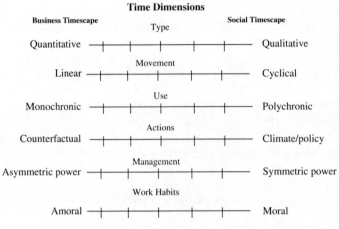

Fig. 1. Organizational Timescapes.

Social Timescape

Organizational social time, or sociotemporal time, as suggested by Fraser (1987) and Zeurubavel (1981), rests upon social and cultural constructions. Organizations socialize by establishing reciprocal, relational networks of people within specific organizations (Major, 2000). Such socialization takes place in constructed events and through integrative processes by exposing newcomers and insiders to company tradition and climate. Such indoctrination conforms to Clark's (2000) description of recurrent action patterns; such patterns feature sequences of actions that are (1) repeated, (2) distributed by communication and authority, (3) spread among several actors, (4) interlocked by role sets, (5) operated on tacit and unarticulated knowledge, and (6) created by emergent routines.

Specifically, social time is event time and concrete: it moves cyclically and attracts integrators who execute a variety of tasks simultaneously and who rely on climate and policy to maintain the present status quo through the use of diffuse, symmetric power. Social time is "lived" time (Minkowski, 1970), occurs in the present, and is public time in the organization (Zeurubavel, 1981). That is to say, time is in the events (Bluedorn, 2002) rather than events being in time. The operationalization of this concept is expressed in organizational rhythm through deliberate actions, paced by human interactions, and bounded by traditions (DiMaggio & Powell, 1983; Leblebici, Salancik, Copay, & King, 1991).

Business Timescape

Bluedorn and Denhardt (1988) expand on Clark's (2000) notion of clock time by stating that it is amenable to exact measurement, moves forward linearly, and flows evenly. Business time is private time (Zeurubavel, 1981) that focuses on individual merit and the future. Urgency and speed drive business time rhythms (Waller, Conte, Gibson, & Carpener, 2000). Certainly business time is the driving force behind organizations' quests to meet their chartered reasons for existing – that is, the business objectives for which they are formed. One can operationalize business time by postulating that (1) business time is even, is abstract, and moves linearly; (2) attracts monadic individuals who prefer to do tasks serially; and (3) uses the past counterfactually to change the future rapidly through the use of asymmetric power.

Timescape Dimensions

Proposition 2. Social and business timescapes have six dimensions in common: type, movement, use, action, management, and work habits.

Using specific organizational questions, organizational timescapes are operationalized through application of the six time dimensions of type, movement, use, actions, management, and work habits to practitioner actions (see Table 1). These questions and dimensions provide a framework for mapping social and business timescapes.

Table 1. Organizational Time Dimensions.

Questions	Dimensions of Time
How do I operate efficiently over time?	Type
How to I operate effectively over time?	
How do I get things off my desk or out the door when I should?	Movement
How do I keep people happy and aligned with company routines?	
Do we learn from the past or do we rely on traditions to determine our actions for the future?	Actions
Do we work better doing tasks serially?	Use
Do we work better in multitasking environments?	
Do we want to have "top management" determine company agendas or do we value broad participation in agenda setting?	Management
Do we operate on the principle of the priority of meeting organizational outcomes or do we operate on social core values?	Work habits

Understanding the complexity of time and its business and social manifestations allows organizational actors to use time more efficiently and effectively across organizations and their boundaries. While the timescapes and their six dimensions (each of which has bipolar parameters) are holistic, organizational actors initially study time serially by relating one organizational issue to one dimension. Applying the wrong time dimension to an issue results in erroneous information. Specific organizational questions relate to specific dimensions, which in turn require dimensions that bring further definition to and create greater clarity in the understanding of organizational time.

Parameters of Timescape Dimensions

Proposition 3. Each dimension is bounded by a social or business timescape parameter.

In time theory, dimensions are often expressed as one of three pairs that can be identified as polar opposites: linear–cyclical (Fine, 1998), qualitative–quantitative (Blount & Janicik, 2001; Bluedorn & Denhardt, 1988), and monochromic–polychronic (Bluedorn, 2000, 2002; Clark, 2000; Hall & Hall, 1987; Reeves-Ellington, 1992). Each of the bipolar indicators provides parameters to the type, movement, and use dimensions of the two timescapes, respectively. Thus we are still missing parameters for actions, management, and work habits. Table 2 proposes parameters for these dimensions: counterfactual–climate, asymmetric power–symmetric power, and amoral–moral, respectively. Each of the dimensions offers insight into organizational time understanding and is used at different levels of the organization and organizational enculturation.

Table 2. Timescape Dimensions and Parameters.

Dimensions	Parameters	
	Business Timescapes	Social Timescapes
Type	Quantitative	Qualitative
Movement	Linear	Cyclical
Use	Monochronic	Polychronic
Actions	Counterfactual	Climate
Management	Asymmetric power	Symmetric power
Work habits	Amoral	Moral

As shown in Table 2, while each timescape shares the same dimensions, the parameter for each is different. Bluedorn and Denhardt (1988) warn that these should not be treated as dichotomous options, but rather as parameters to timescape dimensions. Organizational actors must overcome a sense of dualism by acknowledging that the two timescapes, along with their dimensions and dimensional parameters, are interwoven at every organizational level and arise from the same source – a way of perceiving organizations as envisioned by the tasks they do and the manner in which they do them. A discussion of each time dimension and its social and business parameters follows.

Type of Time: Quantitative and Qualitative
Proposition 4. Business time is discrete, fixed, and universally measured, whereas social time is event driven and subjectively applied.

Quantitative time occurs in a business timescape and refers to clock time that is amenable to precise measurement via discrete division, is subject to a unitary interpretation, moves forward linearly, and flows evenly (Adam, 1998; Bluedorn & Denhardt, 1988). Clock time dominates the Western sense of time (Flanherty, 1999; Gell, 1992; Kern, 1983; McKay, 1968). Efficiency, as a measure of the speed of activities, becomes the objective of clock time use, with the ultimate goal of increasing the value of the firm.

Qualitative (event) time, as a measure of social timescapes, can follow different indeterminate event trajectories, can be subject to multiple interpretations (plurality of meaning), can flow discontinuously, and can be neither measured nor manipulated easily (Bluedorn & Denhardt, 1988). Organizing occurs in qualitative time by the building of consensually validated grammars for process and action, thereby creating organizational effectiveness (Clark, 2000; Giddens, 1984; Reed, 1992).

Movement of Time: Linear and Cyclical
Proposition 5. Organizational business activities flow from the past into the future, as measured by periodic monetary measures, whereas human social activities rely on celebratory, reoccurring, and seasonal events.

Sir Isaac Newton's view of linear time is a major feature of the Western cultural worldview. His mechanistic view of time portrays it as an absolute physical reality and infers that the passage of time is independent of consciousness. In the linear view, time flows like a conveyor belt that moves horizontally from past to present to future at the same unchangeable speed for all of us (Hall, 1983). Linear time is conceived of as an endless process, without beginning but created by a succession of events in which earlier events imply later ones and later events are consequences of earlier ones. Linear time has the ethos of unilateral determinism. Business timescapes are grounded in linear time.

Organizational business actions take place in linear time (Adam, 1995) – the past, present, or future – and each temporal location requires different temporal orientations and different abilities to project into the future through the use of the past and present. Koselleck (1985) suggests temporal categories of space of existence and of horizon of expectation to frame the past–present–future. The space of existence allows for the integration of the past into the present, whereas the horizon of the future reveals the way of thinking about the future. The space of existence constructs itself on a selectively remembered past.

Cyclical time springs from earth and life cycles (Hall & Hall, 1987). It is identified as variable and diurnal (Adam, 1995), seen through a cultural prism (Eliade, 1955), expressed through collective memory (Cohen & Bacdayan, 1994), and expressed as recurrent and periodic (Clark, 2000). Cyclical time is important only in social timescapes, because it is lived time that promotes stability and coherence through processes, such as social rites of passage, and discontinuous events, such as shifting homes or job changes. It has high emotion content. There are two ways of using cyclical time: nostalgia (Boym, 2001) and climate expressed as tradition (Reeves-Ellington, 1997, 1999b).

Use of Time: Monochronic and Polychronic

Proposition 6. Organizational business activities, moving from the past through the present and forecasted into the future, occur serially and quasi-independently one from the other. Organizational social activities often require multitasking.

Bluedorn (2002) argues that only polychronicity in human activities is possible in reality, and that the continuum is, in fact, one of the intensity and number of polychronic activities. The counterargument, as presented in this chapter, states that people prefer monochronic time usage when dealing with business activities, but accept polychronic time usage when interacting with people.

Monochronic time is single-tasked, controlling, imposed on activities, and short-term oriented (Hall & Hall, 1987), and it takes place in personal space. People who prefer monochronic activities tend to work on tight deadlines, are serially task oriented, work monadically, and avoid team activities. Statements such as "First things first," "I'll decide on priorities," and "One thing at a time" express the urge to work monochronically and monadically.

In contrast, polychronic time focuses on multitasking (undertaking two or more tasks simultaneously), outcomes, and the future. People who prefer polychronic work tend to change plans easily, develop more human relationships, have strong organizational commitment (Bluedorn, Kaufman, & Lane, 1992; Hall & Hall, 1987), and use public space as an extension of themselves. Such individuals prefer working integratively. Within organizations, especially within managerial ranks, monochronic behavior is encouraged early in one's career but a plethora of needs quickly causes managers to work in polychronic ways (Bluedorn, 2002).

Actions in Time: Counterfactual Thinking and Climate

Proposition 7. Counterfactual thinking activities lead to change, whereas working with climate and culture projects stability.

The term *counterfactual thinking* refers to classifying information that involves simulating alternatives to past or present factual events or circumstances (Roese, 1997). Each alternative then provides a causal explanation that may serve different functions in planning for future actions that may be preventive or predictive in nature (Byrne, 1997, 2002; Byrne & McEleney, 2000). Counterfactual thinking is the "what if ..." or "if only ..." thinking in which people often engage after some event or outcome has transpired. It has been shown to serve at least two functions: an affective function and a preparatory function (Sanna, 1996, 1998; Sanna & Turley-Ames, 1999). When people mull over the past and think about what might have been, they sometimes construct counterfactual "if only" alternatives or semi-factual "even if" alternatives (Byrne & McEleney, 2000; Sanna & Turley-Ames, 1999). *Additive counterfactuals* provide a new antecedent to the present that was not present in the "real" past. These additives then serve a preparative function, as future changes are predicated upon them. *Subtractive counterfactuals* are facts that are removed from the past in an attempt to reconstruct the current reality. They are affective in that they make the individual feel better by comparing reality to a less desirable outcome that might have occurred.

Within the framework of this study, counterfactual thinking is placed within the horizon of expectation and offers several alternative functions for constructing a future from the past. The two primary counterfactual dimensions are based on direction as it relates to outcomes

- *Upward* represents a more desirable state than expressed by the past reality.
- *Downward* represents a worse state than actuality.

Climate is the internal atmosphere of the organization (Burton, Jorgen, & Borge, 2002) that is grounded in its culture. Timescapes are inherent in all organizational cultures (Reeves-Ellington, 1995; Kluckholn & Strodtbeck, 1961) and acted out in organizational climate by key stakeholders. In other words, timescapes are embedded in organizational systems in ways that have an effect on groups and individuals (Ekvall, 1987; Joyce & Slocum, 1984; Koyes & Decotiis, 1991). Organizational climate, as expressed in timescapes and related activities, constitutes a part of the shared history, expectations, unwritten rules, and social mores that affect the behavior of everyone in an organization (Denison, 2002). More simply, organizational climate is a set of underlying beliefs that are always there to color the perceptions of actions and communications of organizational actors (Schneider, 1990).

The focus is on operational organizational understanding, which requires an examination of members' perceptions of observable practices (Reeves-Ellington, 1992, pp. 95, 97). Such perceptions and practices determine the organizational atmosphere of their workplace, including the complex mixture of norms, values, expectations, policies, and procedures that influence individual and group patterns of behavior.

Zammuto and Krackover (1991) and Burton et al. (2002) believe that organizational climate can be measured by underlying cultural factors. Burton et al. (2002) use two dimensions – tension and change – as the basis for such measurements. They use high and low tension to separate types of tension but generalize its understanding by including trust, conflict, morale, rewards, equity, leader credibility, and scapegoating. High tension is characterized by low trust, low morale, low leader credibility, and low sense of equity; low tension is just the opposite. Burton et al. (2002) posit two basic change modes: episodic and continuous. Furthermore, they classify four organizational types of outcomes, which measure (1) internal processes, (2) rational goals, (3) development, and (4) group activities. Their results explain tension and the resistance to change within a competing values framework and reach the following conclusions:

- The development climate has high trust, low tension, and low resistance to change.
- The rational climate has low trust, high tension, and low resistance to change.
- The internal process climate has low trust, high tension, and high resistance to change.
- The group climate has high trust, low tension, and high resistance to change.

Each of these change models informs organizational timescape preference selection. Those models that include low trust are likely to emphasize a business timescape, whereas those models with high trust will likely utilize a social timescape.

Management of Time: Asymmetric and Symmetric Power
Proposition 8. Organizational business decisions require asymmetric power relationships, whereas organizational social interactions are most successful when symmetric power is assumed.

Hobbes and Machiavelli provide the two significant foundations for each of the power sets – asymmetric and symmetric power. Hobbes is responsible for the Western mainstream power concepts of agency and episodic notions of power (i.e., asymmetric power). Based on the Hobbesian model, power-users seek precision and cast it in individualistic terms (Clegg, 1992). Machiavelli's concerns are quite different from those of Hobbes. To him, power is imprecise, contingent, strategic, and organizational (Clegg, 1992). Hobbes and his successors endlessly focus on what constitutes power and its consequences. Machiavelli and his successors have interpreted what power does.

Hobbes (1962) indirectly states that power comes from regulation "as being *regulated* by desire and design." When discussing what power actually is, he is more direct

> The greatest power is that which is compounded of the powers of men, united by consent in one person, natural or civil, that has the use of all their powers depending on his will. (Hobbes, 1962, p. 160)

Machiavelli states in *The Prince*

> it seemed more suitable to me to search after the effectual truth of the matter rather than its imagined one ... for there is such a gap between how one lives and how one ought to live that anyone who abandons what is done for what ought to be done learns his ruin rather than his preservation. (Griffin, 1991, p.52)

Machiavelli viewed power in the same pluralistic way as he did truth, as reflected in the preceding quote (Clegg, 1992), whereas Hobbes suggested theorized power within an agency model (Ball, 1978). Asymmetric power choice requires acceptance of agency as expressed as a single, predetermined power identification. By contrast, effectual or distributed power is characterized by multiple power centers with distributed agency. Both agency (asymmetric power) and pluralistic power (symmetric power) exist within organizations and compete for application (Griffin, 1991; Jackell, 1989). When operationalizing organizational time management, the model

presented in this chapter assumes that business time works on the consequences of power (Hobbesian) and social time works on the events requiring
power (Machiavellian).

Asymmetric power is reified and located in the leader's office, and it
radiates downward and outward. First, managerial alignment is based on
identification with the leader on issues of key interest and the leader's stated
values and idealized vision. The implication is that "I will attend to your
personal growth and competence but you must be loyal to me" (Kanungo &
Mendonca, 1996). Through consolidation of organizationally sanctioned
power, leaders want power used on their behalf, as discipline wielded to gain
obedience (Etzioni, 1975).

Hobbes and his successors relate concerns for power by way of a common
"agency model" in which ontologically autarchic individuals hold sway
(Ball, 1978). The agency of power in organizations is the organizational
senior person who wields authority. As Hobbesian sovereigns, such leaders
want a world of eurhythmic power (Clegg, 1992). The result is hierarchical
power, with asymmetric power at the apex of each hierarchy (Sinha, 1995).

Symmetric power follows the precepts of Machiavellian power: its use is
strategic for specific contexts and for specific purposes. As purveyors of power,
symmetric power users provide strategies that bind the organization in ways
that unify the organization and provide for wide organizational participation.

Symmetric power in organizations is reflective in that it comes from uniting
organizational members with the broader society. In this sense, successful use
of power is opaque. Heinze (1991), however, suggests that power usage is
intimately related and instrumental to solving vital problems of the community. Successful diffusion of symmetric power causes self-empowerment of
others and alignment of clients with organizational climate and culture.

Leaders using symmetric power encourage others to recreate themselves,
their organizations, and their societies (Pattee, 1989). Their social function
provides social structure understanding as supported by shared communal
myths. They put the benefit of others before their own needs for power
usage motivations that are less likely to be questioned (Heinze, 1991). The
results of such uses of power enhance the well-being of the whole rather than
a separate or particular part.

Within this context, people – both as individuals and as members of
organizations – are subordinate to the community and receive their power
through the agency of community. Power comes from the organization's
community and then by reference from inside the organization. Once agreed
by all actors, cultural morality, as organizationally agreed, creates self-
monitored discipline.

Work in Time: Amoral and Moral

Proposition 9. Companies practicing symmetric management power will select amoral time parameters that focus on business outcomes, whereas companies practicing asymmetric management power will select moral work parameters that focus on people.

An appreciation of amoral and moral time factors requires an understanding of the business task environments as well as the interactional, human, or social side of organizations. The tasks of business are amoral, but the social interactions needed to complete business tasks require morality. Where one spends the most time in organizational activities has a major impact on the individual and, hence, on amoral or morally related activities and behavior. Task and dialogue are both necessary in the modern market-driven organization, thus juxtaposing amoral and moral decisions within the overall organizational timescapes.

When asymmetric power is concentrated at the top of the organization and assumes responsibility for actions, agendas become paramount (Reeves-Ellington & Anderson, 1997a). The resultant agendas lead to the implementation of rational (or rationalized) actions in an effort to increase certainty, organizational uniformity, and centrally controlled individual behaviors. As Reeves-Ellington and Anderson (1997a) infer, the ethic in amorality becomes a business ethic whose interpretation flows from the top down to a generally abstract "workgroup." Such amorality of action lacks a personal relationship. All workgroups must pass through formal organizational circuits of power (Clegg, 1992). As Calvin Coolidge said in a public speech in Washington, DC, on January 17, 1925, "The business of business is business" (Drucker, 1955), and today this idea continues to drive the amoral ethic. Business communications and the more general business operational paradigm (Reeves-Ellington, 1996; Reeves-Ellington & Anderson, 1997a) rely on an "I–it" paradigm driving a producer mentality and strive to avoid social entanglements. Levitt (1958) summed up the business time user's position as follows: "The governing rule in industry should be that something is good only if it pays. Otherwise, it is alien and not permitted."

Pure business, as an ideal type, overemphasizes the economic tasks of wealth creation and their demands for growth, viability, and profitability. The reductionist assumption looks only at wage/price movements for goods, with the goal of acceptable profits as defined by various stakeholders in the organization (Reeves-Ellington & Anderson, 1997a). Task-time pressures are expressed in linear, clock expressions in terms of speed of completion and efficiency. Purely business concerns form the primary purpose of an organization, are transactional in nature, and are managed by laws, rules, and regulations. The development of successive layers and versions of imposed and rationalized legalisms discourages attempts to respond in socially responsible or moral ways.

The emergence of a market-oriented form of capitalism gave rise to new moral habits in the pursuit of profit and the way organizations would function in today's capitalistic systems (Haskell, 1985). Interactions between the modern state, modern capitalism, and the actors in both created a new causal attribution of social responsibility. How purely business matters are transacted became important. How business is done requires the concept of commerce that is based on principles and principled people (Atiyah, 1979), who have an image of a moral, interactive community in this type of organization. Moral behavior springs from a diffuse cultural climate, is internalized, and is highly interactional. Boehm (1993) and Reeves-Ellington and Anderson (1997a, 1997b) would place social timescapes within an older concept of commerce, which can never be morally neutral because of the active presence of persons who are constantly engaging with others through interpretations of others' needs and decisions that are driven by these interpretations. As Heinze (1991) suggests, modern organizations need a more holistic integration of earning a living and a cultural heritage of inwardly social knowledge. Actors' use of the timescapes dimensions of work and its business and social parameters help achieve this balance.

Summary of Timescapes

Timescape theory provides a rich set of concepts with which organizational time can be studied and understood. While timescapes, their dimensions, and their dimension parameters exist in complex organizations, they present researchers and practitioners with choices regarding the appropriate application of each timescape, the preference for a specific timescape dimension, and the parameter weighting that is most apt. While theory and conceptual frameworks inform both researcher and practitioner, they must be contextualized using other research methods and analytical tools. The next section considers such contextualizations.

MULTI-LEVEL TIMESCAPE ANALYSIS

Different levels and ranks of organizational actors use time differently, and each timescape dimension has a primary managerial level responsible for processing and determining the primary use of each time dimension and its parameters. Three traditional management levels (senior, middle, and entry) provide a starting base for multi-level organizational time analysis.

To better understand timescapes and their organizational importance, three categories of multi-level analysis will be examined. By triangulating on organizational time, both the researcher and the practitioner should gain a better understanding of organizational time as it applies to the individual, interpersonal relations, and organization social structures. Triangulation also facilitates an understanding of the ways in which time affects organizations.

The basic multi-level analysis includes individual (self), dyadic (between individuals), and social (organization or society) levels (Dansereau & Yammarino, 1998; Dansereau, Yammarino, & Kohles, 1999; Dansereau, Yammarino, & Markum, 1995; Reeves-Ellington, 2004b). Composition and compilation theories (Kozlowski & Klein, 2000; Kozlowski, Gully, Salas, & Cannnon-Bowers, 2000) and leadership (Dansereau & Yammarino, 1998) explain the manner in which time shapes organizational activities. They provide frameworks to show time usages that integrate people within organizations and time usages that might be organizationally dysfunctional. Composition and compilation also expose organizational processes and behaviors that are affected by time (Hunt, 2004; Hunt & Ropo, 1998; Lundberg, 2004; Mackenzie, 2004).

Situating the three multi-level analytical methods into longitudinal analysis brings an additional depth to complex organizational studies. Only through such an analysis does the richness of organizational time surface.

Multi-level Time Dimensions in Self, Dyadic, and Social Relationships

Conceptualization of time in a vacuum might provide an academic understanding of time but it does not aid a comprehension of organizational time as practiced in specific organizations by individual actors. Researchers and practitioners need to deconstruct the general theories of timescapes and reconstruct them in culturally grounded applications that pertain to specific organizations. The cultural foundations of organizational timescapes transcend defined-level contexts of hierarchy, but, given multi-level variations, the grounding should reflect not only researcher categories but also organizational actors' timescape perceptions. When reconceptualizing organizational timescapes, researchers should incorporate multi-level analysis to include levels of management (entry, middle, and senior), each level's self or dyadic use of time, and the nature, dimensions, and parameters of culturally determined organizational time constructs. As shown in Table 3, time use and definition vary by individual and group needs as well as by hierarchical organizational requirements.

Based on the current state of time studies, the author's experience as a manager, and his anthropological organizational research, the model introduced in this chapter posits that timescape dimensions of management and work habits are led by senior management. After deciding on a management style, senior managers shape themselves in ways that project the chosen managerial power style. Also, senior managers decide on organizational work styles that are either business or socially driven. They then attempt to socialize the rest of the organization in ways that support individual decisions. By comparison, mid-level managers have leadership of dimensions of action and use. Such managers expand on their monadic use of time by focusing on individual business skills but expand their dyadic interpersonal skills through the action dimension. Finally, successful entry-level personnel exhibit leadership along the time dimensions of type and movement. They are expected to master these dimensions by doing things in the "proper" organizational way, by demonstrating mastery of technical business skills, and by learning to work with an immediate supervisor. Only then are they considered qualified to move up in the managerial hierarchy.

Complex organizational needs drive the time leadership dimensions for each managerial level. New hires must learn how business is done and how to socialize in meaningful ways. Mid-level managers must demonstrate mastery of those skills learned during the entry-level years. Senior managers

Table 3.   Organization Multi-Level Business/Social Time Construct.

Levels of Organizational Time Leadership	Business/Social Timescapes	
	Timescape Dimensions	Dimension Parameters
Senior		
Self	Management	Asymmetric power – symmetric power
Social	Work	Amoral – moral
Middle		
Dyadic	Use	Monochronic – polychronic
Self	Actions	Counterfactual – climate
Entry		
Dyadic	Movement	Linear – cyclic
Self	Type	Quantitative – qualitative

must set cultural and climate parameters for how the organization will manage and how it will work.

Senior Managerial Levels

Senior management establishment of preferred managerial and work timescapes and their dimensions should show a bias to the organizational historic climate preference.

Senior managers use the aggregated time data for the constructs of both power and morality. They are responsible for supporting the existing organizational climate or, if desirous of change, for gaining organizational support at the other two managerial levels. Business and social structure maintenance or change requires the use of managerial power, either asymmetric or symmetric in ways that are congruent with past power usage. Also, only senior managers can maintain or develop a dominant organizational work habit climate that is either amoral or moral. These work habits and managerial time use choices are bounded by organizational tradition and use.

Senior managerial leadership sets the social climate for organizations and establishes the criteria for sustaining or altering a given organizational culture. A senior manager's execution of time usage for climate continuation or change constitutes his or her most meaningful use of organizational power. The choice of dimensional parameters is culturally influenced but ultimately is an individual choice of the CEO. Such choices may be driven by personal preference, may follow from board mandates, or may occur in reaction to perceived organizational shortcomings. Through the selection of the primacy of either business or social timescapes comes the automatic selection of working from either an amoral business position or a moral social one. Such choices interact with the organizational societal landscape and the primacy of grounding the organization in amoral business activities or primarily with moral social interactions.

These senior decisions around management style and work habits define a moral or amoral climate and have implications for the entire organizational society. We see, then, that senior managers bear the mantle of leadership for work and management timescape dimensions.

Middle Managerial Levels

The mid-level manager's primary organizational business responsibility is to drive the business forward in terms of goods and services. The business expectations require training entry-level managers in business skills and expanding customer and supplier networks in ways that are based in social interactions. These social, dyadic applications are key for business success and are a primarily measure of mid-level success. The individual and self-actualization skills learned at the entry level are further strengthened at this managerial level.

In a sense, the middle managerial levels of the organization enforce the execution of the business and its social timescapes. For the execution of business activities within business timescape parameters, middle management sets the example for how business tasks are accomplished. These managers bear the responsibility of learning from the past mistakes and successes of others and of adapting those lessons to ensure future successes. In addition, through the use of complex dyadic relationships, middle managers provide examples of how internal and external organizational relationships are created and maintained. They also demonstrate the need to maintain relationships.

There is an inherent tension in trying to manage both social time and business time in the same way – for example, by remaining within a business timescape and seeking to use time to build monochronic personal relationships and to develop business relationships counterfactually. However, middle managers are the backbone of tradition within any organization and are highly supportive of the status quo. As such, they typically support senior managers who work within the traditional organizational society and culture but tend to be nonsupportive of senior managers who lobby and act for change. Hence they have influence over the timescape dimensions of use and actions.

Entry Managerial Levels

Benjamin's (1968) comments describing Klee's painting *The Angel of History* might be considered a metaphor for what is required of entry-level managers

> The face of the angel of history is turned toward the past, where we see a chain of events. The angel would like to stay and make whole what has been smashed. But a storm is blowing. It has got caught in his wings with such violence that the angel can no longer close them. This storm propels him into the future to which his back is turned. This storm is what we call progress. (p. 131)

These are the tensions that the new manager must learn to handle while taking the first steps on the road to organizational success. Coping with these tensions is a skill that successful organizational actors must master early in their careers; they must also internalize the organizationally accepted coping skills prior to applying them widely both within and outside the organization. In short, these skills must become part of each employee's organizational self.

The timescape dimensions of movement and type accommodate the enculturation activities of entry-level managers. They lay the groundwork for learning how to do business and socialize within the company. Within these dimensions (and their parameters), new employees learn how to focus on the linear and quantitative activities required for successful business activities. Managerial tutoring, mentoring, and other dyadic interfaces facilitate organizational teaching and new-hire learning.

Understanding Timescapes and Their Multi-Level Applications Using Composition Theory

Proposition 10. In successful organizations, timescapes and their related dimensions and parameters are aligned vertically across all hierarchical levels of complex organizations.

Composition theory informs the multi-level analysis of time in complex organizations by revealing vertical integration of timescape applications and alignment from senior, through mid-level, to entry-level managers. Composition theory (Kozlowski et al., 2000; Kozlowski & Klein, 2000; Rousseau, 1988) informs discussions of dominant-value orientations of either business or social time as determined at multiple levels of an organization. Business and social time composition reflect what organizational members know, how they learn what they need to know, and how they use what they have learned.

As Kozlowski and Salas (1997) found, levels issues are embedded in two distinct transfer foci: horizontal and vertical transfer. Horizontal *transfer* (Kozlowski & Salas, 1997) refers to transfer of knowledge across different settings or contexts at the same level. Kozlowski and Salas (1997) and Kozlowski et al. (2000) define *vertical transfer* as being concerned with the link between individual outcomes and outcomes or results at higher levels of the organizational system.

Markus and Zajonc (1985) suggest that strong organizational support (as expressed in a tight organizational composition) provides socioemotional order. In other words, organizations with strong composition at multiple organizational levels act in tandem with their cultural and climate strengths. Climate consistency usually provides more business and social transparency and results in improved business results, which in turn lead to more satisfied stakeholders.

In strong organizational cultures, the composition of timescapes and their dimensions and parameters are essentially the same for individuals at all levels and are formulated at the beginning of an employee's career. Assuring this conformity requires a process that inculcates organizational business and social activities at the entry level, strengthens them during mid-level transitions, and reinforces timescape preferences at senior levels of the organization. While flexibility and conflict occur between timescape applications (actors use them at all levels of an organization), organizational personnel are comfortable flexing within limits set by the dominant cultural orientation, whether it be social or business. It is where organizational training and knowledge intersect that temporal preferences for timescapes are formed and internalized in individual employees' self-perceptions. They are then exercised in dyadic relationships and practiced at middle-management levels, and the organization's ingrained temporal face is maintained and nurtured at senior levels.

Understanding Timescapes and Their Multi-Level Applications Using Compilation Theory

Proposition 11. Conflicted organizations' timescapes and their related dimensions and parameters are misaligned vertically across hierarchical levels of complex organizations. Misalignment creates organizational dysfunction.

Attempting a major shift within an organization from a culture grounded in one management or work timescape dimension to a culture driven by the opposite dimension can cause major organizational dysfunction ("Can Procter and Gamble Change," 2002; Graney, 2000; Reeves-Ellington, 1997; Turner, 1995; "Restructuring P&G," 2004). Changes at senior managerial levels often are designed to shift between business timescape primacy and social timescape emphasis (House, Rousseau, & Thomas-Hunt, 1995; Rose, 1989; Schiller, 1997; Sculley with Byrne, 1988). Such attempts at discontinuity should alert both researchers and practitioners to examine shifts in entry-level training, the providers of that training, and retention rates to see whether the discontinuity is causing shifts in entry-level managerial attitudes. Also, examination of mid-level support for such discontinuity is revealing in regard to possible resistance to changes.

If shifts in timescape emphasis are part of entry-level managerial training, the researcher or practitioner is alerted to possible organizational discontinuity. For example, if traditional training has stressed asymmetric power relationships in early training but shifts to focus on symmetric power uses, a shift to business timescape emphasis from social timescape primacy should be researched. In such circumstances, traditional organizational timescape emphasis comes into conflict within the organization. Conflict is greatest when senior managers lead radical change away from the status quo (Chan, 1998) by focusing on entry-level activities.

Such shifts in a specific organization's traditional timescape usage usually originate with senior management, who attempt to bypass middle-manager levels and proceed to influence entry-level managers. By ignoring mid-level managers, the senior group often creates organizational climate tensions, conflicts, and potential dysfunction, for, within the organization, the aggregate mid-level management traditionally influences other organizational individuals in ways that cause resistance to change (Bliese & Halverson, 1998a, 1998b; Kozlowski & Klein, 2000) rather than institute change. Senior managers who want change often respond to resistance by firing those offering it.

Summary of Multi-Level Analysis

In summary, examination of self, dyadic, and social relations reflect how single actors influence complex organizations. Composition theory provides a framework for examining unifying principles that aid in strengthening consistencies within complex organizations, and compilation theory exposes potential and real conflicts within complex organizations. Analyzing individual, dyadic, and social relationships as they apply to specific managerial levels informs the researcher about timescape focus at each of the levels, but such analysis does not provide a framework for understanding the integration of timescape applications or determining where conflicts might occur.

Composition theory informs multi-level complex organizational timescape research by revealing consistencies and overlap across three managerial levels. The theory also informs researchers and practitioners about timescape leadership at each managerial level. In strong organizational cultures, the composition of timescapes and their dimensions and parameters are essentially the same for individuals at all levels and are formulated at the beginning of an employee's career. Assuring this conformity requires a process that inculcates organizational business and social activities at the entry level, strengthens it during mid-level transitions, and reinforces timescape preferences at senior levels of organizations.

Compilation theory provides a tool for highlighting emergent activities that occur across organizational levels in ways that identify organizational discontinuities found at different organizational levels (House et al., 1995). Although a variety of interpretations are possible (Kozlowski & Klein, 2000), compilation theory is viewed here as informing the study of business timescapes and their dimensional parameters by alerting practitioners and researchers to potentially dysfunctional organizational shifts in timescape selection and managerial use of timescape dimensions and parameters.

Understanding which timescape applications might be cohesive and which might be dysfunctional within a particular organization requires longitudinal analysis, as becomes clear in the P&G case study.

RESEARCHING AND UNDERSTANDING
ORGANIZATIONAL TIME USAGE

Thus far, this chapter has elaborated a theorized model of timescape phenotypes, their dimensions, and dimension parameters. This section conducts a preliminary qualitative test of the model using traditional anthropological methods and research tools as applied to a P&G case study. After a brief review of the methods, it provides details from the P&G case that generated the propositions for the model.

The author of *The Life of Pi*, Yann Martel (2003), provides appropriate analogies that frame the research methods employed in this case study. Martel's castaway character, Pi, embraces the Catholic, Muslim, and Buddhist faiths simultaneously. In Pi's opinion, each of the three religious faiths has validity, and the acceptance of all three offers more rewards than the acceptance of only one. One unintended result of Pi's multi-religious acceptance is confusion for those around him. The research presented in this chapter, like Pi's religion, accepts and integrates rather than selects and rejects. Holistic understanding of business and social timescapes, their dimensions, and their dimension parameters results in a clearer understanding of complex organizational time. Avoiding confusion requires the researcher to attempt clarification of the voice of the researchers: academic outsiders, internal practitioners, joint academic practitioners. The voice used here is that of a researcher in the presentations of the models and structure of the data, an internal practitioner and anthropologist for the collection of the data, and an internal academic when clarifying the data through the literature and practitioners.

Grounded Research Methodologies

Gaining contextual cultural and societal information starts by grounding research in specific environments and using qualitative research methods and tools to provide initial insights and understanding. Gaining insights from and about given cultural or societal environments is best accomplished by initially using qualitative research techniques and methods, such as ethnology and participant observation (Reeves-Ellington, 1999b, 2004a; Reeves-Ellington & Anderson, 1997a, 1997b; Spradley, 1981; Zammuto & Krackover, 1991).

The primary practitioner research paradigm employed here is indigenous cognitive mapping (Denzin & Lincoln, 1994). When practitioners map the social knowledge and cultural paradigms of their own operating environments, they are internal academics who, by being organizational practitioners, create the social and cultural realities in ways that provide organizationally important knowledge. Working on the assumption that all knowledge is socially constructed (Menand, 2001) by individuals in specific environments, the research presented here assumes that timescapes are socially constructed. The social construction requires that practitioners who work within large complexities must develop a holistic understanding of the environment in which practitioners find themselves (Comaroff & Comaroff, 1992; Pearce & Branyiczki, 1997).

Applying Research Methods to the Procter & Gamble Company

Field work driving the P&G case study in this chapter is descriptive and based on grounded theory (Strauss & Corbin, 1984) as recommended by Kozlowski and Klein (2000). Research efforts relating to P&G start with qualitative tools that provide basic insights into the subject matter from the perspective of organizational actors and their interrelations with colleagues. In other words, the research attempts to see time through the eyes and understanding of those implementing it rather than through the constructs of independent researchers. By being an insider during the time of the P&G case, the author was able to catch the insider understanding of the company. In short, the case is developed through ethnology and the use of participant observation (Comaroff & Comaroff, 1992; Czarmoawsla, 1999; Finan & Van Willigen, 1990; Flanherty, 1999; Gabriel, 2000; Reeves-Ellington, 2004a, 2004b; Wheeler & Chambers, 1992). With this methodology, the author was able to find out what was important to others (Jorgensen, 1989) and to make accessible what would normally be concealed – mainly back-stage and commonsense information from a P&G point of view. All data gathered while working in P&G involved employees at a variety of sites and in several countries. To help the researcher learn about P&G business and social culture, informants were asked to provide supporting stories, examples, and organizational myths. All willingly obliged, as that is a traditional learning method at P&G.

The following case data and ideas are presented in the order in which the model and supporting theory were introduced throughout this chapter.

EMPIRICAL CASE STUDY

Procter & Gamble Company Qualitatively Researched Timescapes

The remainder of this chapter examines social and business timescapes and their dimensions and parameters by discussing them as they are used in P&G. It examines how timescape dimensions are situated in the three management levels and how actors at each of these levels use them primarily in relation to self, dyadic relationships, or broader organizational socialization. Specifically, P&G information is applied in the analysis outlined in Table 3 through the examination of three levels of management and the way in which each level applies specific dimensions to the self, dyadic relationships, and broader social applications. Using composition and compilation theory, the chapter demonstrates that consistency of timescape use reinforces company success whereas inconsistency results in poor business and social performance at the company. Specifically, it uses compilation theory to examine how overreaching change attempts leads to organizational dysfunction.

This case was developed by using information gained from several sources: participant observation over a 14-year period, materials written by individuals who had operated at all three managerial levels (Artzt, 1990, 1992; Decker, 1998; Dyer, Dalzell, & Olegario, 2004; Brand Resource Handbook, 1990; Kruse, 1984, 1996; Pritchett, 1992, 2003; "Awards and Recognitions," 2002; Schisgall, 1981; Tecklenberg, 1983), publications by outsiders with extensive internal contacts (Swasy, 1993; Walton, 1993), and other external reporting ("P&G's Strong-Arming," 1991; Buckley, 2002; "Can Procter and Gamble Change," 2002; Coolidge, 2004; Graney, 2000; Hopkins, 2004; Jones, 2002; Major, 2000; Merry, 2001; Mortished, 2001;

Rawe, 1991; Safire, 1991; Schiller, 1997; Serwer, 2001; "Shampoo Giant Caught Spying," 2001; Walton, 1993). All data used were confirmed by a minimum of three sources.

Timescapes at Procter & Gamble

Some companies socialize their entry-level employees to think only in business timescapes and reward employees only for business time activities; other companies reward both business and social timescape activities. P&G senior managers traditionally believe that balance and continuity are necessary for the organization to be successful. In other words, timescape dimensions of type choices are not based on dichotomous options but rather substantial flex between the two is possible. However, radical shifts from one timescape to the other are risky and court failure.

Timescape, Dimensions, and Parameters Leadership

The task at hand for entry-level employees and managers is to internalize the P&G way of working with other people in ways that drive the product businesses forward. Entry-level managers have primary responsibility and organizational leadership for timescape dimensions of type and use. They must demonstrate business skills for the timescape dimension of type and develop dyadic relationships with their brand manager and brand colleagues by using the timescape dimension of use. The new manager's focus is to become self-reliant, and he or she must turn inward to accomplish this goal. Learning occurs through a dyadic relationship with the immediate supervisor. If the employee fails to demonstrate mastery of the timescape dimensions of type and use within three years, he or she leaves the organization. With mastery, the employee moves up the managerial hierarchy.

Although this socialization process continues throughout a managerial career (Schisgall, 1981), the importance of timescape dimensions shifts according to the managerial level. Mid-level managers are expected to demonstrate mastery over the timescape dimensions of use and actions, along with their associated parameters. While the ability to work within one's own skills remains important, dyadic relationships come to the fore as employees are expected to apply P&G business and social timescapes in both customer and collegial interactions. Failure to measure up results in separation from P&G, while outstanding performance results in promotion.

Finally, senior managers are responsible for the work climate within business or social timescapes and thus support or change the organizational culture. They must create and maintain the timescape dimensions of management and work and their attendant parameters. Choices around managerial power usage are individual senior decisions that are based on perceptions of self. When such decisions take the organization away from the traditional climate, however, problems arise.

Entry-Level Timescape Leadership

Proposition 12. Organizational entry-level managers' primary responsibility is to master self in terms of using the business and social timescape dimensions of type and movement of time and to learn to apply the proper parameter to each of the timescapes. These managers are supported by a dyadic relationship with their immediate supervisor.

An entry-level employee immediately starts learning how P&G expects work to be done, and the entry-level manager is expected to teach that employee how to become a "proctoid." According to Ed Artzt (a former CEO) "a professional in search of mastery brings an attitude to his or her work that no sacrifice is too great, and no experience or grunt work too menial, all begins with attitude" (Decker, 1998). Former Chairman Owen Butler states the principle another way: "There is no potential business gain, no matter how great, which can be used to justify a dishonest act. The ends cannot justify the means because unethical means can and will destroy an organization" (Schisgall, 1981). Finally, Bob Goldstein, former P&G vice president of advertising, sums up the P&G belief about principles: "A principle isn't a principle unless it costs you something" (Decker, 1998).

P&G's new-employee manual for business conduct asks three questions: "(1) Is my action the right thing to do internally? (2) Would my action withstand public scrutiny? (3) Will my action protect P&G's reputation as an ethical company? If the answers are not an unqualified 'yes,' don't do it" (Decker, 1998). New hires learn these skills through a socialization process that relies on cyclic, qualitative, and polychronic activities that are morally based. Success at P&G is overtly measured by business outcomes but is embedded in company socialization ritual.

Type of Time: Quantitative and Qualitative Parameters
P&G Operating Principle. The interests of the company and the individual are inseparable

- We believe that doing what is right for the business with integrity will lead to mutual success for both the company and the individual.
- Our quest for mutual success ties us together.

Tensions abound regarding which is more important – learning the social or business ropes. One without the other leads to failure, however. Employees are admonished to work to get "it" right before implementation (Decker, 1998) but are also pressured to meet firm volume and financial goals (Dyer et al., 2004). They learn organizational social skills together but are evaluated individually. By creating a sense of family, P&G employees traditionally work to assure that social and business time are tightly interwoven into the psyche of each new employee in ways that embed business within the social boundaries of the company (Schiller, 1997; Swasy, 1993). When successful, employees become "proctoids" (Swasy, 1993); the social rhythms remain hidden through internalization but the business time lines are overt and consciously managed.

Within the business sphere, entry-level employees and managers quickly learn the importance of quantitative business skills. For example, in business discussions, "I think," "in my judgment," and "in my opinion" are expressions that do not count. The facts are expected to lead to clear conclusions. Early business training focuses on single assignments done rapidly, with absolute focus on the task at hand, and factually based on information that the new entrant gleans personally. The new hire receives assignments and training to develop the ability to retain, synthesize, and use qualitative data, facts, and knowledge. Without referencing others, new hires must know key data and information and readily contribute factual information to any management question asked. With this information, the new hire must linearly relate only pertinent information to specific aspects of brand performance. The new hire quickly learns that the time to respond to all questions is "immediately." Becoming an accomplished business manager in P&G requires the newly hired employee to work in isolation, think quantitatively and linearly, think counterfactually, and let amoral data speak for itself. All of this activity occurs in response to "management questions," which are very powerful questions in the life of the new hire.

During the same entry period, the new manager, working in a dyadic relationship with an immediate superior, learns to be a good P&G employee through extensive socialization. The new-hire assignments are often framed in business-like assignments, when the primary task assignment is, in reality, to become enculturated into P&G's work and social worlds. The key lesson for new employees is doing what is right for the company in ways that the company considers to be right. Through memo writing, budget cycles, and P&G College, they learn the cycles of P&G socializing and work life – for example, they learn to live and work in the P&G climate. While learning self-responsibility, they learn that success requires the activities of many.

The employees must become good proctoids if they expect continued employment and retention. The P&G marketing handbook (Brand Resource Handbook, 1990) for training pharmaceutical new hires into the company has, as a first lesson, company vision, values, mission, and strategies; it then moves on to operating principles, and concludes with a discussion of the Division's culture within P&G. Lesson 2 offers "Key Business Tips for New Brand Assistants" that include expected business guidelines but embed them in a P&G cultural context. For example, new hires are exhorted to "Ask questions," "Master the tools of self development," "Know that 'team work is critical'," and "Don't be afraid to express opinions and question what you are told." Cheryl Bachelder provides an example of the importance of learning to work "the Procter way" in doing business: "I learned to get things done with a purpose based on what we were trying to achieve. It makes so much sense if you know how to do it" (Decker, 1998).

Movement of Time: Linear and Cyclical Parameters
P&G Operating Principle. We are strategically focused in our work

- We operate against clearly articulated and aligned objectives and strategies.
- We only do work and only ask for work that adds value to the business.
- We simplify, standardize, and streamline our current work whenever possible ("Purpose, Values, Principles," 2002).

The task at hand for entry-level employees and managers is to internalize the P&G way of working with other people in ways that drive product businesses forward. The operating principles provide a strategic underpinning for time use. The articulated objectives address business timescape requirements for movement, while the focus on the right work entails interactions with and learning from a supervisor. Standardization in the P&G system includes both what to do and how to do it. In traditional marketing activities, P&G uses linear time processes by focusing on product development, creating consumer benefits from the product, and then convincing the public to try the product. These skill sets are part of the entry-level manager training, and mastery of them is key if the new manager is to be promoted. Traditionally, linear thinking is overt, whereas more socially oriented cyclical time is hidden. An example from the Pampers brand illuminates this principle.

In the mid- to late 1980s, the Pampers brand was static and losing market share to Huggies. The brand team had become enamored of business statistics about their key competition, rather than focusing on the product's purchases and the babies who would wear Pampers. The aggregated statistics provided few clues about the decline in market share. Telephone verbatim responses were collected but not reviewed by the team. During this period, the brand team decided to rely on product technical improvements such as absorbing wetness, stopping leakage, and enhancing softness in ways that featured the construction of the diaper. The advertisements were highly schematic in design and lacked the traditional P&G story of problem, solution, and reasons for the solution. The brand group had strayed from a basic tenant of meeting parents' perceived needs for their babies and therefore failed to meet these needs.

By the late 1980s, the brand had stagnated and the traditional arguments seemed to be less convincing as the competition caught up and, in some cases, surpassed the Pampers brand. Rather than middle or senior management taking charge, P&G maintained its traditional learning model (Reeves-Ellington, 2004b) and replaced the entry-level team with another – this time led by a woman rather than the traditional male. The new team shifted to a research strategy that identified and met parents' perceived needs for their babies rather than supporting diaper technical elegance.

The new brand team started by reviewing the verbatim comments in both transcripts and telephone logs. These comments revealed what product users – mainly mothers – thought to be the biggest problem with diapers. Through a more social analysis, the team heard mothers telling them that girl babies wet their diapers in different places than boy babies. The absorptive materials were not always in the right place. This finding was the basis of boy/girl diapers. The revised research technique information led to revised product development and marketing. The Pampers team started their efforts in a social timescape by working with the purchasers' ideas of need for diapers, engaging mothers in a dialogue as the product was developed to their specifications, and then checking with them to be certain that the final product met the need. Adopting a more cyclical approach to customer interactions and emotional needs both improved the product and increased market penetration. The linear use of time continued in the business activities of product development, marketing program development, and sales strategies, but it was no longer the controlling time dimension for the brand.

The Pampers story provides a detailed example of how loss of focus on objectives and straying from usual customer research cost the brand in terms of business share and required total restaffing. The new team brought back the appropriate work habits and trained new entry-level brand people into the "proper" way of doing P&G business.

Mid-Level Timescape Leadership

Proposition 13. Organizational mid-level employees demonstrate that they have learned the lessons of types of time and actions in time in complex dyadic relationships. They continue to be self-reliant when doing business timescape activities.

P&G Operating Principle. We seek to be the best

- We strive to be the best in all areas of strategic importance to the company.
- We benchmark our performance rigorously versus the very best internally and externally.
- We learn from both our successes and our failures ("Purpose, Values, Principles," 2002).

Mutual interdependency is a way of life

- We work together with confidence and trust across functions, sectors, categories, and geographies.
- We take pride in results from reapplying others' ideas.
- We build superior relationships with all the parties who contribute to fulfilling our corporate purpose, including our customers, suppliers, universities, and governments ("Purpose, Values, Principles," 2002).

We are externally focused

- We develop superior understanding of consumers and their needs.
- We create and deliver products, packaging, and concepts that build winning brand equities.
- We develop close, mutually productive relationships with our customers and our suppliers ("Purpose, Values, Principles," 2002).

Three sets of principles guide and influence P&G mid-level managers. The first two continue focusing on the importance of the timescape lessons learned during the early years at P&G. The third moves to prominence the importance of fostering personal relationships and building shared values with outside customers. Mid-level managers use time and take actions in time to meet these operating principles. Within personnel development, the second multi-level uses of time constructs provide temporal settings for undertaking commercial activities (based in qualitative time). The strategic focus on understanding customers and developing close relationships provides a framework for commercial activities. As employees move through the middle-management levels, dyadic relations shift from internal ones to the creation and maintenance of external ones.

Mid-level managerial efforts at pushing forward business activities (quantitative time) are framed by the principle of creating and delivering products as stated in second point of the third externally focused statement. The individual and self-actualization skills learned at the entry level are further strengthened at this managerial level by demonstrating an ability to work with major external customers in ways that meet their needs but in ways that align with P&G culture and work habits. Major brand movement is the business win for both the external customer and P&G.

Two important concepts underpin use and actions in time at P&G: context (the amount of information that a person can comfortably manage) and space (personal and public). Low-context environments are predominantly business ones; high-context environments are found in interpersonal actions at both the dyadic and social levels. Climate and cultural contexts operate on implicit information, whereas business contexts require explicit information. People who prefer to operate in high-context environments have wider networks and stay well informed on many subjects (Hall, 1997), whereas people who prefer low-context environments usually verbalize much more background information and tend to operate linearly and focus on single tasks.

Use of Time: Monochronic and Polychronic Parameters

While monochronic time remains important in the execution of business activities at the middle-management level, personal interactions are of primary importance. The mutual interdependency principles provide the strategic underpinning to support mid-level manager activities.

At mid-level management, work (including R&D, marketing, and sales) efforts are stated in individual terms. Organizational members at all levels understand that mid-level managers are responsible for the company's successes and failures. These managers establish teams, publicly set meetings and agendas, and receive accolades as the leaders of business units. The underlying principle of personal business accountability learned early in a manager's organizational career is reflected in an individual's ability to meet business needs, improve systems, and generally behave like an owner.

Mid-level employees are expected to have a superior knowledge of the business segments in which they work and to master the analytical, strategic, and practical skills needed to apply their business knowledge in terms of brand business growth. They drive specific projects, deadlines, and outcomes (Brand Resource Handbook, 1990). In addition, these employees are responsible for training new managers and making "proctoids" of them. At the middle-management level, business time comes to the fore and is the primary measure for success. While social time activities are important, they have become highly contextualized and exist below the conscious level. Within P&G, mid-level employees have the key job of ensuring that all of their subordinates learn and continue to improve in thinking in the P&G way. Gene Plummex, when a junior brand manager, remembers an advertising manager calling him into his office and complimenting him on a memo he had written: "Instead of saying, 'What a great idea,' he said, 'What a well-written memo!'" (Decker, 1998). The thinking behind the remark is that most company decisions made by management are based on information passed along via P&G memos, which are structured to reflect proper P&G thinking.

Within an organizational sense, however, successful work outcomes are much more polychronic. The company encourages employees to create mutual trust and have confidence in other employees' capabilities and intentions. For example, the company ("P&G's Focus," 2002; "Awards and Recognitions," 2002) works diligently to create a diverse workforce in terms of gender, color, ethnicity, physical abilities, and nationality. Converting encouragement into measurable action plans is the responsibility of mid-level managers. They work simultaneously with environmental groups, ethnic organizations, and women's groups. Awards won in these areas might indicate the results ("Awards and Recognitions," 2002). P&G is ranked (1) within the top 50 companies in terms of percentage of contributions to minorities, (2) among the United States' top 50 corporations for women and minority business enterprises, (3) as one of the best companies for working mothers, (4) among the 25 top companies for executive women, and (5) among the 100 employers for blacks. The company statements of purpose, values, and principles reflect the underlying importance of polychronic behavior within the organizational setting.

To accomplish these tasks, managers must develop and use dyadic relationships across traditional business functions and reach outside the formal company organization to strengthen informal organizational social structures. In all cases, however, these social tasks are expected to underpin P&G business building activities.

Actions of Time: Counterfactual Thinking and Climate Parameters
Counterfactual thinking is the work method that helps mid-level managers meet their self-development in mastering business outcomes. The second and third sets of principles that apply to mid-level management help shift thinking

beyond dyadic relationships to interpersonal actions and organizational socialization. In working with customers, consumers, and the general product
value chain, P&G uses counterfactual thinking to improve its products and
distribution, in particular. Nevertheless, the core of counterfactual applications at P&G focuses on products and service customer chains.

For example, for many years, P&G did not sell to Wal-Mart, because
P&G executives demanded control over retail prices and promotions. Sam
Walton, the CEO and primary owner of Wal-Mart, refused to cede authority over these activities, resulting in his company not buying from P&G.
When P&G senior managers realized that Wal-Mart represented more than
$400 million in potential business, they decided that P&G policies needed
reassessment. They appointed a Southern mid-level sales manager, Lou
Pritchett, to the job of working with Wal-Mart management. After a meeting between Walton and Pritchett, business differences were understood and
reconciled, and a future course of action plotted. One year of work between
the two companies resulted in P&G management agreeing to the pricing
strategies that Walton wanted (Dyer et al., 2004; Martel, 2003; Pritchett,
1992; Walton, 1993). Within the year, P&G had 40 of its employees working
in Wal-Mart's hometown of Bentonville, Arkansas, with reciprocal numbers
of Wal-Mart employees in P&G's headquarters in Cincinnati. Their areas of
cooperation extended from basic supply and pricing, through packaging and
promotions, to sophisticated technological research skills.

Today, Wal-Mart represents 17% of P&G's total worldwide sales volume
(Coolidge, 2004; Hopkins, 2004; McNeill, 2000). Just as important as the
market share is the fact that P&G used the principles outlined earlier in
developing strong relationships with Wal-Mart. In fact, the company now
bases its customer contacts on the principles developed between Pritchett
and Walton.

Mid-level success in P&G requires a manager to have such a success story in
his or her past to be retained and promoted. The success story would necessarily include a business success accomplished by working within P&G's
social structures. The success story usually focuses on working with outside
customers but is inclusionary of P&G personnel. The P&G–Wal-Mart story
makes the point.

Pritchett shifted P&G's sales and customer relations paradigm in a major
way. He made a new box rather than just thinking outside the existing one.
Before his contact with Walton, the company had a reputation of arrogance
toward outside customers that assumed a traditional business attitude
toward them and excluded their managers from traditional P&G internal
socialization. Attitudes toward these outsiders focused on business

timescape dimensions of linear thinking about what is good for P&G, working monochronically as a company, using asymmetric power by assuming the right to dictate to its customer, and acting in amoral ways toward them. In short, P&G fostered attitudes that violated its principle of doing the right thing to others.

Pritchett's "new box" required a socialization process between the employees of the two companies and then moving on to tackle business timescape dimensions. Pritchett and Walton set in motion a more qualitative relationship on a personal level and on an organizational level by ensuring that employees of each company were located on the other party's premises. This co-location altered the climate within each company as well as between the two firms. The power relationships shifted from the traditional P&G one of asymmetry to one of partnership and were based on shared values of doing the right thing.

While the activities were driven by joint socialization into the ways of the two companies, the driver that started the process was the desire for improved business results (Pritchett, 1992, 2003; Walton 1993). However, business improvements followed the socializing activities that led to a more complex, multitasking relationship. Pritchett achieved this feat by arranging, through a mutual friend, to take a canoe trip with Walton in Arkansas. When they first met, their initial conversations searched for shared experiences. The two men soon discovered that they were Eagle Scouts, liked fishing and hunting, grew up during the Depression in the South, and were self-made men. As a mutual friend said, "Never have a pair been better suited" (Pritchett, 1992, 2003; Walton, 1993). During the canoe trip, Pritchett listened to Walton's problems and then explained his vision of how the two companies could and should work in partnership.

Pritchett and Walton agreed that they were soul mates (Pritchett, 1992, 2003; Walton, 1993). Only after establishing a deep dyadic relationship and thereby learning of the cultural similarities was sufficient trust achieved for them to arrange working relationships that resulted in a strong business bond between the two companies. From such climate and cultural sharing emerged a strong business bond between the two organizations that provided a win–win situation for each company in terms of volume, profits, and earnings.

Senior-Level Timescape Leadership

Proposition 14. Organizational senior-level managers construct and support organizational continuity or change through leadership by their individual use of power and the social constructions of morality.

Senior-level employees provide strategic direction for existing businesses (Artzt, 1990; "Can Procter and Gamble Change," 2002; "P&G's Focus," 2002) and acquisition of new businesses, all of which are traditional senior-level activities that are duly noted in the popular press (Jones, 2002; Pritchett, 1992; Swasy, 1993; Zook, 2003). Ed Artzt, a past CEO of P&G, focused heavily on business time activities and saw social time as a hindrance to achieving business objectives. Conversely, ex-CEOs John Pepper (in his second tenure at the P&G helm), and Alan Lafley underpinned business objectives with social timescape activities: career development, leadership, equal opportunity, total quality improvements, and consensus building (Swasy, 1993; Dyer et al., 2004). Traditionally at P&G, senior-level managers are expected to balance between delivering business results and socializing all employees within the confines of acceptable P&G culture.

In the 1990s, John Smale, the firm's CEO at the time, and John Pepper, P&G's president, introduced Covey's (1989) *Seven Habits* within the company worldwide and reinforced the traditional P&G emphasis on social timescape activities. Under the leadership of Pepper, by the late 1990s, the company had incorporated the various strains of the *Seven Habits*, total quality, and *kaisan* into a holistic training program called the "P&G Way" (Imai, 1986; Kinney, 1998; Reeves-Ellington, 1995; Rohrer, 1990). Pepper, was once described as "Jiminy Pepper," acted as the conscience of P&G (Dyer et al., 2004). However, when Smale, stepped down as CEO, he worried that the culture processing and building under Pepper had become too strong. For this reason, he passed over Pepper, who was expected to be the next CEO, and selected Ed Artzt as his replacement, sending Pepper to the international division. The underlying timescape tensions between how to manage and how to work help us to analyze and understand the effects of these managerial decisions at P&G.

Management of Time: Asymmetric and Symmetric Power Parameters
P&G Operating Principle. The interests of the company and the individual are inseparable

- We believe that doing what's right for the business with integrity will lead to mutual success for both the company and the individual. Our quest for mutual success ties us together.
- We encourage stock ownership and ownership behavior ("Purpose, Values, Principles," 2002).

Starting with Ed Harness (P&G CEO from 1974 to 1981) and through Durk Jager (CEO from 1999 to 2000), organizational tensions existed due to shifts of CEO preferences on either asymmetric or symmetric power. Smale, Pepper (in his second senior-level managerial position), and Lafley all sought to adhere to the idea of business activities based in social morality as a way to achieve business success. Harness and Pepper emphasized symmetric power and moral work habits to the virtual exclusion of the business timescape parameters of management and work dimensions. Artzt and Jager, by contrast, honored the principle by ignoring it entirely.

Business performance declined under Harness until his successor, Smale, was named CEO. During Smale's tenure, the company focused on returning to strong business performance, measures that captured performance, and time limits for achieving performance but expected business results to be grounded in traditional P&G climate. Working in tandem with P&G president Pepper, who was known for his commitment to the social organization of the company, Smale reintegrated business timescape attributes to return to a desirable work and social timescape balance (Dyer et al., 2004). When the time came to choose Smale's successor, however, business needs drove the decision leading to the selection of Artzt. Pepper was passed over. At the 1989 annual management review meeting, Pepper was greeted with thunderous applause and Artzt with politeness. The message was clear: the organization wanted symmetric power usage but got asymmetric power.

In 1989, as the newly elected CEO, Artzt laid out a course of action for the entire organization that was grounded in asymmetric power usage. The instructions were thematic and focused: reduce regretted turnover, especially among women; return sales unit volumes to the growth lines of the early 1980s; achieve operating profits that exceeded the industry mean. The power of the CEO in the company provided for implementation of this type of direction. Artzt legislated the course and focus of the company. His unfettered use of personal power laid the foundations for major organizational conflicts. As reported in Swasy (1993), a senior researcher remembers meetings in which Artzt would tell anyone who disagreed with him to report to his office after the meeting. As Pritchett (1992) said, "Artzt believes 'I'm the boss and you're not'." For Artzt, Attila the Hun was the perfect leader type (Swasy, 1993).

As successor to Artzt, Jager speeded things up even more by declaring war on the P&G culture and those who wanted to support it ("Can Procter and Gamble Change," 2002). His motto was "We need to fix things and fix them fast!" At this point, qualitative time activities receded almost entirely. Jager's drive for change in achieving research product output, new product introductions, and acquisitions put the company well on the spectrum of business time and moved it away from the traditional social time within the company. The result: A loss of almost 60% of the company's stock value and the termination of Jager ("P&G's Strong-Arming," 1991; Graney, 2000; Safire, 1991). The language of speed and efficiency drowned out the traditional enculturation language of socializing activities.

Appointed CEO in 2000, Lafley ("Awards and Recognitions," 2002; "P&G's Focus," 2002; "Purpose, Values, Principles," 2002) supported the changes Jager had instituted but indicated that the tone that Jager adopted was not right for the company. He used asymmetric power to achieve the tone that he desired. Although Lafley's action was hailed as a victory for organizational proctoids, a more reasonable interpretation might emphasize the importance of reestablishing the rhythm and language of time and its use in the company. The company's statement of principles on this matter supports the alternative analysis.

While Artzt's and Jager's successors, Pepper and Lafley, recognized Jager's changes, they recognized that his tone had not been appropriate for the company ("Purpose, Values, Principles," 2002). To show why, they explained the mission of P&G College, the company school that is taught by P&G executives and aims to teach leadership and transmit company values. "We are emphasizing heavily the whole area of coaching," said Pepper. After meeting with a number of young managers, Pepper maintained that he was encouraged at the chances they said they were getting to run important parts of the business and the amount of time their bosses were spending with them. "These are the reasons I'm with the company," he said. Schiller (1997) summed up P&G employees' belief in Pepper when he stated in his book, "Hokey as it sounds, from Pepper, it's believable." Lafley concurred with getting P&G people back into the traditional socialization mode and steered a course to return symmetric power balances in the company in ways that would produce desired business results ("P&G Annual Report," 2005; "P&G's Performance," 2003). He believed that command and control methods of operating in P&G were inappropriate (Adam, 1995; "Can Procter and Gamble Change," 2002; Dyer et al., 2004) and needed to be replaced with traditional P&G values and a customer focus. His beliefs, which are summarized in Table 4 (Dyer et al., 2004), reflect an expansion and clarification of the managerial operating principle stated earlier.

Work in Time: Amoral and Moral Parameters
P&G Operating Prinicple. We show respect for all individuals

- We believe that all individuals can and want to contribute to their fullest potential.
- We value differences.

Table 4.   Five Things I Believe: A. G. Lafley.

The customer is boss
- We must understand consumer needs, wants, and dreams and desired consumer experiences to create loyal customers and passionate ambassadors.
- This understanding focuses technology, product, and brand choices so we're more effective and faster to market.
- We must understand total consumer experiences – shopping, usage, bonding – to enable us to build a relationship, be where he or she lives, and become a trusted partner in his or her life.

Power of strategy
- We must make clear choices about where to play and how to win.
- We must exploit core capabilities and P&G strengths.

Power of knowledge and learning
- This power is manifested when turned into superior strategies and business plans.

Power of P&G people
- Without us – P&G people – there are no strategies, no brands, and no execution.
- P&G people are at the center of everything we are and everything we do, and everything we want to become.

Take P&G's statement of purpose, values, and principles seriously
- Values that are particularly important now include leadership, ownership, integrity, trust, and passion for winning.
- P&G principles offer a few opportunities for improvement: respect for individuals, valuing differences, strategically focused, externally focused, and mutual interdependence as a way of life.

- We inspire and enable people to achieve high expectations, standards, and challenging goals.
- We are honest with people about their performance ("Purpose, Values, Principles," 2002).

Connecting to the management of time discussion and its attendant power dimensions, we can see that amoral attitudes are instilled when business time is employed. Early business training at P&G focuses on single assignments done rapidly, with absolute focus on the task at hand, and factually based on information that the new entrant gleaned personally. On the other side of the work time is moral grounding. An entry-level employee immediately starts learning how P&G expects work to be done and the entry-level manager is expected to teach employee that how to become a proctoid. As detailed in the multi-level discussions of the timescape dimensions of type and movement at the managerial entry level, the use of both social and business timescapes is grounded in moral imperatives of work habits

(Decker, 1998; Schisgall, 1981). Senior managers traditionally rely more on asymmetric power to ensure that entry-level managers learn to do the right things. We can see both parameters of the work dimension in the principles. The desire to contribute and achieve high expectations weighs on the amoral side of work, and the demand of honesty and valuing differences comes down on the moral parameter of work.

During the mid- to late 1980s, P&G's pharmaceutical division sold topical anti-infective drugs to both the Iranian and Iraqi armies while their countries were at war. Sales and deliveries to each country were difficult to arrange because unsecured credit was unacceptable to P&G. Neither Iraqi nor Iranian officials wanted to provide credit notes until the goods were delivered and accepted. U.S. law did not ban the sales and delivery of pharmaceuticals; however, on moral grounds, senior managers debated whether P&G should sell to regimes that took actions inimical to the United States. They met to place this conversation in a wider context. While no manager supported Iranian and Iraqi policies, the company was not selling goods that were destructive to life but rather providing goods that could save lives. Also, when all the countries of the world were put on the table for moral consideration of doing business, none were universally agreed to be "good." The company chose to take an amoral stance on the business transactions, even though substantial differences of opinion existed. Further, the managers considered the ethical and moral issues, took a clear position, and believed that they were honest with themselves and others about their position.

In the mid-1990s, P&G decided to integrate the pharmaceutical management and research operations into its home office complexes. This move would leave the town of Norwich, New York, without a major source of employment and substantially reduce the amounts of money spent in the community. The local management team was expected to develop a plan that would enable the town to use the buildings that were to be vacated, encourage alternative employment opportunities in the town, and support the public purse during a period of transition. The company agreed to pay taxes on the properties for five years, renovate the buildings in ways such that they could be used for incubation of new small businesses in the town, and provide management and advertising to help assure success of the plan. The plan worked. The offices were full of tax-paying small businesses after one year. While a 20–30% turnover occurred in the first five years, the start-up success approximated 30%. Fifty percent of the office space was occupied by the same companies for more than five years.

Composition Theory Applications at P&G

To assure systematic composition of the enculturation process, company principles clearly identify the dominant values and ethics for all levels of management and multiple levels of self, dyadic, and social relationships within P&G (Schisgall, 1981; Decker, 1998; Dyer et al., 2004). These public values ("P&G's Focus," 2002), which are initiated at all levels of the organization, are agreed in final form after what might be years of discussion. Ownership of these principles is almost universal, and deviance by any employee results in punishment, either formal or informal (social).

The iterative learning processes are practiced horizontally at each of the managerial levels and vertically across them all: an employee enters a level, learns the skills, is promoted, and then teaches other newcomers (Decker, 1998). During their early years of employment, newcomers learn company routines, interpersonal relationship building, company traditions, and the power of knowledge use. As newcomers become more seasoned employees and move to mid-level positions, they teach recent company hires entry-level skills. Simultaneously, the mid-level employees learn P&G business skills in more depth from the senior levels of the organization. The senior levels, in turn, use their cumulative social skills to assure the continuation of a strong P&G culture and their business skills to work primarily with outsiders, such as stock markets, acquisition experts, banks, and other business institutions. This reoccurring cycle is socially lived time, with business applications, and provides socioemotional order and stability. P&G senior managers believe that for the organization to be successful, balance and continuity are necessary.

Tensions abound in discussions of which educational component is most important – learning the business or learning the social ropes. As noted earlier, the long-term success of P&G seems predicated on the need for both timescapes and their multiple dimensions and parameters. The command is to achieve firm volume and financial goals but in socially accepted ways. When successful, employees become "proctoids" (Swasy, 1993), and the social rhythms remain hidden through internalization while the business time lines are overt and consciously managed.

P&G's socialization and business activity enculturation activities continue throughout an employee's employment and reflect organizational use of both timescapes. To ensure systematic composition of the enculturation process, company principles clearly identify the firm's underlying values and ethics. The results of successful enculturation are widely circulated throughout the company and celebrated through a variety of other public forums ("Awards and Recognitions," 2002).

Underlying these principles are some company tautologies that help to understand the strengths of P&G's complex organization.

Learning the Right Things: Persistence, Knowledge, and Principles

From a P&G insider viewpoint, the issues of persistence, knowledge, and principles are all essential. The entry-level employee in P&G must learn to work to get P&G desired results and do it in the P&G work style. Both learning to work and learning to work together are promoted from the top down.

Persistence

When asked which single personal characteristic would most likely contribute to success at P&G, Harry Tecklenberg, a former senior vice president of P&G, pointed to persistence (Tecklenberg, 1983). In *Rising Tide* (Dyer et al., 2004), that point is made repeatedly. One P&G brand manager (Kadin, 1985) reported that upon joining the company and learning to write in P&G style, "Remarkably simple topics would be revised 10 times before a memo would be worthy of forwarding. I now find myself thinking in terms that I was taught to write in. I learned the importance of persistence and focus in all I do at P&G." Gary Stibel (Decker, 1998), a brand assistant, was assigned to work on a single product. After 30 days on the job, he recommended that the product be discontinued. His boss tried to dissuade him from insisting that the memo go forward on three separate occasions. Stibel persisted. Three higher-level managers forwarded the memo, with each level recommending disapproval. When the memo reached the fourth level, however, a vice president agreed with Stibel and the product was discontinued.

Knowledge

Stibel had facts that could not be ignored, which was what Richard Deupree, a former CEO, said was necessary: "An opinion isn't worth a damn if facts can be ascertained" (Schisgall, 1981). Brad Butler, a former chairman, wrote, "The prevailing attitude is that what is right is far more important than *who* is right. Facts, truth, [and] logic have far more authority at P&G than any individual" (Schisgall, 1981).

Paul Kadin (1985) remembers learning about attention to details when working as a brand assistant. He was responsible for getting all the sales and promotional materials ready for a sales presentation. "There were a hundred things to do. I had done a good job, but forgot to bring the shelf card needed to place under the product on the shelf. My boss was the only one who noticed that the shelf card was missing. Nevertheless, he jumped all over me and stayed on me for a week. You got it right if it's one hundred percent. That is the standard of the place." He continues by noting that to retain and synthesize data is to create knowledge in transmittable form. The resulting knowledge is what grows business at P&G. "The learning of this truth starts on the first day on the job."

When the facts are unknown or contradictory, junior managers must expand the databases that create knowledge in ways that clarify. In the preceding example, Stibel stuck to the facts and persisted in spreading this knowledge. A well-known P&G story makes the point even more forcefully (Decker, 1998). When Rely tampons were associated with toxic shock syndrome in 1980, an all-out effort was launched to find the cause of this link. The Centers for Disease Control and Prevention (CDC) cited an apparent correlation between the disease and Rely, but another group of scientists argued that no reasonable evidence definitively linked the two. CEO Harness asked his scientists and brand group if they could assure him that Rely was not associated with toxic shock syndrome. They could not. The immediate response from Harness was, "Okay, we'll withdraw the product" (Decker, 1998).

Principles
Ed Harness, a previous CEO, defined the art of finding the principle as follows: "Making the hard decision, consistent with principle, usually involves two things – hard thinking by a disciplined mind and short-term sacrifice on the part of the company" (Decker, 1998). Fred Kruse (1984) admonished all new employees to discover the principle at work and argue from that position, based on hard data. Kruse learned this precept from his boss, Harry Tecklenberg, who claimed that all of his successes were predicated on that principle.

To ensure that the new hire learns the right way to do the right thing, P&G operates P&G College. The primary purpose of the college is to ground company thinking, over time, by retelling the company history and personal anecdotes, including stories of predecessors. The faculty of the college consists of the company's CEO and top management. New hires spend about two weeks in the college and are invited back periodically throughout their careers. Attendance is a cyclic rite of passage (Decker, 1998) whose purpose is to create a qualitative environment in which P&G employees feel comfortable, while teaching them how to work with a variety of departments, people, and situations. The basis of the instruction and its application in everyday work activities rely on the idea that the P&G way is the way of moral companies.

Timescape Balance: The Desired Outcome from the Principles

In a newspaper interview ("Can Procter and Gamble Change," 2002), CEO Lafley clearly intended to highlight business results and to publicly forecast business performance. This interview was situated entirely within business timescape dimensions and parameters. In contrast, in an interview for an in-house publication ("P&G's Focus," 2002), Lafley emphasized the importance of P&G employees and those things that they were doing right. This interview was grounded in social timescape dimensions and parameters but tied to business timescapes. In the internal publication, Lafley stated that success derived from people who do the right things; who actively support and implement the company's purpose, values, and principles ("Purpose, Values, Principles," 2002); and who are customer oriented – all points covered in the article. As Lafley concluded, "We need to focus on a common purpose, goal, and a few choices, and then try to unleash the organization, and let them make decisions and do the right things. I can assure you that the 'command and control' method of management doesn't work in the world today" ("P&G's Focus," 2002). The points are supported in Lafley's statement of five things he believes (see Table 4). These are very reassuring words to socialized proctoids.

Lafley, as a CEO steeped in P&G traditions, demonstrates that the principles discussed underlie the primacy of social timescapes and the appropriate dimension leadership at each managerial level. Furthermore, these principles ensure the selection of the appropriate social dimensional parameter. The 1990s saw a major deviation from traditional social timescape activities that resulted in poor business performance and the loss of skilled P&G managers.

Compilation Theory Applications at P&G

Composition theory confirms that traditionally P&G is grounded in social timescapes – particularly its climate and culture – in ways that provide horizontal and vertical binding throughout the company. During the 1990s, this formula was violated with disastrous results by Artzt and Jager. Their actions revealed a discontinuity of senior managerial timescape responsibilities that led to major organizational disruption. Of importance to this case is that discontinuity theory exposes how Artzt and Jager, through their attempts to destroy P&G's traditional social timescape use and replace it with a dominant business timescape position, created company dysfunctions and major shifts in traditional profitability. Of interest is not only what they did, but also why two CEOs, who had spent their entire careers at P&G, would want to attempt such a fundamental timescape change.

Making Business Timescapes Count

Recall that Smale attempted to rebalance asymmetric and symmetric power during his tenure as CEO and attempted to assure the continuity of power balance through his selection of Artzt over Pepper as the next CEO. A *Fortune* report on P&G, discussing a "battle of the proctoids" ("Can Procter and Gamble Change," 2002), strongly supported this selection by emphasizing Pepper's strengths in building and maintaining P&G culture and his lack of drive in achieving a perceived shortfall in business results during the late 1980s. The P&G board of directors concurred with Smale by supporting Artzt, who was known as a business troubleshooter (Swasy, 1993). Artzt's strong European performance was the key factor in his selection as CEO.

In 1990, Artzt became the CEO and set out to design a new work timescape – one that abandoned traditional socialization activities in favor of a perspective that emphasized business results almost exclusively. Amoral business values were to be dominant. After all, that paradigm was what had gotten Artzt to the CEO's chair, so why not transform the entire company? P&G legends create the image of the CEO as not thinking outside the work timescape box but rather changing it.

Making Business Timescapes Paramount

Artzt immediately began to put his imprint on the company: "Clear the dead wood!" As one manager put it, "If we don't like some employees, we'll just go chop down some more trees" (Swasy, 1993). Artzt's (1992) goal was to push for larger profits and increase the value of the firm's stock. He made penalizing mistakes paramount to learning from them.

After assuming the CEO position, Artzt gutted training programs and fired those teaching them in an effort to focus on the message of "Sell more soap" (Kruse, 1996; Pritchett, 2003; Swasy, 1993). He changed the P&G College from a learning climate that taught the P&G way of doing business to a milieu that was nicknamed "Eddie's War College." Its focus was re-directed to technology deployment, advertising, and basic business skills – pushing the what-to-do message and ignoring the how-to-do part of the equation. Artzt's perspective was that he was the boss. In short, the traditional values of persistence, knowledge, and principles were to be replaced by a focused drive to improve the bottom line.

Artzt declared war on the traditional P&G culture and its use of social timescapes and socialization processes (Graney, 2000; Swasy, 1993). As reported by Pritchett (1992), Swasy (1993), and Walton (1993), Artzt terrified the Philippines organization during his visits. Artzt also publicly berated Pepper, both inside and outside the organization, which offended many employees. He almost single-handedly destroyed the sense of family within the P&G organization, even to the point of attacking his protégés and losing more of his senior management team than any CEO in the history of P&G (Swasy, 1993).

In summary, during his tenure as CEO, Artzt's goal was to shift the company culture from one of shared culture to one of an absolute focus on products. As he said of himself, "I am the Johnny Appleseed because I plant the seeds that tell employees why they're enrolled" (Swasy, 1993).

The War Continues

Artzt's protégé, Jager, continued the war on the firm's traditional culture. "He's like General Patton arriving with the Third Army," said Burt Flickinger, a former P&G employee, "except that instead of an opposing army, what's under attack here is P&G itself" ("Can Procter and Gamble Change," 2002). While in Japan, Jager revealed his attitude toward people when he encouraged them "to bust some kneecaps" or not to be afraid to "gutter fight" (Pritchett, 1992; Swasy, 1993).

Ultimately, Pritchett's forecast that Jager "would not be P&G user friendly" proved correct (Pritchett, 1992; Swasy, 1993). Jager was let go after a 17-month stint at the top. The value of P&G's stock was sent lower again, this time for a roughly 6% loss. Quite simply, Jager had brazenly put his job on the line when his company shocked investors and sell-side analysts alike by pre-announcing lower-than-expected fiscal-quarter earnings. By the time he resigned, the company had slammed four profit warnings into two quarters, and its stock value had fallen by 50% in the previous six months, losing $70 billion in market value. Clearly, Jager left the company on unsure footing ("Can Procter and Gamble Change," 2002).

Artzt's and Jager's Focus on Amoral Management and Asymmetric Power

As discussed earlier, amoral relationships are based on asymmetric power and the self's ("I") relationship to the business. In their purest form, interpersonal relationships are abstracted to avoid personal entanglements and maintain the actor identified as "I." Such actors then operate with disdain of others, both within and outside the organization. In the discussion of Artzt's and Jager's use of power, the "I" reached the pinnacle of asymmetric power. The comments of both men reflected a high disdain for people and, through abstraction, put personal relationships into a realm usually inhabited by tools, products, and money.

An example makes the point of how Artzt's misuse of asymmetric power sullied P&G's reputation. In 1991, Artzt was unhappy with the reporting of *The Wall Street Journal* on activities within the company. He decided on a series of actions that were labeled as immoral, unethical, bad, and wrong (Safire, 1991), both within and outside the company. Capitalizing on internal leaks, *The Wall Street Journal* published a series of articles on internal personnel changes at P&G (Ripley, 1991; Swasy, 1993). Artzt took the position that the affair was a business matter of protecting corporate proprietary information. He responded by calling in security personnel and asking them to find the "traitors" at P&G (Swasy, 1993). He further solicited, through company security personnel, the aid of the Cincinnati police and the Cincinnati Bell telephone company. Swasy and others (Rawe, 1991) determined that proprietary information was not really the issue. Rather, Artzt was concerned about internal leaks of matters that he did not want made public. Artzt never admitted to more than an error in judgment in trying to protect the company and its assets.

The task at hand was not to protect trade secrets but rather to catch insiders who were speaking with Swasy, a person outside Artzt's control who was writing about "his" company. Much of *The Wall Street Journal* information exposed Artzt's poor relationships within the company. Many insiders – even senior managers who worked closely with Artzt – were anxious to speak about him with Swasy (Kruse, 1984, 1996; Pritchett, 1992; Ripley, 1991; Swasy, 1993). Insiders were embarrassed and angry at Artzt's tactics and discussed internal problems with Artzt at work, at home, and with outsiders – something that was never done at P&G.

How Artzt Avoided Traditional P&G Training and Still Advanced

Artzt's training and hence his leadership in P&G was unusual in that it was strictly business – amoral, monochronic, quantitative, linear, counterfactual, and entirely steeped in asymmetric power. Artzt quickly replaced almost all of Smale's advisors and senior management with managers from the international division whom Artzt had brought into the company and who had worked for him outside the United States (Swasy, 1993). Jager was not one of the early subordinates to join Artzt in Cincinnati but was specifically brought in from Japan, as heir apparent, near the end of Artzt's CEO tenure.

A Failure in Proctoid Training

How Artzt avoided proctoid indoctrination is a matter of speculation, but Kruse (1996) offers the most compelling argument. Artzt went outside the United States when it was unfashionable to do so and the business was small. As he was successful, he was promoted. As he was promoted, he gained more power. When he returned to the United States as a senior executive, he was sidelined with expectations of Pepper gaining the CEO chair. But when Smale worried over Pepper, Artzt, as a co-vice chairman with Pepper, was the logical alternative.

Artzt's entire early and mid-level career was product focused and took place outside the nurturing environment of the home office. In his first employment in P&G, he skipped the initial brand training in which an entry-level employee was socialized. Instead, Artzt went directly into sales, where moving product was paramount (Swasy, 1993).

As reported in Swasy (1993) and confirmed by a myriad of P&G employees to the author of this chapter, this unusual sales move resulted from Artzt's "invention" of product store counts. When Artzt moved to Cincinnati, after seven months of sales training in the Los Angeles area, he stopped at more than 60 groceries to talk to managers and check stockrooms for P&G brands. Upon arriving in Cincinnati and meeting with his new boss, he reported his findings. According to Artzt, they were astounded at what he knew. As Swasy quotes him, "I was the only one on earth who had an up-to-the minute reading on what our store stocks looked like across the country." Artzt had made his reputation on activities that took place outside Cincinnati and outside the traditional P&G learning model. For Artzt, business activities that were outside the traditional P&G socialization box were the tickets to success. Becoming a proctoid was unimportant to him.

As Artzt moved through his P&G career, his focus remained on selling product. As a brand manager, he rewrote product copy on his own, without gaining company approval. He was severely chastised. Artzt's response was "That goes on in big companies. The little guy comes up with an idea. It sold a lot of soap. This guy wanted to put me back in my box" (Swasy, 1993). Much of his mid-level career was spent acting as a troubleshooter and problem solver for troubled P&G businesses (Swasy, 1993). Artzt's task was to increase the sales of specific products, often working as an outsider to the division that he was assigned to fix.

His entry into senior management was as a company director taking charge of P&G Europe, an area that was experiencing volume and profit difficulties (Pritchett, 1992). Immediately, Artzt emphasized organizational efficiencies rather than organizational effectiveness. He attacked the existence of too many "sacred cow" products, too many long-standing advertising formulae, and too many company traditions (Pritchett, 1992; Swasy, 1993). He acted aggressively to cut prices, axe matrix management systems, consolidate manufacturing, and eliminate layers of management. Along the way, he either ignored or eliminated P&G traditions and personnel concerns. Once again, Artzt avoided being socialized at the senior management levels. His European position paved the way to his role as chief executive, but he was not used to having to answer to shareholders, interact with his colleagues in home office, or deal with tradition (Swasy, 1993).

P&G Organizational Response to Artzt

The use of asymmetric power to effect work habit change from a moral parameter to an amoral parameter was a level of discontinuity that inspired outrage in long-term U.S.-based P&G employees (Swasy, 1993). Artzt's and Jager's self-focused and narcissistic approaches to management and work dimensions business timescapes were viewed as distinctly amoral when seen through the cultural lenses of proctoids and their external sympathizers. Smale, a good P&G proctoid who is representative of traditional P&G employees, was reported not to "unlock his jaw for a month" (Swasy, 1993) after Artzt's self-centered performances. Traditional proctoids believed that the job of the CEO was to lead the organization in achieving flex and balance between business and social timescapes – not to radically change P&G to a company based on business timescape dominance. A key learning from this case study is that a CEO can flex the operating timescape fundamental to the social structure of an organization but cannot drastically alter it from above: there are too many enculturated employees to battle and overcome.

In summary, Artzt had 34 years of P&G employment, during which he had learned the language of the company and often sounded like a traditional proctoid to outsiders. Insiders, however, recognized him as lacking sufficient company enculturation and therefore deemed him not to be deeply trusted. The resultant discontinuities introduced by Artzt were perceived as needed by the outside business world, but as dysfunctional by most senior and mid-level management. Artzt's radical actions as CEO led to major company personnel losses, loss of traditional profit levels, and loss of investor confidence.

Longitudinal Performance

If the P&G analysis were limited to the decade of the 1980s or 1990s or a time span starting with the end of Jager's tenure, the researcher might be misled by short-term problems of timescape use. For example, a study of the Harness era of the early 1980s might reveal a company that was too focused on the way things used to be done (Kruse, 1996) and not enough on market changes and growth strategies. A look at the Smale era might produce an analysis of the balance of business and social time, but with business being grounded in social time. A study of P&G in the 1990s would lead an investigator to believe that the bottom line was driving the company and that Artzt, in particular, made major successful shifts from a social-timescape-based company to a business-timescape-focused company. The Lafley era would reflect a company that was secure in going about its business using a strong, traditional P&G culture. Thus, to understand which timescape best suits P&G, one must take a longer view.

CEOs who wanted to ground P&G in a business timescape (Artzt and Jager) were often supported by the business press (Graney, 2000; Safire, 1991), while insiders supported those who grounded company activities in social timescapes (Harness, Smale, Pepper in his second stint at the top, and Lafley) (Pritchett, 1992; Swasy, 1993).

The data in Table 5 suggest that CEOs who support traditional P&G socialization and organizational behaviors lead the company to better business performance than those who solely promote a business timescape focus.

In spite of his laser focus on profit, Artzt produced growth rates that were 40% lower than those achieved under CEOs who relied on traditional timescape applications. Graney (2000) reported a 10% drop in the value of P&G shares just on the news of Jager's appointment as CEO, foreshadowing the loss of 60% of the company's share value a few months later. As reported in a *Financial Times* article (Buckley, 2002), under Lafley P&G once again approached its traditional growth rates. Buckley reported that Lafley refocused the company on its big brands – its 10 best sellers that accounted for more than 50% of its total revenues. These brands received top priority in terms of talent, money, and research. "It's a basic strategy that worked for me in the Navy and here at P&G," said Lafley. "I learned there that even when you've got a complex business, there's a core, and the core is what generates most of the cash, most of the profits. The trick was to find the few

Table 5. CEO Time Type and Performance Indicators.

President and Chief Executive	Years	Primary Time Type	Average Net Earnings per Year ($ millions)	Average Shareholders Equity
John Smale	1986–1990	Balanced, socially underpinned	1,216 (10%/year)	13%/year increase
Edwin Artzt	1990–1995	Business	917 (6%/year)	9%/year increase
John Pepper	1995–1998	Social	3,157 (10%/year)	13%/year increase
Durk Jager	1999–2000	Business	−500	60%/year decrease
John Pepper Alan G. Lafley	2000–2004	Balanced, socially underpinned	5,246 (14%/year)	11%/year increase

things that were really going to sell, and sell as many of them as you could" ("Can Procter and Gamble Change," 2002). The plan was simple and everyone in the company understood that selling more Tide was less complicated than trying to invent a new Tide. P&G culture knows that game and is socialized to succeed with it.

CONCLUSIONS

Business and social timescapes that are situated in specific contexts influence the ability of individuals, their relationships, and their broader societies to remain stable or to affect paced changes. Change studies require an understanding of complex time in its operations in both individual and dyadic contexts and through complex organizational interactions in a wider social environment. Multi-level research provides several theoretical frameworks for organizing data and understanding and using timescapes in ways that permit multi-level hypotheses to be created, tested, and implemented.

This chapter has highlighted four critical points, each of which is a hypothesis that needs to be tested by teams of mixed disciplines for richness. These teams also should test each hypothesis in a variety of ethnic and organizational cultures for assurance of generality. Of particular importance for understanding organizational timescape usage is the involvement of employees within the system to provide discussion – not just a number-two pencil with which to circle numbers.

First, social timescapes and their attendant dimensions and parameters are learned through dyadic relationships and socially distributed in a top-down fashion in complex organizations. Because of this social distribution, learners of social time applications are often not consciously aware of such learning. Researchers have more difficulty in studying socially driven organizational activities.

Second, business timescapes and their attendant dimensions and parameters are individually learned and practiced. Business timescape applications demand monadic work practices, serial tasks, and counterfactual reasoning to change the present course of events in ways that will yield future changes. They require asymmetric power applications to task assignments.

Third, both business and social timescapes are found at entry, middle, and senior managerial levels, but each of these levels has a primary responsibility or organizational leadership for certain dimensions. When dimensional leadership is blurred or shifts among the three managerial levels, organizational confusion occurs.

Fourth, understanding the value of horizontal and vertical timescape congruence or change requires longitudinal studies. As demonstrated in the P&G case, if a researcher had studied the administrations of either Artzt and Jager or Pepper and Lafley, substantial errors might arise in the research findings. Such research is time-intensive, both in terms of the length of time required and the depth of understanding needed. Without longitudinal timescape studies, multi-level analysis will be shortchanged and provide less insight than might otherwise be possible.

REFERENCES

Abbott, A. (2001). *Time matters*. Chicago: University of Chicago Press.

Adam, B. (1995). *Timewatch: The social analysis of time*. Cambridge, UK: Polity Press.

Adam, B. (1998). *Timescapes of modernity: The environment and invisible hazards*. Oxford: Routledge.

Albert, S. (1995). Towards a theory of timing: An archival study of timing decisions in the Persian Gulf War. *Research in Organizational Behavior, 17*, 1–70.

Ancona, D. G., Okhuysen, G. A., & Perlow, L. A. (2001). Taking time to integrate temporal research. *Academy of Management Review, 26*(4), 512–529.

Anon. (2002). P&G's focus making a difference. *P&G Champions*, September 2005, pp. 1–2.

Artzt, E. (1990). *Video address to senior P&G management*. Cincinnati: Procter & Gamble Company.

Artzt, E. (1992). *CEO report to year end management meeting.* Cincinnati: Procter & Gamble Company.

Atiyah, P. S. (1979). *The rise and fall of freedom of contract.* New York: Oxford Press.

Awards and Recognitions. (2002). Retrieved August 7, 2003, from http://www.pg.com/about_pg/overview_facts/awards_recognition.jhtml

Ball, T. (1978). Two concepts of cohesion. *Theory and Society, 5,* 97–112.

Benjamin, W. (1968). In: H. Arendt (Ed.), *Illuminations* (pp. 121–140). New York: Harcourt Brace Jovanovich.

Bliese, P. D., & Halverson, R. R. (1998a). Group size and measures of group-level properties: An examination of eta-squared and ICC values. *Journal of Management, 24,* 157–172.

Bliese, P. D., & Halverson, R. R. (1998b). Individual and nomothetic models of job stress: An examination of work hours, cohesion, and well-being. *Journal of Applied Social Psychology, 28,* 563–580.

Blount, S., & Janicik, G. (2001). When plans change: Examining how people evaluate timing changes in work organizations. *Academy of Management Review, 26,* 556–584.

Bluedorn, A. C. (2000). Time and organizational culture. In: N. M. Ashkanasy & M. F. Peterson (Eds), *Handbook of organizational culture and climate* (pp. 117–125). Thousand Oaks, CA: Sage.

Bluedorn, A. C. (2002). *The human organization of time: Temporal realities and experience of time.* Stanford: Stanford Press.

Bluedorn, A. C., & Denhardt, A. (1988). Time and organizations. *Journal of Management, 14,* 299–320.

Bluedorn, A. C., Kaufman, C. F., & Lane, P. M. (1992). How many things do you like to do at once? An introduction to monochronic and polychronic time. *Academy of Management Executive, 6,* 17–26.

Boden, D. (1997). Temporal frames: Time and talk in organizations. *Time and Society, 6,* 5–53.

Boehm, C. (1993). Egalitarian behavior and reverse dominance hierarchy. *Current Anthropology, 37*(5), 227–240.

Boym, S. (2001). *The future of nostalgia.* New York: Basic Books.

Brand Resource Handbook. (1990). *Brand resource handbook.* Cincinnati: Procter & Gamble Company.

Buckley, N. (2002). Rebounding P&G beats Q4 profits and forecasts. *Financial Time,* August 6, p. 15.

Burton, R. M., Jorgen, L., & Borge, O. (2002). *Tension and resistance to change in organizational climate: Managerial implications for a fast paced world.* Retrieved August 30, from http://www.lok.cbs.dk/departments/mpp/lok/publikationer/os99-1213.pdf

Byrne, R. M. J. (1997). Cognitive processes in counterfactual thinking about what might have been. In: D. L. Medin (Ed.), *The psychology of learning and motivation: Advances in research and theory* (Vol. 37, pp. 105–154). San Diego: Academic Press.

Byrne, R. M. J. (2002). Mental models and counterfactual thinking. *Trends in Cognitive Sciences, 6,* 405–445.

Byrne, R. M. J., & McEleney, A. (2000). Counterfactual thinking about actions and failures to act. *Journal of Experimental Psychology: Learning Memory and Cognition, 26,* 1318–1331.

Can Procter and Gamble Change. (2002). Can Procter and Gamble change its culture, protect its market share, and find the next Tide? Retrieved January 5, 2004, from http://www2.una.edu/sborah/MBA/procter.htm

Chan, D. (1998). The conceptualization and analysis of change over time: An integrative approach incorporating longitudinal mean and covariance structures analysis (LMACS) and multiple indicator latent growth modeling (MLGM). *Organizational Research Methods, 1*, 421–483.

Clark, P. A. (1985). A review of theories of time and structure for organizational sociology. *Research in Sociology of Organizations, 4*, 35–79.

Clark, P. A. (2000). *Organizations in action: Competition between contexts.* London: Routledge.

Clegg, S. R. (1992). *Frameworks of power.* Thousand Oaks, CA: Sage.

Cohen, M., & Bacdayan, P. (1994). Organizational routines are stored as procedural memory: Evidence from a laboratory study. *Organizational Science, 5*, 554–568.

Comaroff, J., & Comaroff, J. L. (1992). *Ethnography and the historical imagination.* Boulder, CO: Westview.

Coolidge, A. (2004). Prilosec OTC may top sales target. Retrieved August 10, from http://www.cincypost.com/2004/01/10/prilo011004.html

Covey, S. (1989). *The seven habits of highly effective people.* New York: Simon and Schuster.

Czarmoawsla, B. (1999). *Writing management: Organizational theory as a literary genre.* Oxford: Oxford Press.

Dansereau, F., & Yammarino, F. J. (Eds). (1998). *Leadership: The multiple-level approaches.* London: JAI Press.

Dansereau, F., Yammarino, F. J., & Kohles, J. (1999). Multiple levels of analysis from a longitudinal perspective: Some implications for theory building. *Academy of Management Review, 24*, 346–357.

Dansereau, F., Yammarino, F. J., & Markum, S. E. (1995). Leadership: The multiple-level approaches. *Leadership Quarterly, 6*, 251–263.

Decker, C. (1998). *Winning with P&G 99.* New York: Pocket Books.

Denison, D. (2002). What is the difference between organizational culture and organizational climate: A native's point of view on a decade of paradigm wars. Retrieved July 30, 2003, from http://www.denisonculture.com/articles/paradigm_wars.pdf

Denzin, N., & Lincoln, Y. (1994). *Handbook of qualitative research.* Thousand Oaks, CA: Sage.

DiMaggio, P. J., & Powell, W. W. (1983). The iron cage revisited: Institutional isomorphism and collective rationality in institutional fields. *American Sociological Review, 48*, 147–160.

Drucker, P. F. (1955). *The practice of management.* London: William Heinemann.

Dyer, D., Dalzell, F., & Olegario, R. (2004). *Rising tide: Lessons from 165 years of brand building at Procter & Gamble.* Cambridge, MA: Harvard Business School Press.

Ekvall, G. (1987). The climate metaphor in organizational theory. In: B. Bass & P. Drenth (Eds), *Advances in organizational psychology* (pp. 177–190). Beverly Hills, CA: Sage.

Eliade, M. (1955). *The sacred and the profane.* New York: Harcourt, Brace, Jovanovich.

Etzioni, A. (1975). *A comparative analysis of complex organizations: On power, involvement, and their correlates.* New York: Free Press.

Finan, T. J., & Van Willigen, J. (1990). The pursuit of social knowledge: Methodology and practice of anthropology. In: J. V. Willigen & T. J. Finan (Eds), *Soundings: Rapid and reliable research methods for practicing anthropologists* (pp. 1–9). Washington, DC: American Anthropological Association.

Fine, C. H. (1998). *Clockspeed: Winning industry control in the age of temporary advantage.* New York: Perseus.

Flanherty, M. (1999). *A watched pot: How we experience time.* New York: New York University Press.

Fraser, J. T. (1987). *Time, the familiar stranger*. Redmont, WA: Tempus.

Gabriel, Y. (2000). *Storytelling in organizations*. Oxford: Oxford Press.

Gell, A. (1992). *The anthropology of time*. Oxford: Berg.

George, J. M., & Jones, G. R. (2000). The role of time in theory and theory building. *Journal of Management, 26*, 657–684.

Giddens, A. (1984). *The constitution of society*. Cambridge: Polity Press.

Goodman, P. S. (2000). *Missing lineages in organizational research*. Newbury Park: Sage.

Goodman, P. S., Lawrence, B. S., Ancona, D. G., & Tushman, M. L. (2002). Introduction. *The Academy of Management Review, 26*(4), 507–512.

Graney, B. (2000). Procter & (failed) Gamble (June 8). Retrieved October 3, 2005, from http://www.fool.com/news/foolplate/2000/foolplate000608.htm

Griffin, G. R. (1991). *Machiavell Machiavell Machiavelli on management*. New York: Praeger.

Hall, E. T. (1983). *The dance of life*. New York: Doubleday.

Hall, E. T. (1997). *Beyond culture*. Garden City, NY: Anchor Press/Doubleday.

Hall, E. T., & Hall, R. H. (1987). *Hidden differences: Doing business with the Japanese*. New York: Anchor.

Haskell, T. S. (1985). Capitalism and the origins of the humanitarian sensibility, part 2. *American Historical Review, 90*, 547–566.

Hatch, E. (1997). The good side of relativism. *Journal of Anthropological Research, 53*, 371–381.

Heinze, R.-I. (1991). *Shamans of the 20th century*. New York: Irvington Publishers, Inc.

Hobbes, T. (1962). *English works of Thomas Hobbes*. London: Bart, Scientia Aalen.

Hopkins, J. (2004). Wal-Mart's influence grows. Retrieved August 10, from http://usatoday.print-this.clickability.com/pt/cpt?action=cpt&expire=&urlID=5243978&fb=Y&partnerID=1661

House, R., Rousseau, D. M., & Thomas-Hunt, M. (1995). The meso paradigm: A framework for the integration of micro and macro organizational behavior. In: L. L. Cummings & B. M. Straw (Eds), *Research in organizational behavior* (Vol. 16, pp. 71–114). Greenwich: JAI Press.

Hunt, J. G. (2004). Making strange knowledge more intelligible. In: F. J. Yammarino & F. Dansereau (Eds), *Multi-level issues in organizational behavior and processes* (Vol. 3, pp. 443–455). Oxford: Elsevier.

Hunt, J. G., & Ropo, A. (1998). Multi-level leadership: Grounded theory and mainstream theory applied to the case of general motors. In: F. Dansereau & F. J. Yammarino (Eds), *Leadership: The multiple-level approaches* (pp. 289–326). London: JAI Press.

Imai, M. (1986). *Kaizen: The key to Japan's competitive success*. New York: Random House.

Jackell, R. (1989). *Moral mazes*. New York: Oxford University Press.

Jones, A. (2002). Final curtain call for Pepper. *Financial Times*, April 11, p. 9.

Jorgensen, D. L. (1989). *Participant observation: A methodology for human studies*. Newbury Park, CA: Sage.

Joyce, W. F., & Slocum, J. (1984). Collective climate: Agreement as a basis for defining aggregate climate in organizations. *Academy of Management Journal, 27*, 721–742.

Kadin, P. (1985). *Persistence pays*. Norwich, NY: Procter & Gamble Company.

Kanungo, R. N., & Mendonca, M. (1996). *Ethical dimensions of leadership*. Thousand Oaks, CA: Sage.

Kern, S. (1983). *The culture of time and space*. Cambridge, MA: Harvard University Press.

Kinney, J. (1998). Policy management: A beginner's perspective. Paper presented at the American Supplier Institute conference on Policy Management, September, Cincinnati, OH.

Kluckholn, F. R., & Strodtbeck, F. L. (1961). *Variations in value orientations*. Evanston: Row, Peterson.

Koselleck, R. (1985). *Futures past* (K. Tribe, Trans.). Cambridge, MA: MIT Press.

Koyes, D., & Decotiis, T. (1991). Inductive measures of psychological climate. *Human Relations, 44,* 265–285.

Kozlowski, S. W., Gully, S. M., Salas, E., & Cannnon-Bowers, J. A. (2000). Team leadership and development: Theory, principles, and guidelines for training leaders and teams. In: D. J. M. Beyerlein & S. Beyerlein (Eds), *Advances in interdisciplinary studies of work teams: Team leadership* (Vol. 3, pp. 251–289). Greenwich: JAI Press.

Kozlowski, S. W., & Klein, K. J. (2000). A multi-level approach to theory and research in organizations. In: K. J. Klein & S. W. Kozlowski (Eds), *Multi-level theory, research, and methods in organizations* (pp. 3–90). San Francisco: Jossey-Bass.

Kozlowski, S. W., & Salas, E. (1997). *Improving training effectiveness in working organizations*. Mohunk, NJ: Lawerce Erlbaum Associates.

Kruse, F. (1984). Personal communication, April 29.

Kruse, F. (1996). Personal communication, October 3.

Leblebici, H., Salancik, G. R., Copay, A., & King, T. (1991). Institutional change and the transformation of interorganizational fields: An organizational history of the U.S. radio broadcasting industry. *Administrative Science Quarterly, 36,* 333–363.

Levitt, T. (1958). The dangers of social responsibility. *Harvard Business Review, 36*(5), 41–50.

Lundberg, C. C. (2004). Standing back to better appreciate: On multi-level process theorizing. In: F. J. Yammarino & F. Dansereau (Eds), *Multi-level issues in organizational behavior and processes* (Vol. 3, pp. 435–442). Oxford: Elsevier.

Mackenzie, K. D. (2004). The process approach to multi-level organizational behavior. In: F. J. Yammarino & F. Dansereau (Eds), *Multi-level issues in organizational behavior and processes* (Vol. 3, pp. 347–418). Oxford: Elsevier.

Mainemelis, C. (2001). When the muse takes it all: A model for the experience of timelessness in organizations. *Academy of Management Review, 26,* 248–265.

Major, D. A. (2000). Effective newcomer socialization. In: N. M. Ashkanasy, C. P. M. Wilderrom & M. F. Peterson (Eds), *Handbook of organizational culture and climate* (pp. 355–368). Thousand Oaks, CA: Sage.

Markus, H., & Zajonc, R. (1985). The cognitive perspective in social psychology. In: G. Lindsey & E. Aronson (Eds), *Handbook of social psychology* (Vol. 15, pp. 137–231). New York: Random House.

Martel, Y. (2003). *The life of Pi*. Orlando, FL: Harcourt.

McKay, J. T. (1968). *The management of time*. Englewood Cliffs, NJ: Prentice-Hall.

McNeill, R. G. (2000). Hospitality sales management. Retrieved August 10, 2004, from http://jan.ucc.nau.edu/~rgm/ha400/class/customer/relationships/Relationship%20article2.html

Menand, L. (2001). *The metaphysical club: A story of ideas in America*. New York: Farrar, Straus and Giroux.

Merry, S. E. (2001). Changing rights, changing culture. In: J. K. Cowan, M. B. Dembour & R. A. Wilson (Eds), *Culture and rights* (pp. 31–55). Cambridge, UK: Cambridge University Press.

Minkowski, E. (1970). *Lived time: Phenomenological and psychopathological studies* (N. Metzel, Trans.). Evanston, IL: Northwestern Press.

Mitchell, T. R., & James, L. R. (2001). Building better theory: Time and the specification of when things happen. *Academy of Management Review, 26,* 530–547.

Mortished, C. (2001). Shampoo giants tell spies to wash and go (September 1). Retrieved November 17, 2004, from http://www.commondreams.org/headlines01/0901-03.htm

P&G Annual Report. (2005). Retrieved June 15, from http://www.eu.pg.com/downloads/PG2004AnnualReport_Online.pdf

P&G's Focus. (2002). *P&G's focus making a difference*. Cincinnati: P&G Champions, July.

P&G's Performance. (2003). P&G's performance exceeds expectations. Retrieved June 15, 2004, from http://static.highbeam.com/h/householdamppersonalproductsindustry/november012003/pampgsperformanceexceedsexpectationsfinancialnews/

P&G's Strong-Arming. (1991). *Cincinnati Post*, August 15, Editorial Page.

Pattee, R. (1989). Neo-shamanism: A source of creativity for our time. In: R. I. Heinze (Ed.), *Proceedings of the fifth International conference of the Study of Shamanism and Alternate Modes of Healing* (pp. 98–110). Berkeley: Independent Scholars of Asia.

Pearce, J. L., & Branyiczki, I. (1997). Legitimacy: An analysis of three Hungarian – West European collaborations. In: P. W. Beamish & J. P. Killing (Eds), *Cooperative strategies: European perspectives* (pp. 300–322). San Francisco: New Lexington Press.

Pritchett, L. (1992). Fostering organizational change. Breakfast meeting (November), Binghamton School of Management, Binghamton, NY.

Pritchett, L. (2003). *Stop paddling and start rocking the boat*. New York: Harper Collins.

Purpose, Values, Principles. (2002). Retrieved August 5, 2004, from http://www.pg.com/about_pg/overview_facts/value_principles.jhtml?document=%2Fcontent%2Fen_US%2Fxml%2Fcorporate%2Fcorp_pvp_principles.xml

Rawe, D. (1991). P&G calls in police to probe journal leak. *Cincinnati Post*, August 12, p. 7.

Reed, M. (1992). *The sociology of organizations*. Brighten: Harvester Wheatsheaf.

Reeves-Ellington, R. H. (1992). Using cultural skills for cooperative advantage in Japan. *Human Organization, 52*, 203–215.

Reeves-Ellington, R. H. (1995). Anthropology and total quality management: Improving sales force performance in overseas markets. In: J. Sherry (Ed.), *Contemporary marketing and consumer behavior* (pp. 169–208). Thousand Oaks, CA: Sage.

Reeves-Ellington, R. H. (1996). Liberal arts education in Bulgaria: A vehicle for change. *International Education, 25*, 5–33.

Reeves-Ellington, R. H. (1997). Cross cultural organizational stress – the American University in Bulgaria. *Human Organization, 57*, 94–107.

Reeves-Ellington, R. H. (1999a). From command to demand economics: Bulgarian organizational value orientations. *Practicing Anthropology, 21*, 5–13.

Reeves-Ellington, R. H. (1999b). Local value orientations and global customer chains: A Bulgarian case study. *South East Europe Review for Labour and Social Affairs, 2*, 105–122.

Reeves-Ellington, R. H. (2004a). Cultural bases of research: Integrating research cultures for complex problems. In: F. J. Yammarino & F. Dansereau (Eds.), *Multi-level issues in organizational behavior and processes* (Vol. 3, pp. 167–180). Oxford: Elsevier.

Reeves-Ellington, R. H. (2004b). Trustscapes and distrustscapes: A multi-level approach for understanding stability and change. In: F. J. Yammarino & F. Dansereau (Eds.), *Multi-level issues in organizational behavior and processes* (Vol. 3, pp. 91–148). Oxford: Elsevier.

Reeves-Ellington, R. H., & Anderson, A. (1997a). *Beyond agenda: Culture, commerce and social responsibility*. Lewiston, NY: Edwin Mellon Press.

Reeves-Ellington, R. H., & Anderson, A. (1997b). The ethnology of information systems. *Accounting, Management, and Information Technologies, 7*, 168–190.

Restructuring P&G. (2004). Retrieved June 18, 2005, from http://icmr.icfai.org/casestudies/catalogue/Business%20Strategy1/BSTR068.htm

Ripley, K. (1991). On second thought. Retrieved November 18, 2004, from http://www.find-articles.com/p/articles/mi_hb323/is_199109/ai_hibm1G111228584

Roese, N. J. (1997). Counterfactual thinking. *Psychological Bulletin, 121*, 133–148.

Rohrer, T. C. (Ed.) (1990). *A continuing series for implementing total quality*. Cincinnati, OH: Procter & Gamble Company.

Rose, F. (1989). *West of Eden: The end of innocence at Apple Computer*. Harmondsworth, UK: Penguin Press.

Rousseau, D. M. (1988). The construction of climate in organizational research. In: C. L. Cooper & I. Robertson (Eds), *International review of industrial and organizational psychology* (pp. 139–158). New York: Wiley.

Safire, W. (1991). At P&G: It sinks. *The New York Times*, September 16, p. A19.

Sanna, L. J. (1996). Defensive pessimism, optimism, and simulating alternatives: Some ups and downs of prefactual and counterfactual thinking. *Personality and Social Psychology Bulletin, 23*, 1020–1036.

Sanna, L. J. (1998). Defensive pessimism and optimism: The bittersweet influence of mood on performance and prefactual and counterfactual thinking. *Cognition and Emotion, 12*, 635–666.

Sanna, L. J., & Turley-Ames, K. J. (1999). Mood, self-esteem, and simulated alternatives: Thought-provoking affective influences on counterfactual direction. *Journal of Personality and Social Psychology, 76*, 543–558.

Schiller, Z. (1997). An old coach with new discipline. *Business Week*, September, p. 51.

Schisgall, O. (1981). *Eyes on tomorrow*. New York: Doubleday.

Schneider, B. (1990). *Organizational climate and culture*. New Delhi: Sage.

Sculley, J., with Byrne, J. A. (1988). *Odyssey: Pepsi to Apple … A journey of adventure, ideas, and the future*. New York: Harper & Row.

Serwer, A. (2001). P&G comes clean on spying operation (August 30). Retrieved November 18, 2004, from http://www.business2.com/b2/web/articles/0,17863,513968,00.html

Shampoo Giant Caught Spying. (2001). Retrieved November 18, 2004, from http://news.bbc.co.uk/1/hi/business/1518901.stm

Sinha, J. B. P. (1995). *The cultural context of leadership and power*. New Delhi: Sage.

Spradley, J. (1981). *Participant observation*. New York: Holt, Rinehart and Winston.

Strauss, A., & Corbin, J. (1984). Grounded theory methodology. In: N. K. D. Y. S. Lincoln (Ed.), *Handbook of Qualitative Research* (pp. 273–286). London: Sage Press.

Swasy, A. (1993). *Soap opera*. New York: Random House.

Tecklenberg, H. (1983). Personal communication, August 12,.

Turner, T. (1995). Neoliberal ecopolitics and indigenous people: The Kayapo, the "rainforest harvest" and the Body Shop. In: G. Dicum (Ed.), *Local heritage in the changing tropics: Innovative strategies for natural resource management and control* (Vol. Bulletin Series 98, Yale School of Forestry and Environmental Studies, pp. 113–123). New Haven, CT: Yale University Press.

Waller, M. J., Conte, J. M., Gibson, C. B., & Carpener, M. A. (2000). The effect of individual perceptions of deadlines on team performance. *Academy of Management Review, 26*, 586–600.

Walton, S. (1993). *Made in America*. New York: Bantam.

Wheeler, D. J., & Chambers, D. S. (1992). *Understanding statistical process control.* Knoxville, TN: SPC Press.

Zammuto, R. F., & Krackover, J. Y. (1991). Quantitative and qualitative studies in organizational behavior. *Research in Organizational Change and Development, 5,* 83–111.

Zeurubavel, E. (1981). *Hidden rhythms: Schedules and calendars in social life.* Chicago: University of Chicago Press.

Zook, C. (2003). Gushers of growth. *The Wall Street Journal,* December 4, p. B4.

A SYSTEM DYNAMICS PERSPECTIVE ON TIMESCAPES IN ORGANIZATIONS

J. Christian Broberg, Adam D. Bailey and James G. (Jerry) Hunt

ABSTRACT

This chapter uses a system dynamics approach to do a constructive replication (Lykken, 1968; Kelly, Chase, & Tucker, 1979; Hendrick, 1990) and extension of Reeves-Ellington's (this volume) timescape theory illustrated in his case study carried out at different hierarchical levels in Procter & Gamble. The timescape theory of temporal fit consists of two time perspectives – business time and social time – that compete for application. The senior-management level plays a key role in determining which timescape dominates. Reeves-Ellington argues that his findings show that organizational performance diminishes when there is a lack of fit between the timescapes of senior management and those of other levels of management. Our system dynamics model tests this notion and finds that the timescape case does not allow sufficient time to clearly demonstrate the hypothesized fit effects. In addition to timescape fit, environmental consumer demand aspects, which were not considered in the original case, are argued to affect Reeves-Ellington's performance measures. The system dynamics model's general emphasis on temporality and

Multi-Level Issues in Organizations and Time
Research in Multi-Level Issues, Volume 6, 317–330
Copyright © 2007 by Elsevier Ltd.
All rights of reproduction in any form reserved
ISSN: 1475-9144/doi:10.1016/S1475-9144(07)06014-6

feedback provide especially for the constructive replication and extension of the timescape theory.

INTRODUCTION

The notion of timescapes in organizations is a potentially important one, and Richard Reeves-Ellington has put together an interesting treatment of the idea. In the spirit of constructive replication (Lykken, 1968; Kelly, Chase, & Tucker, 1979; Hendrick, 1990) and extension, in this chapter we revisit selected aspects of Reeves-Ellington's work using a system dynamics approach (Forrester, 1961; Sterman, 2000). Using Eden's definition, a constructive replication is "research that tests the same hypothesized relationships among the same theoretical constructs as a given earlier study but varies the 'operationalization' of those constructs (Eden, 2002, p. 842)." Our study takes aspects of Reeves-Ellington's theory and operationalizes it by using system dynamics. We see system dynamics as now coming into its own, after some earlier ebbs and flows (Hunt & Ropo, 2003), in the organizational behavior or the broader organization studies arena. System dynamics is a part of computational modeling, or what some have called the "third scientific discipline" (Hunt & Ropo, 2003; Ilgen & Hulin, 2000), with the first two being experimentation and regression-based work (Cronbach, 1957, 1975).

The nature of system dynamics studies varies widely both conceptually and in terms of data. Works involve extensions of case studies, survey data, data based on inventories, units of production, prices, person-hours, rework, measures of charisma, and grounded theory approaches, to name only a few examples (Black, Carlile, & Repenning, 2004; Davis, 2005; Repenning & Sterman, 2002; Rudolph & Repenning, 2002; Sastry, 1997). Many times, theories are conceptualized in terms of counts of dynamic measures of motivation, goal setting, and the kinds of variables commonly used in traditional organization studies. In fact, instead of linear conceptualizations and traditional statistical approaches, the research demonstrates oscillations, S-shaped growth curves, and the like derived from computer simulations of mathematical formulations reflecting conceptual representations.

In summary, system dynamics research varies widely both across and within studies using a wide range of data sources (Anderson & Johnson, 1997; Sterman, 2000). In this sense, system dynamics research is much like a series of jet engines that can run on fuels ranging from kerosene to high-octane aviation fuel. As a consequence, studies examining complex environmental segments such as global warming and the effects of increasing oil usage may be contrasted with relatively simple ones, such as our study (to be described shortly), that incorporate relatively few variables and assumptions. Our system dynamics model was formulated to reflect selected aspects of Reeves-Ellington's theory with a very different methodology and allow for the constructive replication and extension that is so important in the organization studies field. Similar to Davis's (2005) research involving the routinization of charisma, we therefore examine aspects of Reeves-Ellington's theory with constructive replication and extension in mind.

WHAT IS SYSTEM DYNAMICS?

Before applying a system dynamics approach, a word may be said about the characteristics underlying what Sterman (2000, p. 22) terms "dynamic complexity." Such characteristics as dynamic, tightly coupled, governed by feedback, and nonlinear provide a good place to start:

- *Dynamic* – while everything changes, the change occurs at many different timescales that often interact.
- *Tightly coupled* – the actors in the system have strong interactions with one another and with the outside world.
- *Governed by feedback* – the activities feed back on themselves.
- *Nonlinear* – cause and effect are rarely proportional and what happens near the current operating point often does not apply in other states of the system.

At the same time, systems meet the following criteria:

- *History dependent* and *path dependent* – taking one road precludes taking others; doing and undoing often have fundamentally different time constants.
- *Self-organizing* – the dynamics of systems arise spontaneously from their internal structure (e.g., market structures).

Finally, systems demonstrate the following characteristics:

- *Adaptive* – decision rules change over time, and there is selection and proliferation.
- *Counterintuitive* – cause and effect are different in time and space.

- *Policy resistant* – because of complexity, many seemingly obvious problem solutions fail or worsen the situations.
- *Characterized by trade-offs* – high-leverage policies often generate transitory improvement before a problem grows worse.

These characteristics clearly are different from the underlying linearity assumptions in the traditional Newtonian perspectives that continue to drive much current organizational work (Hunt & Ropo, 2003). In a nutshell, dynamism, nonlinear, cause and effect, and strong emphasis on feedback convey the essence of the system dynamics approach used in our analysis of Reeves-Ellington's work.

HIGHLIGHTS OF REEVES-ELLINGTON'S THEORY AND CASE

A key focus of Reeves-Ellington's work is an attempt to bring together multiple levels and temporality to explain the performance of the consumer products giant, Procter & Gamble (P&G). The levels that are utilized are not the increasingly popular analytical levels of analysis, but rather the hierarchical levels within the organization (Hunt, 1991). Reeves-Ellington's three levels of analysis are entry-level managers and employees, mid-level managers, and senior-level managers. He uses two time perspectives, which are referred to as timescapes: business time and social time. These two timescapes represent two different ways of experiencing and perceiving time. Reeves-Ellington uses longitudinal qualitative and quantitative data in an effort to show that the different time perspectives and levels of management interact to affect firm performance.

According to Reeves-Ellington (this volume), both business and social timescapes exist within organizations and compete for application. The senior-management level plays a pivotal role in determining which timescape dominates, as these managers have the power to sustain or change the organizational climate. As he writes, "senior managers decide on organizational work styles [timescapes] that are either business or socially driven. They then attempt to socialize the rest of the organization in ways that support individual decisions" (p. 274). Reeves-Ellington posits that this use of organizational power is the most meaningful one for senior managers.

Reeves-Ellington further explains that middle managers do not change timescapes but rather enforce timescape execution within the organization. However, middle managers tend to defend the status quo and do not readily support change. Even so, these managers are sometimes forced to change as a result of senior-management pressures. Reeves-Ellington cites the example of one business timescape CEO who fired any employee who disagreed with him. Middle managers are the "face" of the organization to entry-level managers; through interaction with these individuals, they facilitate the socialization of entry-level managers, leading these employees to adopt the dominant organizational timescape.

Reeves-Ellington theorizes that each level of management has a different resistance rate to change. The longer managers have been socialized to practice the dominant organizational timescape, the more vigorously they will resist change. Entry-level managers are still learning the dominant timescape, so they will be less resistant than middle managers to timescape change. Senior managers who seek to change organizational timescapes will virtually always encounter some resistance, but the resistance will be the greatest when the senior managers bypass the middle-manager levels and work directly with the entry-level managers. Although this action is taken in an attempt to overcome the status quo defending middle managers, in fact, it increases the intensity of middle-manager resistance.

Reeves-Ellington (this volume) uses the P&G case to demonstrate that "consistency of timescape use reinforces company success and that inconsistency results in poor business and social performance at the company" (p. 282). The basic idea is that organizational performance diminishes when there is lack of fit between the timescapes of senior management and the other levels of management. Reeves-Ellington seeks to "demonstrate that radical shifts from one timescape to the other are risky and court failure" (p. 283).

Reeves-Ellington's (this volume) case study indicates that even though both business and social timescapes are incorporated within the P&G culture, the dominant timescape in the organization is the social timescape. He notes:

> Composition theory [which he finally defines on p. 277] confirms that traditionally P&G is grounded in social timescapes, particularly its climate and culture, in ways that provide horizontal and vertical binding throughout the company. During the 1990s this formula was violated with disastrous results by Artzt and Jager. Their actions revealed a discontinuity of senior managerial timescape responsibilities that led to major organizational disruption. (pp. 301)

Reeves-Ellington further contends that the diminished performances of P&G during the tenures of Artzt and Jager are largely due to their business temporal timescapes not fitting with the social timescapes of the organization. He notes that, "Of importance to this case is that discontinuity theory [discussed on p. 278 of Reeves-Ellington's case] exposes how Artz and Jager, through their attempts to destroy P&G's traditional social timescape use and replace it with a dominant business timescape position, created company dysfunctions and major shifts in traditional profitability" (p. 301). Thus the cause of poor performance is postulated to be the misfit in timescapes between the CEO and the organization.

Reeves-Ellington (this volume) uses performance data in an effort to show that "CEOs who support traditional P&G socialization and organizational behaviors lead the company to better business performance than those who solely privilege the business timescape focus" (p. 307). Therefore, our system dynamics constructive replication and extension of Reeves-Ellington's theory seeks to answer the following questions: Does Reeves-Ellington's analysis make sense? Is poor performance due to misfit and good performance due to fit? Is it possible for an organization to change its dominant timescape? If so, how long would it take to enact change?

METHODOLOGY OF THE SYSTEM DYNAMICS APPROACH

One of the basic assumptions from Reeves-Ellington's theory is that when there is a match between the timescape of the CEO and the dominant timescape of the organization, the overall organizational performance is greater than when a mismatch occurs. We sought to test this basic assumption using the previously mentioned system dynamics approach (Sterman, 2000). System dynamics is a computer-simulated modeling approach that is effective in modeling complex phenomena dynamically. It is especially useful, according to Sterman (2000), for analyzing situations in which management policy has created resistance. To test the basic assumption, we modeled timescape fit among three different levels: CEO, middle management, and employees (see Fig. 1 for the system dynamics model).

The system dynamics model in Fig. 1 consists of a series of stocks (represented by boxes) that are accumulations of the differences between inflows and outflows. For the purposes of our model, the stocks are the individual timescapes of managers and employees. The double-lined arrows with values pointing toward and away from the stocks (boxes) are rates that determine the speed at which individuals enter or exit a particular timescape. Single-lined arrows in the model input specific information into rates that enables the mathematical calculation of the speed of exit or entry. "Multiplier tabs" are one piece of information entered into the rate equations; these table

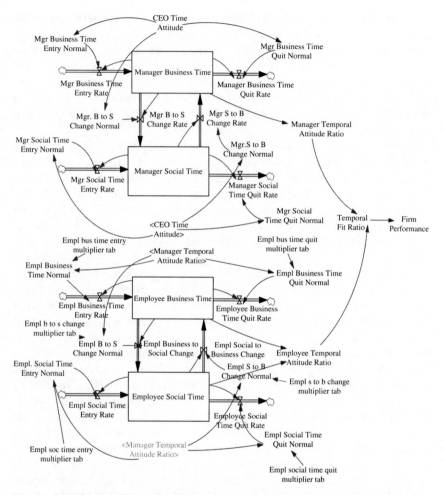

Fig. 1. Multi-Level Timescape Change System Dynamics Model. (*Note:* The model involves a series of stocks (boxes) and flows (double-lined arrows with heads pointing toward and away from stocks. Stocks are accumulations of the differences between inflows and outflows of individuals with particular timescapes. Rates determine the speed at which individuals enter or exit a particular timescape. Single-lined arrows supply information that enable the mathematical calculation of rates. Multiplier tabs introduce assumptions of nonlinearity into the exit and entry rates over time. Ratios are included in the model to determine the ratio of business to social timescape employees and managers over time and to determine the point in time when organizational timescape fit is achieved with CEO.)

functions (Sterman, 2000) introduce assumptions of nonlinearity into the model. Table functions include pairs of x and y values that are nonlinear – in our case based on assumptions – that regulate the rate at which individuals flow in and out of specific timescapes. Finally, the model includes ratios, which enable the calculation of the point in time at which the CEO timescape fits with the organization timescape (managers and employees). In our model, organizational fit occurs when a majority of managers and employees possess the same timescape as the CEO.

Unlike in Reeves-Ellington's model, we grouped the notion of mid-level and entry-level managers into middle management and included employees. We decided that including employees was vital to testing the CEO and organization timescape fit because employees embody the majority of the workforce and arguably do the majority of the work. We tested how long it would take for the organization's dominant social timescape to change into a business timescape, assuming that the CEO has a business timescape orientation.

According to Reeves-Ellington, P&G has a dominant timescape of social time. We, therefore, made the assumption that 70% of managers had a social timescape and 30% of managers had a business timescape. We assumed that the same distribution of timescapes existed among the employees. Based on average employee counts at P&G over the last 10 years (Mergent Online, 2005), we assumed a total number of 100,000 employees for our model.

Although we did not have data on the ratio of managers to employees, for our purposes we assumed an employee-to-manager ratio of 9:1. The 70% to 30% ratio of social timescape to business timescape seems to be reasonable, given the information from the case. These percentages represent a dominant position for the social timescape while simultaneously allowing for the existence of business timescape orientation among the employees. Several pieces of information from the case, in fact, point to the existence of the business timescape within P&G. For example, one business timescape manager, whose quantitative business analysis was dismissed by his manager, found that this analysis was later used by an upper-level executive to make an important business decision. The fact that two of the internally promoted CEOs have had a business timescape and thrived in various divisions within P&G also signals the existence of a business timescape in at least some areas within the company.

The Reeves-Ellington theory of temporal fit posits that a fit between the CEO's timescape and the dominant organizational timescape results in superior performance, as compared to a misfit. However, Reeves-Ellington did not take into account the time it would potentially take to change the temporal orientation of an organization. Using system dynamics, we attempted to determine how long it would take P&G to implement a change of this magnitude.

For managers, we theorized that given a change at the CEO level, there would be a change in the dominant temporal orientation of managers from two directions. First, there would be voluntary turnover of managers whose timescape did not fit with that of the current CEO. Second, some managers would change timescapes to conform to the new regime. This managerial change would come both from being convinced of the advantages of the new timescape and from compliance and adoption of the new timescape orientation in an effort to keep their jobs.

This change would probably not occur suddenly, but rather would take place gradually due to the voluntary turnover and the change in attitude to change a misfit into a fit. However, we do assume that a change could occur over time. Eventually, a new CEO with a timescape misfit could create a fit with the organization and improve performance, if the timescape orientation of the organization changed. Reeves-Ellington's case discussed the asymmetrical use of power by CEOs whose business timescapes conflicted with the overall social timescapes of P&G. The initial reaction to these CEOs was negative, and average overall performance was less than that achieved under the tenures of more social-oriented CEOs.

It might be expected that such a cultural change would be met with opposition and resistance (Oreg, 2003; Watson, 1971). To enact change in an expeditious manner, CEOs might have to rely on heavy-handed measures that would not be perceived positively by employees in the short term. However, given enough time, we hypothesize that CEOs could ultimately create a fit between their timescape and the organization and thereby improve performance.

To model this hypothesis, we tested how long it might take for a new business timescape CEO to transform a social timescape culture so that it fits with his or her business timescape orientation. In modeling this hypothesis, we made several assumptions about the rate of timescape change at both the manager and employee levels. For managers, when a new business timescape CEO takes charge, we assumed that the exit rate of social timescape managers increases and the exit rate of business timescape managers decreases due to a better fit with the new CEO's timescape. Conversely, the hiring rate of social timescape managers decreases and the hiring rate of new business timescape managers increases. The change rate between business managers to social managers (i.e., the rate at which business-oriented managers are persuaded to become social-oriented managers) decreases and the transfer rate between social-oriented managers to business managers increases as more managers decide to change their timescape to better fit with the new leadership or, in some cases, to maintain employment and position.

Given these assumptions, Fig. 2 shows how the aggregate manager timescape changes over time. This behavior over time chart (Burns, 2000) is derived from the system dynamics model and its underlying assumptions. According to assumptions in the model, in approximately quarter 12 (i.e., year 3), the business timescape becomes the dominant temporal orientation within the organization for managers.

For the employees, because of their relative numbers and distance from the CEO level, we assumed that it would take longer to enact a timescape change among them. We incorporated the same assumptions as we made for the managers with respect to entry, exit rates, and transfer rates for business and social timescapes, except that the rates of change from a social to business timescape were slower. We thought it reasonable to assume that employee timescape change would be delayed somewhat and would be a function of the employee timescape fit with manager and CEO, with the fit with managers having the greatest direct influence on the employee timescape change.

Figure 3 shows the employee timescape change over time between social and business timescapes. Similar to Fig. 2, Fig. 3 is generated from our system dynamics model based on the rate of change assumptions, given the introduction of a business timescape CEO. Although the time required to achieve a majority of business timescape managers is approximately 3 years

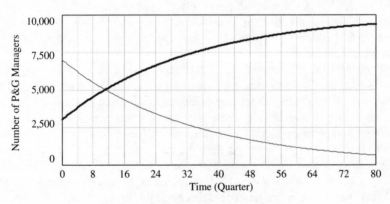

Fig. 2.   Manager Timescape Change over Time.

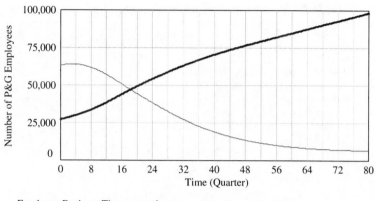

Fig. 3. Employee Timescape Change over Time.

in our model, the time necessary for a majority of the employees to adopt a business time orientation is about 18 quarters, or 4.5 years.

To calculate the length of time needed to achieve a fit between a CEO and the organization such that organizational performance is not disadvantaged, we created a function of the ratio of business timescape managers to business timescape employees. Although employees probably would have less influence as compared to managers, we postulate that, given their sheer numbers, employees would exert a greater influence on the performance of the organization with respect to timescape fit. For this reason, we decreased the weight of the manager's influence on the performance calculation. Applying the performance function to our model, it took approximately 5.5 years to achieve CEO and organizational fit. Given this estimate, we postulate that it will take approximately 5–6 years for a business timescape CEO to change the organization from a majority social timescape to a majority business timescape.

This estimate appears reasonable when one looks at the performance information for P&G's business timescape CEOs. The case provided the average earnings for the tenure of each CEO from 1986. Those CEOs with a business timescape achieved lower earnings than those with a more balanced or social timescape. This finding is to be expected given that the business timescape is a misfit with the social timescape that dominates the P&G culture. However, analysis of the year-to-year earnings for the business timescape CEO Artzt (Table 1) reveals that during the last year of his tenure as CEO his earnings increased by almost 20%.

Table 1.   Procter & Gamble Yearly Earnings by CEO.

CEO	Temporal Timescape	Year	Earnings ($ billion)	Yearly Earnings Change
Lafley	Balanced/social	2005	7,257	0.12
Lafley	Balanced/social	2004	6,481	0.25
Lafley	Balanced/social	2003	5,186	0.19
Lafley	Balanced/social	2002	4,352	0.49
Lafley	Balanced/social	2001	2,922	−0.18
Jager	Business	2000	3,542	−0.06
Jager	Business	1999	3,763	0.00
Pepper	Social	1998	3,780	0.11
Pepper	Social	1997	3,415	0.12
Pepper	Social	1996	3,046	0.15
Artzt	Business	1995	2,645	0.20
Artzt	Business	1994	2,211	2.37
Artzt	Business	1993	−656	−1.35
Artzt	Business	1992	1,872	0.06
Artzt	Business	1991	1,773	

Source: Procter & Gamble annual reports, June 1991–June 2005 (Mergent Online, 2005).

This increase in earnings rivals those in the very best years achieved by balanced and social timescape CEOs. This finding seems to fit with our system dynamics model, which indicates that it takes a substantial amount of time to change the timescape orientation of an organization. The other business-oriented CEO, Jager, enjoyed only two years at the helm before he was dismissed. We contend that this span was not enough time to change the timescape orientation of the organization.

Especially interesting to note is that Jager's first year of negative performance also fits with a substantial decrease in consumer spending on personal care items among U.S. households (U.S. Department of Labor Bureau of Labor Statistics, 2005). This personal care area represents the largest product category in P&G's largest market. Such a finding suggests that more than just the timescape fit between the CEO and the organization affects firm performance; other exogenous factors may also loom large.

DISCUSSION AND CONCLUSIONS

Our application of the system dynamics model is quite simple, yet still calls for several kinds of underlying assumptions – for example, entry rates and exit rates. Even with our simplified model, starting with a different set of assumptions would likely yield different findings. Similar to Sterman and Wittenberg's (1999) constructive replication of Kuhn's theory of scientific revolutions, our system dynamics model is not comprehensive, nor does it capture the subtleties of Reeves-Ellington's theory. However, using system dynamics to constructively replicate aspects of his theory does identify some deficiencies in the theory. Obviously, we would have preferred to use actual data rather than assumptions for as many of these variables as possible. Armed with such data, we could have gone much further with our analysis. Nevertheless, even such a simple model and its attendant assumptions demonstrates the usefulness of a system dynamics approach and allows us to constructively replicate and extend Reeves-Ellington's theory.

Clearly, many variables other than timescape fit would have affected Reeves-Ellington's choice of average net earnings per year or average shareholder equity. Our choice of variable – consumer spending by household unit per year – is, of course, just one example. Furthermore, a system dynamics approach, even in its simplified form, allowed for a much more explicit treatment of temporality as compared with the Reeves-Ellington theory. Finally, a much more detailed and specific treatment of the various time dimensions included in Reeves-Ellington's theory, while adding complexity, could open up new opportunities for additional insights. On balance, Reeves-Ellington's theory, while contributing to levels approaches in its own right, quite readily lends itself to an alternative form of analysis in a temporally oriented journey toward constructive replication and extension.

ACKNOWLEDGMENT

We thank A-Team members Donna Hunt, John N. Davis, and especially James R. Burns for their assistance with this manuscript.

REFERENCES

Anderson, V., & Johnson, L. (1997). *Systems thinking basics, from concepts to causal loops.* Waltham, MA: Pegasus Communications.

Black, L. J., Carlile, P. R., & Repenning, N. P. (2004). A dynamic theory of expertise and occupational boundaries in new technology implementation: Building on Barley's study of CT scanning. *Administrative Science Quarterly, 49,* 572–607.

Burns, J. R. (2000). *Causal loop diagrams, stock and flow diagrams, VENSIM mechanics.* Available from the College of Business Administration, Texas Tech University, Lubbock, TX.

Cronbach, L. J. (1957). The two disciplines of scientific psychology. *American Psychologist, 12*, 671–684.

Cronbach, L. J. (1975). Beyond the two disciplines of scientific psychology. *American Psychologist, 30*, 116–127.

Davis, J. N. (2005). *How is charisma routinized? A new look at an old question.* Unpublished dissertation, Texas Tech University, Lubbock, TX.

Eden, D. (2002). Replication, meta-analysis, scientific progress, and AMJ's publication policy. *Academy of Management Journal, 45*(5), 841–846.

Forrester, J. W. (1961). *Industrial dynamics.* Cambridge, MA: MIT Press.

Hendrick, C. (1990). Replications, strict replications, and conceptual replications: Are they important? *Journal of Social Behavior and Personality, 5*(4), 41–50.

Hunt, J. G. (1991). *Leadership: A new synthesis.* Newbury Park, CA: Sage.

Hunt, J. G., & Ropo, A. (2003). Longitudinal organizational research and the third scientific discipline. *Group and Organization Management, 28*(3), 315–340.

Ilgen, D. R., & Hulin, C. L. (Eds). (2000). *Computational modeling of behavior in organizations: The third scientific discipline.* Washington, DC: American Psychological Association.

Kelly, C. W., Chase, L. J., & Tucker, R. K. (1979). Replication in experimental communication research: An analysis. *Human Communication Research, 5*, 338–342.

Lykken, D. T. (1968). Statistical significance in psychological research. *Psychological Bulletin, 70*, 151–159.

Mergent Online. (2005). *Procter & Gamble annual reports.* Retrieved November 9, 2005, from http://www.mergentonline.com/compdetail.asp?company=1&company_mer=6814&type=compdetail

Oreg, S. (2003). Resistance to change: Developing an individual differences measure. *Journal of Applied Psychology, 88*(4), 680–693.

Reeves-Ellington, R. H. (this volume). Timescapes: A multi-level approach for understanding time in complex organizations. In: F. Dansereau & F. J. Yammarino (Eds.), *Multi-level issues in organizations and time* (Vol. 6). Oxford: Elsevier.

Repenning, N. P., & Sterman, J. D. (2002). Capability traps and self-confirming attribution errors in the dynamics of process improvement. *Administrative Science Quarterly, 47*, 265–295.

Rudolph, J. W., & Repenning, N. P. (2002). Disaster dynamics: Understanding the role of quantity in organizational collapse. *Administrative Science Quarterly, 47*, 1–30.

Sastry, M. A. (1997). Problems and paradoxes in a model of punctuated organizational change. *Administrative Science Quarterly, 42*, 237–275.

Sterman, J. D. (2000). *Business dynamics: Systems thinking and modeling for a complex world.* Boston: McGraw-Hill.

Sterman, J. D., & Wittenberg, J. (1999). Path dependence, competition, and succession in the dynamics of scientific revolution. *Organization Science, 10*(3), 332–341.

U.S. Department of Labor Bureau of Labor Statistics. (2005). *Consumer expenditure annual reports.* Retrieved November 9, 2005, from http://www.bls.gov/cex/home.htm

Watson, G. (1971). Resistance to change. *American Behavioral Scientist, 14*(5), 745–766.

FRUIT FLIES LIKE A BANANA (OR, WHEN RIPENESS IS ALL): A MEDITATION ON MARKETS AND TIMESCAPES

John F. Sherry

ABSTRACT

This essay uses Reeves-Ellington's discussion of the timescape as a departure point for describing one way in which marketing managers have responded to consumers' lived experience of time. It focuses on the retail theatrics of the retroscape as a source of meaning for beleaguered consumers. It then extends the notion of the liminal to account for the temporal orientation that consumers display with regard to both clock time and cosmic time. It concludes with some observations on pluritemporality in postmodern culture.

> I wasted time, and now doth time waste me.
> —Richard II, V,5,112

At a formative point in my own very strange career, I recall recapturing refracted bits of Shakespeare and Vonnegut from the prism of Bob Textor's notion of the tempocentric – our tendency to view the world from an

Multi-Level Issues in Organizations and Time
Research in Multi-Level Issues, Volume 6, 331–337
Copyright © 2007 by Elsevier Ltd.
All rights of reproduction in any form reserved
ISSN: 1475-9144/doi:10.1016/S1475-9144(07)06015-8

impoverished temporal perspective that discounts the future – and refocusing them in repurposed fashion to imagine that one goal of the ethnographer might be to become unstuck in time. If, as business strategists claim, corporations are chiefly (if not solely) vehicles for implementing plans in the service of colonizing the future, then time travel must be part of the job description for any anthropologist attempting to understand such organizations. Whether negotiating the frenetic nanoculture of high-tech firms or the geological pace of academic departments, the ethnographer must account for the quality of time that informs emic experience and etic analysis.

In his treatment of corporate timescapes, Richard Reeves-Ellington provides us with a template for such ethnographic time travel – or rather a *templait*, if the pun be accepted. For anthropologists, context is the *sine qua non* of understanding. Context is a joining or weaving of experiential strands, the creating of a structure. Context is shaped and reflected by duration, bracketed on each end by reverie, either retrospective or anticipatory. The ethnographer apprehends the lived experience of others through prolonged engagement and immersion. The longitudinal study is an account of that experience unfolding, the story of the braiding of multiple experiences of time (from empirical to mythic) into a templait, a pattern or mold much like the part of the loom that keeps the cloth of context properly stretched. The plait that such timeweaving produces is of such a piece with the patchwork quilt of culture that it typically goes unexamined in our analyses (the work of Textor, Geertz, and a few others being the remarkable exceptions).

Reeves-Ellington's privileged position as a corporate insider, abetted by his ethnographic penchant for holistic comparison, permits him to inhabit the chronotopes of his informants as if these zones were temporal worlds, in a way that reveals the heterochronic nature of the complex organization. He demonstrates the theoretical value of his templait as he unravels the temporal filaments of formal and informal social organization within the firm, and illustrates the practical value of his templait in the reproduction of ever more effective Proctoids. It is by dwelling in the moments of his colleagues at all levels of the firm that Reeves-Ellington is able to convey so compellingly the timescapes that limn the firm at large.

In my own recent work in consumer research, I have practiced an analogous dwelling, albeit in more nomadic fashion. Along with my colleagues (most notably, Rob Kozinets and Stephen Brown), I have tracked brandscapes across commercial culture and counterculture over the past decade, seeking to understand local accommodation and resistance to the global forces of consumption. As retail theater in commercial culture and spectacle in counterculture increasingly converge and give rise to hybrid forms, consumers find the heterotopias available to them distinguished ever more precisely along temporal lines.

Given the time famine experienced by consumers in the United States, and the inherent inefficiencies and dissatisfactions of multitasking, it comes as no surprise to discover that few of us ever actually live – in the sense of an embodied dwelling – in the present. Rather, American consumers more commonly inhabit the future. This aspirational erewhon is configured by a reconfiguring of the past; the undiscovered country is simultaneously skirted and visited. We're always going back to the future.

The term my colleagues and I have used to describe this nostalgic (re)turn is "retroscape." Corporations of private, public, and nonprofit cast, ever eager to emplace and embody their brands in ways that consumers will introject, have used the evocation of times past to create an experience in the present that consumers, in turn, use to negotiate their futures. These sites are temporal portals, part high tech and part nostalgia, that reassure anxious contemporary consumers of the inevitability of the updated eternal return, and afford brand stewards the chance to forge a product life circle.

The retrofuturism of clicks-and-mortar telematic flagship brandstores such as ESPN Zone and of paraprimitive cyber-utopian temporary autonomous zones such as the Burning Man Project, represents consumers' Mobius strip grasp of time that meaning managers – marketers, designers, artists, politicians, and so on – are desperate to manipulate. They invite us to a tamed "there," encourage us to dwell in a reprised or redacted "then" and offer us identity renewal in the bargain. By transforming our sense of the present from a discontinuous flow of fragmented immediacy into one of future possibilities that collectively signify the fruition of the past's unrealized promise, experienced engineers give the retroscape the aura of authenticity. We move forward into a familiar future, comforted by its continuity with a past that never was.

The retroscape is the edifice complex of a more pervasive phenomenon in consumer culture that my colleagues and I have labeled retrobranding. To the extent that brands are our contemporary household gods, and to the degree that brands constitute a principal symbolic and material screen through which we apprehend and build the world, the entire marketing effort that sustains brands – product design, advertising, distribution systems, and pricing decisions, at the very least – is subject to these pressures of time famine, future orientation, and fungibility. In a marketplace of functional parity, those brands that embody and convey the most compelling story (about the meaning they enable consumers to harness) rank among the most competitive and successful. Increasingly, that story is nostalgically utopian, and the channels that deliver it, though bleeding-edge relevant, are absolutely beholden to a romanticized past apotheosized.

The retrobrand promises the benefits of an idyllic past that never was to contemporary consumers who are besieged by threats from all quarters that make the present so untenable. Retrobrands are portals to the good old days of the future. They commute the devolutionary premise of hyperindustrial life and make the postmodern palatable. The names of the retrobrand are legion: American Girl, Nike, Volkswagen, Coca-Cola, Alka-Seltzer, Guinness, Cunard, Las Vegas, Celebration, Willow Creek, Black Rock City, Colonial Williamsburg, Chuck Taylors, Beeman's chewing gum, and Schwinn bicycles. The retrobrand spans all manners of fast-moving consumer package goods and quick-service restaurants, museums and megachurches, services and festivals. It comprises the personae of media and civic celebrity alike. I'll return to this Janusian theme of portality in just a moment.

The complex organizations that market the retrobrand must synchronize the internal timescapes that Reeves-Ellington has described, and synchronize them in turn with those of their supply-chain partners. Such balletic chronography must be choreographed still further to harmonize with the calendar of commercial culture, which itself is often, ironically, tied inextricably to a liturgical cycle (which itself, again ironically, in a multicultural marketplace is becoming increasingly commoditized, as in the accelerating assumption of the commercial ethos of Christmas by Chanuka and Ramadan). All the while, these firms are steering a course by looking in the rearview mirror. Achieving effective time management in a corporate context is clearly no mean feat. Nor is it merely logistical in nature. As individuals in ever greater numbers seek the experience of immanence and transcendence in the realm of consumption, corporate engagement with time moves into the eschatological.

This brings us back to portals. As William Gibson has reminded us, the future is already here – it's just not evenly distributed. Like Janus, consumers surmount a temporal doorway, from which they are able to regard the future as well as the past, arguably at the expense of the present. While anthropologists as a rule have not been attentive to this vantage point from the lintel, one in particular has paid close attention to the view from the sill. Victor Turner has masterfully unpacked that eternal moment of the threshold, or limen, in his study of the rite of passage, itself the quintessentially temporal dimension of place. His analysis of the liminal phase – the antistructural juncture between fixed states that is both the engine of cultural stability and change and the barometer of cultural health – is the source of my understanding of the way in which marketing firms bridge the gap from Reeves-Ellington's logistical chronotopes to eschatological time.

In returning to my anthropological roots to theorize about the significance of spectacle to consumer research, I have explored the role of ludic agency in the evolution of liminality. In Turner's view, the ludic arises in tribal society in a liminal setting ultimately to affirm the status quo, and in modern society in a liminoid setting as a potentially subversive and independent source of innovation. The liminoid is a peripheral zone of independent, genred, optional activity outside the culture's central political and economic processes. I have argued that postmodernity gives rise to the liminate, as the ludic, manifesting itself through spectacle, abets the collapse of the liminal and the liminoid into absolute political and economic centrality, then re-emerges as an uncritical – if provocative – reinforcer of the status quo. The play is now the thing. Retail theater epitomizes the liminate and becomes the play space of the consumer bent upon creating an idiotopia from the do-it-yourself materiel the marketer provides. Thus is the brand animated, and thus does it animate in turn.

These marketized liminate spectacles – of which the retroscape is a particular example – lie at the heart of brand relations in the twenty-first century. And, as much as they satisfy, they also alienate, by inviting consumers to seek similar resonance in ostensibly more authentic countercultural venues. This emigration is only apparently spatial; it is more properly understood as temporal. Nomadic consumers are pilgrims, intent upon returning to the source. They seek to abandon clock time (whatever its former ties to natural cycles) and embrace cosmic time. They pursue a taste of final things, the fullness of time that only a mythological charter can endow. They push the liminate back to the liminal, to sacred time officially recognized, and not merely bootlegged or skunk-worked into the pluritemporal corporation.

As I complete the writing of this essay, I am acutely aware of my (meta)physical surroundings. The business school at Notre Dame is situated strategically between a mammoth, new performing arts center (a twenty-first-century technological wonder encased in a collegiate gothic megastructure) and a refurbished football stadium whose hallowed confines have been preserved in the updating (imparting a 1930s feel to the millennial-class infrastructure and amenities), on a tract of land some of my colleagues disparage as the "entertainment quad." From a stairwell window, I can see both the spire of the basilica and the Golden Dome; with a little bit of craning, I can also view the Touchdown Jesus mural on the library. Once Studebaker country, this is now Hummer territory. Built and driven locally, these high-tech stagecoach skeuomorphs (part atavism, part anachronism) are visually stunning as they motor past the horse-drawn buggies in nearby Amish country.

Spring break beckons, and while many students will head to China to witness the Middle Kingdom wrestle with consumer culture, many others will make a pilgrimage to Cabo to reenact some ancient ritual of excess. I'll go home tonight, hunker down with the dogs in front of my 40" LCD electronic hearth, and watch some of the Bard's best, updated for my Pomo sensibilities. I write from the heart of a retroscape whose identity I help to craft even as it largely crafts my own identity. I like to imagine that the progressive/conservative dialectic driving our academic enterprise is fundamentally anthropological in character, and that the thrum of the retroscape is music to our ethnographic ears.

Whither our proleptic paradise? Let me conclude by returning to the occult title of my essay. My early training as a business anthropologist entailed an immersion in the workplace so prolonged that a sense of humor became less an adaptive strategy than a literal survival skill. This experience will be familiar to every ethnographer who has ever done fieldwork. An ardent Groucho Marxist in my appreciation of koans, I came across one of the master's gems that I have used as a mantra ever since the sleep-deprived days of my apprenticeship: "Time flies like an arrow. Fruit flies like a banana." Serendipity synergized this saying, as I read concurrently in the literature of the sociology of work.

For a doctoral student yoked to corporate offices, conveyor belts, assembly lines, foundries, and the sundry servicescapes of manufacturing communities, a periodic rereading of Don Roy's essay on "Banana Time" was a life-affirming exercise on the order of a plenary indulgence. His description of the appropriation and re-parsing of wage time by workers striving to reduce boredom – a ritual of rebellion now refined to an art form at all levels of the corporation in an era of globalized markets – coincided with my own observations and practices in the moment. It became a portent of my current research pursuits as well.

Arrow time begets banana time. Corporate timescapes beget consumer time famine, which begets a market-mediated future orientation. Our ludic impulse follows a reframed past as a lodestar, even as it steers by a utopian beacon. Structure inexorably summons antistructure as a playmate. Stressed-out consumers prefer nostalgic comfort brands that exude the contemporaneity of shrewd updating. The retroscape is the dwelling of choice of these beleaguered consumers, who are all struggling to return home for the first time. If there is a call of the mall, it is this siren song of sweet surrender.

FURTHER READING

Brown, S. F. X., Kozinets, R. V., & Sherry, J. F., Jr. (2003). Sell me the old, old story: Retromarketing management and the art of brand revival. *Journal of Customer Behavior*, *2*(2), 133–147.

Brown, S. F. X., Kozinets, R. V., & Sherry, J. F., Jr. (2003). Teaching old brands new tricks: Retro branding and the revival of brand meaning. *Journal of Marketing*, *67*(3), 19–33.

Brown, S., & Sherry, J. F., Jr. (Eds) (2003). *Time, space, and the market: Retroscapes rising*. New York: M.E. Sharpe.

Kozinets, R. V., Sherry, J. F., Jr., Storm, S., Duhachek, A., Nuttavuthisit, K., & Deberry-Spence, B. (2004). Ludic agency and retail spectacle. *Journal of Consumer Research*, *31*(3), 658–672.

Roy, D. F. (1959). Banana time: Job satisfaction and informal interaction. *Human Organization*, *18*, 158–168.

Sherry, J. F., Jr. (2005). Brand meaning. In: T. Calkins & A. Tybout (Eds), *Kellogg on branding*. New York: Wiley.

Sherry, J. F., Jr. (2005). We might never be post-sacred: A tribute to Russell Belk on the occasion of his acceptance of the Converse award. In: A. Griffin & C. Otnes (Eds), *The sixteenth Paul D. Converse symposium* (pp. 67–77). Chicago: American Marketing Association.

Sherry, J. F., Jr., & Kozinets, R. V. (2003). Sacred iconography in secular space: Altars, alters, and alterity at the Burning Man project. In: C. Otnes & T. Lowrey (Eds), *Contemporary consumption rituals: A research anthology* (pp. 291–311). Mahwah, NJ: Lawrence Erlbaum.

Textor, R. (1980). *A handbook on ethnographic futures research*. Stanford, CA: Stanford University School of Education and Department of Anthropology.

Turner, V. (1974). Liminal to liminoid in play, flow and ritual: An essay in comparative symbology. *Rice University Studies*, *60*(3), 53–92.

LET US THEORY BUILD RATHER THAN THEORIZE

Richard Reeves-Ellington

ABSTRACT

This chapter discusses a complex research model that accommodates qualitative organizational learning methods and permits researchers to formulate clear research questions that are then explored through quantitative methodologies. Using a multitiered research model, it reinterprets the Procter & Gamble case material presented in "Time-scapes: A Multi-level Approach for Understanding Time Use in Complex Organizations" and addresses the issues discussed in Sherry's and Broberg, Bailey, and Hunt's commentaries (both found in this volume).

INTRODUCTION

In their commentaries, Sherry (this volume) and Broberg, Bailey, and Hunt (this volume) find my chapter on "timescapes" (this volume) relevant to extending organizational understanding. Their responses challenge neither the concepts of social and business timescapes nor the factors used to identify them. Instead, Sherry extends their usage, and Broberg et al. use alternative

Multi-Level Issues in Organizations and Time
Research in Multi-Level Issues, Volume 6, 339–353
Copyright © 2007 by Elsevier Ltd.
All rights of reproduction in any form reserved
ISSN: 1475-9144/doi:10.1016/S1475-9144(07)06016-X

methods to test their applicability. Sherry requires researchers to understand the historiography and cultural specificity of particular organizations to gain organizational timescape understanding, whereas Broberg and colleagues are more interested in theory testing of organizational timescape change, using quantitative methods and tools.

In his elegant and provocative remarks, Sherry emphasizes temporal applications of timescapes in ways that create more effective organizations. Specifically, he appreciates the strength of a complex organizational cultural *templait* that supports Procter & Gamble's (P&G's) efforts to turn out ever more effective Proctoids. He values the need for organizational temporal understanding by examining timescape phenomena through organizational eyes at a variety of organizational levels. Sherry emphasizes social time by examining the ways in which marketing managers use social temporality to create brand space and by exploring consumer responses to brand space in terms of both social and business timescapes.

Broberg et al. emphasize business timescapes through the examination of a CEO's ability to change an organization's reliance from one timescape to another. These authors take the position of an outside scientist looking for universal understandings. The P&G case is too complex for their modeling techniques, which causes them to limit the number of variables: Their variables test only traditional business activities or traditional power hierarchical concepts and ignore cultural items. Relying on a system dynamics mathematical model, they take my research methodology to task for "being a bit behind the times" by using multi-level theory analysis rather than "the increasingly used analytical levels of analysis."

Both responses have merit and suggest that organizational time usage requires different research tools and methodologies for understanding social time and business time. My initial use of qualitative research methods reveals organizationally constructed timescapes and multi-level variations. Sherry's application of social timescapes to brand development supports qualitative efforts, albeit in a new direction. Broberg et al., using quantitative tools, suggest organizational rates of change for organizational timescapes. Each of us has theorized our work but we lack an organized theory construct that would provide an improved and broader understanding of organizational timescape usage. Adapting Rousseau's (2006) admonition to work with specific managerial evidence, we require a complex research model that will accommodate qualitative and quantitative evidence in ways that lead to complex theory building.

BUILDING COMPLEX RESEARCH MODELS

Theory-Building Models

Carlile and Christensen (2005) provide a complex research model that extends the usefulness of the timescapes concept. Using their research model, this chapter addresses the need for a theory that is (1) driven by both intellectual rigor and practicality (Hambrick, 1994; Simon, 1976; Solow, 1985; Staw & Sutton, 1995); (2) capable of capturing changing circumstances (Carlile & Christensen, 2005); and (3) able to coordinate efforts of theory constructs that bridge qualitative and quantitative data. Both qualitative and quantitative data must be gathered in ways that capture organizational webs of socially constructed, taken-for-granted prescriptions of appropriate conduct (DiMaggio, 1988; Greenwood & Suddaby, 2006; Meyer & Rowan, 1977; Scott, 2000) as well as the rationale for those activities (DiMaggio, 1988; Greenwood & Suddaby, 2006). Working with the Carlile and Christensen model, I demonstrate the importance of starting with the qualitative research methods espoused by Sherry and myself and suggest ways to integrate the more analytical methodologies offered by Broberg and colleagues.

Carlile and Christensen (2005) offer a sound process that creates a common research vocabulary and requires qualitative and quantitative methodologies to interact. They suggest that theory building proceeds in two major stages: the descriptive stage and the normative stage. Each of these stages, in turn, involves its own set of sub-steps. Furthermore, they argue, substantial theory exists only through a body of understanding gained by progressing through each major stage and each sub-step of their model.

Stage One

The first stage of Carlile and Christensen's theory building begins with a preliminary description based on observation (phenomena), progresses through classification (frameworks and typologies of phenomena), and ends by defining relationships (models that are statements of association). Initially, much of the observation entails the trial and error of data collection until patterns begin to emerge. Using ethnographic information and emergent patterns, the researcher then formulates meaning attributes. Within the Carlile and Christensen system, attribute-based categorizations are required to create substantive theory as described by Glaser and Strauss (1967). According to Sherry, the models develop shape and reflect duration that is bracketed by introspective or anticipatory reverie. Stopping with descriptive material and not moving on to develop a theory that has predictive ability produces only half a theory (Carlile & Christensen, 2005; Gephart, 2003; Glaser & Strauss, 1967; Berson, Avolio, & Kahai, 2003). While qualitative data can be predictive, a combination of both qualitative and quantitative data at the normative stage builds a stronger theory (Carlile & Christensen, 2005; Gephart, 2003; Reeves-Ellington, 1997). A complete theory requires reviewing, refining, and expanding on the inductive materials using deductive and analytical methodologies.

Stage Two
The second stage of Carlile and Christensen's model (2005) hypothesizes a statement of causality derived from the hypotheses as framed in the descriptive stage of theory building. Carlile and Christensen agree with Lawrence and Lorsch (1967) that contingency theory drives this part of their model. By applying contingency theory, the researcher reinvestigates the original and new observations, descriptions, and measures of the phenomena considered to provide necessary and sufficient data for the hypotheses being tested. If anomalies occur between statements of causality and descriptive stages of research, or between statements of causality and the underlying observed phenomena, researchers must recategorize circumstances. This recategorization remains based on specific phenomena – either newly found or reexamined from the descriptive stage. Predictive success requires alignment of the descriptive material, statements of causality, and categorization of phenomena.

Given that circumstance-defined categorization is necessary to achieve a successful normative theory, determination of the boundaries of the categories is of paramount importance. Specifically, if managers find themselves in a circumstance in which they must change organizational actions to achieve the outcome of interest, they know that a salient boundary between categories has been crossed (Carlile & Christensen, 2005).

Model Application Requirements

The Carlile and Christensen research model requires a mix of researchers skilled in qualitative and quantitative research methods, who together form and test hypotheses using both types of research methodologies. Given the sequential requirements of the research model, the study, by definition, must be longitudinal and involve all researchers throughout the study.

APPLYING THE MODEL TO TIMESCAPE ORGANIZATIONAL THEORY

Inserting Descriptive Theory

In the interests of theory building, this chapter reexamines my P&G case material (this volume) using the Carlile and Christensen model. Specifically, in agreement with Sherry's comments on the importance of holistic under-standings of organizations, the descriptive theory provides a strong frame-work for understanding how a specific complex organization, P&G, uses social and business timescapes. Working as an insider provides what Sherry values as a lived experience through prolonged engagement and immersion; this experience, in turn, allows the researcher to understand and speak from a position of understanding the internal organizational voices. Also, according to Sherry, immersion exposes organizational patterns or molds that might otherwise be missed.

Through inductive reasoning, the case study grounded the theoretical work in ways that were intended to make the theory more transparent. Inductive reasoning began with formulating observations, progressed through categorization, and ended with statements of correlation. Table 1 provides information relating to the descriptive phenomena, categories, and correlations discussed in my chapter on understanding and using time.

Preparation of the timescape chapter required a decade's worth of grounded observations (Reeves-Ellington, 2004a; Wells, 1995) using ethnographic meth-odologies (Reeves-Ellington, 1993, 1995, 1997) as well as pertinent extant literature. Using the field and literature research, I developed frameworks and categories that reflected causal relationships of importance to P&G managers at three levels of management. These managerial categories provided the basis for understanding the overarching concepts of social and business timescapes and their multi-level use, leading me to two primary statements of association:

1. The priority of timescapes is dyadically learned, socially disseminated, and internalized by individuals.
2. Every organizational manager operates using both timescapes, but one is the preferred dominant timescape, and each managerial level has primary responsibility for each timescape aspect.

Once these associations are created in a holistic organizational description, the next research step of normative theory can follow.

Table 1.   Reeves-Ellington's Descriptive Theory Analysis Based on
                  Carlile and Christensen's Categories.

Statements of correlation	• Social timescapes and their attendant dimensions and parameters are learned through dyadic relationships, socially distributed in complex organizations, and internalized by individuals • Both business and social timescapes are found at entry, middle managerial, and senior managerial levels, but each of these levels has primary responsibility or organizational leadership for certain timescape dimensions • Understanding the value of horizontal and vertical timescape congruence or change requires longitudinal study
Categorize by attributes of phenomena	• Two complex time constructs interact within organizations: social time and business time • Each timescape has six dimensions. Three levels of management use timescapes and methods of their organizational transmission • Three social relation constructs function within managerial levels: self, dyadic, and social relationships • Organizational learning systems provide organizational business and social learning
Observe and describe phenomena	Triangulation of data through action research used: • Participant observation provided my input • Indigenous cognitive mapping provided P&G actors' viewpoints • Internal and external printed materials provided external and internal perspectives

Inserting Normative Theory

Using the concept of constructive replication (Eden, 2002), Broberg et al. state that they want to apply the same set of hypotheses and theoretical constructs that I apply in the timescape chapter. Furthermore, they follow Eden's advice by varying operationalization of the concepts – that is, they apply a quantitative systems dynamic, which includes a component of computational modeling. But whereas I found a relationship between managerial timescape alignment and organizational performance, Broberg et al. found no strong relationship.

An underlying cause of such a basic anomaly lies in their focusing on CEO business strategies for changing timescape preference at the expense of examining organizational cultural factors at work. To more fully understand this anomaly, we require a comparison of congruence statements, an examination of categorizations and their rationale, a clarification of the underlying observations, and, perhaps more importantly, a comparison and evaluation of the predictability of our respective congruence hypotheses. Initial teamwork might have helped us avoid such a basic anomaly, thereby permitting us to build better hypotheses.

Let's start by examining our congruence statements, so that we know whether we are looking at the same normative hypotheses.

Congruence Statement Comparisons

Building on the deductive data set and categorization in the descriptive theory I developed, I concluded that organizational performance weakens when there is an incongruity of timescapes within and across managerial hierarchies, whereas congruencies of managerial timescape dominance strengthen performance. These conclusions are drawn as normative statements of causality in Table 2. Other than offering some limited financial data to support the major thrust of the chapter, my work did not progress much past the causality statements. This is where Broberg et al. take up the discussion by working with a more quantitative model.

Broberg, Bailey, and Hunt provide causality statements based on my P&G observations, statements of correlation, and statements of congruence (see Table 2). Their intent is to use a constructive replication of analysis of the P&G case material in the timescape chapter by implementing Eden's (2002) requirements for testing the same hypothesized relationships among the same theoretical constructs as a given. They vary the operationalization of those constructs, however. Rather than continuing with descriptive theory, they turn to a systems dynamics approach that allows for a more explicit (meaning "quantitative") treatment of temporality than my own approach, which relied almost exclusively on normative types of information. They then categorize circumstances that would permit predicting organizational outcomes based on the phenomena they collected or hypothesized. Table 2 summarizes their findings using a normative theory model.

Sense-Making Orientations

As reflected in the first statement in Table 2, we agree on a research question. However, rather than applying their quantitative modeling to this agreed research question, Broberg et al. raise another question concerning

Table 2. Normative Theory Analysis.

Carlile and Christensen	Reeves-Ellington	Broberg, Bailey, and Hunt
Statement of causality	• Organizational performance diminishes when there is a lack of fit between senior management timescapes and the timescapes of other levels of management • When there is a match between the timescape of the CEO and the dominant timescape of the organization, the overall organizational performance is greater than when there is a mismatch	Interpretation of Reeves-Ellington: • Organizational performance diminishes when there is a lack of fit between senior management timescapes and the timescapes of other levels of management • Multiple levels and temporality explain the performance of the consumer products giant, Procter & Gamble Hypothesis: • Given enough time, CEOs will ultimately create a fit between their timescape and the timescape of the organization to improve performance
Categorization of circumstances	• Contingency of timescape to organizational cultural timescape preference and managerial alignment	• CEO-driven change based on (1) nonlinear cause and effect and (2) CEO feedback power
Observe and describe phenomena	Business Data: • Published financial • Internal financial Social Data: • Informant feedback on causality statements • Published materials • Organizational learning of preferred timescapes through multi-level managerial analysis and applications	Business Data: • Published financial Social Data (assumptions for hypothesis): • 70% of managers had a social timescape; 30% of managers had a business timescape • Job security dependent upon fitting with the CEO timescape preference by CEO enforcement of timescape preference of managerial alignment through turnover • Category quit rates or assumptions that regulate an individual's adoption of specific timescapes, based on (1) exit rates of conflicted-timescape employees increase and (2) hiring of aligned-timescape managers increases as the exit rates of conflicted-timescape managers increase

the sense making of my analysis. The question of "Sense making to whom?" is not addressed, but the context indicates that they are interested in sense making to themselves as researchers. If so, that shifts the discussion away from an examination of what is sense making to internal employees. Dick Clark, CEO of Merck and Company, sums up the importance of sense making to internal employees with a comment on the importance of corporate culture:

> And the fact is culture eats strategy for lunch ... You can have a good strategy in place, but if you don't have the culture and the enabling systems that allow you to successfully implement that strategy ... the culture of the organization will defeat the strategy. (Bowes, 2006)

Broberg et al. give preeminence to CEO business strategies and their implementation for determining successful timescape change. By ignoring important cultural determinants of change in their analytical model, however, they fail to recognize specific organizational boundaries, identities, and interactions that might be called "institutional logics" (DiMaggio, 1988; Greenwood & Suddaby, 2006; Rao, Monin, & Durand, 2003; Thornton, 2004). This failure leads to their focus on business time and rational analysis that ignores social time use and implications in P&G, which, in turn, leads to their misunderstanding of how the company responds to organizational activities and business practices.

From Research Question to Hypothesis

Broberg et al. also attribute a broader causality to me than the one I actually espoused (Table 2). Their question, "Is poor performance due to misfit and good performance due to fit?", is a straw man in terms of testing the same congruency statements. All of us would agree that performance cannot be attributed solely to timescape alignment or misalignment, but that does not negate its impact. Managers who choose social time as a primary timescape employ business practices that vary dramatically from the business practices of managers who explore business time as the fundamental organizational driver.

The key to Broberg, Bailey, and Hunt's chapter is the hypothesis that they set out to demonstrate: "Given enough time, CEOs will ultimately create a fit between their timescape and organization to improve performance." They expand this hypothesis by asking, "If so, how long would it take to enact change?" Although a fascinating hypothesis, this point has nothing to do with my study. The change question is the one to which they apply their quantitative model, not the two congruence statements mentioned earlier. As a consequence, they have not addressed my hypothesis and therefore have neither proved nor disproved my congruence statements.

By setting out to test one theory through the use of another, Broberg et al. pursue theorizing rather than theory building. That is, they set out to test one aspect of my theory by substituting another aspect of my theory. If I have properly presented their statements here, it is unclear how Broberg et al. use constructive replication, as they did not test my hypothesis. That said, we both share the same (albeit unspoken) congruence statement: Timescape conflicts can occur in organizations, and change to an aligned position results in improved performance.

Table 2 summarizes both of our normative analyses and shows the differences between our work. The differences shown indicate that we have theorized timescapes differently. To work from the same set of congruence statements, we need to work from an integrated theory-building model. This would resolve the anomalies between our expected outcomes.

Normative Categories
Broberg, Bailey, and Hunt accept that timescapes are salient boundaries for ways in which organizations operate and that organizational nonalignment of timescapes influences organizational performance. Their unstated premises – that timescape change rates apply to all organizations and that meaningful change is CEO driven and controlled – fail to meet Carlile and Christensen's (2005) contingency requirements for good theory building. Certainly, if one accepts the premise that social and cultural constructs limit organizational choices, Broberg et al. need to incorporate some categorization that captures organizational contingencies (Kramer, 1994, 1995). An examination of the third major normative theory component – observation and description of phenomena – provides some insights for the need for grounded and specific organizational information.

Supporting Phenomena
Broberg et al. acknowledge that they lack P&G-specific data for their model. As they state, one would expect that starting with a different set of assumptions would likely result in obtaining different findings. An examination of the conflicts between the two sets of underlying assumptions is therefore in order.

The lack of relevant social information inputs in their model invalidates three areas of assumptions concerning P&G: timescape divisions among managers and employees, personnel turnover, and hiring. One could argue that the failure to test social data and constructs and over-reliance on traditional business information warped their ability to test timescapes, as timescapes are basically cultural phenomena.

As noted in my chapter, the CEO has only limited power and authority in personnel matters. Given P&G's entry-level hiring policy and practice of total promotion from within, the CEO's power to change P&G culture is contingent upon the traditional company hiring and promotion policies. P&G's annual turnover is a tiny 2%, a rate that has not changed substantially over a 20-year period (Fisher, 2006). Many, if not most, P&G employees have 25 or 30 years of longevity. Such tenure reflects a promote-from-within culture, which requires hiring the right people in the first place. To assure such hiring, P&G has three Ph.D. psychologists on staff who oversee a rigorous testing process based on 20 years of records that measure what makes a successful Proctoid.

When CEO Artzt attempted initially to surround himself with managers he brought from Europe, he expected support (Reeves-Ellington & Anderson, 1997) for making the business timescape the predominant factor. However, these executives reverted to P&G enculturation and resisted such a fundamental change in organizational culture (Pritchett, 1995). CEO Jager, by contrast, had more success in surrounding himself with direct reports who were business timescape operators; however, within a year of his demise, they had all voluntarily retired. This outcome does raise a point for further investigation: Are social timescape operators more organizationally resilient than business timescape operators?

Examining Expected Outcomes

Using a system dynamics model, Broberg et al. tested "how long it would reasonably take for a new business timescape CEO to transform a social timescape culture to fit with his or her business timescape orientation." Given the hypothesis, the model would presumably work if the CEO wanted to move from a dominant business timescape to a dominant social timescape. Also, it appears that Broberg et al. universalize the dynamics to fit all companies, even though they mention only P&G. There are no restrictive caveats concerning their conclusions.

Predictive Requirements

Effective models and associated theories must have predictive capabilities. Within the scope of my chapter, the descriptive material and subsequent attribute categories of P&G material are predictive, whereas Broberg et al.'s normative data lack predictability. A review of their findings suggests that P&G has only one valid timescape change circumstance. For example, given their results, at the end his tenure Artzt should have converted P&G from having a social timescape to adopting a business timescape, with business timescape managers serving at all levels of the organization. This outcome did not occur. Instead, outside of a narrow senior level, the dominant timescape preference remained social. An example demonstrates the lack of serious total organizational timescape change at P&G.

The current head of P&G marketing, Jim Stengel (a social timescape manager who stayed with the organization throughout the Artzt and Jager tenures), now works to extend P&G's social timescape dominance to include the company's entire value chain. He describes the process as a "consumer-learning journey" aimed at "touching lives and improving lives" (Silverman, 2006). This description fits into Sherry's retroscape analysis and deserves a closer examination of how timescapes operate in such an environment. As reported in the *Financial Times* (Silverman, 2006), Stengel is asking P&G to expand its role in society "to be as neighbourly as his father."

Internally, P&G is strengthening its social timescape by publishing (at its own expense) and distributing throughout the company, John Pepper's *What Really Matters* (2005). The cover copy, "Reflections on my career at Procter & Gamble with guiding principles for success in the company and in life," and the picture showing Pepper next to William Procter, who was the original social timescape CEO (1890–1929), reflect the strength of the social timescape at P&G (Pepper, 2005). To gain insight into the anomalies of what the model predicts and what actually happens requires an examination of the normative classifications and underlying data. Even at the senior level, the board of directors replaced Artzt, a business-timescape-driven manager, with Pepper, a truly social timescape operator. If the company had been converted to and was satisfied with a dominant business timescape, such a replacement would not seem reasonable.

The strength of social timescape use during Pepper's tenure is an additional consideration when assessing the validity of Broberg et al.'s theorizing. According to these authors, Pepper's one year at the helm of P&G would be too short a period to replace Artzt's preferred timescape. Given such a scenario, why would Jager require an additional five years to once again put a preferred business timescape back in place? The data seem inconsistent with Broberg and colleagues' theoretical expectations. Their failure to include social data in their theorizing might explain their problems. A review of operational philosophies of P&G CEOs from William

Procter (1890) through John Lafley (2006) (Pepper, 2005) reveals a strong social and cultural bias at P&G. All but two executives had tenures of a decade or more as CEO and President. The two exceptions on both counts were Artzt and Jager.

CONCLUSION

Business research has focused, all too exclusively, on business data and organizational assumptions that agree with Herbert Hoover's assertion that the business of business is business. Developing both business and culture requires researchers to return to the ancient concept of *commerce* (Reeves-Ellington & Anderson, 1997), a term that provides an umbrella for understanding both social and business timescapes. Such an approach requires expanding theorizing to complex theory building in ways that include both qualitative and quantitative methodologies (Reeves-Ellington, 2004a, 2004b). The resulting theory should not only be able to explain the past but also offer some reasonable future projections.

My work attempts to provide both descriptive and normative aspects to build a theory of identifying organizational timescapes and their role within an organization in a systematic way that Sherry deems important. Like me, Sherry believes that only through a multi-level research program that results in a multi-level analysis can organizational temporal understanding be achieved. However, my chapter is overly reliant on qualitative information. Broberg et al.'s quantitative efforts have merit, but, by limiting their discussion to the business side of commerce to predict social change, their material is the mirror image of my chapter's limitations. Also, by creating a general and universal set of conclusions that are extended to all organizational levels, they lose important nuances. The lesson one can take away is that better theory building by a team of researchers who use complex research methods and address an agreed-upon research agenda will provide stronger theoretical frameworks for us all.

ACKNOWLEDGMENTS

I thank John Sherry for his penetrating comments and for providing a roadmap for moving forward and Christian Broberg, Adam Bailey, and Jerry Hunt for taking my material into a quantitative analytical dimension. I thank Paul R. Carlile for sharing with me an unpublished manuscript that provides the framework of this chapter. Fran Yammarino and Fred Dansereau forced clarity of thought, and Barbara Reeves-Ellington contributed to making the paper readable.

REFERENCES

Berson, Y., Avolio, B., & Kahai, S. (2003). Level specification: Using triangulation in a grounded theory approach to construct validation. In: F. Dansereau & F. J. Yammarino (Eds), *Multi-level issues in organizational behavior and strategy* (Vol. 2, pp. 80–112). Oxford: Elsevier.

Bowes, C. (2006). The man who has to shake up Merck. *The Financial Times*, March 27, p. 8.

Broberg, J., Bailey, A., & Hunt, J. (this volume). A system dynamic perspective on timescapes in organizations. In: F. Dansereau & F. J. Yammarino (Eds), *Multi-level issues in organizations and time* (Vol. 6). Oxford: Elsevier.

Carlile, P. R., & Christensen, C. M. (2005). *Practice and malpractice in management research*. Unpublished manuscript, Boston.

DiMaggio, P. (1988). Interest and agency in institutional theory. In: L. Zucker (Ed.), *Institutional patterns and organizations: Culture and environment* (pp. 3–22). Cambridge: Ballinger.

Eden, D. (2002). Replication, meta-analysis, scientific progress, and AMJ's publication policy. *Academy of Management Journal*, 45(5), 841–846.

Fisher, A. (2006). *How admired companies find the best talent*. New York: Fortune.

Gephart, R. P. J. (2003). Grounded theory and the integration of qualitative and quantitative research. In: F. Dansereau & F. J. Yammarino (Eds), *Multi-level issues in organizational behavior and strategy* (pp. 113–125). Oxford: Elsevier.

Glaser, B., & Strauss, A. (1967). *The discovery of grounded theory: Strategies and qualitative research*. London: Wiedenfeld and Nicholson.

Greenwood, R., & Suddaby, R. (2006). Institutional entrepreneurship in mature fields: The Big Five accounting firms. *Academy of Management Journal*, 49(1), 27–48.

Hambrick, D. (1994). 1993 Presidential address: What if the Academy actually mattered? *Academy of Management Review*, 19, 11–16.

Kramer, R. M. (1994). Cooperation and organizational identification. In: M. Murnighan (Ed.), *Social psychology in organizations: Advances in theory and research* (pp. 2224–2268). Englewood Cliffs, NJ: Prentice-Hall.

Kramer, R. M. (1995). Divergent realities and convergent disappointments in the hierarchic relation. In: R. M. Kramer & T. R. Tyler (Eds), *Trust in organizations: Frontiers of theory and research* (pp. 216–245). Thousand Oaks, CA: Sage.

Lawrence, P. R., & Lorsch, J. W. (1967). *Organization and environment*. Boston: Harvard Business School Press.

Meyer, J. W., & Rowan, B. (1977). Institutionalized organizationals: Formal structure as myth and ceremony. *American Journal of Sociology*, 83, 440–463.

Pepper, J. (2005). *What really matters*. Cincinnati: Colophon.

Pritchett, L. (1995). *Stop paddling and start rocking the boat*. Bangalore: East West Books.

Rao, H., Monin, P., & Durand, R. (2003). Institutional change in Toque Ville: Nouvelle cuisine as an identity movement in French gastronomy. *American Journal of Sociology*, 108, 795–843.

Reeves-Ellington, R. (1993). Using cultural skills of cooperative advantage in Japan. *Human Organization, 52*, 203–215.

Reeves-Ellington, R. (1995). Organizing for organizational effectiveness: Ethnicity and organizations. *Human Organization, 53*, 249–263.

Reeves-Ellington, R. (1997). Cross cultural organizational stress–the American University in Bulgaria. *Human Organization, 57*, 94–107.

Reeves-Ellington, R. (2004a). Cultural bases of research: Integrating research cultures for complex problems. In: F. J. Yammarino & F. Dansereau (Eds), *Multi-level issues in organizational behavior and processes* (Vol. 3, pp. 167–177). Oxford: Elsevier.

Reeves-Ellington, R. (2004b). Trustscapes and distrustscapes: A multi-level approach for understanding stability and change. In: F. J. Yammarino & F. Dansereau (Eds), *Multi-level issues in organizational behavior and processes* (Vol. 3, pp. 91–148). Oxford: Elsevier.

Reeves-Ellington, R., & Anderson, A. (1997). *Beyond agenda: Culture, commerce, and social responsibility*. Lewiston, NY: Edwin Mellon Press.

Rousseau, D. M. (2006). Is there such a thing as "evidence-based management"? *Academy of Management Journal, 31*(2), 256–259.

Scott, W. R. (2000). *Institutions and organizations*. Thousand Oaks, CA: Sage.

Sherry, J. (this volume). Fruit flies like a banana (Or, when ripeness is all: A meditation on markets and timescapes). In: F. Dansereau & F. J. Yammarino (Eds), *Multi-level issues in organizations and time* (Vol. 6). Oxford: Elsevier.

Silverman, G. (2006). How may I help you? *The Financial Times,* February 4, pp. W21–22.

Simon, H. (1976). *Administrative behavior* (3rd ed). New York: Free Press.

Solow, R. M. (1985). Economic history and economics. *The American Economic Review, 75*, 328–331.

Staw, B., & Sutton, R. I. (1995). What theory is not? *Administrative Science Quarterly, 40*, 371–384.

Thornton, P. H. (2004). *Markets from culture*. Stanford: Stanford University Press.

Wells, W. D. (1995). Afterword. In: J. Sherry (Ed.), *Contemporary marketing and consumer behavior* (pp. 446–450). Thousand Oaks, CA: Sage.

PART V:
JUSTICE CLIMATE

JUSTICE CLIMATE PAST, PRESENT, AND FUTURE: MODELS OF STRUCTURE AND EMERGENCE

Deborah E. Rupp, Michael Bashshur and Hui Liao

ABSTRACT

This chapter reviews research on multi-level organizational justice. The first half of the chapter provides the historical context for this issue, discusses organizational-level antecedents to individual-level justice perceptions (i.e., culture and organizational structure), and then focuses on the study of justice climate. A summary model depicts the justice climate findings to date and gives recommendations for future research. The second half of the chapter discusses the process of justice climate emergence. Pulling from classical bottom-up and top-down climate emergence models as well as contemporary justice theory, it outlines a theoretical model whereby individual differences and environmental characteristics interact to influence justice judgments. Through a process of information sharing, shared and unique experiences, and interactions among group members, a justice climate emerges. The chapter concludes by presenting ideas about how such a process might be empirically modeled.

Multi-Level Issues in Organizations and Time
Research in Multi-Level Issues, Volume 6, 357–396
Copyright © 2007 by Elsevier Ltd.
ISSN: 1475-9144/doi:10.1016/S1475-9144(07)06017-1

INTRODUCTION

As recently as 2000, reviews of the justice literature were noting the virtually complete absence of multi-level analyses of organizational justice (Konovsky, 2000). Only a few multi-level justice studies were in print at that time, and the justice community knew very little about justice at the unit level (Ehrhart, 2004). Just five years later, a number of multi-level justice studies have been published, and many see this multi-level trend as a fruitful and exciting challenge for the justice community. This chapter seeks to outline this challenge explicitly, reviewing what we know at present and outlining ways in which research in this area might proceed.

We will begin our journey with a brief overview of the justice literature, leading up to what we consider to be significant precursors to the multi-level justice movement. We then review in detail the multi-level justice literature to date, which includes both unit-level antecedents to individual-level justice perceptions (i.e., culture and organizational structure) and unit-level justice perceptions (i.e., justice climate) as antecedents of multi-level outcomes. Next, we discuss the processes by which a justice climate emerges and the theories particularly pertinent to this phenomenon. The chapter concludes with an identification of areas that might be fruitful candidates for future research and presents a theoretical model that might serve as a catalyst for future hypothesizing about justice climate.

THE HISTORY OF JUSTICE AS AN INDIVIDUAL-LEVEL CONSTRUCT

Types of Justice

The topic of workplace justice has risen to become a major area of inquiry within the organizational sciences (Colquitt, Greenberg, & Scott, 2005; Cropanzano & Rupp, 2003). For decades, the term *justice* has referred to employees' individual perceptions of how fairly they individually feel they are treated at work (Colquitt & Shaw, 2005). Justice has not been treated as an attitude, motive, or emotion per se, but rather as a class of motivated behavior (Cropanzano, Byrne, Bobocel, & Rupp, 2001a). That is, employees are said to experience and respond to events that take place at work, and the sense of (in)justice that results from these experiences guides their subsequent attitudes and behaviors. Furthermore, research has shown that justice reactions are fueled by a number of motives, including self-interest, relational concerns, and morality (see Cropanzano, Rupp, Mohler, & Schminke, 2001b, for a review).

Over the decades, three classes of events have been identified as especially relevant in this psychological process. The first class includes outcomes such as pay, promotions, and the like. The perceived fairness of outcomes is referred to as *distributive justice* and has its roots in research on equity theory (Adams, 1965). A second class of events entails the procedures that are used to arrive at such outcomes. Known as *procedural justice*, these fairness judgments were largely described by Thibaut and Walker's (1975, 1978) control theory, and were advanced with the criteria proposed by Leventhal (1976, 1980), which included consistency, correctability, lack of bias, representativeness, and ethicality. A final class of behaviors evaluated by employees involves the general treatment that employees receive from those in authority over them. Proposed by Bies and Moag (1986), this type of justice is referred to as *interactional justice*. Greenberg (1993a, 1993b) later proposed a subdivision of interactional justice that includes fairness judgments made about the information provided about procedures (*informational justice*) and the basic interpersonal behaviors directed at the employee (*interpersonal justice*).

This classic typology of justice perceptions has served as a conceptual backbone for the field. Although there has not always been agreement on the distinctiveness of these constructs (see Ambrose & Arnaud, 2005; Bies, 2005), empirical research clearly supports a four-factor structure (Colquitt, 2001), and meta-analytic evidence shows that the four types show different patterns of relationships with both antecedents and consequences (Colquitt, Conlon, Wesson, Porter, & Ng, 2001).

The meta-analytic evidence also suggests that the various types of justice judgments are quite influential in predicting a wide range of important workplace outcomes (Bartel & Hays, 1999; Cohen-Charash & Spector, 2001; Colquitt et al., 2001; Viswesvaran & Ones, 2002). These include outcomes of relevance to organizations, such as job performance, citizenship behaviors, organizational commitment, employee theft, workplace aggression, turnover, and counterproductivity, as well as outcomes of relevance to employees, such as job satisfaction, health, and stress. Reflecting the broad influence of employee justice perceptions, the discussion of justice has begun infiltrating research on selection and staffing (Gilliland, 1993), performance appraisal (Korsgaard & Roberson, 1995), conflict resolution (Shapiro & Rosen, 1994), layoffs (Konovsky & Brockner, 1993), sexual harassment (Adams-Roy & Barling, 1998), discrimination claims (Goldman, 2001), labor relations (Skarlicki & Latham, 1996), and many other topics within industrial/organizational psychology, organizational behavior, and human resources management. If one theme has emerged from the last 40 years of research, it is that justice matters.

Sources of Justice

A more recent wrinkle in the justice literature has been a theoretical push to increase the specificity with which justice constructs are measured (Colquitt & Shaw, 2005). That is, justice researchers of late have lobbied the research community not only to carefully consider and measure the type of justice (i.e., distributive, procedural), but also to measure its source. This approach has been termed the *multifoci* approach (Cropanzano et al., 2001a, 2001b), in that it argues that justice stems from multiple foci within the organization, including supervisors, the organization as a whole, coworkers, customers, and other parties. Indeed, employees might be treated quite fairly by one source, but rather unfairly by another. Hence, failing to specify the source of justice in justice measures, or averaging across sources, could at worst lead to spurious results or at best yield justice effects that are difficult to interpret.

Malatesta and Byrne (1997) were the first to propose the multifoci idea, positing that procedural justice is an organizationally referenced variable, because policies and procedures are typically seen as being passed down from the organization, whereas interactional justice is a supervisory-referenced variable, because the supervisor is often the direct contact and therefore the source of interpersonal treatment. Consequently, it was hypothesized that procedural justice should best predict outcomes directed at the organization, whereas interactional justice should best predict outcomes directed at the supervisor. There is a certain eye-for-an-eye flavor to these notions. That is, a basic assumption within this model is that injustice is reciprocated to the source of the injustice as opposed to other sources. This notion has been supported for the most part (e.g., see Masterson, Lewis, Goldman, & Taylor, 2000), although "spillover" to other sources has been detected in some studies (Rupp & Cropanzano, 2002; Liao & Rupp, 2005).

Byrne (1999) eventually expanded the multifoci model by crossing justice type (i.e., procedural, interactional) with justice source (i.e., organization, supervisor), arguing that employees can make multiple types of justice judgments about multiple sources. Empirical support for this notion has been promising. For example, Rupp and Cropanzano (2002) found that supervisor-focused procedural and interactional justice predicted supervisory-directed citizenship behaviors, job performance, and organizationally focused citizenship behaviors, whereas organizationally focused procedural and interactional justice predicted organizationally directed citizenship behaviors only. Likewise, Liao and Rupp (2005) measured procedural, informational, and interpersonal justice coming from both the supervisor and the organization. They found (with a few exceptions) these variables to predict multifoci commitment, satisfaction, and citizenship. Rupp et al. (2004) extended this research by including coworkers as a source of justice. They found, using a sample of prison guards, that coworker-focused procedural and interactional justice predicted commitment to and satisfaction with coworkers. Finally, Rupp and Spencer (in press) introduced customers as a source of justice, finding in a laboratory study that interactional justice coming from customers affected participants' emotional labor.

The multifoci justice research has made a theoretical contribution as well. Beginning with the work of Masterson et al. (2000), multifoci justice research took a solid social exchange perspective. That is, it was argued that acts of injustice are reciprocated to their original source because justice engenders social exchange relationships, and the quality of these relationships, in turn, mediates multifoci justice effects. For example, Masterson et al. (2000) found leader–member exchange to mediate the effect of interactional justice on supervisory-directed outcomes, and they perceived organizational support to mediate the effect of procedural justice on organizationally directed outcomes. Cropanzano, Prehar, and Chen (2002) obtained similar results. Rupp and Cropanzano (2002) found that social exchange with a supervisor mediates supervisor-focused procedural and interaction justice effects, whereas social exchange with the organization mediates organizationally focused procedural and organizationally focused justice effects. Finally, Rupp et al. (2004) found coworker-focused procedural and interactional justice effects to be mediated by team member exchange.

Shifting from Individual- to Unit-Level Considerations

Although multifoci justice research was not multi-level in either its conception or in its onset, it is important to understand this research from a historical perspective (at least for us) because it has served as an impetus for multi-level justice considerations. That is, the multifoci movement, along with the increased attention paid to teams in organizations (Cohen & Bailey, 1997; Colquitt, Zapata-Phelan, & Roberson, 2005; Cropanzano & Schminke, 2001; Devine, Clayton, Philips, Dunford, & Melner, 1999; Konovsky, 2000; Kozlowski & Bell, 2003) and the rise in multi-level research in general (Kozlowski & Klein, 2000) caused justice researchers to shift their attention away from the *what* of justice and toward the *who* of justice. In considering the perpetrator (i.e., the source of justice), we became inherently aware that employees must interact with and form relationships with many people, groups, and entities at work. This web of relationships – the quality of which is largely determined by the justice stemming from each source – can create unique social environments for individuals.

The next logical step in this theoretical line of reasoning was to ask two questions:

- How do the various sources of justice interact with one another to form an overall atmosphere regarding how well employees perceive themselves to be treated?
- To what extent do individuals who have common relational webs (e.g., work on the same team, have the same boss) come to share perceptions about how fairly they as a group are treated?

Research questions surrounding the issue of unit-level justice or justice climate have certainly been incubating, just waiting to evolve.

THE EMERGENCE OF MULTI-LEVEL JUSTICE RESEARCH

Organizational-Level Antecedents to Individual-Level Justice Perceptions

Before embarking on a larger discussion of justice climate, it is necessary to point out that this is not the only multi-level application addressed by the justice literature. Indeed, an important collection of studies have considered multi-level antecedents of individual-level justice perceptions. At large, these studies surround the effects of both culture (Leung, 2005) and organizational structure (Ambrose & Schminke, 2003) on fairness perceptions. We will briefly discuss these two avenues of research before turning our attention to unit-level justice perceptions.

The Effects of Culture
Research that has considered the influence of culture on employee justice perceptions has argued that substantial culturally based differences are present in the justice perception formation process, the relative importance placed on the various justice types, and the behavioral and attitudinal reactions following a perceived injustice (James, 1993; Greenberg, 2001; Lam,

Schaubroeck, & Aryee, 2002). The empirical evidence to date is generally supportive of these arguments.

For example, Blader, Chang, and Tyler (2001) found culture to moderate the effect of procedural injustice on workplace retaliation, with employees in Taiwan showing less of a propensity to retaliate. Pillai, Williams, and Tan (2001) presented evidence that procedural and distributive justices were related to satisfaction, commitment, and trust across four different cultures, but the relative importance of the justice types varied by culture. Brockner et al. (2001) showed voice (a key component of procedural justice) to be more important to individuals in low-power-distance (versus high-power-distance) cultures.

Li (2004) reported results from a meta-analysis that synthesized the cross-cultural justice research to date. His findings suggested that although distributive and procedural justice perceptions were related to employee attitudes in all cultures, the magnitude of the correlations varied across cultures – most notably, across those cultures that differed in terms of their power distance. Finally, Bashshur and Rupp (2004) studied the measurement equivalence of justice across four cultures. Justice measures were shown to be metrically equivalent across cultures. Further, results indicated that the construct of justice can be measured in the same way across cultures, and that both the factor structure and the strength of the relationships between manifest indicators and latent constructs are equivalent across cultures. However, in line with previous cross-cultural justice work, the experience of a specific just or unjust behavior was heavily influenced by the expectations related to treatment in the workplace. In other words, depending on what was typically expected to occur in the workplace, the same behavior by a supervisor could be rated as very unfair or as neutral by respondents from different cultures.

The Effects of Organizational Structure
Cropanzano and Greenberg (1997) were among the first to propose theoretically that employees' environmental contexts help shape their justice perceptions. Ambrose, Schminke, and their colleagues have shown empirically across several studies that a number of structural aspects within an organization affect workplace fairness. In a study analyzing samples from 11 different organizations, Schminke, Ambrose, and Cropanzano (2000) found a relationship between the concentration of authority within an organization (termed "centralization") and the perceptions of procedural justice. That is, more injustice was perceived when employees had fewer opportunities to participate in decision making and when power to make decisions was concentrated among those high in the authority hierarchy. Organizational size was also discovered

to make a difference, with more interactional justice being found among employees in larger organizations.

Schminke, Cropanzano, and Rupp (2002) extended these findings by considering the role of organizational structure on three types of justice (distributive, procedural, and interactional) using a sample of employees grouped into 45 departments across 35 organizations. Their results reaffirmed that centralization exerted effects on employee justice perceptions. These researchers also found main effects for formalization – that is, the extent to which policies and procedures are well documented by the organization – with more fairness being perceived in departments with higher levels of formalization. Lastly, these authors found that many of the main effects were moderated by the employees' level within the organization, with a weaker effect of structure occurring among those employees at higher hierarchical levels. This finding was interpreted through the lens of social exchange theory (Blau, 1964). That is, the authors posited that employees at higher levels in the organizational hierarchy are more likely to be engaged in high-quality social exchange relationships with the organization, and therefore are less influenced by structure.

Another multi-level study of the influence on organizational structure on workplace justice was conducted by Ambrose and Schminke (2003). This time, rather than structure acting as an antecedent to the formation of justice perceptions, structure moderated reactions to injustice. Taking both a multifoci and a social exchange perspective, this study, which was conducted in 102 departments of 68 organizations, revealed that interactional justice predicted supervisory trust most strongly in organic organizations (i.e., organizations with decentralized, loose, flexible structures), whereas procedural justice predicted perceived organizational support most strongly in mechanistic organizations (i.e., organizations characterized by centralized power, hierarchical communication, uniformity, and formality). Based on the results of these studies, it appears that policy makers should consider how the structure and design of workplace environments shape how organizations and the people in them influence individual employees.

The Evolution of Justice Climate Research

For the purpose of this chapter, the research on organizational and cultural effects on justice perceptions is very important. Not only does it represent two lines of multi-level justice research, but, like the research on multifoci justice described earlier, this research has also served to "broaden the minds" of those trained with a strict "micro" orientation. That is, it has made us aware of environmental influences in both forming justice judgments and moderating reactions to unfair events. Furthermore, these multi-level designs required the collection of data from employees who could be clustered in meaningful groups (e.g., teams, departments, organizations). It was only natural that the research community shift its thinking toward not only how individuals working within the same team, group, or organization might have *shared* perceptions regarding their treatment by authorities, but also how a *climate* for justice could emerge within groups that might predict outcomes above and beyond the effects of individual-level justice perceptions.

This shift in thinking was simultaneously spurred by other trends occurring within the organizational sciences at that time. First, the last decade has observed an increase in the use of team-based work systems within organizations, and as a result, an increase in the amount of research focused on team settings (Cohen & Bailey, 1997; Colquitt et al., 2005; Cropanzano & Schminke, 2001; Devine et al., 1999; Konovsky, 2000). Second, multi-level perspectives have been very much on the rise, as single-level analyses have been recognized to represent incomplete methods for understanding complex organizational phenomena. Organizations are now (correctly) being treated as integrated systems with individual and organizational characteristics that interact and combine to shape individual and organizational outcomes (Kozlowski & Klein, 2000). Third, contemporary theoretical models of workplace justice have revealed that justice concerns are not always self-interested (Folger, Cropanzano, & Goldman, 2005); instead, people also care about the treatment of others (Colquitt, 2004), and "third-party" justice effects (i.e., emotional, attitudinal, or behavioral reactions upon witnessing another being treated unfairly) are far more common than was once thought (Folger & Cropanzano, 2001).

Together, these influences have catalyzed the development of a very exciting new line of inquiry within workplace justice: that of justice climate. The following sections review the justice climate research to date. The remainder of the chapter then seeks to integrate these findings into a theoretical model and makes suggestions for fruitful areas of future research.

Justice Climate

General Justice Climate
To our knowledge, the first study that took justice beyond individual-level perceptions was carried out by Mossholder, Bennett, and Martin (1998). These authors argued for the existence of a "context" for procedural justice.

This paper was based on the arguments of Tyler and Lind (1992), who stated that when the organization violates procedural norms with respect to one employee, this action can easily be seen as a violation to all members of the work unit. Mossholder et al. further argued that when multiple group members perceive themselves as being treated in a similar way by authorities, "justice perceptions ... may emerge in the aggregate" (1998, p. 132). This study was influential not only as the first justice climate paper, but also because Mossholder and colleagues, in setting-up the theoretical justification for their hypotheses, brought together past research findings from yet another area of justice research that has great implications for the study of justice climate – namely, third-party justice effects (Ambrose, Harland, & Kulik, 1991; Colquitt, 2004; Folger, Rosenfield, Grove, & Corkran, 1979; James & Cropanzano, 1994; Miller, Jackson, Mueller, & Schersching, 1987; Steil, 1983). Collectively, this research has shown that the treatment of others often affects one's own justice judgments.

In their study, Mossholder et al. hypothesized that a climate for procedural justice would emerge within workgroups and that unit-level procedural justice would predict individual-level job attitudes (satisfaction and commitment). Random coefficients modeling (RCM) (via hierarchical linear modeling, HLM) was employed on a sample of employees within 53 bank branches. The authors found support for their predictions, with procedural justice climate predicting 20% of the variance in job satisfaction (no multilevel effect was found for commitment).

Naumann and Bennett (2000) extended the Mossholder et al. findings by placing more emphasis on the definition and measurement of procedural justice climate as well as the development of justice climate within workgroups. Pulling from the workgroup climate literature, these researchers defined procedural justice climate as "a distinct group-level cognition about how a work group as a whole is treated" (Naumann & Bennett, 2000, p. 882) and measured their climate variable via an aggregate of how group members perceived the group to be treated in terms of procedural justice. They predicted that group cohesion, demographic similarity among group members, and the manager's visibility would increase the likelihood of an emergence of justice climate; and that procedural justice climate would predict organizational commitment and helping behavior. Using a sample of employees taken from 40 bank branches, HLM analyses revealed that cohesion and visibility – but not demographic similarity – predicted the emergence of procedural justice climate. As in the work of Mossholder et al., procedural justice climate did not predict commitment, although it did predict employee-helping behaviors.

Ehrhart (2004) expanded the Naumann and Bennett findings by testing a model whereby procedural justice climate predicted *unit-level* helping behaviors (organizational citizenship behaviors, OCB). This model proposed that the relationship between servant leadership and unit-level OCB would be mediated by procedural justice climate. It was tested using an employee sample from a grocery store chain. Employees were grouped into one of 249 departments. Using structural equations modeling (SEM), Ehrhart found that this unit-level model fit the data well. The model was not compared with an individual-level model, however, hindering our ability to determine the relative strength of the unit-level effects above and beyond the individual-level effects.

Justice Climate within Team Settings
Other justice climate research has turned its attention to teams. That is, rather than simply testing for justice climate effects within departments or work units, this line of research has considered how a context for procedural justice emerges within intact teams (e.g., manufacturing teams, project teams, product development teams). For example, Colquitt, Noe, and Jackson (2002) conducted a study using 88 semiautonomous teams within 6 automobile parts manufacturing plants. These authors proposed several hypotheses based on the extant justice theories (e.g., the relational model, the instrumental model, fairness heuristic theory) linking procedural justice climate within teams to team performance. Regression analyses revealed that smaller, more collective teams were shown to possess more favorable procedural justice climate levels, and procedural justice climate level positively predicted team performance and negatively predicted team-level absenteeism. This investigation was the first study of its kind to measure both justice and performance at the team level of analysis.

Research has continued to explore justice within team settings, although these studies have not necessarily incorporated multi-level methodology (see Colquitt et al., 2005, for a comprehensive review of this research). For example, a study by Colquitt (2004) looked at the consistency between how team members feel they are personally treated and how they feel their teammates are treated in terms of procedural justice. Results from both a student team sample and a laboratory study showed that this consistency matters. Consistency predicted role performance, especially in interdependent teams consisting of members who were sensitive to equity concerns. As will be discussed later, the target of justice (i.e., the focal "victim" or referent) is quite relevant both theoretically and psychometrically to the study of justice climate.

Organizational-Level Justice Climate

Simons and Roberson (2003) extended the findings of Mossholder et al., Naumann and Bennett, and Colquitt et al. by expanding their focus to the *organizational* level of analysis and considering not only procedural justice climate, but also interpersonal justice climate within organizations. Using a very large sample of employees from nearly 100 hotel properties, these authors used SEM to test a model whereby procedural and interpersonal justice predicted commitment and satisfaction, which in turn predicted outcomes such as discretionary service behavior, intent to remain, guest service satisfaction, and employee turnover.

This model was tested by collapsing the data in three ways: as individual-level data, as aggregated by department, and as aggregated by organization (i.e., hotel property). Although this analytical strategy (i.e., using SEM rather than HLM) did not allow the authors to test for incremental unit- and organizational-level effects (over and above individual-level effects – that is, nested models – were not compared), and although the models did not show exactly parallel prediction of outcomes, for the most part all three models fit the data quite well. This outcome provides evidence for the existence of justice climate within both teams and organizations.

Multitype Multifoci Multi-level Justice

To review, the justice climate research supports the existence of both procedural justice climate and interpersonal justice climate, and these justice climates predict a wide range of outcomes such as job attitudes, performance, and citizenship behaviors. Liao and Rupp (2005) sought to further expand the justice climate research by explicitly integrating the multifoci justice literature model discussed earlier with that described in the multilevel justice literature. These authors proposed that a number of justice climates exist within workgroups surrounding the multiple types and sources of justice. They argued for the existence of six distinct justice climate variables: *organizationally focused* procedural, informational, and interpersonal justice climate, and *supervisory-focused* procedural, informational, and interpersonal justice climate.

Consistent with the multifoci justice literature (Malatesta & Byrne, 1997; Masterson et al., 2000; Rupp & Cropanzano, 2002), Liao and Rupp hypothesized that the organizationally focused justice climate variables would predict individual-level attitudes and behaviors directed at the organization, and that the supervisory-focused justice climate variables would predict individual-level attitudes and behaviors directed at the supervisor. In addition, their work was among the first multi-level justice studies to incorporate an individual difference variable as a moderator. That is, Liao and Rupp predicted that the effects of multifoci justice climate on multifoci outcomes would be moderated by individual differences in group members' justice orientations (the extent to which they internalize justice as a moral virtue and pay attention to issues of justice around them).

This model was tested using RCM (via HLM) on a sample of 49 workgroups taken from 9 different organizations. Results were generally supportive, albeit with many exceptions. In general, organizationally focused justice climate (procedural, informational, and interpersonal) was found to predict commitment to the organization, whereas supervisory-focused justice climate (procedural, informational, and interpersonal) was found to predict both commitment to and satisfaction with the supervisor. Organizational citizenship behavior was predicted by organizationally focused procedural and informational justice climate only.

Liao and Rupp's work, of course, was only a preliminary study of multilevel multifoci justice research in that differential hypotheses were not made for the different types of justice climate, nor for the same type of justice at multiple levels of analysis. Indeed, we have merely begun to scrape the surface in terms of understanding the world of justice as it manifests itself at levels beyond that of individual employees.

Where Do We Go from Here?

The justice literature is, at present, perfectly situated in its evolution to take on a systematic investigation into the antecedents and consequences of justice climate. The literature is rich and comprehensive, and some multi-level investigations have already been embarked upon. At this point, a summary model serves to illustrate what we know with regard to the multi-level nomological network that contains justice climate.

Fig. 1 graphically depicts this model. It is nothing more than a summary of the links between constructs that have been shown thus far in past research. Readers can imagine this figure floating in three-dimensional space, with the four levels depicted hovering over one another. Individuals are over-arched by groups, which are over-arched by organizations, which are over-arched by culture. Indeed, the research to date implies a nomological net for each level (although the nets are incomplete at some levels). Research also implies several cross-level effects whereby a variable at one level (e.g., justice climate) affects constructs at other levels (e.g., individual-level attitudes and behaviors). Readers will notice that the nomological networks are

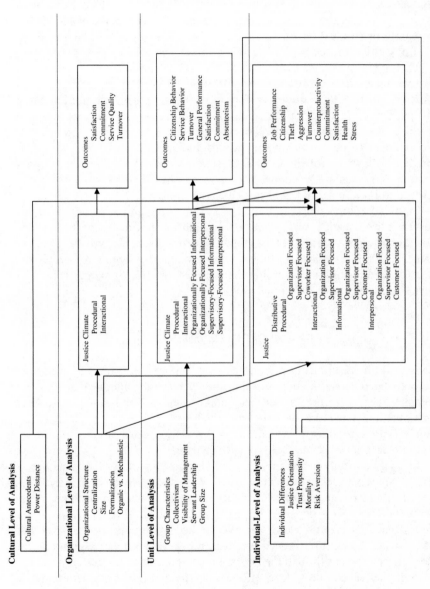

Fig. 1. Generalized Summary Model of Justice Climate's Nomological Network.

incomplete at some levels. For example, at the individual level of analysis, we see that there are no foci under distributive justice, and coworker justice is only listed under procedural justice. This is not to suggest that any foci are not relevant to any individual type of justice, but rather, this is all the justice community has explored thus far.

In addition, the model is grossly overgeneralized in that it simply links groups of constructs but does not illustrate the specific connections between specific variables. It does, however, give a sense of where attention has been directed to date. Indeed, justice considerations have been taken into account at the individual, group/team, and organizational levels of analysis, and some attempt has been made to distinguish between types and sources of justice at each of these levels. Research has also begun to explore the links between justice climate and outcomes at multiple levels of analysis. Some attention has been devoted to both the contextual and the individual difference variables that affect justice climates. Finally, a small amount of research has been conducted that considers culture and personality as moderators of justice effects. Despite these advances, several untested areas remain within justice climate's nomological network. The following sections outline five areas that are in need of attention as the research on justice climate moves forward.

Multifoci Research and More Differential Hypotheses

First, more research is needed that explores justice climate from a multifoci perspective. At present, the multifoci literature is especially well situated to extend itself theoretically into multi-level investigations. Whereas some initial headway has made here (e.g., Bashshur, Rupp, & Christopher, 2004; Liao & Rupp, 2005; Ng, Rupp, & Drasgow, 2005), the research undertaken to date has merely scratched the surface of what could become a much more comprehensive collection of research propositions. The major need at present is an investigation of the *differential* effects of different types and sources of justice climate at the unit level of analysis (indeed, this type of research is needed in the general, individual-level multifoci justice literature as well) and an examination of the *differential* effects of the justice climate at different levels of analysis.

This last point – that is, theorizing about how the effects of justice are *different* at different levels of analysis – is of particular importance. For example, Dietz, Robinson, Folger, Baron, and Schulz (2003) were unsuccessful in predicting workplace aggression with procedural justice climate. Assuming this failure was not due to a Type II error, this finding is actually quite pertinent to future multi-level justice research, in that it shows that justice climate is much more than individual-level justice perceptions averaged up. Rather, justice at different levels of analysis might have both different antecedents and different outcomes, and future research will need to further explore both the process of emergence and the construct validity of multi-level justice.

Boundary Conditions
Second, future multi-level justice research needs to examine the boundary conditions of justice climate effects. As Hall and Rosenthal (1991, p. 447) pointed out, "If we want to know how well we are doing in the biological, psychological, and social sciences, an index that will serve us well is how far we have advanced in our understanding of the moderator variables of our field." Similarly, to advance our understanding of *how* and *when* justice climate influences multi-level outcomes, future research needs to go beyond assessing its main effects and examine potential moderators of such effects.

The work of Ambrose and Schminke (2003) is especially relevant to an exploration of situational moderators. These authors found that the effects of individual-level justice perceptions on organizational trust were moderated by organizational structure. Future research might consider linking the levels of analysis to an even greater extent and theorizing about how structural variables such as the ones explored by these authors might moderate justice climate effects. In terms of individual differences, the limited studies along this line show that the effects of justice climate and justice context on individual attitudes and behaviors are contingent on enduring individual characteristics such as justice orientation (Liao & Rupp, 2005) and social value orientation (Liao, Rupp, Ko, Nam, & Bashshur, 2005). Additional theory-driven efforts might further our understanding of which factors may constrain or enhance the effects of justice climate. The work of Colquitt, Judge, Scott, and Shaw (2004) might be a great place to start in extending this line of research. These authors were among the first to show compelling results for a set of theoretically derived personality variables (i.e., trust, morality, risk aversion) as moderators of individual-level justice effects. Future research looking at moderators of justice climate may want to begin with these variables in forming hypotheses based on contemporary justice theories.

The Measurement of Justice Climate
Our third recommendation as research on the antecedents and consequences of justice climate moves forward is to carefully consider how justice climate is best operationalized and consequently measured. Using the classic multi-level

terminology, researchers need to develop *composition models*. Chan (1998) specified a number of composition models, which link constructs at different levels. *Direct consensus* models are probably the most commonly used models for aggregation (Chan, 1998). This approach typically focuses on the group level, but uses aggregations of responses from individuals given some minimal level of within-group agreement of scores. Mossholder et al. (1998), Simons and Roberson (2003), Liao and Rupp (2005), and Bashshur et al. (2004) used this type of composition model to measure justice climate. This approach involves collecting procedural and/or interactional justice perceptions from individuals and aggregating these perceptions to the group level. Employees are asked individually how fairly they feel *they themselves* are treated (e.g., an item might read "*I* am treated with dignity and respect," to which the employee responds by indicating his or her level of agreement). After item ratings are averaged to obtain an overall justice rating for each individual employee, and assuming that there exists sufficient within-group agreement and between-group dissimilarity, the scores for employees within a team, department, or organization are then averaged to form a justice climate variable for that unit.

The *referent shift* approach differs in terms of the referent of interest. Instead of simply aggregating each group member's assessment of his or her treatment into some group-level construct (as is done in the direct consensus approach), the referent shift approach refers specifically to the treatment that the group receives. Again, akin to the direct consensus approach, there is a shared component to the referent shift approach: Some minimal level of agreement in the perceptions of group members must be observed to say that a climate exists. This approach, however, results in a new form of the conceptual construct that is distinct from the original one. For example, while justice climate using a referent shift approach assesses the justice experiences of the group, the outcome is not the same thing as the sum of each individual's treatment within the group. This composition model was used by Naumann and Bennett (2000), Colquitt et al. (2002), Dietz and colleagues (2003), and Ehrhart (2004) to measure justice climate.

In an effort to explore the issue of composition model choice in the study of justice climate, Bashshur et al. (2004) compared the within- and between-group agreement indices using an array of composition models as well as general and specific sources of justice (direct consensus, multifoci direct consensus, referent shift, and multifoci referent shift models). Results indicated that referent shift models led to more agreement within groups and a better ability to distinguish between groups than did direct consensus models. In addition, the process of focusing respondents' attentions on a specific source for justice seemed to increase within-group agreement for both direct consensus and referent shift approaches.

An interesting result of this approach was that it became possible to observe patterns of agreement levels for each type and source of justice. The largest increases in average group agreement levels when moving from a direct consensus approach to a referent shift approach arose when assessing interpersonal and distributive justice climates (e.g., the average r_{wg} value jumped from 0.60 to 0.78 when moving from a general direct consensus model to a general referent shift model). Theoretically, this is an interesting trend. Equity theory research (Adams, 1965) suggests that it is one's own outcome versus some relevant target that is important in assessing distributive justice – that perceptions of distributive justice are, in fact, relative. This idea implies that by focusing items intended to measure a group-level construct (justice climate) at the individual level (as is done with the direct consensus approach), we are introducing noise into the construct, because each individual in the group may achieve different outcomes. By forcing all respondents to focus on the same target (i.e., the group as a whole), the referent shift approach increases within-group agreement and more accurately assesses the group-level nature of the construct.

The same might be said for the assessment of interpersonal justice climate. Given that employees in the same group can experience dramatically different relationships with their supervisors, the fact that within-group agreement indices were lower in the direct consensus approach as compared to the referent shift approach should not be surprising. Again, the referent shift approach forces all respondents to focus on the same level of interest – the group. An individual may have a negative relationship with his or her supervisor, yet, when asked about how the group as whole is treated, may respond quite positively.

Given these findings, although direct consensus measures have been used with some success in the literature (even by us), we do not feel they are theoretically ideal for measuring justice climate because of the disconnect between the true referent of interest (the group) and the actual referent alluded to in the items (the self). Because the referent shift approach uses the group rather than the individual as the construct's referent (Chan, 1998; Chen, Mathieu, & Bliese, 2004), measurement and theory are more closely linked in that the justice items, although still rated by employees individually, refer to the experiences of the group as opposed to the experiences of the individual employee. Given that justice climate researchers are interested in what group-level justice perceptions are and how they affect important outcomes, we find ourselves agreeing with the recent recommendations of multi-level researchers (Hofmann & Jones, 2004; Kozlowski & Klein, 2000) that the referent shift approach, with its explicit focus on the group level, is the more appropriate approach for measuring climate in general and justice climate in particular.

Climate Strength
Alternatively called "climate consensus" (Lindell & Brandt, 2000), *climate strength* (Chan, 1998) refers to the basic notion that the amount of within-group agreement should, independently of the mean level of agreement (Lindell & Brandt, 2000), affect organizational outcomes (or at the very least moderate the effect of mean levels of climate on outcomes). To date, the findings have been mixed, with some researchers reporting strong effects for climate strength (Colquitt et al., 2002) and others reporting no incremental explanatory power for the construct (Lindell & Brandt, 2000).

Part of the problem with assessing the effects of climate strength may lie in the fact that climate strength is at least partially dependent on mean levels of climate. As the mean for the group increases, there results a certain restriction of range such that levels of agreement also increase. This multicollinearity makes it difficult to partial out the effects of climate strength from climate level. Although a variety of indices (e.g., $r_{wg(j)}$, James, Demaree, & Wolf, 1984) have been offered to assess climate strength, each seems to have its own set of problems.

Ostroff, Kinicki, and Tamkins (2003) offer a different approach to assessing climate strength that is independent of many of the problems that trouble the typical measures of agreement. They discuss three aspects of climate strength: agreement-based strength, system-based strength, and alignment-based strength. *Agreement-based strength* deals with the issues of climate strength as they have been discussed thus far. It simply assesses the extent to which group members agree in their perceptions of the environment. System-based strength and alignment-based strength, however, involve a different focus. *System-based strength* refers to the extent to which the climate is pervasive in an organization. An organization is said to possess high system-based strength when it has strong socialization and training programs in place and sanctions for behaving in ways not congruent with the group norms. *Alignment-based strength* deals with the extent to which organizational climate is aligned with actual organizational practices. It is an assessment of the congruence between organizational foci. In situations characterized by a lack of congruence across foci, the contingencies are "ambiguously interpreted across individuals ... and do not generate uniform expectancies concerning the desired behavior" (Ostroff et al., 2003, p. 583).

Given that we have argued for multiple sources of justice climate, we extend this idea of alignment-based strength to include the idea that, aside from an alignment between policies and actual practices, climates from different sources (for example, a justice climate from supervisors versus a justice climate from the organization) may be out of alignment. Note that this approach to strength is independent of mean levels, as it is simply the amount of alignment that is hypothesized to affect the strength of climate on outcomes. Groups with misaligned climates are deemed to have *inconsistent climate*. However, when all sources (e.g., supervisor, organization) are either very just or very unjust, then the prediction of outcomes – whether it be in a positive or a negative direction – will be stronger.

Bashshur et al. (2004) examined this proposition by comparing groups according to their levels of justice climate. These researchers assessed climate according to the Naylor, Pritchard, and Ilgen (1980) climate model described later in this chapter. That is, justice climate was assessed based on the likelihood of punishments or rewards given specific justice behaviors coming from supervisors versus coworkers. In only 10 of 47 groups in the sample did participants, on average, report that a negative relationship or no relationship between supervisor and coworker contingencies. In other words, in 10 of 47 groups, the same type of behavior was rewarded or punished by supervisors, but ignored by colleagues. In the remaining groups, the relationship between supervisor rewards and coworker rewards was measured as $r = 0.70$ at the least. In a nonparametric test of the differences in means on a variety of outcomes, aligned groups were found to have higher levels of satisfaction with supervision, affective commitment, normative commitment, and supervisor-rated organizational citizenship than did nonaligned groups.

This initial test of the effects of alignment strength on climate–outcome relationships provides some encouraging support for this new approach to climate strength. While the results are not conclusive (we did not find circumstances in which one climate was positive while another was negative), it does represent a tentative step toward a theoretically interesting and new approach.

Statistically Modeling Multi-level Hypotheses
As the theoretical thinking about justice becomes increasingly multi-level, it becomes necessary to think critically about the statistical techniques employed to test hypotheses. Typically, in justice climate research, the conceptual model is multi-level or cross-level in nature, with predictors

spanning both the individual level (e.g., individual-level justice perceptions) and the group level (e.g., group-level justice climate). In addition, the data are often hierarchical in nature, with employees nested in higher-level units such as workgroups. Thus observations from the same workgroup may be interdependent of each other, violating the statistical independence assumption of ordinary least squares (OLS) regression. As a result, the OLS estimates of standard errors may be biased, and test statistics may not be valid. To avoid these potential problems, researchers may adopt RCM and cross-level operator analysis (CLOP). A comparison of the similarities and differences among these methods can be found in Klein et al. (2000).

For example, HLM is an RCM technique that has been used in extant multi-level justice research. HLM explicitly accounts for the nested nature of data and can simultaneously estimate the effects of factors at different levels on individual-level outcomes while maintaining appropriate levels of analysis for the predictors (Bryk & Raudenbush, 1992). HLM can be applied to test a *two-level incremental model* of the justice climate effects. In this case, researchers are interested in the *incremental* effects of the group-level justice climate on individual attitudinal and behavioral outcomes after controlling for individual-level justice perceptions. In the justice climate literature, such a technique was used in the studies of Mossholder et al. (1998), Naumann and Bennett (2000), and Liao and Rupp (2005). These studies found an incremental effect of justice climate on outcomes over and above the effects of individual-level justice perceptions.

HLM can also be applied to test a *cross-level moderation model* of the justice climate effects. In this case, researchers may be interested in whether the group-level justice climate moderates the relationship between an individual-level predictor and an individual-level outcome variable. For example, Liao and Rupp (2005) detected an interaction between supervisor-focused procedural justice climate and individual differences in justice orientation on supervisory-directed commitment and satisfaction. An even more direct illustration of this type of model was presented by Ng et al. (2005), who found that the relationship between conscientiousness and contextual performance (specifically, job dedication and dutifulness) was moderated by organization-focused justice climate. Interestingly, and in line with this chapter's discussion of emergence, no effects were found for individual-level justice–conscientiousness interactions. As such, these results evidence the utility of cross-level theorizing in organizational behavior. A more detailed discussion of testing multi-level incremental models and cross-level moderation models can be found in Bryk and Raudenbush (1992) and Hofmann and Gavin (1998).

THE PROCESS OF EMERGENCE

We now turn our attention to the process by which a climate for justice emerges within workgroups. The following sections present several theories that offer different perspectives on how such a process might occur. These perspectives can be divided into two major categories:

- *Bottom-up* models, which posit processes by which individuals within workgroups come to develop a shared cognition about how the group as a whole is treated.
- *Top-down* models, which posit processes by which the organization imposes structures and contingencies on the group, which causes climate to emerge.

We categorize the various theoretical perspectives as best we can, although – as is obvious from our writing – many of the perspectives make mention of both top-down and bottom-up influences.

Bottom-Up Processes of Climate Emergence

Although justice perceptions have their origin at the individual level of analysis, the collection of individual perceptions within groups may lead to the formation of a shared, collective cognition or climate. This type of emergence process has been referred to as *bottom-up* emergence in multi-level research (see Kozlowski & Klein, 2000). Several theories provide the theoretical underpinnings for the bottom-up emergence of justice climate, including theories of social information processing (Salancik & Pfeffer, 1978), socialization (Ostroff & Kozlowski, 1992), and attraction–selection–attrition (ASA) (Schneider, 1975). Empirical research has provided evidence for the hypothetical processes proposed by each of these perspectives in the formation of other climate variables (e.g., technical updating climate, Kozlowski & Hults, 1987; innovation climate, Anderson & West, 1998; safety climate, Hofmann & Stetzer, 1996; and service climate, Schneider, 1990). Below we briefly describe how each of these perspectives is relevant to the study of justice climate.

Social Information Processing Theory
Social information processing theory (Salancik & Pfeffer, 1978) argues that individuals use information gathered from others in their direct social contexts to form judgments about organizational practices, values, and norms.

Given that members of the same group are exposed to the same policies, leaders, and other contextual characteristics (Naumann & Bennett, 2000), they will possess shared information and form common perceptions regarding how fairly they are treated by multiple parties within the organization. In other words, this perspective would argue that because group members are often affected by the same procedures, may receive similar outcomes or re-wards, and may be treated in a similar fashion by supervisors, the organ-ization, customers, and other parties, a shared evaluation of distributive, procedural, and interactional justice may form about each of these sources. A similar phenomenon – that of *contagious justice* – has been proposed in the justice literature. This perspective argues that "the often ambiguous and emotionally charged nature of justice events compels organizational actors to engage in social talk and arrive at a shared, socially constructed interpretation of justice" (Degoey, 2000, p. 51).

Attraction–Selection–Attrition
The ASA perspective (Schneider, 1975) proposes that individuals of similar characteristics are attracted to, selected into, and retained by the same group. Consequently, this model implies that over time, a workgroup will consist of individuals with similar values and perceptions. In the words of Schneider (1987), "The people make the place." Rooted in the work of Payne and Pugh (1976) and Naylor et al.(1980), this intriguing theoretical perspective places special emphasis on the similarity of individual differences between members of a workgroup. As individuals with similar backgrounds, values, and inter-ests are selected into or attracted to the group, homogeneity is said to in-crease. As homogeneity increases, individuals are expected to perceive the work environment in a similar manner. While a compelling theory, only limited support has been found for this model in the general climate literature.

However, pertinent to the present investigation is the question of which individual differences might group members come to be similar on through an ASA process, which will lead them to form similar justice perceptions. Whereas the justice literature has shown that broad personality constructs are generally not predictive of justice perceptions (Colquitt et al., 2004), a small set of justice-related individual difference constructs might fit this category, including equity sensitivity (Huseman, Hatfield, & Miles, 1987), sensitivity to befallen injustice (Schmitt, 1996; Schmitt & Dörfel, 1999), justice orientation (Rupp, Byrne, & Wadlington, 2003; Liao & Rupp, 2005), and morality (Folger et al., 2005; Rupp, 2003).

Further, Colquitt et al. (2004) showed that the effect of individual-level justice perceptions on task performance and theft were moderated by morality, trust propensity, and risk aversion. An ASA perspective would argue that perhaps over time, this interaction of personality and individual justice perceptions might influence the emergence of justice climate within groups. Of course, both the notion of similarity on justice-relevant personality characteristics predicting justice climate and the idea of a personality × justice perception interaction affecting justice climate emergence are in need of empirical testing before strong conclusions can be drawn regarding these ideas.

Socialization
We know from the socialization literature that coworkers are the key agents in the socialization process, and that a new employee will come to learn, via interactions with existing members, the procedures dictating how things are generally carried out and how people are generally treated in their work-groups (see Louis, Posner, & Powell, 1983; Ostroff & Kozlowski, 1992; Trice & Beyer, 1993). Similarly, Kozlowski and Bell (2003) point out that through social- and work-based interactions among group members, workgroups tend to develop relatively stable mental models and shared meanings. Consequently, climate formation occurs through a reciprocal process by which the group influences the individual through socialization, and the individual attempts to influence the group, "to accommodate to their unique attributes and needs" (Kozlowski & Bell, 2003, p. 341). This constitutes a slight divergence from the traditional ASA framework, which would argue that unique individuals would seek to leave the group. ASA may work to homogenize the workgroup to some extent, but the socialization process discussed by Kozlowski and Bell may maintain a group's climate dynamic as members seek to exert their influence.

The question then becomes, How would the socialization process affect the emergence of justice climate? We believe the process would be similar to that described in our discussion of the social information possessing model, with a slightly different twist. That is, a socialization perspective, like the social information processing perspective, would suggest that a climate for justice would emerge within a workgroup simply because group members are likely to be recipients of the same experiences (e.g., outcomes, processes, interpersonal treatment by various sources). However, this approach would argue that, in addition to climate being influenced by shared experiences, group members will attempt to exert influence on the climate based on their unique set of experiences and personality characteristics. Thus, the justice climate emerges as a result of the shared *and* unique justice perceptions experienced by group members.

Top-Down Processes of Climate Emergence

Many climate researchers have pointed out that individuals do not exist in a vacuum (James & Jones, 1974; Kozlowski & Klein, 2000). Just as group members interact to share perceptions, meanings, and interpretations, which over time may stabilize around some common view of the organizational climate, so, too, do *top-down* processes such as organizational policies, practices, and procedures influence how climates are formed within groups. In discussing top-down climate emergence, we will focus on a classic model of climate, the Naylor et al. (1980) model, which has important implications for the study of justice climate in particular.

Drawing on earlier work (Campbell, Dunnette, Lawler, & Weick, 1970; James & Jones, 1974; Schneider, 1975), Naylor et al. proposed a model of climate emergence that specifies a role for both the external environment and the individual in shaping climate perceptions. These researchers argued that climate exists at three levels: the objective environment (Level 1 climate), the individual perceptions of that objective environment (Level 2 climate), and the evaluation of the psychological characteristics based on that objective environment (Level 3 climate). Climate was said to be measurable at any or all of these levels.

Pulling from Campbell et al. (1970), it was argued that psychological climate (Level 3 climate in their terminology) is based on the individual perceptions of climate contingencies in the environment. Climate contingencies refer to the pattern in which behaviors relevant to the focal construct are rewarded and punished in the work environment. Of course, this pattern of rewards and punishments does not emerge spontaneously. That is, features of the organization such as structure (e.g., size, centrality) act as antecedents to the *formal* policies, which in turn shape the *actual* policies in the organization, and eventually the system of rewards and punishments. Indeed, our earlier discussion of the effect of organizational structure on justice perceptions is certainly relevant here as well.

Most important to our discussion of justice climate is that, according to this model, climate at Level 1 and Level 2 are at least partially defined in terms of specific contingencies. For example, Hulin, Fitzgerald, and Drasgow (1996) developed a measure of tolerance for sexual harassment based on the Naylor et al. (1980) model of climate. Their measure of the contingencies inherent in an organization for sexually harassing behavior predicted occurrences of sexual harassment as well as work-related psychological and physical outcomes. Although Naylor et al. preferred to think about climate as a construct that exists only at the individual level (now commonly referred to as psychological climate), as has been amply discussed through this chapter, subsequent research has demonstrated that, in fact, the average of the group members' perceptions, given a certain threshold of variability and agreement, is useful in predicting both group and individual behavior and attitudes.

Naylor et al. were not alone in emphasizing the importance of organizational attributes in shaping climate. Payne and Pugh (1976) postulated a model that placed organizational context and structure as antecedents of organizational climate. They argued that the purpose, size, and resources of an organization (the context), in combination with the authority system, status system, and structure of roles (organizational structure), should drive the extent to which a climate emerges. For example, an organization that prides itself on being on the cutting edge and that has a relatively flat organizational structure should lead to the emergence of a risk-taking climate. To date, however, this top-down model of climate emergence has received only modest support (Jones & James, 1979; Payne & Pugh, 1976).

In terms of justice climate, we argue that, although in general justice climate might emerge through both bottom-up and top-down influences, differential propositions can be made regarding which type of emergence process will be more influential in the formation of different types of justice climate. Recall from this chapter's historical overview of the justice literature that multiple types (distributive, procedural, interactional) and sources (organization, supervisor, coworkers) have been identified as differentially relevant in the prediction of important outcomes. For example, whereas procedural and distributive justice climate might emerge via a top-down process because policies and outcomes are often handed down from above, interactional justice climate might emerge from the bottom-up as employees experience interpersonal treatment personally while at the same time witnessing how others around them, both internal and external to the group, are treated, creating a venue for shared cognitions to materialize. It is somewhat more difficult to postulate where source-based justice climates might fall in terms of emergence. The next section devotes further attention to this issue.

Multiple Sources of Climate

Early models of organizational climate emphasized the top-down, leader-driven nature of climate. As Kozlowski and Doherty (1989) argued, leaders can act as filters for all of the organizational policies, procedures, and practices. However, it is important to consider the argument implicit in the work of many modern climate researchers (e.g., Anderson & West, 1998; Kidwell & Bennett, 1993; Kozlowski & Bell, 2003) – namely, that punishment and rewards can come from the workgroup as well. Indeed, the climate shaped by the workgroup is expected to be more informal than that shaped by the leader or organization. The rules are not encoded in organizational policies, but there is a clear understanding of the punishments, such as social ostracism, and the rewards, such as an invitation to lunch, that exist for specific behaviors.

As a result, one set of values and beliefs that the organization espouses may be filtered through the leader, while simultaneously another set of values or beliefs *around the same construct* may emerge from within the workgroup. Indeed, Schneider (1975) has long argued that the concept of organizational climate is not unidimensional. Our work, which provides evidence for distinct justice climate constructs, crossed by type and source/foci, is based on this notion (Bashshur et al., 2004; Liao & Rupp, 2005). From the perspective of Naylor et al. (1980), this is actually a reasonable proposition. If climate predominantly comes from shared perceptions of punishments and rewards, then it is possible to have two separate climates for the same construct. One behavior may be punished or rewarded by the leadership, while the same behavior is differentially punished or rewarded by coworkers.

Of course, these two sources of climate need not be incongruent. To the extent that employees agree with the values or policies of management, these two influences on climate are likely to be complementary. In contrast, if conflict exists between employees and management, these sources are likely to contradict each other. Looking at climate from this multifoci perspective provides a multitude of interesting, yet untested research questions and makes for a range of interesting possibilities, not the least of which is the intriguing idea of interactions among sources of climate. Some work has already begun that examines how aligned and misaligned sources influence individual employees' behavior (e.g., see Bashshur et al., 2004; Ostroff et al., 2003).

How Does Justice Climate Relate to Other Climates?

Katz and Kahn (1978) define climates as collective beliefs. These beliefs are transferred to new group members via a combination of socialization processes interacting with the physical and social environments. As such, climate is said to develop in a process similar to Schneider's ASA theory – that is, it originates from the types of people attracted, selected, and retained by an organization. In addition, climate is a product of physical layout, traditions, history, methods of communication, and so on. Similarly, Schneider defined climate as the "shared perceptions of employees concerning the practices, procedures, and kinds of behaviors that get rewarded and supported in a particular setting" (1990, p. 384). He argued that because multiple climates can exist simultaneously in the same organization, one must think of climate as a specific construct with a specific referent. Climates have to be climates "for something" (e.g., innovation, service).

This early argument that a climate must be "for something" has led to the proliferation of "climates" noted in the literature. Currently there exist climates "for" constructs ranging from a climate for safety to a climate for top management, including, it must be admitted, a number of climates for justice. These "specific climates" (Carr, Schmidt, Ford, & DeShon, 2003, p. 605) focus on a rather narrow bandwidth of the climate construct space. Of course, it is this very specificity that makes them so useful in predicting outcomes (e.g., climates for safety predict safe behavior; Carr et al., 2003). The downside of this process is that researchers are left with a "staggering number" (Parker et al., 2003, p. 391) of climate dimensions to deal with when trying to assess the influence of the work environment on employees. Any attempt to synthesize or integrate climate perceptions is hampered by the sheer numbers of climate dimensions. If for nothing else than to reduce overlap among constructs and to impose some order on the range of climate dimensions, it becomes important to place this array of climates into some sort of taxonomy. Also of interest for the purposes of this chapter is a determination of where justice climate fits within this cornucopia of climates. Fortunately, at least three such taxonomies already exist.

Kopelman, Brief, and Guzzo (1990) argue that five dimensions cover the common aspects of psychological climate (note that at least two of these three taxonomies focus on psychological climate–individual perceptions, but there is no reason that these dimensions cannot be said to reside at the organizational level as well given sufficient agreement among group members). These dimensions – *means emphasis, goals emphasis, task support, reward orientation,* and *socioemotional support* – do seem to relate to employee attitudes and motivations. In addition, as Lindell and Brandt (2000) point out, the core climates (such as a strong goal emphasis) that emerge from these functions do not prohibit the emergence of specific climates. The fact that an organization has a strong goal emphasis alone does not specify which goal (e.g., safety or service – in other words, which specific climate) is being emphasized. As such, each specific climate can be classified within a particular core dimension. However, the rather narrow range of dimensions in the Kopelman et al. classification scheme does not seem to capture all possible manifestations of climate (not even justice climate).

Alternatively, Ostroff (1993) proposed a framework consisting of 12 dimensions of climate with three higher-order facets: *affective, cognitive,* and *instrumental.* The affective higher-order facet relates to involvement with people and encompasses the lower-order dimensions of *participation, cooperation, warmth,* and *social rewards.* The cognitive facet relates to the self's or others' psychological involvement in work and encompasses the dimensions of *growth, innovation, autonomy,* and *intrinsic rewards.* Finally, the instrumental facet relates to task involvement and getting things done; it encompasses the lower-order dimensions of *achievement, hierarchy, structure,* and *extrinsic rewards.* While some researchers have enjoyed success when using this taxonomy as an organizing framework (Carr et al., 2003), it is frequently difficult to make a judgment regarding where a particular specific climate should be assigned. For example, justice climate, with its dimensions of interpersonal, informational, procedural, and distributive justice, could fit into any one of the three higher-order facets.

Finally, James and colleagues (Jones & James, 1979; James & James, 1989; James & McIntyre, 1996) proposed a five-dimensional structure of workplace perceptions (psychological climate): *leader support and facilitation* (leader characteristics); *role stress and lack of harmony* (role characteristics); *job challenge and autonomy* (job characteristics); *workgroup cooperation, warmth, and friendliness* (workgroup characteristics); and *organization and subsystem* (organizational characteristics). Each of these dimensions includes at least three lower-order dimensions and seems to be invariant over a large number of organizations (James & James, 1989; James & Sells, 1981). Further, James and coauthors have asserted that the correlations they have observed among the four first-order factors are best explained by some higher-level, general psychological climate factor, a "PC_g." This general factor is said to reflect the idea that people respond to their environments based on their perceptions of the potential benefits or harm to them inherent in that environment (James & McIntyre, 1996). This notion echoes the earlier contentions of Schneider (1990) and Naylor et al. (1980) that climate reflects some assessment of the rewards and punishments inherent in a system. James simply takes this point, which initially referred to a specific climate, and applies it to climate in general.

The intuitive appeal of this approach lies in the fact that it clearly links climate to organizational attributes, much as earlier theories regarding specific climates tried to link those perceptions to organizational features. Given the definitions of climate as assessments of organizational contexts, this approach, as contrasted to the two prior approaches, demonstrates how organizational attributes such as job features or leader features translate into climate dimensions. In addition, given the focus on organizational attributes, this taxonomy is both broad enough and flexible enough to subsume most, if not all, of the specific justice climates currently proposed. For example, as noted earlier, justice climate can be looked at as coming from a supervisor, from the organization, or from both. In the James et al. approach, a climate for justice, if deemed to be coming from the supervisor, would fit within the leader support and facilitation factor; by contrast, a climate for justice shaped by the organization would fit under the organizational characteristics factor.

In essence, this framework provides a structure of climate dimensions. Specific climates, such as a climate for justice, fit within broader climate dimensions that are based on characteristics of the environment such as leader support and facilitation. By placing the specific climates such as climate for justice within a broader taxonomy, we hope to clarify how the different climates "for something" relate to one another and coexist within the broader general climate space.

In their discussion of PC_g, James and colleagues were concentrating solely on the level of the individual – on the perceptions of each individual of his or her environment. Nevertheless, there is no reason that PC_g and its four subfacets should not exist at the organizational or group level. Given enough agreement within groups, leader support and facilitation, role stress and lack of harmony, and so on, there should be something that researchers can aggregate to the group level and examine for its effects on group and individual attitudes and behaviors. This endeavor would mean that there may be something we can call C_g – a general higher-order climate. Of course, this work has yet to be done.

Proposing a Model of Justice Climate Emergence

Whereas the extant multi-level justice research has begun to give solid attention to the antecedents and consequences of justice climate (as noted earlier in this chapter), far-less emphasis has been placed on the psychological process by which justice climate emerges. Although the concept of justice climate is firmly grounded in organizational theories such as social informational processing (Salancik & Pfeffer, 1978), attraction–selection–attrition (Schneider, 1975), and socialization (Louis et al., 1983; Ostroff & Kozlowski, 1992; Trice & Beyer, 1993), future research should test explicitly the emergence of justice climate using longitudinal or experimental designs, and incorporate factors at the individual level (e.g., individual past justice experiences), group level (e.g., group norms), and organizational level (e.g., organizational structure) to examine their joint impact on the formation of justice context. The work of Naumann and Bennett (2000), which considered the antecedents of group cohesion and visibility of management; the work of Ehrhart (2004), which considered servant leadership; the work of Colquitt et al. (2002), which examined the role of team size and collectivism; and, of course, the research on organizational structure's effects on justice perceptions (Ambrose & Schminke, 2003) represent positive steps in this direction.

That said, the authors of this chapter have been struggling both with theoretically laying out a process model for justice climate emergence and with identifying solid methodological procedures for modeling the emergence process itself. Our first (public) attempt at a theoretical model is presented in Fig. 2.

This model not only pulls from the bottom-up and top-down theories of climate emergence presented earlier in this chapter, but also reflects Cropanzano et al.'s (2001a, 2001b) integrative model of organizational justice. It integrates two major paradigms through which justice has been explored over the decades: the *event paradigm*, in which individuals evaluate isolated events, resulting in state-like justice perceptions, and the *social entity paradigm*, whereby individuals make more stable judgments about a particular social entity (e.g., supervisors) across events and situations. Our model posits that both individual differences and environmental characteristics affect how events are perceived by individuals and, over time, influence their social entity justice judgments. Individuals then come together, bringing along these judgments. Through the processes of information sharing, experience sharing, socialization, and individual influences, these persons collectively form a shared perception of social entity justice. This same process would occur to form shared justice perceptions regarding each type (e.g., procedural, interactional) and source (e.g., supervisor, customers) of justice climate. As explained earlier, each of these climates may be similar or different depending on the events leading up to the individual justice judgments and the interactions between group members over time. Furthermore, these climates might be hierarchically arranged according to the taxonomic model presented in the last section.

Empirically Modeling Justice Climate Emergence

The emergence of even a single justice climate variable is complex and dynamic, making the task of empirically modeling emergence quite a daunting undertaking. Whereas we do not have a clear answer about how exactly one

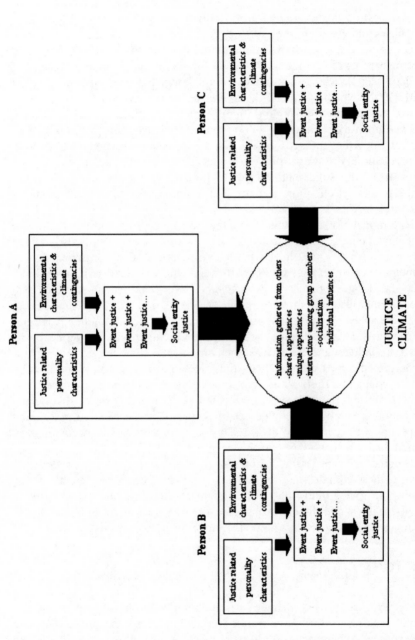

Fig. 2. Proposed Model of Justice Climate Emergence.

might empirically trace the emergence of justice climate, we have some ideas that might catalyze a dialogue on the topic. To model climate emergence, multiple measurement techniques and methodologies must be employed. Trait measurement will be needed to tap individual differences. Experience sampling could be used to model the process by which event judgments lead to social entity evaluations over time within persons. Social network mapping could be used to tap the shared and unique experiences and relational patterns between persons.

Finally, another potentially useful technique is the NK model of rugged fitness landscapes (Kauffman, 1993). Originating in physics and now being applied in biology to model evolutionary processes, this technique has yet to be applied to the modeling of psychological phenomenon. N refers to the n traits that an individual is composed of (expressed as a vector), and K refers to the episodic links that enable or constrain the expression of n traits. Such a process would involve developing a solid theory or theories regarding the justice climate emergence process, building a decision model based on the parameters implied in the theory, conducting a simulation study based on the theoretical model (which would simulate longitudinal, within-persons data), and comparing a cross-sectional employee sample to the simulated sample to test for emergence. Admittedly, much remains unknown about this method, but it might show promise for the study of multi-level justice.

CONCLUSION

This chapter has reviewed issues pertinent to multi-level justice research and ideally will serve as a catalyst for future research in this area. Multi-level justice has emerged as an exciting new area of research within organizational justice. A burgeoning body of literature has examined the multi-level antecedents of individual justice perceptions, the emergence of justice climate from individual justice perceptions, and the effects of justice climate on multi-level workplace outcomes above and beyond the effects of individual-level justice perceptions. In addition, the models proposed by the organizational climate and multi-level literatures align nicely with the theoretical arguments made within the justice community. Over the past few years, justice researchers have come a long way in conceptualizing and empirically examining multi-level justice issues, yet much more needs to be done to further our understanding of how justice fits into the inherently multi-level, integrated systems of organizations. We look forward to watching the literature on multi-level justice unfold and evolve from this pivotal point in its existence.

ACKNOWLEDGMENTS

We thank Yoichiro Hayashi, Silke Holub, and Alex Alverio for their assistance with this manuscript.

REFERENCES

Adams, J. S. (1965). Inequity in social exchange. In: L. Berkowitz (Ed.), *Advances in experimental social psychology* (Vol. 2, pp. 267–299). New York: Academic Press.
Adams-Roy, J., & Barling, J. (1998). Predicting the decision to confront or report sexual harassment. *Journal of Organizational Behavior, 19*, 329–336.
Ambrose, M. L., & Arnaud, A. (2005). Are procedural justice and distributive justice conceptually distinct? In: J. A. Colquitt & J. Greenberg (Eds), *Handbook of organizational justice* (pp. 59–84). London: Lawrence Erlbaum Associates.
Ambrose, M. L., Harland, L. K., & Kulik, C. T. (1991). Influence of social comparisons on perceptions of organizational fairness. *Journal of Applied Psychology, 76*, 239–246.
Ambrose, M. L., & Schminke, M. (2003). Organization structure as a moderator of the relationship between procedural justice, interactional justice, perceived organizational support, and supervisory trust. *Journal of Applied Psychology, 88*, 295–305.
Anderson, N. R., & West, M. A. (1998). Measuring climate for work group innovation: Development and validation of the team climate inventory. *Journal of Organizational Behavior, 19*, 235–258.
Bartel, S. A., & Hays, B. C. (1999). Organizational justice and work outcomes: A meta-analysis. Paper presented at the 14th annual meeting of the society for industrial and organizational psychology, Atlanta, GA, April–May.
Bashshur, M., & Rupp, D. E. (2004). Social exchange as a mediator of justice effects across culture. Paper presented at the 19th annual meeting of the society for industrial and organizational psychology, Chicago, IL.
Bashshur, M., Rupp, D. E., & Christopher, J. (2004). Theoretically-based strategies for defining and measuring justice climate: Implications for multi-level research in organizational justice. Paper presented at the 64th annual meeting of the academy of management, New Orleans, LA.
Bies, R. J. (2005). Are procedural justice and interactional justice conceptually distinct? In: J. A. Colquitt & J. Greenberg (Eds), *Handbook of organizational justice* (pp. 85–112). Mahwah, NJ: Lawrence Erlbaum Associates.
Bies, R. J., & Moag, J. S. (1986). Interactional justice: Communication criteria for fairness. In: B. Sheppard (Ed.), *Research on negotiation in organizations* (Vol. 1, pp. 43–55). Greenwich, CT: JAI Press.
Blader, S. L., Chang, C. C., & Tyler, T. R. (2001). Procedural justice and retaliation in organizations: Comparing cross-nationally the importance of fair group processes. *International Journal of Conflict Management, 12*, 295–311.
Blau, P. M. (1964). *Exchange and power in social life*. New York: Wiley.
Brockner, J., Ackerman, G., Greenberg, J., Gelfand, M. J., Francesco, A. M., & Chen, Z. X. (2001). Culture and procedural justice: The influence of power distance on reactions to voice. *Journal of Experimental and Social Psychology, 37*, 300–315.

Bryk, A. S., & Raudenbush, S. W. (1992). *Hierarchical linear models.* Newbury Park, CA: Sage.

Byrne, Z. S. (1999). How do procedural and interactional justice influence multiple levels of organizational outcomes? Paper presented at the 14th annual meeting of the society for industrial and organizational psychology, Atlanta, GA, April.

Campbell, J. P., Dunnette, M. D., Lawler III, E. E., & Weick, K. E. (1970). Managerial behavior, performance, and effectiveness. New York: McGraw-Hill.

Carr, J. Z., Schmidt, A. M., Ford, K., & DeShon, R. P. (2003). Climate perceptions matter: A meta-analytic path analysis relating molar climate, cognitive and affective states, and individual level work outcomes. *Journal of Applied Psychology, 88,* 605–619.

Chan, D. (1998). Functional relations among constructs in the same content domain at different levels of analysis: A typology of composition models. *Journal of Applied Psychology, 83,* 234–246.

Chen, G., Mathieu, J. E., & Bliese, P. D. (2004). A framework for conducting multi-level construct validation. In: F. J. Dansereau & F. Yammarino (Eds), *Research in multi-level issues: The many faces of multi-level issues* (Vol. 3, pp. 273–303). Oxford, UK: Elsevier Science.

Cohen, S. G., & Bailey, D. E. (1997). What makes teams work: Group effectiveness research from the shop floor to the executive suite. *Journal of Management, 23,* 239–290.

Cohen-Charash, Y., & Spector, P. E. (2001). The role of justice in organizations: A meta-analysis. *Organizational Behavior and Human Decision Processes, 86,* 278–321.

Colquitt, J. A. (2001). On the dimensionality of organizational justice: A construct validation of a measure. *Journal of Applied Psychology, 86,* 356–400.

Colquitt, J. A. (2004). Does the justice of the one interact with the justice of the many? Reactions to procedural justice in teams. *Journal of Applied Psychology, 89,* 633–646.

Colquitt, J. A., Conlon, D. E., Wesson, M. J., Porter, C. O. L. H., & Ng, K. Y. (2001). Justice at the millennium: A meta-analytic review of 25 years of organizational justice research. *Journal of Applied Psychology, 86,* 425–445.

Colquitt, J. A., Greenberg, J., & Scott, B. A. (2005). Organizational justice: Where do we stand? In: J. A. Colquitt & J. Greenberg (Eds), *Handbook of organizational justice* (pp. 589–620). Mahwah, NJ: Lawrence Erlbaum.

Colquitt, J. A., Judge, T. A., Scott, B. A., & Shaw, J. C. (2004). Justice and personality: Deriving theoretically-based moderators of justice effects. Paper presented at the 19th annual meeting of the society for industrial and organizational psychology, Chicago, IL.

Colquitt, J. A., Noe, R. A., & Jackson, C. L. (2002). Justice in teams: Antecedents and consequences of procedural justice climate. *Personnel Psychology, 55,* 83–109.

Colquitt, J. A., & Shaw, J. C. (2005). How should organizational justice be measured? In: J. Greenberg & J. Colquitt (Eds), *Handbook of organizational justice* (pp. 113–152). Mahwah, NJ: Lawrence Erlbaum Associates.

Colquitt, J. A., Zapata-Phelan, C. P., & Roberson, Q. M. (2005). Justice in teams: A review of fairness effects in collective contexts. In: J. Martocchio (Ed.), *Research in personnel and human resources management* (Vol. 24, pp. 53–94). Oxford, UK: Elsevier.

Cropanzano, R., Byrne, Z. S., Bobocel, D. R., & Rupp, D. E. (2001a). Moral virtues, fairness heuristics, social entities, and other denizens of organizational justice. *Journal of Vocational Behavior, 58,* 164–209.

Cropanzano, R., & Greenberg, J. (1997). Progress in organizational justice: Tunneling through the maze. In: C. L. Cooper & I. T. Robertson (Eds), *International review of industrial and organizational psychology* (Vol. 12, pp. 317–372). New York: Wiley.

Cropanzano, R., Prehar, C. A., & Chen, P. Y. (2002). Using social exchange theory to dis-
    tinguish procedural from interactional justice. *Group and Organizational Management*,
    27, 324–351.
Cropanzano, R., & Rupp, D. E. (2003). An overview of organizational justice: Implications for
    work motivation. In: L. W. Porter, G. A. Bigley & R. M. Steers (Eds), *Motivation and
    work behavior* (7th ed., pp. 82–95). Burr Ridge, IL: McGraw-Hill Irwin.
Cropanzano, R., Rupp, D. E., Mohler, C. J., & Schminke, M. (2001b). Three roads to or-
    ganizational justice. In: J. Ferris (Ed.), *Research in personnel and human resource man-
    agement* (Vol. 20, pp. 1–113). New York: JAI Press.
Cropanzano, R., & Schminke, M. (2001). Using social justice to build effective work groups. In:
    M. Turner (Ed.), *Groups at work: Advances in theory and research* (pp. 143–171).
    Hillsdale, NJ: Erlbaum.
Degoey, P. (2000). Contagious justice: Exploring the social construction of justice in organ-
    izations. *Research in Organizational Behavior*, *22*, 51–102.
Devine, D. J., Clayton, L. D., Philips, J. L., Dunford, B. B., & Melner, S. B. (1999). Teams in
    organizations: Prevalence, characteristics, and effectiveness. *Small Group Research*, *30*,
    678–711.
Dietz, J., Robinson, S. L., Folger, R., Baron, R. A., & Schulz, M. (2003). The impact of
    community violence and an organization's procedural justice climate on workplace ag-
    gression. *Academy of Management Journal*, *46*, 317–326.
Ehrhart, M. G. (2004). Leadership and procedural justice climate as antecedents of unit-level
    organizational citizenship behavior. *Personnel Psychology*, *57*, 61–94.
Folger, R., & Cropanzano, R. (2001). Fairness theory: Justice as accountability. In: J. Greenberg
    & R. Folger (Eds), *Advances in organizational justice* (pp. 1–55). Lexington, MA: New
    Lexington Press.
Folger, R., Cropanzano, R., & Goldman, B. (2005). What is the relationship between justice
    and morality. In: J. A. Colquitt & J. Greenberg (Eds), *Handbook of organizational justice*
    (pp. 215–246). Mahwah, NJ: Lawrence Erlbaum Associates.
Folger, R., Rosenfield, D., Grove, J., & Corkran, L. (1979). Effects of "voice" and peer opin-
    ions on responses to inequity. *Journal of Personality and Social Psychology*, *37*, 2253–
    2261.
Gilliland, S. W. (1993). The perceived fairness of selection systems: An organizational justice
    perspective. *Academy of Management Review*, *18*, 694–734.
Goldman, B. (2001). Toward an understanding of employment discrimination-claiming: An
    integration of organizational justice and social information processing theories. *Person-
    nel Psychology*, *54*, 361–386.
Greenberg, J. (1993a). The social side of fairness: Interpersonal and informational classes of
    organizational justice. In: R. Cropanzano (Ed.), *Justice in the workplace: Approaching
    fairness in human resource management* (pp. 79–103). Hillsdale, NJ: Lawrence Erlbaum
    Associates.
Greenberg, J. (1993b). Stealing in the name of justice: Informational and interpersonal mod-
    erators of theft reactions to underpayment inequity. *Organizational Behavior and Human
    Decision Processes*, *54*, 81–103.
Greenberg, J. (2001). Studying organization justice cross-culturally: Fundamental challenges.
    International Journal of Conflict Management, *12*, 365–377.
Hall, J. A., & Rosenthal, R. (1991). Testing for moderator variables in meta-analysis: Issues and
    methods. *Communication Monographs*, *59*, 437–448.

Hofmann, D. A., & Gavin, M. B. (1998). Centering decisions in hierarchical linear models: Implications for research in organizations. *Journal of Management, 24,* 623–641.

Hofmann, D. A., & Jones, L. M. (2004). Some foundational and guiding questions for multi-level construct validation. In: F. J. Dansereau & F. Yammarino (Eds), *Research in multi-level issues: Multi-level isssues in organizational behavior and processes* (Vol. 3, pp. 305–316). Oxford, UK: Elsevier Science.

Hofmann, D. A., & Stetzer, A. (1996). A cross-level investigation of factors influencing unsafe behaviors and accidents. *Personnel Psychology, 49,* 307–339.

Hulin, C. L., Fitzgerald, L. F., & Drasgow, F. (1996). Organizational influences on sexual harassment. In: M. S. Stockdale (Ed.), *Sexual harassment in the workplace* (pp. 127–150). Thousand Oaks, CA: Sage.

Huseman, R. C., Hatfield, J. D., & Miles, E. W. (1987). A new perspective on equity theory: The equity sensitivity construct. *Academy of Management Review, 12,* 222–234.

James, K. (1993). The social context of organizational justice: Cultural, intergroup, and structural effects on justice behaviors and perceptions. In: R. Cropanzano (Ed.), *Justice in the workplace: Approaching fairness in human resource management* (pp. 21–50). Hillsdale, NJ: Lawrence Erlbaum Associates.

James, K., & Cropanzano, R. (1994). Dispositional group loyalty and individual action for the benefit of an ingroup: Experimental and correlational evidence. *Organizational Behavior and Human Decision Processes, 60,* 179–205.

James, L. A., & James, L. R. (1989). Integrating work perceptions: Explorations into the measurement of meaning. *Journal of Applied Psychology, 74,* 739–751.

James, L. A., & McIntyre, M. D. (1996). Perceptions of organizational climate. In: K. Murphy (Ed.), *Individual differences and behavior in organizations* (pp. 416–450). San Francisco, CA: Jossey-Bass.

James, L. R., Demaree, R. G., & Wolf, G. (1984). Estimating within-group interrater reliability with and without response bias. *Journal of Applied Psychology, 69,* 85–98.

James, L. R., & Jones, A. P. (1974). Organizational climate: A review of theory and research. *Psychological Bulletin, 81,* 1096–1112.

James, L. R., & Sells, S. B. (1981). Psychological climate: Theoretical perspectives and empirical research. In: D. Magnusson (Ed.), *Toward a psychology of situations: An interactional perspective* (pp. 275–295). Hillsdale, NJ: Lawrence Erlbaum Associates.

Jones, A. P., & James, L. R. (1979). Psychological climate: Dimensions and relationships of individual and aggregated work environment perceptions. *Organizational Behavior and Human Performance, 23,* 201–250.

Katz, D., & Kahn, R. L. (1978). *The social psychology of organizations.* New York: Wiley.

Kauffman, S. A. (1993). *The origins of order: Self-organization and selection in evolution.* New York: Oxford University Press.

Kidwell, R. E., & Bennett, N. (1993). Employee propensity to withhold effort: A conceptual model to intersect three avenues of research. *Academy of Management Review, 18,* 429–456.

Klein, K. J., Bliese, P. D., Kozlowski, S. W. J., Dansereau, F., Gavin, M. B., Griffin, M. A., & Yammarino, F. J. (2000). Multi-level analytical techniques: Commonalities, differences, and continuing questions. In: K. J. Klein & S. W. J. Kozlowski (Eds), *Multi-level theory, research, and methods in organizations: Foundations, extensions, and new directions* (pp. 512–553). San Francisco, CA: Jossey-Bass.

Konovsky, M. (2000). Understanding procedural justice and its impact on business organizations. *Journal of Management, 26,* 489–511.

DEBORAH E. RUPP ET AL.

Konovsky, M. A., & Brockner, J. (1993). Managing victim and survivor layoff reactions: A procedural justice perspective. In: R. Cropanzano (Ed.), *Justice in the workplace: Approaching fairness in human resource management* (pp. 133–153). Hillsdale, NJ: Lawrence Erlbaum Associates.

Kopelman, R. E., Brief, A. P., & Guzzo, R. A. (1990). The role of climate and culture in productivity. In: B. Schneider (Ed.), *Organizational climate and culture* (pp. 282–318). San Francisco, CA: Jossey-Bass.

Korsgaard, M. A., & Roberson, L. (1995). Procedural justice in performance evaluation: The role of instrumental and non-instrumental voice in performance appraisal discussions. *Journal of Management, 21,* 657–669.

Kozlowski, S. W. J., & Bell, B. S. (2003). Work groups and teams in organizations. In: W. C. Borman & D. R. Ilgen (Eds), *Handbook of psychology: Industrial and organizational psychology* (pp. 333–375). New York: John Wiley.

Kozlowski, S. W. J., & Doherty, M. L. (1989). Integration of climate and leadership: Examination of a neglected issue. *Journal of Applied Psychology, 74,* 546–553.

Kozlowski, S. W. J., & Hults, B. M. (1987). An exploration of climates for technical updating and performance. *Personnel Psychology, 40,* 539–563.

Kozlowski, S. W. J., & Klein, K. J. (2000). A multi-level approach to theory and research in organizations: Contextual, temporal, and emergent processes. In: K. J. Klein & S. W. J. Kozlowski (Eds), *Multi-level theory, research, and methods in organizations: Foundations, extensions, and new directions* (pp. 3–90). San Francisco, CA: Jossey-Bass.

Lam, S. S. K., Schaubroeck, J., & Aryee, S. (2002). Relationship between organizational justice and employee work outcomes: A cross-national study. *Journal of Organizational Behavior, 23,* 1–18.

Leung, K. (2005). How generalizable are justice effects across cultures? In: J. A. Colquitt & J. Greenberg (Eds), *Handbook of organizational justice* (pp. 555–588). London: Lawrence Erlbaum Associates.

Leventhal, G. S. (1976). The distribution of rewards and resources in groups and organizations. In: L. L. Berkowitz & E. Walster (Eds), *Advances in experimental social psychology* (Vol. 9, pp. 91–131). New York: Academic Press.

Leventhal, G. S. (1980). What should be done with equity theory? In: K. J. Gergen, M. S. Greenberg & R. H. Willis (Eds), *Social exchange: Advances in theory and research* (pp. 27–55). New York: Plenum.

Li, A. (2004). Are reactions to justice cross-culturally invariant? A meta-analytic review. Paper presented at the 19th annual meeting of the society for industrial and organizational psychology, Chicago, IL.

Liao, H., & Rupp, D. E. (2005). The impact of justice climate and justice orientation on work outcomes: A cross-level multifoci framework. *Journal of Applied Psychology, 90,* 242–256.

Liao, H., Rupp, D. E., Ko, J., Nam, K., & Bashshur, M. (2005). How they are treated matters too, sometimes: Self-focused justice perceptions and individual differences as moderators of other-focused justice effects. Paper presented at the 20th annual meeting of the society of industrial organizational psychology, Los Angeles, CA.

Lindell, M. K., & Brandt, C. J. (2000). Climate quality and consensus as mediators of the relationship between organizational antecedents and outcomes. *Journal of Applied Psychology, 85,* 331–348.

Louis, M. R., Posner, B. Z., & Powell, G. N. (1983). The availability and helpfulness of socialization practices. *Personnel Psychology, 36,* 857–866.

Malatesta, R. M., & Byrne, Z. S. (1997). The impact of formal and interactional procedures on organizational outcomes. Paper presented at the 12th annual meeting of the society for industrial and organizational psychology, St. Louis, MO.

Masterson, S. S., Lewis, K., Goldman, B. M., & Taylor, M. S. (2000). Integrating justice and social exchange: The differing effects of fair procedures and treatment on work relationships. *Academy of Management Journal, 43*, 738–748.

Miller, C. E., Jackson, P., Mueller, J., & Schersching, C. (1987). Some social psychological effects of group decision rules. *Journal of Personality and Social Psychology, 52*, 325–332.

Mossholder, K. W., Bennett, N., & Martin, C. L. (1998). A multi-level analysis of procedural justice context. *Journal of Organizational Behavior, 19*, 131–141.

Naumann, S. E., & Bennett, N. (2000). A case for procedural justice climate: Development and test of a multi-level model. *Academy of Management, 43*, 881–889.

Naylor, J. C., Pritchard, R. D., & Ilgen, D. (1980). *A theory of behavior in organizations.* New York: Academic Press.

Ng, Z. W., Rupp, D. E., & Drasgow, F. (2005). Justice climate as a moderator of the conscientiousness–contextual performance relationship. Paper presented at the 20th annual meeting of the society for industrial and organizational psychology, Los Angeles, CA.

Ostroff, C. (1993). The effects of climate and personal influences on individual behavior and attitudes in organizations. *Organizational Behavior and Human Decision Processes, 56*, 56–90.

Ostroff, C., Kinicki, A. J., & Tamkins, M. M. (2003). Organizational culture and climate. In: W. C. Borman & D. R. Ilgen (Eds), *Handbook of psychology: Industrial and organizational psychology* (Vol. 12, pp. 565–593). New York: John Wiley.

Ostroff, C., & Kozlowski, S. W. (1992). Organizational socialization as a learning process: The role of information acquisition. *Personnel Psychology, 45*, 849–874.

Parker, C. P., Baltes, B. B., Young, S. A., Huff, J. W., Altman, R. A., Lacost, H. A., & Roberts, J. E. (2003). Relationships between psychological climate perceptions and work outcomes: A meta-analytic review. *Journal of Organizational Behavior, 24*, 389–416.

Payne, R. L., & Pugh, D. S. (1976). Organizational structure and climate. In: M. D. Dunnette (Ed.), *Handbook of industrial and organizational psychology* (pp. 1125–1173). Chicago, IL: Rand McNally.

Pillai, R., Williams, E. S., & Tan, J. J. (2001). Are the scales tipped in favor of procedural or distributive justice? An investigation of the US, India, Germany, and Hong Kong (China). *International Journal of Conflict Management, 12*, 312–332.

Rupp, D. E. (2003). Testing the moral violations component of fairness theory: The moderating role of value preferences. Paper presented at the 18th annual meeting of the society for industrial and organizational psychology, Orlando, FL.

Rupp, D. E., Bashshur, M., Smith, R. S., Mattern, K., Spencer, S., & Holub, A. S. (2004). Person and situational antecedents to social exchange-based justice effects: A consideration of multiple perpetrators. Paper presented at the 19th annual meeting of the society for industrial and organizational psychology, Chicago, IL.

Rupp, D. E., Byrne, Z. S., & Wadlington, P. (2003). Justice orientation and its measurement: Extending the deontological model. Paper presented at the 18th annual meeting of the society for industrial and organizational psychology, Orlando, FL.

Rupp, D. E., & Cropanzano, R. (2002). Multifoci justice and social exchange relationships. *Organizational Behavior and Human Decision Processes, 89*, 925–946.

Rupp, D. E., & Spencer, S. (in press). When customers lash out: The effects of customer interactional injustice on emotional labor and the mediating role of discrete emotions. *Journal of Applied Psychology.*

Salancik, G. J., & Pfeffer, J. (1978). A social information processing approach to job attitudes and task design. *Administrative Science Quarterly, 23,* 224–253.

Schminke, M., Ambrose, M. L., & Cropanzano, R. (2000). The effect of organizational structure on perceptions of procedural fairness. *Journal of Applied Psychology, 85,* 294–304.

Schminke, M., Cropanzano, R., & Rupp, D. E. (2002). Organization structure and fairness perceptions: The moderating effects of organizational level. *Organizational Behavior and Human Decision Processes, 89,* 881–905.

Schmitt, M. (1996). Individual differences in sensitivity to befallen injustice (SBI). *Personality and Individual Differences, 21,* 3–20.

Schmitt, M., & Dörfel, M. (1999). Procedural injustice at work, justice sensitivity, job satisfaction and psychosomatic well-being. *European Journal of Social Psychology, 29,* 443–453.

Schneider, B. (1975). Organizational climates: An essay. *Personnel Psychology, 40,* 437–454.

Schneider, B. (1987). The people make the place. *Personnel Psychology, 40,* 437–453.

Schneider, B. (1990). The climate for service: An application of the climate construct. In: B. Schneider (Ed.), *Organizational climate and culture* (pp. 383–412). San Francisco, CA: Jossey-Bass.

Shapiro, D., & Rosen, B. (1994). An investigation of managerial interventions in employee disputes. *Employee Responsibilities & Rights Journal, 7,* 37–51.

Simons, T., & Roberson, Q. (2003). Why managers should care about fairness: The effects of aggregate justice perceptions on organizational outcomes. *Journal of Applied Psychology, 88,* 432–443.

Skarlicki, D. P., & Latham, G. P. (1996). Increasing citizenship behavior within a labor union: A test of organizational justice theory. *Journal of Applied Psychology, 81,* 161–169.

Steil, J. M. (1983). The response to injustice: Effects of varying levels of social support and position of advantage or disadvantage. *Journal of Experimental Social Psychology, 19,* 239–253.

Thibaut, J., & Walker, L. (1975). *Procedural justice: A psychological analysis.* New York: Erlbaum/Wiley.

Thibaut, J., & Walker, L. (1978). A theory of procedure. *California Law Review, 66,* 541–566.

Trice, H. M., & Beyer, J. M. (1993). *The cultures of work organizations.* Upper Saddle River, NJ: Prentice-Hall.

Tyler, T. R., & Lind, E. A. (1992). A relational model of authority in groups. In: M. P. Zanna (Ed.), *Advances in experimental social psychology* (Vol. 25, pp. 115–191). San Diego, CA: Academic Press.

Viswesvaran, C., & Ones, D. S. (2002). Examining the construct of organizational justice: A meta-analytic evaluation of relations with work attitudes and behaviors. *Journal of Business Ethics, 38,* 193–203.

EXAMINING JUSTICE CLIMATE: ISSUES OF FIT, SIMPLICITY, AND CONTENT

Maureen L. Ambrose and Marshall Schminke

ABSTRACT

The chapter by Rupp, Bashur, and Liao (in this volume) is rich with ideas for the study of a justice climate. This comment on their chapter focuses on three areas that flow from their presentation: issues in modeling climate strength, complexity and simplicity in conceptualizing a justice climate, and an alternative conceptualization of a justice climate. Specifically, it describes how polynomial regression and response surface methodology may assist researchers in examining climate fit. The comment also describes the benefits of a simplified view of a justice climate – one focusing on the overall justice climate. Finally, it develops a framework for examining a climate for justice – a climate that promotes fair behavior in organizations.

INTRODUCTION

The chapter by Rupp, Bashur, and Liao (this volume) is rich with ideas for the study of a justice climate. This comment on their chapter focuses on

Multi-Level Issues in Organizations and Time
Research in Multi-Level Issues, Volume 6, 397–413
Copyright © 2007 by Elsevier Ltd.
All rights of reproduction in any form reserved
ISSN: 1475-9144/doi:10.1016/S1475-9144(07)06018-3

three areas that flow from their presentation: issues in modeling climate strength, complexity and simplicity in conceptualizing a justice climate, and an alternative conceptualization of a justice climate. We hope that our commentary adds to Rupp et al.'s discussion of justice climate and similarly stimulates future research.

MODELING CLIMATE STRENGTH

One of the areas receiving the most interest in current climate research is that of climate strength. As Rupp, Bashur, and Liao note, most research on climate strength focuses on the agreement among organizational members about climate level – that is, the mean rating of individual perceptions of the climate. Even within this area, additional research would be useful. For example, whereas researchers have examined correlates of climate strength (e.g., group cohesiveness), little research considers the process by which climate strength develops. We commend Rupp et al. for tackling the emergence of justice climate, and suggest that a model of how climate strength develops would also benefit the field.

Rupp et al. extend our understanding of climate strength in another way. One of the most interesting ideas offered in the chapter involves considering alternative perspectives on the meaning of climate strength. Following Ostroff, Kinicki, and Tamkins (2003), the authors identify three distinct aspects of climate strength: the traditional agreement-based strength (whether group members agree on perceptions of the climate), plus two alternatives – system-based strength (whether a climate is pervasive throughout an organization) and alignment-based strength (whether a fit exists between organizational climate and organizational practices). They further extend the concept of alignment-based strength to include questions of alignment between different sources of climate, such as alignment between the justice climate emanating from supervisors and that emanating from the organization.

This adaptation of alignment-based climate strength suggests an intriguing set of possibilities for crafting theoretical models involving climate in general and justice climate in particular. That is, they trigger interest in questions common to other areas of organizational "fit" research (e.g., person–organization fit), such as the relative effects of fit (and misfit) on various outcomes. In considering these questions, we must also consider the methodological issues involved in exploring questions of fit.

Traditionally, questions of fit have been addressed empirically by calculating "difference scores," which reflect the numerical gap between, say, individual- and department-level evaluations of some construct of interest, such as values (e.g., Meglino, Ravlin, & Adkins, 1996). However, numerous potential problems with difference scores have been identified (see Edwards, 1994, 2001, or Edwards & Parry, 1993 for a more complete discussion). Among the most critical of these problems for the current application is that difference scores impose artificial – and oftentimes unrealistic – constraints on the relationships between the constructs of interest.

One of these constraints requires that researchers treat all forms of fit or alignment as being equal. For example, consider the case of group-level justice climate perceptions. Suppose, as Rupp and colleagues suggest, we assess both supervisor procedural justice (SPJ) climate and organizational procedural justice (OPJ) climate on a 7-point Likert-type scale. Utilizing a difference scores perspective, if both SPJ climate and OPJ climate receive ratings of "1," the result would be defined as being in alignment. Of course, the same would be true if both received ratings of "4" or "7." That is, perfect alignment would exist in each of these cases. We believe that alignment resulting from joint evaluations of "1" should not necessarily exert similar influences on outcomes as joint evaluations of "7." Rather, we suggest that the question of how alignment at low, moderate, or high levels of justice climate might result in different outcomes represents an important problem – both theoretically and empirically – for researchers to explore.

Similarly, traditional difference scores methodologies require researchers to live with the assumption that all forms of misfits are equal. For example, misfit resulting from higher levels of SPJ climate than OPJ climate is treated the same as misfit resulting from higher levels of OPJ climate than SPJ climate. Again, not only are such assumptions unrealistic, but they also rob researchers of the opportunity to craft theoretical rationales for *why* different forms of misfit might exert very different influences on individual and organizational outcomes.

Fortunately, alternative methodologies exist that allow researchers to theorize about the effects of different types of alignment and misalignment on outcomes. One such approach relies on polynomial regression and response surface methodology.

Polynomial regression analysis develops a quadratic regression model in which the two variables involved in the alignment question are independent variables (X and Y) and some outcome variable (Z) is the dependent variable. The result is the following full polynomial equation:

$$Z = b_0 + b_1 X + b_2 Y + b_3 X^2 + b_4 XY + b_5 Y^2 + e$$

As an example, let us assume that X represents an individual justice perception, Y represents a supervisory justice perception, and Z represents organizational citizenship behavior (OCB). Our general belief might be that alignment between individual and supervisory justice perceptions would lead to enhanced OCBs, whereas misalignment would result in decreased OCBs. However, this methodology allows a researcher to theorize at a finer-grained level about the relationship between the two justice perceptions and OCBs. For example, we might predict that all forms of alignment will not be equal: Alignment at relatively low levels of justice would not be likely to result in enhanced OCBs, whereas alignment at higher levels of justice would. Furthermore, we might predict that all forms of misalignment will not be the same. For example, misalignment resulting from higher supervisory justice perceptions might be expected to exert a more detrimental influence on OCBs than misalignment resulting from higher individual justice perceptions (or vice versa).

The unique feature of the polynomial equation given earlier is that, rather than resulting in a 2D representation of the relationships between the three variables, it generates a 3D surface reflecting that set of relationships. Although these surfaces might seem somewhat confusing at first glance, more careful consideration allows one to draw strong inferences from them in relatively straightforward ways.

Consider the situation depicted in Fig. 1, Panel 1. The figure contains three axes, labeled X, Y, and Z. Let us assume that the X-axis represents the value of employee justice perceptions and the Y-axis represents the value of supervisory justice perceptions. These two axes constitute the X, Y plane, or the "floor," of our 3D figure. OCBs are indicated on the vertical (Z) axis extending upward from the floor. The resulting surface "floats" above the floor and illustrates the level of OCBs expected to result from any particular combination of employee (X) and supervisor (Y) justice perceptions. Its shape indicates which combinations of X and Y result in the highest (and lowest) levels of OCBs.

This surface may be further analyzed via response surface methodology (Edwards, 1994, 2001). For example, questions regarding the effects of justice alignment on OCBs require exploring the shape of the surface along the lines of interest. The line along which employee and supervisory perceptions are equal and, therefore, in perfect alignment is the $X = Y$ line in Fig. 1. It is represented in Panel 1 with the solid arrow, which extends from the nearest corner to the farthest corner of the X, Y plane.

Conversely, for questions regarding the effect of justice misalignment on OCBs explore the shape of the surface along the $X = -Y$ line. Represented

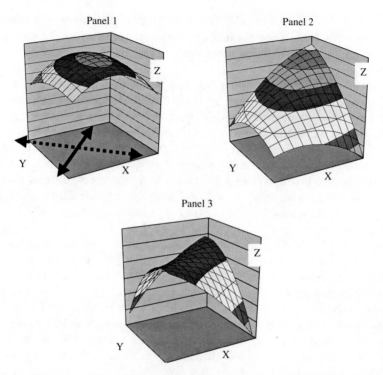

Fig. 1. Samples of Response Surfaces Resulting from Polynomial Regression Analyses.

in Panel 1 by the dashed arrow, this line extends from the left corner to the right corner of the X, Y plane. Along this line, employee and supervisory justice perceptions are unequal and, therefore, misaligned. More specifically, points on the left side of the X, Y plane (to the left of the solid arrow) reflect X, Y combinations in which supervisory perceptions exceed employee perceptions. Points on the right side of the plane (to the right of the solid arrow) reflect X, Y combinations in which employee perceptions exceed supervisory expectations.

Panels 2 and 3 in Fig. 1 depict two hypothetical sets of relationships that one might predict would exist between employee justice perceptions (X), supervisor justice perceptions (Y) and OCBs (Z). For example, the surface illustrated in Panel 2 would support a hypothesis that suggested that not all types of alignment are the same. Observe that as we move along the line of perfect alignment (the $X = Y$ line, extending from the nearest to the farthest corner, as indicated by the solid arrow in Panel 1), the value of Z (OCBs) increases. This trend suggests that alignment at high levels of justice perceptions exerts a much stronger influence on OCBs than alignment at low levels of justice.

Likewise, the surface illustrated in Panel 3 is consistent with a hypothesis that misalignment would result in lower OCBs. Notice that this surface appears to have "wings." That is, OCBs decline as we move away from the line of perfect alignment (the $X = Y$ line) and toward either the left or right side of the figure. These wings represent the decline in OCBs that results from misalignment. Consider the shape of this surface along the $X = -Y$ line (the dashed arrow in Panel 1). This line represents a series of points, each reflecting a single combination of X and Y values. At the leftmost end of the line, the values of Y greatly exceed the values of X. Here, OCB is low. As we move to the right along the $X = -Y$ line, X and Y become more closely aligned, and OCBs increase. At the point at which we cross the $X = Y$ line, X and Y are perfectly aligned, and OCBs are at their peak. As we continue toward the right end of the $X = -Y$ line (the right corner of Panel 1), the values of X greatly exceed the values of Y. As that gap increases, OCBs again decline. Although it is not obvious in Panel 3, a surface such as this could also reflect a situation in which misfit on one side of the surface more strongly influences OCB decline than misfit on the other side. This scenario would be manifested by a more severely dipped wing on one side of the figure than on the other.

Of course, response surface methodology involves more than just simple visual evaluations of these surfaces. Edwards and his colleagues (Edwards, 1994, 2001; Edwards & Parry, 1993; Edwards & Rothbard, 1999) have identified a series of F-tests that allow researchers to explore the statistical significance of these surface characteristics. The tests compare the explanatory power of the unrestricted polynomial regression equation presented earlier with that of various "restricted" models that capture the constraints involved in hypotheses offered by the researcher (e.g., whether all forms of alignment are hypothesized to exert an equal influence on Z, or whether all forms of misfit – such as higher X or higher Y – are thought to be the same). Edwards (1994, 2001) and Edwards and Parry (1993) offer excellent illustrations of the mechanics of these tests, and Schminke, Ambrose, and Neubaum (2005) provide an additional illustration involving fit between employee and leader ethics.

Polynomial regression and response surface methodologies represent a potentially valuable tool for researchers interested in asking – and answering – questions involving the alignment of different types of justice climate. The examples provided here involved only the alignment between individual and supervisory evaluations of justice. Of course, these methods are not limited to that question alone. With these methodologies, researchers are free to theorize about, hypothesize about, and empirically test for relationships between all types and sources of justice. In doing so, we might be able to shed considerable light on complex questions involving the alignment between, say, climates for procedural and interactional justice, climate perceptions of individuals and coworkers, or climate perceptions of supervisors and the organizations for which they work. Virtually any pairing of justice climate type, source, or level could be explored using these tools.

COMPLEXITY AND SIMPLICITY IN JUSTICE CLIMATE RESEARCH

A dominant theme in the Rupp et al. chapter is the potential value of a multifoci perspective on justice climate. In this conceptualization, climates emerge not only around types of justice (distributive, procedural, interpersonal, and informational), but also around the sources of decisions and behaviors (coworkers, supervisors, organizations, and customers).

As a field of research evolves, that evolution often includes investigation that reveals finer distinctions within the construct. In justice research, this development has been exemplified by the distinction made between distributive justice and procedural justice, followed by the distinction made between procedural justice and interactional justice, and most recently by the distinction within interactional justice made between interpersonal justice and informational justice. The multifoci approach draws similar within-construct distinctions by taking these subdimensions of justice and expanding them across sources. We agree with Rupp et al. that such an approach may prove useful when the questions it uses to address are based on strong theory. However, our enthusiasm for a multifoci approach, and its application to justice climate, is perhaps more tempered. In this section, we describe the basis for our more restrained reaction and delineate a path for justice climate research based on greater simplification, not increased complexity.

Our more tempered enthusiasm for the multifoci approach to climate stems both from our general concern about the benefits of increased complexity in the conceptualization of justice and from specific questions about the robustness of the multifoci model. Two specific issues about the multifoci model concern us: the applicability of justice across all "sources" and the empirical support for the model.

The initial conceptualizations of the multifoci model examined procedural and interactional justice from supervisors and procedural and interactional justice from the organization (Malatesta & Byrne, 1997; Rupp & Cropanzano, 2002). An extensive review of the literature that led to these examinations is beyond the scope of this commentary, but suffice it to say that this perspective was part of a stream of research examining the differential effects of procedural and interactional justice. Specifically, the initial work attempted to clarify whether research demonstrating a stronger relationship between procedural justice/organizational outcomes and interactional justice/supervisory outcomes was a function of the focus of the justice questions (procedural justice typically identified the organization as the source, whereas interactional justice items typically identified the supervisor as the source), and if both types of justice could occur at both the levels.

Conceptually, this extension is appealing. Both organizations and supervisors make allocation decisions (distributive justice), enact procedures (procedural justice), and engage in behavior during the enactment of those procedures (interactional justice). However, as the sources of justice expand to include coworkers and customers, the fit of justice constructs to the source becomes a bit more strained. Certainly, in some circumstances (e.g., self-managing work teams) coworkers make allocation decisions, enact procedures, and engage in behavior during the enactment of those procedures. In most work settings, however, allocation decisions and the procedures used to make those decisions are not the role of coworkers. Thus, the quality of interpersonal treatment is the primary type of "justice" that is relevant in this case. The same is true to an even greater extent for customers: Justice perceptions for customers must be based nearly exclusively on the quality of interpersonal treatment. In the main, employees do not have a foundation for developing perceptions about the distributive fairness and procedural fairness of customers. By extension, conceptualizing a justice climate for these individual-level constructs is problematic. This difficulty may leave researchers questioning the prudence of pursuing these concepts.

A multifoci model that does not fully cross the source of justice and the type of justice is also problematic. First, such a model seems to be constructed on an ad hoc basis, as researchers must intuitively determine the relevant types of justice for each source of interest. Second, and more importantly, if the only relevant construct for a source is interpersonal treatment, it seems more appropriate to label it as "quality of interpersonal treatment" rather than "justice."

Our second concern with a multifoci approach to climate relates to the current empirical support for the approach. As Rupp et al. note, only limited empirical research on the multifoci model has been conducted to date. Whereas this research has provided support for the approach, the results are both mixed and complicated. For example, in one of the few published articles on this topic, Rupp and Cropanzano (2002) not only found some support for the model, but also noted high correlations between constructs. Specifically, the correlation for supervisor procedural justice and supervisor interactional justice was found to be 0.91. The correlation for organizational procedural justice and organizational interactional justice was 0.88. Rupp and Cropanzano note that this result calls into question the independence of procedural and interactional justice within a source.

Liao and Rupp's (2005) work at the climate level has similarly yielded mixed findings. Liao and Rupp hypothesized that an organization-focused procedural justice (OPJ) climate, interpersonal justice (OIPJ) climate, and informational justice (OIFJ) climate would predict organization-directed commitment, satisfaction, and citizenship behavior. Similarly, they predicted that a supervisor-focused procedural justice (SPJ) climate, inter-personal justice (SIPJ) climate, and informational justice (SIFJ) climate would predict supervisor-directed commitment, satisfaction, and citizenship behavior. Although Liao and Rupp found some support for their predictions, the results were complicated. Of the nine possible significant effects for organization-focused climates, only three were significant (OPJ predicted commitment and citizenship, and OIFJ predicted satisfaction). Of the nine possible effects for supervisor-focused climates, only three were significant (SPJ predicted commitment and satisfaction, and SPIJ predicted commitment). Indeed, fewer than half of the hypothesized relationships were as predicted. Before extending this work further at the climate level by considering a greater number of sources, it seems useful to clarify the relationships at the individual level and to demonstrate clearer support for supervisor and organization foci at the climate level.

Our tempered enthusiasm for the multifoci approach to climate is also a function of our belief that the interest in justice research of making increasingly finer-grained, within-construct distinctions should be balanced by an interest in pursuing a more global approach to justice. Specifically, we suggest the field may benefit from a focus on overall justice judgments. We have described this approach in detail elsewhere (Ambrose & Arnaud, 2005; Ambrose & Schminke, 2005). We briefly summarize our thoughts here and discuss them in relation to justice climate.

In the recent organizational justice literature, a number of researchers have suggested a shift in focus from different types of justice (distributive, procedural, and interactional) toward more global justice judgments

(Hauenstein, McGonigle, & Flinder, 2001; Lind, 2001; Tornblom & Vermunt, 1999). (See Ambrose & Schminke, 2005, for a detailed discussion.) Such an approach offers several benefits. First, the inclusion of overall justice judgments in justice models appears to provide a more accurate description of individuals' justice experiences (Ambrose & Schminke, 2005). Second, a focus on overall justice allows us to compare the relative effects of the total justice experience (i.e., overall justice judgments) to the effects of other variables. A focus on specific types of justice "misses" the total effect by examining the *unique* variance accounted for, rather than the total variance. A concern for justice is only one of many motivational forces that influence individuals at work (Greenberg, 2001; Leventhal, 1980; Lind, 2001). Focusing on the total effect of justice allows researchers to compare more easily the effects of justice to the effects of other variables. Finally, use of an overall justice construct provides a more parsimonious approach to examining justice. Justice researchers often make identical predictions about the effect of some moderating or mediating variable on all three subtypes of justice. In these cases, the underlying construct appears to be "justice" rather than the specific justice subtype. An overall justice judgment provides a better indicator of that underlying construct and, therefore, represents a more parsimonious approach to justice judgments.

We believe each of these benefits applies to justice climate research as well. For example, although individuals may be able to distinguish between types of justice and sources of justice, and respond to each, research on overall justice suggests that individuals use these experiences to form an overall justice judgment (Ambrose & Schminke, 2005; Lind, 2001). Similarly, although individuals may be able to recognize a supervisory procedural justice climate and an organizational interactional justice climate, they are likely to respond to an overarching justice climate. If the relationships found at the individual level hold true at the climate level, this overall justice climate would mediate the relationship between the specific types of climate suggested by Rupp et al. and the outcomes thereof. Of course, this recognition raises two issues: how the different subclimates might combine to affect the overall justice climate and how contextual variables might affect the relative influence of the subclimates on overall justice climate. The strong theory-driven research suggested by Rupp et al., about the types of subclimates and their relationship to organizational characteristics (e.g., task interdependence, customer contact, centralization) would be useful in this area.

As Rupp and colleagues note, climate researchers recognize a wide range of climate types. Rupp et al. provide a conceptual framework for categorizing the various climate types and place justice climates within this framework. However, the existence of a range of climate types raises its own set of issues. For example, climate research rarely considers the interactions between different climates or the relative effect of one climate type versus another on individual, group, and organizational outcomes. A focus on overall justice climate provides a foundation for these types of comparisons by allowing a straightforward examination of the influence of the total effect of justice climate on (or relative to) other organization climates.

We support Rupp et al.'s call for theory-driven research examining the effects of different types of justice climate on different outcomes. At the same time, we recognize that researchers often expect the same types of effects for different justice climates on outcomes. In such cases, a more parsimonious approach that examines overall justice climate is appropriate. Indeed, without strong theory to guide differential predictions, one wonders about the benefit of a fine-grained analysis of justice climate versus a global justice climate measure. Consider the simplest multifoci model of justice climate, which would cross supervisor and organization with distributive justice climate, procedural justice climate, interpersonal justice climate, and informational justice climate. This approach results in eight types of justice climates. Add coworkers and customers to the mix, and the number of climate types doubles. Could employees really identify and respond to so many different justice climates? Moreover, could any researcher hope to adequately conceptualize the relationship between 16 types of justice climates and outcomes? Interpreting empirical results would be similarly daunting. Overall justice climate may prove equally – or more – able to explain employees' experiences.

As at the individual level, we do not suggest that all work on specific types of justice climates and their effects on outcomes should cease. Rather, we suggest that organizational justice climate research could benefit from a contemporaneous line of research that focuses on overall justice climate. As research on organizational justice climate continues, a balance between focusing on finer distinctions within the justice climate construct and seeking a more holistic justice climate construct might prove productive as well.

A CLIMATE FOR JUSTICE

This final section considers an anomaly between the conceptualization of justice climate and other types of climate. This anomaly lies with the content of the climate construct and its relationship to outcomes. Climate is typically conceptualized as shared perceptions among organizational members about the organizational environment that informs role behavior. Specifically, it is the shared perception of the behaviors that are rewarded, supported, and expected in a particular organizational setting (Reichers & Schneider, 1990).

Most climate research focuses on individuals' perceptions about how things should be done. That is, climate deals with what the appropriate behaviors in the organization are, what is valued, and what is expected. For example, customer service climate is defined as "shared perceptions of the policies, practices and procedures that are rewarded, supported, and expected concerning customer service" (Schneider, Salvaggio, & Subirats, 2002; Schneider, White, & Paul, 1998). Safety climate refers to the degree to which safety is valued in an organization (Zohar, 2000). Learning climate captures the extent to which learning is expected and valued (Cunningham & Iles, 2002). Ethical climate captures shared perceptions of the ethical principles that govern decisions and behavior; it provides organizational members with information about "what they should do" when faced with ethical issues (Schminke et al., 2005; Treviño, Butterfield, & McCabe, 1998). Moreover, the typical outcome variables in studies examining each of these climates are behaviors that are climate relevant (e.g., customer service behavior, safety behavior, learning behavior, ethical behavior). Not surprisingly, research demonstrates that these climates are good predictors of the climate-relevant behavior (Schneider et al., 1998, 2002; Treviño et al., 1998; Wimbush, Shepard, & Markham, 1997; Zohar, 2000).

Justice climate is conceptualized as the shared perception of how fairly *treated* individuals feel. It is the shared perception of the actions of others. Rather than predicting whether individuals will engage in more fair behaviors, it predicts individuals' attitudes and performance. Missing from justice climate research are studies that examine a climate *for* fairness – that is, the climate that guides fair behavior in organizations. Of course, this omission is understandable given that organizational justice research at the individual level does not generally examine why individuals choose to behave fairly or unfairly. Instead, it focuses on individuals' reactions to the actions of others.

Next, we consider the elements that contribute to a climate for justice. Specifically, drawing on the literature in ethical decision making (Rest, 1986), we suggest that four distinct factors will influence a climate for justice. We begin by reviewing the process at the individual level and then move on to discuss the climate level.

Rest (1986) examined the process by which ethical decision making results in ethical action. He suggests four psychological processes that must exist for ethical behavior to occur: moral sensitivity, moral judgment, moral motivation, and moral character.

Moral sensitivity involves an individual's assessment and interpretation of a situation that involves moral content. It includes both awareness that a moral issue exists and a capacity for putting oneself in the place of the individuals involved in the resolution of the situation. Moral sensitivity includes the ability to imagine which alternative actions are possible in the setting and to evaluate the consequences of those actions in terms of how they would affect others and who would be affected by those actions.

Moral judgment refers to the process by which a person determines the correct moral course of action in a situation. It involves making a judgment about what is morally right and utilizing some sort of individual ethical decision-making framework (e.g., deontological, teleological) to arrive at the moral decision believed to be correct.

Moral motivation involves values. In particular, it recognizes that ethical values are merely one set of personal values that help guide individual behavior. Competing values, such as power or achievement, may sometimes take precedence over an individual's ethical values. Moral motivation refers to the extent to which ethical values dominate other values in an individual's decision-making process.

Moral character refers to whether – even if the other components of ethical action are in place (an individual recognizes that a moral dilemma exists, has made a judgment about the correct course of action, and has ethical values as a priority) – an individual possesses the moral courage to carry through on those factors and execute the ethical action. That is, the person must have sufficient individual fortitude (e.g., perseverance, ego strength, will) and implementation skills so as to overcome obstacles to following through on ethical intent.

We suggest that these four components might also apply to individuals' decisions to behave fairly. Specifically, we believe that justice sensitivity, justice judgment, justice motivation, and justice character, all play a role in determining individuals' fair behavior. Furthermore, we argue not only that these four components of justice occur at the individual level, but also that climates for each exist at the social system level, reflecting shared perceptions that could involve teams, departments, or entire organizations (Payne, 1990). The result would be distinct climates for justice sensitivity, justice judgment, justice motivation, and justice character.

Justice sensitivity climate reflects a shared awareness that fairness represents an important component of organizational life. It involves shared perceptions that organizational events regularly involve issues of fairness, and that members of the organization do (and should) regularly encounter issues of distributive, procedural, and interactional fairness in their working days. Rupp et al. describe several individual-level constructs related to justice sensitivity that have appeared in the literature in the past – for example, equity sensitivity (Huseman, Hatfield, & Miles, 1987), sensitivity to befallen injustice (Schmitt, 1996; Schmitt & Dörfel, 1999), and justice orientation (Liao & Rupp, 2005). Each of these is relevant at the individual level. We argue that similar constructs may exist at the climate level.

Justice judgment climate reflects a shared belief that as issues of fairness appear on the organizational "radar screen" (justice sensitivity), organizational members ought to be thoughtful in their assessments of those issues. It involves a shared sense of strategies for dealing with issues of fairness when they arise and determining what the appropriate outcomes to these issues should look like. That is, justice judgment climate entails a shared understanding of the rules and norms that govern fair behavior (e.g., equity, equality, need, voice, consistency, neutrality, interpersonal sensitivity, justification). We expect climates to vary both in terms of which norm dominates (e.g., equity versus equality, procedural justice versus distributive justice) and how strongly those norms are embraced.

Justice motivation climate involves the degree to which organizational values of justice dominate other values of importance in organizational settings. Issues such as safety, customer service, innovation, ethics, learning, entrepreneurship, and profitability represent important considerations for most organizations. To be sure, climates for many of these issues are known to exist (e.g., Schneider et al., 2002; Tracey, Tannenbaum, & Kavanaugh, 1995; Victor & Cullen, 1988). Therefore, just as individual values for ethicality, achievement, power, and so on compete for an individual's attention, so too do organizational values like these vie for attention.

Finally, justice character climate reflects the shared will to carry through on strategies designed to ensure organizational fairness. Organizational policy makers may understand that fairness issues exist. They may recognize effective strategies for creating and maintaining organizations, departments, and workgroups that are distributively, procedurally, and interactionally fair. The organization may even value fairness at or near the top of the various aspects of organizational life that compete for managerial attention and organizational resources. Beyond these factors, however, managers and employees must exhibit the perseverance and implementation skills needed to carry through on such desires. At the climate level, this ability reflects the shared understanding of the importance of standing up for fairness.

Of course, our commentary here has provided only thumbnail sketches of what our four components of justice climates might look like. Much additional theoretical work is needed to flesh out these constructs more fully and to anticipate the theoretical and empirical challenges that thinking about justice in this way might entail. Nevertheless, these components provide a stepping-off point for additional conversations about a broader view of justice and justice climate – one that considers a climate that guides fair behavior.

SOME FINAL THOUGHTS

Research on justice climate is thriving. This interest reflects the broader understanding of the importance of multi-level issues and research in the organizational sciences. Based on Rupp et al.'s chapter, we have identified several areas we believe provide fertile ground for future research: the development of climate strength, polynomial regression and response surface methodology approaches to climate fit, the examination of overall justice climate, and the investigation of a climate for fairness. We hope our observations complement the ideas presented by Rupp and colleagues and stimulate new and interesting research on justice climate and multi-level issues.

REFERENCES

Ambrose, M. L., & Arnaud, A. (2005). Are procedural justice and distributive justice conceptually distinct? In: J. Greenberg & J. Colquitt (Eds), *The handbook of organizational justice: Fundamental questions about fairness in the workplace* (pp. 59–84). Hillsdale, NJ: Erlbaum.

Ambrose, M. L., & Schminke, M. (2005). Overall justice: Some empirical observations. Paper presented at the society for organizational behavior meeting, Minneapolis, MN.

Cunningham, P., & Iles, P. (2002). Managing learning climates in a financial services organization. *Journal of Management Development, 21*, 477–492.

Edwards, J. R. (1994). The study of congruence in organizational behavior research: Critique and a proposed alternative. *Organizational Behavior and Human Decision Processes, 58*, 51–100.

Edwards, J. R. (2001). Alternatives to difference scores: Polynomial regression analysis and response surface methodology. In: F. Drasgow & N. W. Schmitt (Eds), *Advances in measurement and data analysis* (pp. 350–400). San Francisco: Jossey-Bass.

Edwards, J. R., & Parry, M. E. (1993). The use of polynomial regression equations as an alternative to difference scores in organizational research. *Academy of Management Journal, 36*, 1577–1613.

Edwards, J. R., & Rothbard, N. P. (1999). Work and family stress and well-being: An examination of person–environment fit in the work and family domains. *Organizational Behavior and Human Decision Processes, 77*, 85–129.

Greenberg, J. (2001). Setting the justice agenda: Seven unanswered questions about "what, why, and how". *Journal of Vocational Behavior, 58*, 210–219.

Hauenstein, N. M. T., McGonigle, T., & Flinder, S. W. (2001). A meta-analysis of the relationship between procedural justice and distributive justice: Implications for justice research. *Employee Responsibilities and Rights Journal, 13*, 39–56.

Huseman, R. C., Hatfield, J. D., & Miles, E. W. (1987). A new perspective on equity theory: The equity sensitivity construct. *Academy of Management Review, 12*, 222–234.

Leventhal, G. S. (1980). What should be done with equity theory? In: K. J. Gergen, M. S. Greenberg & R. H. Willis (Eds), *Social exchange: Advances in theory and research* (pp. 27–55). New York: Plenum.

Liao, H., & Rupp, D. E. (2005). The impact of justice climate and justice orientation on work outcomes: A cross-level multifoci framework. *Journal of Applied Psychology, 90*, 242–256.

Lind, E. A. (2001). Fairness heuristic theory: Justice judgments as pivotal cognitions in organizational relations. In: J. Greenberg & R. Cropanzano (Eds), *Advances in organizational justice* (pp. 56–88). Stanford, CA: Stanford University Press.

Malatesta, R. M., & Byrne, Z. S. (1997). The impact of formal and interactional justice on organizational outcomes. Poster session presented for the 12th annual conference of the society for industrial and organizational psychology, St. Louis, MO.

Meglino, B., Ravlin, E., & Adkins, C. (1996). Value congruence between co-workers and its relationship to work outcomes. *Group and Organization Management, 21*, 439–461.

Ostroff, C., Kinicki, A. J., & Tamkins, M. M. (2003). Organizational culture and climate. In: W. C. Borman & D. R. Ilgen (Eds), *Handbook of psychology: Industrial and organizational psychology* (Vol. 12, pp. 565–593). New York: Wiley.

Payne, R. L. (1990). Method in our madness: A reply to Jackofsky and Slocum. *Journal of Organizational Behavior, 11*, 77–80.

Reichers, A. E., & Schneider, B. (1990). Climate and culture: An evolution of constructs. In: B. Schneider (Ed.), *Organizational climate and culture* (pp. 5–39). San Francisco: Jossey-Bass.

Rest, J. R. (1986). *Moral development: Advances in research and theory.* New York: Praeger.

Rupp, D. E., Bashur, M., & Liao, H. (this volume). Justice climate past, present, and future: Models of structure and emergence. In: F. Dansereau & F. J. Yammarino (Eds), *Research in multi-level issues.* Oxford: Elsevier.

Rupp, D. E., & Cropanzano, R. (2002). Integrating psychological contracts and multifocused organizational justice. *Organizational Behavior and Human Decision Processes, 89*, 925–946.

Schminke, M., Ambrose, M. L., & Neubaum, D. (2005). The effect of leader moral development on ethical climate and employee attitudes. *Organizational Behavior and Human Decision Processes, 97*, 135–151.

Schmitt, M. (1996). Individual differences in sensitivity to befallen injustice (SBI). *Personality and Individual Differences, 21*, 3–20.

Schmitt, M., & Dörfel, M. (1999). Procedural injustice at work, justice sensitivity, job satisfaction and psychosomatic well-being. *European Journal of Social Psychology, 29,* 443–453.

Schneider, B., Salvaggio, A. N., & Subirats, M. (2002). Climate strength: A new direction for climate research. *Journal of Applied Psychology, 87,* 220–229.

Schneider, B., White, S. S., & Paul, M. C. (1998). Linking service climate and customer perceptions of service quality: Test of a causal model. *Journal of Applied Psychology, 83,* 150–163.

Tornblom, K. Y., & Vermunt, R. (1999). An integrative perspective on social justice: Distributive and procedural fairness evaluations of positive and negative outcome allocations. *Social Justice Research, 12,* 39–64.

Tracey, J., Tannenbaum, S., & Kavanaugh, M. (1995). Applying trained skills on the job: The importance of the work environment. *Journal of Applied Psychology, 80,* 239–252.

Treviño, L. K., Butterfield, K. D., & McCabe, D. L. (1998). The ethical context in organizations: Influences on employee attitudes and behavior. *Business Ethics Quarterly, 8,* 447–476.

Victor, B., & Cullen, J. B. (1988). The organizational bases of ethical work climates. *Administrative Science Quarterly, 33,* 101–125.

Wimbush, J. C., Shepard, J. M., & Markham, S. E. (1997). An empirical investigation of the relationship between ethical climate and ethical behavior from multiple levels of analysis. *Journal of Business Ethics, 16,* 1705–1716.

Zohar, D. (2000). A group-level model of safety climate: Testing the effect of group climate on microaccidents in manufacturing jobs. *Journal of Applied Psychology, 85,* 587–596.

INTRAUNIT JUSTICE AND INTERUNIT JUSTICE AND THE PEOPLE WHO EXPERIENCE THEM

Russell Cropanzano, Andrew Li and Keith James

ABSTRACT

In their chapter, Rupp, Bashshur, and Liao (this volume) have made an impressive contribution to the literature on multi-level justice. These authors have provided both a precise conceptual definition of justice climate and a measurement strategy (referent shift) that will greatly smooth the progress of future empirical inquiry. The goal of this commentary is to expand these important ideas by moving in two directions. First, we discuss what it means to be an individual when justice is experienced as a member of a team. Toward this end, we describe research on social identity theory and social categorization theory, emphasizing how these paradigms could further increase our knowledge. Second, we discuss two new manifestations of multi-level justice that have hitherto been neglected: intraunit justice (group perceptions regarding how team members generally treat one another) and interunit justice (perceptions regarding the way one group treats another). All of these multi-level justice concepts are organized into a new taxonomy.

Multi-Level Issues in Organizations and Time
Research in Multi-Level Issues, Volume 6, 415–437
Copyright © 2007 by Elsevier Ltd.

ISSN: 1475-9144/doi:10.1016/S1475-9144(07)06019-5

INTRODUCTION

In recent years, justice researchers have added a new tool to their repertoire of ideas: They have begun to seriously consider unit-level justice perceptions. The mathematics is straightforward enough, but the theoretical question is less tractable. When justice is considered as a group-level phenomenon, what does it mean? One answer is that aggregated fairness ratings are indicative of something called "justice climate." Justice climate has been defined as a "group-level cognition about how a work group as a whole is treated" (Naumann & Bennett, 2000, p. 882). Ehrhart (2004, p. 67) cites this definition favorably, and Roberson and Colquitt (2005, p. 596) seem to concur, although they refer to it as "shared team justice." Although these are important steps, still more interesting work remains to be done.

Building on the important ideas presented by Rupp, Bashshur, and Liao (this volume), we will direct our comments into two directions. First, an emphasis on justice climate has a counterintuitive implication: It compels us to think more seriously about *individual* identities. After taking up the issue of individual identity, our remarks will proceed in the other direction. That is, we will return to the group, suggesting that unit-level justice comes in at least three varieties: Justice climate (shared perceptions of how the group as a whole is treated), intraunit justice (shared perceptions of how group members treat one another), and interunit justice (shared perceptions of how groups treat other groups).

We begin with intraunit justice. We define the concept, distinguish it from justice climate, and review potential measurement strategies. We then organize all three unit-level fairness concepts into a new taxonomy. From this taxonomy we derive and explore interunit justice, reviewing literatures that could benefit by application of this perspective.

JUSTICE CLIMATE AND SOCIAL IDENTITY

Focusing on unit-level analyses should not lead us astray by ignoring the role of individuals within a unit. The relationship between individuals and their group can be viewed as continuously interacting and mutually reinforcing dynamics. On the one hand, individuals' perceptions and behaviors are shaped by the immediate context in which they are embedded. On the other hand, rather than being passively exposed to external influence, individuals actively shape the external environment in the service of their goal. Such dynamics can be explicated in the context of justice climate. Specifically, justice climates may shape an individual's self-concept as well as that person's view on his or her relationships with other members of the same unit. Justice climate may also trigger strategic responses from individuals in their proactive attempts to maintain a positive self-concept. Because justice climate is a relatively new idea in the pantheon of fairness constructs, its influence on individuals has been relatively understudied by justice researchers. Fortunately, there is a long scholarly tradition to help inform our thinking. Research on social identity theory and social categorization theory (cf., Turner & Haslam, 2001) is especially useful in this regard.

Social identity theory (SIT; see Tajfel & Turner, 1979) and social categorization theory (SCT; see Turner, 1985) are two related but somewhat different theoretical conceptions dealing with membership in groups (i.e., intragroup membership) and individuals' self-concepts (Brown, 2000). Social identity theory is the broader approach. Its central idea is that individuals, motivated by the desire to maintain a desirable social identity, engage in intergroup comparison and self-serving bias, manifested as favoring one's in-groups and derogating one's out-groups. In essence, the theory argues that invoked intragroup patterns and individual identity act as mediators of intergroup relations (Hogg & Terry, 2000; Tajfel & Turner, 1979).

Social categorization theory, by contrast, starts with a focus on the cognitive mechanisms and examines their effects on individual identity. A central concept of SCT is the prototype, which represents stereotypic/normative characteristics that define category memberships. These prototypes facilitate social categorization through which individuals within the same category come to resemble one another in terms of their attitudes, feelings, and behaviors, yet remain distinct from those in other social categories, a process that is termed "depersonalization." SCT looks at intragroup and intergroup phenomena as both *outcomes of* cognitive self-categorization and potential contextual *influences on* cognitive self-categorization (Oakes, 1987; Turner, 1985).

Despite these differences, both SIT and SCT have implications for research on justice climate. These theories, along with the research programs they have spawned, point to three distinct sets of issues regarding justice climate. The first set ties into the SIT and SCT principles that identity is always comparative. To the extent that work identities are related to justice climate, it may also be best to understand one's justice climate by comparing it to other climates. The second connection suggests that active identity type may mediate the relationship between justice climate and work-related outcomes. The third set raises an alternative – the possibility that identity could moderate the impact of climate on work-relevant outcomes. We next briefly examine each of these three sets of issues.

How Individuals Come to Understand Their Justice Climate

Let us begin with perhaps the most basic issue – an individual's identity as a member of a work team. One basic insight from SIT and SCT is that what transpires external to a group may influence how an individual views his or her identity with respect to the work team. For example, both theories stress that identity is a comparative process (e.g., Brickson, 2000; Hogg & Terry, 2000). The existence of an in-group to which one belongs makes sense only within the context of one or more out-groups to which one does not belong.

Similarly, justice climate will be most clearly perceived – as well as exert the strongest cognitive, affective, and behavioral effects – only to the extent that a different justice climate exists either in another group or at a different level of the organization. Along the same line of reasoning, and as Rupp and her colleagues discuss, the strength, consistency, and implications of group-level justice climate can best be understood by comparing them to the strength, consistency, and implications of the justice climate in other groups or at other levels of the organization. Stated somewhat differently, whether justice climate is conceived favorable within a focal group depends, to a great extent, on the justice climate in other groups.

Collective Identity as a Mediator of Justice Climate Effects

Both SIT and SCT indicate that personal and group-based identities are two fundamental categories of identity (for detailed discussions of this point, see Brickson, 2000; Hogg & Terry, 2000; Triandis, 1995). In other words, people conceptualize themselves in different ways – either as an individual or as a part of a large collective. Moreover, individuals can be part of several different collectives (a work team or the entire organization). Each of these collectives may, under certain conditions, provide the entity that an individual can be identified with.

Besides being interesting in its own right, these observations regarding individual and group identifications have implications for research on justice climate. As we have already noted, how one's team is treated is likely to influence the extent to which an individual comes to identify with the team. One example, based on SIT/SCT, of why this is true is that justice patterns seem to influence the perceived status of one's in-group (James, in press; Tyler, 1999); this perception may, in turn, determine the extent to which individuals are inclined to either identify with the in-group or try to separate themselves from it (Brown, 2000).

Consider the predicament faced by a worker whose work team is treated relatively poorly (low justice climate), and who can see that other work teams are treated relatively more favorably. In such a situation, the employee will be inclined to vest his or her identity at a different level, unless circumstances block the individual from doing so (Tyler, 1999; see Tajfel & Turner, 1979 and Brown, 2000, for additional discussion of this process and of potential circumstantial influences on it). For example, if a person witnesses other groups being treated better than her own, an employee may emphasize her personal identity as an individual ("I'm not like them!").

Fig. 1 illustrates the implications of this argument. Justice climate affects identity, such that an unfavorable justice climate leads an employee to identify less with his or her group. Conversely, a more favorable climate leads to a stronger collective identification. The strength of collective identification, in turn, has behavioral and attitudinal consequences. For instance, a weaker collective identification is associated with fewer citizenship behaviors to benefit the team, a higher likelihood of turnover from the team, and more derogation of teammates. A stronger collective identification, by contrast, is associated with more citizenship behaviors to benefit the team, reduced turnover, and less derogation of teammates (Clayton & Opotow, 2003).

Fig. 1 raises an interesting possibility. Upper management, by not being supportive of a team, may wreak havoc on justice climate. This turn of events may then cause the team to unravel. This interesting possibility has important implications for both theory and practice. However, a closer look at identity in the context of SIT and SCT suggests another potential outcome.

Moderator Effects of Identity Activation

According to SIT and SCT, one individual can have multiple identities. Not all of these identities can be active at the same time, however. An active identity is one that is cognitively prominent *and* evocative of an emotional attachment to the group. When a group-based identity is active, individuals will be likely to "feel positive about accepting ingroup norms" and "feel concerned about their ... ingroups" (Triandis, 1989, p. 325; see also

Fig. 1. Type of Identity as a Mediator of Justice Climate Effects.

Turner, 1985; Tyler, 1999), including the in-group's norms pertaining to justice (Wenzel, 2000, 2002). However, this speaks only to the group identity. Employees also have personal identities.

When personal identities are salient and important, the opposite may occur. Individuals "feel ambivalent and even bitter about accepting ingroup norms" and "find it completely natural to do their own thing and disregard the needs of community, family, or work group" (Triandis, 1989, p. 325). In addition to ignoring the needs of others, self-focused individuals are apt to neglect the norms and values of their collectives (James, in press; Tyler, 1999). These possibilities are displayed in Fig. 2.

Notice how this analysis differs from our earlier discussion. Previously, we had raised the possibility that a collective identity may be more or less likely to form depending on the justice climate experienced by one's in-group. Now, however, the focus is on a circumstance in which both collective and personal identities exist in tandem, but one is active while the other is not. The active identity, be it personal or collective, should exert a stronger influence on employee reactions than the inert identity does.

Rupp and her colleagues have done an excellent job of demonstrating that how one's team is treated (i.e., justice climate) causes attitudinal and behavioral responses on the part of workers. Although we agree, we further suggest – based on SIT and SCT – that the active identity moderates the relationships. Specifically, when employees think of themselves as members of a collective, then justice climate is anticipated to produce more profound responses. These effects will be attenuated when personal identity is active.

Some Closing Thoughts

All of the preceding points need to be examined further empirically. In addition, space constraints do not allow us to fully delineate the general

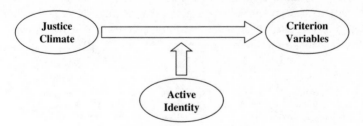

Fig. 2. Active Identity as a Moderator of Justice Climate Effects.

connections between SIT/SCT and justice climate, and they limit us to providing only a few examples of the larger number of specific mechanisms and outcomes implicated by these links. Much additional conceptual/ theoretical work is clearly needed on the topics touched on in this section. We hope these suggestive ideas will point to potential avenues for future research.

Now we will move away from the individual and back to the group. In the next few sections, we turn our attention to other unit-level concepts that could enrich our understanding of organizational justice.

THE PROBLEM OF INTRAUNIT JUSTICE

Two Hypothetical Work Groups

Rupp and her colleagues make an interesting observation with respect to climate: The climate within an organization may not necessarily agree with the climate within a particular work unit (for a related perspective, see Liao & Rupp, 2005). This observation is important, because it creates an interesting opportunity for scholars.

To understand our predicament, consider two hypothetical work groups. Within Group A, everyone treats one another well, but the group as a whole experiences injustice at the hands of upper management. Within Group B, everyone treats one another badly, but upper management is fairly benign. How are we to understand their experiences? If we assess their reactions with the referent shift methodology, we are likely to find that the unit-level justice scores for Group A are lower than those for Group B. However, if we utilize direct consensus, the scores are likely to be similar, because all individuals experience roughly the same level of unit-level injustice, though in the former case unfairness comes from upper management and in the latter case it is from fellow coworkers. Consequently, our conclusions change dramatically based on which measure we employ. Such a situation is awkward, for the matter is more than a lack of precision. Workers in our two hypothetical groups are likely to have very different psychological experiences. In Group B, the collection of individuals can scarcely be called a team (cf., Katzenbach & Smith, 1993) because the unit's climate is utterly dysfunctional. Conversely, members of Group A seem to get along well and may be further united by their common managerial adversary. Hence, members of each group will have a distinct understanding of, and response to, the injustice they have experienced.

This is where Rupp and her colleagues have rescued us. Their approach resolves this paradox in a straightforward way. Because justice climate refers to how one's *group* is treated, then we should rely on the referent shift method to make inferences about justice climate: Group A has a more favorable justice climate than Group B. Consequently, our conclusions are clear, so long as we understand that we are talking about justice climate and that justice climate concerns the treatment received by the work group.

While it is clear Groups A and B differ on justice climate (operationally defined by referent shift), they differ on something else as well: their intraunit climates. Group A is treated worse by upper management than is Group B, but the coworkers in Group A behave more favorably toward one another than do their Group B counterparts. In other words, the key problem is that "justice climate" is only one phenomenon in the domain of unit-level justice. In short, this simple example suggests that we need to consider how coworkers typically relate to one another. We term this parameter *intraunit justice*. Like justice climate, intraunit justice is an aggregate or group-level variable. Unlike justice climate, intraunit justice refers to what goes on *inside* the team, rather than how the team is treated by outsiders.

Evidence for Intraunit Justice

As both justice climate and intraunit justice are new ideas, little research has sought to compare them. Fortunately, an experimental study by Branscombe, Spears, Ellemer, and Doosje (2002) sheds light on this problem. Branscombe and her colleagues used a bogus task to sort research participants into two groups. Every subject was therefore a member of an in-group but also recognized the presence of an out-group. With these divisions having been created, the authors then manipulated two independent variables.

Roughly half of all participants were told that they had the personal respect of their fellow in-group members, while the other half were told that they did not. Notice how this manipulation is similar to what we have been calling intraunit justice, with one exception. Intraunit justice concerns how individuals typically treat one another. In Branscombe et al.'s (2002) study, the authors were concerned with how an individual was treated by a unit.

The other independent variable was group prestige. Some participants were told that their in-group was respected by the out-group; others were told that the out-group did not respect them. Notice how this group prestige manipulation corresponds to justice climate, but only when justice climate concerns one group's mistreatment of another group. This is reasonable, although an unjust climate can also come from mistreatment by an individual (as we shall argue later). While Branscombe and her colleagues' manipulation of group prestige is appropriate for our analysis, other manipulations might also suffice.

Branscombe et al. (2002) found that the two forms of threat – from within the in-group and from the out-group – interacted to predict sundry criterion variables. When compared to their counterparts in other conditions, participants who were respected by their in-group (in our language, high intragroup justice) but disrespected by the out-group (low justice climate) were especially unlikely to allocate rewards to the out-group, but especially likely to expend effort to improve their in-group's image. Conversely, participants who were disrespected by their in-group (low intragroup justice) but respected by the out-group (high justice climate) did not show an in-group bias when dividing benefits. Also, these individuals would expend effort for their in-groups only when it benefited them personally.

We readily concede that Branscombe et al. (2002) have provided only preliminary evidence on this concept. Nevertheless, their study is a creative and important one. It suggests that justice climate and intraunit justice are distinguishable constructs with distinct nomological nets. Given this evidence, we develop these ideas further. We first consider how intraunit justice can be best measured by researchers. We then turn our attention to theoretical matters, exploring the nomological network (cf., Cronbach & Meehl, 1955; Schwab, 1980) for intraunit justice.

MEASURING INTRAUNIT JUSTICE: REFERENT SHIFT AGAIN!

Rupp and her colleagues suggested that, although both the direct consensus approach and the referent shift model can be used to measure unit-level justice, employing the referent shift paradigm may be the preferred choice. These authors cite two essential reasons in support of their argument. First, referent shift provides a less equivocal assessment of the constructs of interest. Second, when respondents rate a single referent for evaluation (in this case, the group as a whole), scales tend to have superior psychometric properties than when the referent is not held constant (Bashshur, Rupp, & Christopher, 2004).

Following Rupp and her colleagues' advice, we consider that the referent shift composition model may ultimately provide a superior strategy for assessing intraunit justice. Of course, the items would need to be worded some differently than they are when the referent shift approach is used to assess justice climate. In using a referent shift approach to assess intraunit justice, the survey items should refer specifically to the general behavior of team members toward one another, rather than to the treatment that the respondent personally receives. For instance, items might contain the following opening stems: "In my work group, people typically ..." or "Among my teammates, people generally ... ." Notice that the items still pertain directly to what goes on within the unit, which is the *sine qua non* of intraunit justice. These items also refer to general behavior among individuals, rather than particular behavior directed toward the research participant.

What to Measure? Part I: Intraunit Justice for Distributions, Procedures, and Interactions

It is important to understand the concept of intraunit justice in the context of various types of justice investigated in previous literature. Traditionally, three types of justice have been examined in the literature: distributive, procedural, and interactional justice (Cropanzano, Rupp, Mohler, & Schminke, 2001). While most of the previous research has primarily focused on justice perceptions about one's supervisors, upper management, or the organization as a whole, these perceptions may also potentially be influenced by one's interaction with coworkers. For example, an employee may have low distributive justice when his or her coworkers take credit for things they do not deserve and reap the subsequent benefits. Similarly, an individual may have low procedural justice when he or she is ostracized from the decision-making process by coworkers. Finally, low interactional justice may result when one is treated rudely by coworkers. Given these considerations, we believe that groups form intraunit justice perceptions for distributive, procedural, and interactional justice.

What to Measure? Part II: The Third Variable Problem and the Need to Assess Both Intraunit Justice and Justice Climate

Rupp and her colleagues reviewed a variety of top-down and bottom-up processes that could influence justice climate. We were struck, however, by the possibility that many of these antecedents could influence intraunit justice as well. For example, social information processing theory (Degoey, 2000; Salancik & Pfeffer, 1978) predicts that individuals in a group will form common perceptions. This could be as true of how they treat one another (intraunit justice) as it is of how they are collectively treated by the organization (justice climate). Likewise, socialization processes may enhance group harmony and promote conflict management skills. This could facilitate both the emergence of intraunit justice within a work unit and a more favorable justice climate.

These effects are interesting in their own right, but they also have a statistical implication. It is likely that justice climate and intraunit justice, though distinct concepts, are moderately correlated. Consequently, if the two are not measured separately, the effects of one might be partially attributable to the other. This dilemma is a variant of the well-known "third-variable" problem. Failure to take account of one construct – either intraunit justice or justice climate – could lead one to overestimate the effect of the other construct. To solve this problem, it would be useful for scholars to include both variables in their research. At the very least, there is a need to examine the effects of intraunit justice beyond the better-established effects of justice climate.

INTRAUNIT JUSTICE, INTERUNIT JUSTICE, AND A NEW TAXONOMY FOR MULTIUNIT JUSTICE EFFECTS

Let us take stock of where we are. A good deal of prior literature has treated justice as an individual-level phenomenon, in which one person is wronged (or righted) by another. Added to this body of evidence, we find the work of Rupp and her colleagues, arguing for the existence of justice climate. A group can be treated (un)fairly, much as can an individual. In this chapter, we have added a third consideration: intraunit justice. *Intraunit* refers to the characteristic way that coworkers interact. It is worthwhile to organize these three classes of justice, as shown in Fig. 3, and establish whether we are missing something.

In Fig. 3, the vertical axis is the one we have so far emphasized. It corresponds to the level of analysis (individuals or unit) applied to the recipient. The victim of an injustice may be either an individual or a group. Justice climate research examines the way that a work unit is treated. As we have already seen from the chapter by Rupp and her colleagues, considerable evidence suggests that a person can distinguish an injustice directed toward him or her from an injustice directed toward a group of which that

Entity 2: Transgressor

	Individual		*Unit*
Individual	**Cell 1** *Typical Justice Study*		**Cell 3** *Intraunit Justice*
Unit	**Cell 2** *Justice Climate*		**Cell 4** *Interunit Justice*

Entity 1: Recipient

Fig. 3. Taxonomy of Justice Studies: Individual and Unit.

person is a member. Indeed, Brickman, Folger, Goode, and Schul (1981) created the term "microjustice" to refer to the former and "macrojustice" to refer to the latter. Later research has supported the distinction between microjustice and macrojustice (James & Cropanzano, 1990; Taylor, Wright, Moghaddam, & LaLonde, 1990), though this work was conducted only at the individual level of analysis.

Rupp and her colleagues have also provided insights regarding the horizontal axis shown in Fig. 3. In their discussion of multifoci justice, these authors remind us that it is important to consider the transgressor, which can also be either a person or a unit. For example, research suggests that employees can distinguish the treatment provided by a supervisor from the treatment provided by the organization as a whole (Cropanzano, Prehar, & Chen, 2002). Moreover, this effect has been exhibited at both the individual (Rupp & Cropanzano, 2002) and group (Liao & Rupp, 2005) levels of analysis.

Building on the ideas presented by Rupp and her colleagues, this evidence suggests that we need to consider multiple levels of analysis for both parties: group versus individual victims, and group versus individual transgressors. Fig. 3 illustrates the results of these musings. Notice, for example, that an individual can victimize an individual (cell 1, as is commonly studied) or an individual can victimize a group (cell 2, much justice climate research could fit here). In the second column we see that a unit-level actor can menace both individuals (cell 3, as in intraunit justice research) and other groups (cell 4).

This analysis presents us with something interesting. The three situations we have discussed so far –individual, justice climate, and intraunit – can easily be organized into a 2×2 matrix, with the organizing continua anchored by individual and group. However, using this taxonomy suggests a fourth expression of workplace fairness: the way that groups treat other groups. We will consider each of these possibilities in more detail, paying special attention to cell 4.

Cell 1: Individual-to-Individual Treatment

Cell 1 encapsulates the most commonly examined situation in justice research: the treatment of one individual by another. This represents the typical justice studies reviewed by scholars (Cohen-Charash & Spector, 2001; Colquitt, Conlon, Wesson, Porter, & Ng, 2001). Speaking only from a methodological (instead of a theoretical or practical) point of view, nothing needs be aggregated and only individual level data are used. We will not belabor ourselves here, as thorough reviews of this point can be found elsewhere (Cropanzano, Byrne, Bobocel, & Rupp, 2001; Cropanzano et al., 2001; Folger & Cropanzano, 1998). However, we should reiterate Rupp and her colleagues' observation that teams research can be conducted at the individual level (e.g., Phillips, Douthitt, & Hyland, 2001).

As an example, consider a field experiment by Korsgaard, Schweiger, and Sapienza (1995). Korsgaard and her colleagues examined 20 intact management teams while they were attending an executive education program. Some team leaders were trained to show considerate interpersonal behavior, whereas others were trained to show less considerate behavior. Team members reported more procedural justice when they were treated considerately than when they were not. These teams also made better decisions.

A similar example of group research with an individual level of analysis is presented in an interesting experiment by De Cremer, van Knippenberg, van Knippenberg, Mullenders, and Stinglhamber (2005, Study 2). Undergraduate subjects reported to a laboratory for a study of "group behavior" (p. 7). Participants worked individually on a creative language task, with the belief that their individual efforts would be combined into a group score. De Cremer and his colleagues found that two sets of leader behavior interacted – procedural justice and rewarding leadership (i.e., acknowledging and appreciating the efforts of workers). When both of these behaviors were high, participants showed relatively high self-esteem. When either or both were low, self-esteem was diminished.

The Korsgaard et al. and De Cremer et al. studies demonstrate that one can study teams without aggregating data into unit-level scores. We now turn our attention to studies with at least one group-level variable.

Cell 2: Individual-to-Group Treatment

General Considerations

In cell 2, we refer to studies investigating the treatment of a group by an individual. The prototypical situation here pertains to studies that have examined manager's behavior and its influence on aggregate justice perceptions. Such studies usually focus on the behavior of a formal manager. For example, several scholars have written about supervisory behavior and justice perceptions among their reports (e.g., Jones & Lindley, 1998; Kirkman, Jones, & Shapiro, 2000; Kirkman, Shapiro, Novelli, & Brett, 1996).

In this cell, we also find some work on justice climate. An excellent example of an individual-to-group study was conducted by Ehrhart (2004). Exploring citizenship behavior among grocery store employees, Ehrhart found that servant–leadership behavior by supervisors engendered a favorable procedural justice climate among employees. A key strength of Ehrhart's study is that justice climate was assessed using the referent shift methodology. Hence, his study examined how workers felt their unit was treated. Consistent with Ehrhart's expectations, procedural justice climate predicted group-level citizenship behavior.

An Important Caveat before Moving On

With respect to justice climate research, it might be worthwhile for future scholars to think about the type of entity that influences the work teams. When that entity is an individual, as in the Ehrhart (2004) study, then justice climate research fits nicely into cell 2. However, when the transgressing party is a group, such as an upper management team or perhaps an organization as a whole, then the study would probably fit better in cell 4.

Cell 3: Group-to-Individual Treatment

General Considerations

When we speak about effects that run from groups to individuals, there are two distinct theoretical positions worth considering. The most obvious pertains to situations in which a large and external body takes an action that harms or benefits an individual. The second, and more subtle position, concerns actions that take place within a work unit. In this situation, coworkers – perhaps united into informal bands – treat one another with more or less justice. This second theoretical approach is where we would locate intraunit justice. We discuss each of these two perspectives in more detail next.

Group as an External Structure

Cell 3 is the home of any phenomenon whereby a group mistreats an individual. Any study that treats a group as a transgressor would seem relevant, so long as one examines the effects that this transgression has on separate persons. Consider, for example, research on justice and downsizing decisions (e.g., Brockner, 1994). The transgressor is a large collective – an organization – that may inflict harm on workers. In this line of inquiry, a group (i.e., a firm) is acting against individuals (i.e., employees). This paradigm is appropriate for cell 3, because the action is taken by the collective, while the resulting harm is experienced (or at least measured) at the individual level. Moreover, this approach has been profitable for our learning. Generally speaking, employees affected by downsizing respond less negatively to workforce reductions when they are informed in advance (Mansour-Cole & Scott, 1998) and the reasons for the layoffs are adequately explained (Brockner, DeWitt, Grover, & Reed, 1990; Brockner, Konovsky, Cooper-Schneider, Folger, Martin, & Bies, 1994; Gopinath & Becker, 2000; Konovsky & Folger, 1991; Mellor, 1992).

Internal Dynamics Within a Work Unit: Intraunit Justice

Cell 3 is also a good location to consider intraunit justice, as this cell refers to how people treat one another within a work unit. That is, intraunit justice describes how each individual believes people are treated by group members in general. Unfortunately, as intraunit justice is a new concept, it is difficult to locate research that precisely fits into this cell.

Nevertheless, some research has examined the way one is treated by coworkers. An example is provided by the development of the Perceptions of Fair Interpersonal Treatment Scale (PFIT; Donovan, Drasgow, & Munson, 1998). The PFIT is concerned with general perceptions of the work environment. It has two dimensions: one pertaining to supervision (perhaps belonging to cell 1 or 2), and the other pertaining to the manner in which coworkers treat one another. Items include "Coworkers help each other," "Coworkers argue with each other," "Coworkers put each other down," and "Coworkers treat each other with respect." The study is consistent with the ideas expressed here, though Donovan et al. did not aggregate them into a unit-level score. Future research should explore this possibility.

A second relevant example was presented by Howes, Cropanzano, Grandey, and Mohler (2000). This study examined 136 workers who were serving on 25 different quality teams. Howes and his collaborators found that individuals could distinguish the support they received from their teammates (intraunit) from the support the organization provided for the team (somewhat similar to justice climate). Unfortunately, this study falls short for our present purposes, as it emphasized support – but not justice – perceptions.

Cell 4: Group-to-Group Treatment

General Considerations

As mentioned at the outset of this section, we term group-to-group inter-actions *interunit justice*, to distinguish it from intraunit justice while emphasizing the complementary nature of the two concepts: *Intraunit* is how group members treat one another; *interunit* is how they treat other groups. (It seems a behavioral science truism that every *intra* implies a complementary *inter*.) The study of interunit justice takes workplace fairness research into the realm of intergroup relations (Marks, DeChurch, Mathieu, Panzer, & Alonso, 2005). Although this topic is important, justice researchers have not considered it in detail.

Our belief is that this approach holds great promise. In fact, justice climate research could fit into the category, depending on which type of entity has inflicted the relevant harm (or provided the relevant benefit). Justice climate, as we have seen, refers to how the group as a unit believes they are being treated. The relevant question for our taxonomy is this: Treated by whom or by what? As we saw from our earlier comments, if the actor is a person, then the justice climate study would be individual-to-group and belongs in cell 2. If the actor is another group, then the study would be group-to-group and fit in cell 4. The justice climate literature lends itself to either possibility, because the identity of the transgressor is not always explicitly given.

While we acknowledge that more work in this area is needed, available research indicates that work teams formulate both individual-to-group and group-to-group perceptions. Liao and Rupp's (2005) findings indicate that justice climate perceptions can result from either the activities of one's supervisor (cell 2 – an individual) or from the organization as a whole (cell 4 – a group). Viewing these findings through the prism of our present tax-onomy suggests that research on justice climate could be further subdivided by considering the source of the treatment as well as the victim.

Regardless, the notion of group-to-group injustice has considerable poten-tial. To illustrate, we will consider three literatures that can enrich our thinking and, we hope, can be enriched by unit-level justice research. The first example concerns dynamics within a single workgroup. The next two examples treat the unit more broadly and are pertinent to organizations as a whole.

Climate for Prejudice

One obvious example of group-to-group injustice can be found in research on racial discrimination. The "groups" here are not necessarily work units. Rather, they are demographic categories, such as white and black Americans. In an important set of studies, Brief, Dietz, Cohen, Pugh, and Vaslow (2000) had a putative superior indicate a preference for a white applicant over a similarly qualified black applicant. Brief and his colleagues found that when this leader-established norm "justified" discrimination, participants gave black job candidates lower ratings. This effect was strongest when research participants were high in modern racism (see also Brief, Buttram, Elliott, Reizenstein, & McCline, 1995). This dynamic seems close to what we are interested in here, as a leader seems to be instituting an organizational climate favoring one ethnicity over another.

The idea of climate for discrimination was tested even more directly by Ziegert and Hanges (2005). Using a role-playing methodology, participants pretended that they worked in a hypothetical firm. In one experimental condition, the organization was predominantly white and wished to remain so. Similar to the results obtained by Brief et al., participants indicated that the climate for discrimination interacted with individual racism to influence subjects' treatment of black job applicants. Participants showed more discrimination when the climate allowed them to express their own prejudice.

Deviance and Social Accounts

A sizable body of literature on corporate social responsibility demonstrates that organizations sometimes behave in a less than appropriate manner (e.g., Aguilera, Rupp, Williams, & Ganapathi, in press; Dalla Costa, 1998; Ermann & Lundman, 1987). Cropanzano, Chrobot-Mason, Rupp, and Prehar (2004) and Rupp, Ganapathia, Aguilera, and Williams (in press) have suggested that this problem can be approached from the perspective of organizational justice. It seems that the behavior of large firms can be interpreted in much the same way as the behavior of individuals. For example, to hold a corporation accountable for an injustice, one would need to ask three questions: What *would* have happened if the organization had behaved differently? What *could* the organization have done differently? How *should* the organization have behaved? These three questions seem to underpin judgments of unfairness and could provide rich avenues for future research.

A related literature looks at how organizations formulate reputation-saving social accounts when they are at risk (Gatewood, Gowan, & Lautenschlager, 1993). Research in this area has found that organizations expend great effort to define the way they are perceived by others. For example, Dutton and

Dukerich (1991) explored how the New York and New Jersey Port Authority dealt with criticism pertaining to the way it treated the homeless population. The Port Authority was taking measures to reduce the presence of homeless people in its facilities, an action that aroused concern from some quarters. In response, the Port Authority initially denied the more severe behavior and, failing that, engaged in legitimating actions to restore its damaged reputation. Similar studies have examined social activist organizations (Elsbach & Sutton, 1992) and the California cattle industry (Elsbach, 1994). Research of this kind underscores that these organizations, acting as corporate entities, are sometimes blamed for injustice and, as a result, take steps to mitigate the blame.

Networks and Alliances
Neither public nor private sector organizations operate in a contextual vacuum. Rather, they are part of a community of collaborating and competitive corporate bodies. Many form cooperative networks (Koput, Smith-Doerr, & Powell, 1997; Provan & Sebastian, 1998). Potentially, these networks can help their members deal with institutional pressures (Provan, Isett, & Milward, 2004), improve firm performance (Powell, Koput, Smith-Doerr, & Owen-Smith, 1999), promote organizational learning (Powell, Koput, & Smith-Doerr, 1996; Suarez, 2005), and produce innovations (Smith-Doerr, Owen-Smith, Koput, & Powell, 1999).

Although research on interorganizational networks has only just begun to take a workplace fairness perspective, this line of inquiry seems promising. For example, work by Provan, Lamb, and Doyle (2004) suggests that network growth is facilitated by building legitimacy. Social justice, of course, has been found to promote legitimacy among decision makers (Tyler, 1997) and institutions (Tyler, 1990). In a more direct test, Luo (2005) examined 124 cross-national alliances in China. When alliance partners had high perceptions of procedural justice, profitability was superior to that obtained when procedural justice perceptions were low. These effects were enhanced when members of the alliance had a greater cultural distance.

Final Thoughts

Fig. 3 presented individual and unit victims alongside individual and unit transgressors. For descriptive purposes, we have treated each case separately. However, at any given time, more than one set of interactions could be operative in a work environment (Rupp & Cropanzano, 2002). These considerations have obvious relevance to Rupp and colleagues' important work on multifoci justice, though these considerations are beyond the scope of this present chapter. It should be a high priority for scholars to further articulate these linkages.

CONCLUSION

In reviewing the emerging literature on justice climate, Rupp and her colleagues have done our discipline a great service. These authors have thoroughly reviewed the literature and addressed prevailing definitional confusion. Even more important, they have provided a solid foundation upon which future scholarship can rest. Our efforts here have sought to build upon their work.

We began by considering what it means to be an individual when one is part of a group. Justice climate, as we have seen, may affect individuals' identities. We then presented a construct called intraunit justice. Intraunit justice is a collective concept, designating how workers treat their comrades *within* their groups. By discussing intraunit justice in the context of social identity theory, we sought to distinguish it from justice climate. We also attended to composition models, suggesting that the referent shift model might be an optimal choice. Finally, we set out to categorize current justice research into a new taxonomy. Our efforts in this regard led us to specify a fourth type of fairness: interunit justice. We then reviewed the taxonomy and discussed several literatures worth examining from an interunit justice perspective. We hope that our observations will further contribute to this rich and exciting research area.

REFERENCES

Aguilera, R. V., Rupp, D. E., Williams, C. A., & Ganapathi, J. (in press). Putting the S back in corporate social responsibility: A multi-level theory of social change in organizations. *Academy of Management Review.*

Bashshur, M., Rupp, D. E., & Christopher, J. (2004). Theoretically based strategies for defining and measuring justice climate: Implications for multi-level research in organizational justice. Paper presented at the 64th annual meeting of the Academy of Management, New Orleans, LA.

Branscombe, N. R., Spears, R., Ellemer, N., & Doosje, B. (2002). Intragroup and intergroup evaluation effects on group behavior. *Personality and Social Psychology Bulletin, 28,* 744–753.

Brickman, P., Folger, P., Goode, E., & Schul, Y. (1981). Microjustice and macrojustice. In: M. J. Lerner & S. C. Lerner (Eds), *The justice motive in social behavior* (pp. 173–202). New York: Plenum.

Brickson, S. (2000). The impact of identity orientation on individual and organizational outcomes in demographically diverse settings. *Academy of Management Review*, *25*, 82–101.

Brief, A. P., Buttram, R. T., Elliott, J. D., Reizenstein, R. M., & McCline, R. L. (1995). Releasing the beast: A study of compliance with orders to use race as a selection criteria. *Journal of Social Issues*, *51*, 171–193.

Brief, A. P., Dietz, J., Cohen, R. R., Pugh, S. D., & Vaslow, J. B. (2000). Just doing business: Modern racism and obedience to authority as explanations for employment discrimination. *Organizational Behavior and Human Decision Processes*, *81*, 72–97.

Brockner, J. (1994). Perceived fairness and survivors' reactions to layoffs, or how downsizing organizations can do well by doing good. *Social Justice Research*, *7*, 345–363.

Brockner, J., DeWitt, R. L., Grover, S., & Reed, T. (1990). When it is especially important to explain why: Factors affecting the relationship between managers' explanations of a layoff and survivors' reactions to layoffs. *Journal of Experimental Social Psychology*, *26*, 389–407.

Brockner, J., Konovsky, M., Cooper-Schneider, R., Folger, R., Martin, C., & Bies, R. J. (1994). Interactive effects of procedural justice and outcome negativity on victims and survivors of job loss. *The Academy of Management Journal*, *37*, 397–409.

Brown, R. (2000). Social identity theory: Past achievements, current problems, and future challenges. *European Journal of Social Psychology*, *30*, 745–778.

Clayton, S., & Opotow, S. (2003). Justice and identity: Changing perspectives on what is fair. *Personality and Social Psychology Bulletin*, *7*, 298–310.

Cohen-Charash, Y., & Spector, P. E. (2001). The role of justice in organizations: A meta-analysis. *Organizational Behavior and Human Decision Processes*, *86*, 278–321.

Colquitt, J. A., Conlon, D. E., Wesson, M. J., Porter, C. O. L. H., & Ng, K. Y. (2001). Justice at the millennium: A meta-analytic review of 25 years of organizational justice research. *Journal of Applied Psychology*, *86*, 425–445.

Cronbach, L. J., & Meehl, P. H. (1955). Construct validity in psychological tests. *Psychological Bulletin*, *52*, 281–302.

Cropanzano, R., Byrne, Z. S., Bobocel, D. R., & Rupp, D. E. (2001). Moral virtues, fairness heuristics, social entities, and other denizens of organizational justice. *Journal of Vocational Behavior*, *58*, 164–209.

Cropanzano, R., Chrobot-Mason, D., Rupp, D. E., & Prehar, C. A. (2004). Accountability for corporate injustice. *Human Resource Management Review*, *14*, 107–133.

Cropanzano, R., Prehar, C. A., & Chen, P. Y. (2002). Using social exchange theory to distinguish procedural from interactional justice. *Group and Organizational Management*, *27*, 324–351.

Cropanzano, R., Rupp, D. E., Mohler, C. J., & Schminke, M. (2001). Three roads to organizational justice. In: G. R. Ferris (Ed.), *Research in personnel and human resource management* (Vol. 20, pp. 1–113). Greenwich, CT: JAI Press.

Dalla Costa, J. (1998). *The ethical imperative: Why moral leadership is good business*. Reading, MA: Addison-Wesley.

De Cremer, D., van Knippenberg, B., van Knippenberg, D., Mullenders, D., & Stinglhamber, F. (2005). Rewarding leadership and fair procedures as determinants of self-esteem. *Journal of Applied Psychology*, *90*, 3–13.

Degoey, P. (2000). Contagious justice: Exploring the social construction of justice in organizations. *Research in Organizational Behavior*, *22*, 51–102.

Donovan, M. A., Drasgow, F., & Munson, L. J. (1998). The perceptions of fair interpersonal treatment scale: Development and validation of a measure of interpersonal treatment in the workplace. *Journal of Applied Psychology, 83,* 683–692.

Dutton, J. E., & Dukerich, J. M. (1991). Keeping an eye on the mirror: Image and identity in organizational adaptation. *Academy of Management Journal, 34,* 517–554.

Ehrhart, M. G. (2004). Leadership and procedural justice climate as antecedents of unit-level organizational citizenship behavior. *Personnel Psychology, 57,* 61–94.

Elsbach, K. D. (1994). Managing organizational legitimacy in the California cattle industry: The construction and effectiveness of verbal accounts. *Administrative Science Quarterly, 39,* 57–88.

Elsbach, K. D., & Sutton, R. I. (1992). Acquiring organizational legitimacy through illegitimate actions: A marriage of institutional and impression management theories. *Academy of Management Journal, 35,* 699–738.

Ermann, M. D., & Lundman, R. J. (1987). *Corporate and governmental deviance: Problems of organizational behavior in contemporary society* (3rd ed.). Oxford, UK: Oxford University Press.

Folger, R., & Cropanzano, R. (1998). *Organizational justice and human resource management.* Beverly Hills, CA: Sage.

Gatewood, R. D., Gowan, M., & Lautenschlager, G. J. (1993). Corporate image, recruitment image, and initial job choice decisions. *Academy of Management Journal, 36,* 414–427.

Gopinath, C., & Becker, T. E. (2000). Communication, procedural justice, and employee attitudes: Relationships under conditions of divestiture. *Journal of Management, 26,* 63–83.

Hogg, M. A., & Terry, D. J. (2000). Social identity and self-categorization processes in organizational contexts. *Academy of Management Review, 25,* 121–140.

Howes, J. C., Cropanzano, R., Grandey, A. A., & Mohler, C. J. (2000). Who is supporting whom? Quality team effectiveness and perceived organizational support. *Journal of Quality Management, 5,* 207–223.

James, K. (in press). Antecedents, processes, and outcomes of collective (group-level) politics in organizations. In: E. Vigoda-Gadot & A. Drory (Eds), *The handbook of organizational politics.* Cheltenham, UK: Elgar.

James, K., & Cropanzano, R. (1990). Focus of attention and locus of control as moderators of fraternal justice effects. *Social Justice Research, 4,* 169–185.

Jones, R. G., & Lindley, W. D. (1998). Issues in the transition to teams. *Journal of Business and Psychology, 13,* 31–40.

Katzenbach, J. R., & Smith, D. K. (1993). The discipline of teams. *Harvard Business Review,* March–April, pp. 111–120.

Kirkman, B. L., Jones, R. G., & Shapiro, D. L. (2000). Who do employees resist teams? Examining the "resistance barrier" to work team effectiveness. *International Journal of Conflict Management, 11,* 74–92.

Kirkman, B. L., Shapiro, D. L., Novelli, L., Jr., & Brett, J. M. (1996). Employee concerns regarding self-managing work teams: A multidimensional justice perspective. *Social Justice Research, 9,* 47–67.

Konovsky, M. A., & Folger, R. (1991). The effects of procedures, social accounts, and benefits level on victims' layoff reactions. *Journal of Applied Social Psychology, 21,* 630–650.

Koput, K. W., Smith-Doerr, L., & Powell, W. W. (1997). Strategies of learning and industry structure: The evolution of networks in biotechnology. In A. Huff (Ed.), *Advances in strategic management research* (Vol. 14, pp. 229–254). Greenwich, CT: JAI Press.

Korsgaard, M. A., Schweiger, D. M., & Sapienza, H. J. (1995). Building commitment, attach-
    ment, and trust in strategic decision-making teams: The role of procedural justice.
    Academy of Management Journal, 38, 60–84.
Liao, H., & Rupp, D. E. (2005). The impact of justice climate and justice orientation on work
    outcomes: A cross-level multifoci framework. *Journal of Applied Psychology,
    90,* 242–256.
Luo, Y. (2005). How important are shared perceptions of procedural justice in cooperative
    alliances?. *Academy of Management Journal, 48,* 695–709.
Mansour-Cole, D. M., & Scott, S. G. (1998). Hearing it through the grapevine: The influence of
    source, leader-relations, and legitimacy on survivors' fairness perceptions. *Personnel
    Psychology, 51,* 25–54.
Marks, M. M., DeChurch, L. A., Mathieu, J. E., Panzer, F. J., & Alonso, A. (2005). Teamwork
    in multiteam systems. *Journal of Applied Psychology, 90,* 964–971.
Mellor, S. (1992). The influence of layoff severity on postlayoff union commitment among
    survivors: The moderating effect of the perceived legitimacy of a layoff account.
    Personnel Psychology, 45, 579–600.
Naumann, S. E., & Bennett, N. (2000). A case for procedural justice climate: Development and
    test of a multi-level model. *Academy of Management, 43,* 881–889.
Oakes, P. (1987). The salience of social categories. In: J. C. Turner and Associates (Eds),
    Rediscovering the social group: A self-categorization theory (pp. 117–141). Oxford,
    UK: Blackwell.
Phillips, J. M., Douthitt, E. A., & Hyland, M. M. (2001). The role of justice in team member
    satisfaction with the leader and attachment to the team. *Journal of Applied Psychology,
    86,* 316–325.
Powell, W. W., Koput, K. W., & Smith-Doerr, L. (1996). Interorganizational collaboration and
    the locus of innovation: Networks of learning in biotechnology. *Administrative Science
    Quarterly, 41,* 116–145.
Powell, W. W., Koput, K. W., Smith-Doerr, L., & Owen-Smith, J. (1999). Network position
    and firm performance: Organizational returns to collaboration in biotechnology. In:
    D. Knoke (Ed.), *Research in the sociology of organizations* (Vol. 15, pp. 129–160).
    Stamford, CT: JAI Press.
Provan, K. G., Isett, K. R., & Milward, H. B. (2004). Cooperation and compromise: A network
    response to conflicting institutional pressures in community mental health. *Nonprofit and
    Voluntary Sector Quarterly, 33,* 489–514.
Provan, K. G., Lamb, G., & Doyle, M. (2004). Building legitimacy and the early growth of
    health networks for the uninsured. *Health Care Management Review, 29,* 117–128.
Provan, K. G., & Sebastian, J. G. (1998). Networks within networks: Service link overlap,
    organizational cliques, and network effectiveness. *Academy of Management Journal,
    41,* 453–463.
Roberson, Q. M., & Colquitt, J. A. (2005). Shared and configural justice: A social network
    model of justice in teams. *Academy of Management Review, 30,* 595–607.
Rupp, D. E., Bashur, M, & Liao, H. (this volume). Justice climate past, present, and future:
    Models of structure and emergence. In: F. Dansereau & F. J. Yammarino (Eds),
    Research in multi-level issues. Oxford: Elsevier.
Rupp, D. E., & Cropanzano, R. (2002). Multifoci justice and social exchange relationships.
    Organizational Behavior and Human Decision Processes, 89, 925–946.

Rupp, D. E., Ganapathia, J., Aguilera, R. V., & Williams, C. A. (in press). Employee reactions to corporate social responsibility: An organizational justice perspective. *Journal of Organizational Behavior.*

Salancik, G. J., & Pfeffer, J. (1978). A social information processing approach to job attitudes and task design. *Administrative Science Quarterly, 23,* 224–253.

Schwab, D. P. (1980). Construct validity in organizational behavior. In: B. M. Staw & L. L. Cummings (Eds), *Research in organizational behavior* (Vol. 2, pp. 3–43). Greenwich, CT: JAI Press.

Smith-Doerr, L., Owen-Smith, J., Koput, K. W., & Powell, W. W. (1999). Networks and knowledge production: Collaborating and patenting in biotechnology. In: R. Leenders (Ed.), *Corporate social capital* (pp. 331–350). Boston: Kluwer Academic Publishers.

Suarez, F. R. (2005). Network effects revisited: The role of strong ties in technology selection. *Academy of Management Journal, 48,* 710–720.

Tajfel, H., & Turner, J. C. (1979). An integrative theory of inter-group conflict. In: W. G. Austin & S. Worchel (Eds), *The social psychology of inter-group relations* (pp. 33–47). Monterey, CA: Brooks/Cole.

Taylor, D. M., Wright, S. C., Moghaddam, F. M., & LaLonde, R. N. (1990). The personal/group discrepancy: Perceiving my groups, but not myself, to be a target of discrimination. *Personality and Social Psychology Bulletin, 16,* 254–262.

Triandis, H. C. (1989). The self and social behavior in differing cultural contexts. *Psychological Review, 96,* 506–520.

Triandis, H. C. (1995). *Culture and social behavior.* New York: McGraw-Hill.

Turner, J. C. (1985). Social categorization and the self-concept: A social-cognitive theory of group behavior. In: E. J. Lawler (Ed.), *Advances in group processes* (Vol. 2, pp. 77–122). Greenwich, CT: JAI Press.

Turner, J. C., & Haslam, S. A. (2001). Social identity, organizations, and leadership. In: M. E. Turner (Ed.), *Groups at work: Theory and research* (pp. 25–65). Mahwah, NJ: Lawrence Erlbaum Associates.

Tyler, T. R. (1990). *Why people obey the law: Procedural justice, legitimacy, and compliance.* New Haven, CT: Yale University Press.

Tyler, T. R. (1997). The psychology of legitimacy: A relational perspective on voluntary deference to authority. *Personality and Social Psychology Review, 1,* 323–345.

Tyler, T. R. (1999). Why people co-operate with organizations: An identity-based perspective. In: B. M. Staw & R. Sutton (Eds), *Research in organizational behavior* (Vol. 21, pp. 201–246). Greenwich, CT: JAI Press.

Wenzel, M. (2000). Justice and identity: The significance of inclusion for perceptions of entitlement and the justice motive. *Personality and Social Psychology Bulletin, 26,* 157–176.

Wenzel, M. (2002). What is social about justice? Inclusive identity and group values as the basis of the justice motive. *Journal of Experimental Psychology, 38,* 205–218.

Ziegert, J. C., & Hanges, P. J. (2005). Employment discrimination: The role of implicit attitudes, motivation, and a climate for racial bias. *Journal of Applied Psychology, 90,* 553–562.

JUSTICE CLIMATE: CONSIDERATION OF SOURCE, TARGET, TYPE, SPECIFICITY, AND EMERGENCE

Deborah E. Rupp, Michael Bashshur and Hui Liao

ABSTRACT

This chapter seeks to integrate and expand on the ideas presented by Cropanzano, Li, and James (this volume), Ambrose and Schminke (this volume), and Rupp, Bashshur, and Liao (this volume). First, it summarizes and comments on the key insights made by each set of authors. It then presents five propositions, along with some preliminary evidence supporting each: (1) employees can and do make source-based justice judgments; (2) justice treatment is directed at different targets (including individuals and groups, both internal and external to the organization); (3) global justice climate may be a useful approach to studying justice once the relationship between more specific justice climates (e.g., interunit or intraunit justice climate) is better understood; (4) it is necessary to study both general and specific justice climates to understand the unfolding of justice reactions over time; and (5) a climate for justice can be behaviorally measured and trained.

Multi-Level Issues in Organizations and Time
Research in Multi-Level Issues, Volume 6, 439–459
Copyright © 2007 by Elsevier Ltd.
All rights of reproduction in any form reserved
ISSN: 1475-9144/doi:10.1016/S1475-9144(07)06020-1

INTRODUCTION

The series of papers presented in this volume represent a treatise on the theoretical and methodological advances we have made over the decades as well as a discourse on the exciting new opportunities that lay on the horizon. Indeed, these works show evidence that we are thinking critically about the definition, measurement, and emergence of justice and justice climate. In addition, we have learned from these authors that the organizational sciences are rich with theory and methodology that stand to push our understanding of justice phenomena to new levels (no pun intended). The sections that follow review the major tenants of each individual paper, seeking to integrate ideas within and across papers. To further this goal, the exposition concludes with the presentation of five propositions, along with preliminary evidence supporting each one.

SUMMARY OF THE KEY POINTS MADE IN THIS VOLUME

Rupp, Bashshur, and Liao: Structure and Emergence of Justice Climate

We first began this dialogue by tracing justice taxonomies over time. We began with the more traditional, individual-level, multitype conceptualization consisting of employees' individual perceptions of distributive, procedural, and interactional justice. Evidence suggests that employees can make these discrete judgments between types of justice, and that justice measured this way predicts a wide range of important outcomes (Colquitt, Wesson, Porter, Conlon, & Ng, 2001; Cohen-Charash & Spector, 2001). We then moved on to discuss multifoci/multitype distinctions, arguing that these distinct types of judgments can be made about multiple entities with whom employees interact (Liao & Rupp, 2005; Rupp & Cropanzano, 2002). This led us to a discussion of justice climate – that is, shared perceptions of fairness among employees working together. We summarized research showing that unit-level justice (i.e., justice climate) predicts variance in outcomes above and beyond the effects of individual-level justice (Colquitt, Noe, & Jackson, 2002), and that justice climate might also be multitype/ multifoci in nature, with separate justice climates forming about treatment received by the group from different entities (Liao & Rupp, 2005).

To summarize, and as other commentators have pointed out, this argument leaves us with a very large number of variables that we can potentially

Table 1. The Many Ways in Which Justice Can Be Operationalized.

Level	Type	Foci/Source	Target
Individual	Distributive	Organization	Self
Unit	Procedural	Top management	Coworkers
Organization	Informational	Human resources	Customers
Culture	Interactional	Supervisor	Labor market
		Coworker	Local community
		Customer	Industry
			Environment

measure, as illustrated in Table 1. With one to four possible levels of analysis (individual, unit, organization, culture), one to four types of justice (distributive, procedural, interpersonal, informational), and an infinite number of foci (e.g., organization, top management, human resources, supervisor, coworkers, customers), the number of constructs is staggering – and, indeed, unrealistic for inclusion in any one study. Also included in Table 1 is the notion of multiple *targets* of justice, whereby an employee might be privy not only to how well he or she is treated personally, but also to how well others are treated in the organization. We will return to this point later in the chapter; for now, however, we will simply point out that we can empirically detect distinctions between this myriad of variables, suggesting at least two things.

First, it is evident that we should use more precision in our measurements. We may not have the need to measure everything, but we should clearly operationalize and measure our variables, specifying the type, source, target, and level, such that our effects are not attenuated by inadvertently collapsing variables that are unrelated or, even worse, negatively related to one another. Second, perhaps we should be alarmed by such a copious set of variables. Their proliferation calls into question whether we truly know what is going on in the heads and hearts of employees. Are our sets of items nothing more than primes? Which is more salient, type or source? Maybe we should treat these variables less as constructs and more as pieces of information that combine in ways we do not yet understand. Perhaps source is more salient than type; perhaps climate is more salient than individual-level perceptions. These questions have yet to be tested empirically and will require more fine-grained measurement (as well as qualitative and policy-capturing types of studies) to investigate. We will elaborate on this need for further research in subsequent sections.

In the second half of the chapter by Rupp, Bashshur, and Liao (this volume), we outlined several strategies and recommendations for measuring justice climate. We argued there for a multifoci, referent-shift composition model and discussed options for measuring climate strength (alignment-based strength). As we will discuss later in the current chapter, our colleagues greatly expanded on these points and have taken us farther in our exposition on these matters than did our original arguments.

The final issue we raised was that of climate emergence. We argued that there already exists a substantial theoretical basis upon which to test our theories of climate emergence (e.g., Kozlowski & Klein, 2000; Payne & Pugh, 1976; Salancik & Pfeffer, 1978; Schneider, 1975). In fact, we would argue that the literature, rather than simply focus on whether research need be more fine-grained or more broad-based, should direct substantially more attention to the unfolding processes of justice and justice climate. In other words, we believe that researchers should engage in more longitudinal studies of how justice perceptions evolve, at both the group and the individual levels. In fact, we believe that a longitudinal approach may reconcile the "splitters" and the "globalizers" in many interesting ways. For example, an individual (or a group) may subdivide justice judgments by type and source initially. However, "an unfair event has the potential to create a series of ripples" that echo from one form of justice perception to another form of justice perception (Cropanzano, Byrne, Bobocel, & Rupp, 2001, p. 179). Therefore, over time different types and sources of justice perceptions jointly shape the overall justice judgment emphasized by Cropanzano and Ambrose (2001), Ambrose and Arnaud (2005), and Ambrose and Schminke (this volume).

Cropanzano, Li, and James: Intraunit Justice, Interunit Justice, and Multiple Identities

Cropanzano and his colleagues (this volume) provide several insights, theoretical extensions, and new ideas in their chapter. First, they use social identity theory and categorization theory to argue that the level of justice climate within a group depends on the justice climate of other groups, implying that justice is largely a comparative process (i.e., groups consider how well they are treated based partially on how they perceive other groups to be treated). Indeed, these authors argue that climate influences the formation of group identity and that the effect of justice climate on outcomes is moderated by whether the group identity is active at the time the judgment is made (as opposed to other active identities). These arguments lead us to consider a number of issues.

First, we wonder if the comparative process described by Cropanzano et al. is a necessary requirement for justice climate to emerge or if it is solidifying mechanism. We base this question on a contemporary model of justice termed the *deonance model* (Cropanzano, Goldman, & Folger, 2003; Folger, 2001; Folger & Cropanzano, 2001; Folger, Cropanzano, & Goldman, 2005). This model posits that justice is an internalized moral virtue that regulates interpersonal behavior. Unlike some justice theories, such as equity theory and the relational model, which argue that justice reduces to self-interest or concerns for status in groups, the deontic model posits that justice is not only a means to an instrumental or relational end, but also an end in and of itself – that it is simply important to humans (and other primates) that fairness is enacted in society. This model is able to explain third-party reactions to observed injustices and individuals' willingness to make personal sacrifices in the name of fairness. Returning to our ideas regarding the comparative process proposed by Cropanzano et al., the deontic model suggests that whereas justice judgments may stem from a comparative process (whether it be a comparison with an actual referent other or an idealized cognitive referent), individuals or, in the present case, groups of individuals may also hold potential transgressors up to some objective, moral standard of conduct. It would be interesting to sort these issues out empirically, exploring the comparative and noncomparative influences on justice climate formation.

A second intellectual exercise that Cropanzano et al.'s series of arguments forced us to partake in involved the case of intraunit justice, interunit justice, and multiple identities. If, as purported by social identity and social categorization theories (Tajfel & Turner, 1979; Turner, 1985), employees see themselves as members of multiple groups with which they may or may not identify, and these varying identities may be active or inactive at different times, we wonder to what extent justice climate within these groups influences the activation of identity. That is, in addition to active identity moderating justice climate effects as proposed by Cropanzano et al., might an unfair climate coming from a group that was once fair lead individuals to dis-identify with this group? In this case, active identity would be both a mediator *and* a moderator of justice climate effects. Furthermore, this mediating effect might be heightened when intraunit injustice is at work. As was implied by Cropanzano and colleagues, when team members agree that everyone treats all other team members poorly, chances are good that pride and affiliation in one's groups will be stifled.

The work of Skitka may also shed some light on these issues (Skitka, 2003; Skitka & Bravo, 2005). This work argues that the identities that an individual might hold can differ in terms of how fairness is viewed and dealt with. Using the terminology of the multiple needs model of justice (Cropanzano et al., 2001), this argument implies that justice might be instrumentally, relationally, or morally motivated, depending on why justice is important to a particular active identity. Skitka takes this notion further in explaining that such differences in how fairness is defined depend on which aspect of the self (material, social, moral) dominates the working self-concept. This factor would then influence how an incident is perceived in terms of justice as well as how criterion variables are affected based on said perceptions. The same line of reasoning also implies the mediated moderated relationship proposed earlier. Justice effects differ depending on which identity is activated, and differences in active identity, the self, and the self-concept can also explain why differential reactions to injustice may occur.

Again, it is important to note that modeling this process dynamically would be superior to cross-sectional tests in that the focus is on the unfolding and changing of identities over time. We agree with Cropanzano et al. that the literature on networks and alliances may shed some light on these issues. Although the focal independent variable in this case is intraunit justice, the allegiances that an individual or a band of individuals might form across groups involve interunit justice.

Ambrose and Schminke: Climate Strength, Global Justice, and Climate for Justice

Like Cropanzano et al. (this volume), Ambrose and Schminke (this volume), in their commentary, not only provide a plethora of points that challenge our thinking, but also offer some suggestions for resolving methodological problems that have bedeviled justice climate researchers. Here we briefly summarize five of the major contributions made by these authors and offer some additional thoughts on these issues.

Climate Strength
Ambrose and Schminke have provided an immense extension to our discussion of climate strength. Further, they describe polynomial regression and response surface methodology as a way of modeling strength. Cheers erupted in our laboratory upon reading this section. Not only was this one of the most elegant descriptions of the method we had seen to date (something the justice community desperately needed so as to take the fear out of a method many are starting to hear about, but may not be familiar

with), but we have also been examining this method as a tool for exploring the interaction between justice climates surrounding different foci.

We have recently incorporated this method in a study where we sought to explore the relationship between multifoci justice climates (Bashshur & Rupp, 2006). Research to date has not explored the nature of the relationship between justice climates. That is, are climates (e.g., supervisory justice climate versus coworker justice climate/interunit climate) cumulative? Are they compensatory? Are they multiplicative? We explored the interaction between justice climate (climate alignment) using polynomial regression and response surface methodology on a sample of employees in a large state university. Our results told an interesting story. Basically, our response surface graphs showed very clearly that misaligned climates caused more visceral employee reactions than when climates were all low. It seems that employees would rather be treated in a consistently unfair manner by multiple transgressors than treated fairly by one group but unfairly by another (see Fig. 1 for an example of the effects of misalignment on organizational citizenship behaviors). We interpreted these findings through the lens of the met-expectations hypothesis (Wanous, 1977; Wanous, Stumpf, & Bedrosian, 1979). Essentially, we argue that treatment by one source of justice in the workplace shapes employee expectations for treatment from other sources. When treatment from multiple sources is negative, the negative treatment becomes expected and employees tolerate it.

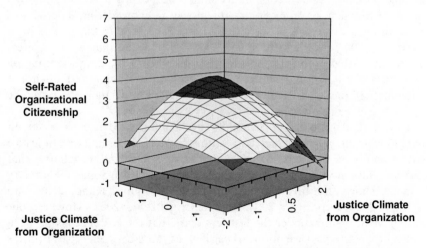

Fig. 1. Relationship between Group Climates from Supervisor and the Organization and Individual-Level Organizational Citizenship Behaviors

Conversely, when treatment by one source is positive while treatment from another source is negative, employees experience what we call a "misalignment shock" and react negatively toward the source of injustice.

We hope that this presentation by Ambrose and Schminke and the preliminary empirical work incorporating this method will inspire researchers to use polynomial regression to explore how employees' shared perceptions about various transgressors interact to influence subsequent attitudes and behaviors.

Global Justice

A second assertion made by Ambrose and Schminke was that the justice community should consider measuring and studying justice as a more global construct. They question the practicality of models that fully cross justice type and justice source (and we would add justice target). The authors point out the paradox that although a fully crossed model is theoretically unreasonable (for example, coworkers may not have influence on outcomes or procedures), a partially crossed model (i.e., incorporating different types of justice with different foci – namely, those that make theoretical sense) may seem post hoc.

Whereas this paradox has credence, the problem is highlighted by Ambrose and Schminke's third important assertion, which is that the justice community rarely develops differential hypotheses for the different types of justice. We agree that this phenomenon has greatly constrained the field and is something that we as a community should be tackling head on. Although some researchers have explored this issue by considering interactions between justice facets (e.g., see Cropanzano, Slaughter, & Bachiochi, 2005; Goldman, 2003; Skarlicki & Folger, 1997), we argue that a more direct approach to this problem is to begin serious theory building surrounding how different types and sources of justice affect similar and dissimilar outcomes. If this effort can be carried out effectively, then the post hoc problem can be resolved.

That said, Ambrose and Schminke also remind us that such a pursuit might be in vain given the high correlations between different types of justice within and between sources. We could not agree more and were happy that this fact has now been formally placed on the table. Some preliminary evidence shows that this assumption holds (Bashshur & Rupp, 2006; Liao & Rupp, 2005; Rupp et al., 2004; Rupp & Cropanzano, 2002). However, our data have also shown over the last few years that the correlations between sources (across types) are not nearly as high as those between types. For this reason, and relevant to Ambrose and Schminke's argument for a global as opposed to specific justice, a discussion of construct validity is necessitated.

For ease of comprehension, the reader might consider thinking about type and source of justice in a multitrait/multimethod matrix (Campbell & Fiske, 1959). The matrix in Table 2, for example, treats type of justice as "traits" and source of justice as "method." Thus, for each source of justice, multiple types of justice might be measured (if, as argued earlier, it is deemed theoretically reasonable). If a fully crossed model is viable, then we should find evidence for both convergent and discriminant validity. That is, each individual type of justice should correlate more highly with itself across sources (depicted by the y's in Table 2) than the different types of justice correlate with each other within a source (depicted by the x's in Table 2). In support of Ambrose and Schminke's propositions, this outcome is not exactly what we have been finding – the types of justice seem to act very similarly both in general and within sources.

But all is not lost. What we observe in extant studies that measure both justice sources and types is construct validity evidence for source. If we were to aggregate across type (i.e., average distributive, procedural, and inter-actional justice together), we would see that the correlations between foci are not nearly as high as the correlations between types either within source or overall. The same is true for the correlations of single types of justice across sources.

Although this point is not directly argued in these papers, the results discussed here can be gleaned by the correlations presented. For example, Bashshur, Rupp, and Christopher (2004) found across two samples that within the same source the average correlation between types of justice was 0.69 for supervisor-focused justice perceptions and 0.63 for organization-focused justice perceptions. In contrast, within the same type of justice across the two sources, the average correlation was 0.49. Similarly, Liao and Rupp (2005) reported that within the same source of organization-focused justice, the average correlation among procedural, informational, and interpersonal justice was 0.70; within the same source of supervisor-focused justice, the average correlation among different types of justice was 0.77. Within the same type of justice, however, the average correlation across the two different sources was only 0.36. In addition, in a series of confirm-atory factor analyses of the justice items, Liao and Rupp reported that a greater improvement in model fit over a single-factor model came from differentiating various sources of justice, rather than from differentiating various types of justice. While the generalizability and robustness of this pattern of results need to be confirmed in formal analyses, the extant evidence suggests that individuals have an easier time distinguishing justice sources than types.

Table 2. A Multitrait/Multimethod Matrix Approach to Understanding the Construct Validity of Justice (Type and Source/Foci).

	Organization				Supervisor				Coworkers			
	DJ	PJ	InfoJ	IntJ	DJ	PJ	InfoJ	IntJ	DJ	PJ	InfoJ	IntJ
Organization DJ	y											
PJ	x	y										
InfoJ	x	x	y									
IntJ	x	x	x	y								
Supervisor DJ	y	x	x	x	y							
PJ	x	y	x	x	x	y						
InfoJ	x	x	y	x	x	x	y					
IntJ	x	x	x	y	x	x	x	y				
Coworkers DJ	y	x	x	x	y	x	x	x	y			
PJ	x	y	x	x	x	y	x	x	x	y		
InfoJ	x	x	y	x	x	x	y	x	x	x	y	
IntJ	x	x	x	y	x	x	x	y	x	x	x	y

DJ, Distributive justice; PJ, procedural justice; InfoJ, informational justice; IntJ, interpersonal justice.

We posit that such findings make perfect sense. Why? Because different people and groups may very well treat employees differently (Cropanzano et al., this volume). It would be unrealistic to expect the quality of treatment by supervisors, customers, coworkers, human resources, and other parties to be identical. What might be more reasonable to expect, however, is that different types of treatment (interactional, procedural) would be similar coming from a particular source – because it is the source, not the type, that is the transgressor. This leaves us with a situation where global justice might be more reasonable in terms of type, but specific justice with regard to source. We will return to this point in the next section.

Climate for Justice

Finally, Ambrose and Schminke (this volume) make the astute observation that the justice climate construct, as it has been treated in the literature, is different in nature from climate of other varieties (e.g., safety climate, Hofmann & Stetzer, 1996; service climate, Schneider, 1990). That is, climate – as it is treated in other literatures – refers to perceptions regarding how things should be done (e.g., safety protocols), which then are sought to predict whether such things are actually done (e.g., safety behaviors). This is vastly different from our practice of looking at the extent to which groups of employees agree with one another about how fairly the group is treated, and whether this factor ends up making the group work harder, be happier, or be better citizens. As a result, Ambrose and Schminke call for the study of climate *for* justice. This endeavor would involve asking employees (in this case, supervisors or managers might be an appropriate sample) how they feel employees *should* be treated, and exploring if such a climate for justice predicts whether such behaviors are, indeed, carried out.

We have attempted to measure this variable (Bashshur et al., 2004). We developed a measure of justice climate that assessed the extent to which just behaviors were rewarded and unjust behaviors were punished within work-groups. Grounding ourselves in the theoretical work of Naylor, Pritchard, and Ilgen (1980), we defined climate as employee perceptions of contingencies for specific behaviors. In essence, we examined whether there was agreement that things should be done in a particular way within work-groups. The focus was on observable behaviors at the level of the supervisor. To the extent that all employees could observe the behaviors of their supervisors and that the behaviors in question were clearly identifiable (in this case, rebukes and disapproval versus praise and recognition), there should have been fairly high agreement around how things should be done.

Unfortunately, given the characteristics of our sample, the majority of our participants did not have enough opportunities to observe the interactions of their supervisors with their supervisors' colleagues, their own immediate supervisors, or upper management (and as such could not assess the extent to which their supervisors' behaviors were punished or rewarded). In the case of this sample, it might have been more fruitful to ask the participants to report the likelihood of punishment or reward (from colleagues or supervisors) for the behaviors of their own colleagues. We believe that a focus on contingencies for behavior is more in the spirit of the idea of justice climate as a climate *for* justice. Given the appropriate focus in level and source of treatment, we think that this may still be a fruitful avenue to explore. We also look forward to seeing future research that explores climate for justice further, including the measurement of justice sensitivity, judgment, motivation, and character, as described by Ambrose and Schminke.

FIVE PROPOSITIONS WITH PRELIMINARY EVIDENCE

In summary, we thank Cropanzano et al. (this volume) and Ambrose and Schminke (this volume) for their commentaries on our ideas, and we thoroughly appreciate the additional theoretical assertions both sets of authors have made. Although we have provided several rejoinder comments already, we conclude this chapter with the presentation of five propositions that are grounded in the positions taken in all three chapters as well as our subsequent thinking on these issues (see Table 3). We also summarize the results of some recent empirical studies to lend some preliminary support to the arguments made thus far, to show how exciting pursuing some of these new lines of research can be and to inspire subsequent exploration of these important topics.

Proposition 1. Employees can and do make specific justice judgments and form specific relationships with multiple individuals and groups, and sources of justice/injustice include more than just supervisors and the organization as a whole.

As we have argued in this chapter and in our last paper (Rupp et al., this volume), taking a multifoci approach to the study of justice is both theoretically and empirically sound. Certainly, treatment coming from multiple actors within the organization will never be perfectly consistent. Whereas

Table 3. Five Propositions Regarding the Study of Justice and Justice Climate.

Proposition 1. Employees can and do make specific justice judgments and form specific relationships with multiple individuals and groups, and sources of justice/injustice include more than just supervisors and the organization as a whole

Proposition 2. Workplace justice has multiple targets, including individuals and groups of individuals, and internal and external stakeholders. Employees may be influenced by justice treatment targeted to them individually and by justice treatment targeted to their coworkers and other groups of employees; their own behaviors may also have justice implications for other organizational stakeholders

Proposition 3. Global justice climate may be useful for the prediction of important workplace outcomes, but not until we understand how justice climates interact

Proposition 4. Both global and specific justice climates may be necessary to understand how justice climate forms, unfolds, and stabilizes over time

Proposition 5. Climate *for* justice forms among managers, can be measured by behaviors (reported by subordinates), and can be trained

climate for justice may be imparted via a top-down process, even organizations with strong "global" justice climates would be expected to vary in terms "justice from whom." As long as organizations are run by humans, we argue that variance will exist in both individual- and unit-level justice across foci, and the data presented thus far seem to support this contention (e.g., Bashshur & Rupp, 2006; Liao & Rupp, 2005; Rupp et al., 2004; Rupp & Cropanzano, 2002). Furthermore, we have replicated these findings in Korea, Japan, and Singapore (Hayashi, Rupp, & Shin-ichiro, 2006; Liao, Rupp, Ko, Nam, & Bashshur, 2005; Ng, Rupp, & Drasgow, 2005).

In addition, we have begun to explore what we have been calling "coworker-focused justice," which aligns with Cropanzano et al.'s (this volume) concept of intraunit justice. That is, justice perceptions made about the treatment received from one's team members constitute a distinct factor and predict relevant outcomes (see Rupp et al., 2004). What we have yet to do is to aggregate individual perceptions of intraunit justice to the group level to test whether this type of climate variable explains incremental variance above and beyond the effects of individual level coworker-focused perceptions. Such an exploration would both be interesting and open the door to explorations into self versus other interunit justice perceptions.

Finally, we have begun to explore customers as a source of justice (Holub, Rupp, & Spencer, 2006; Rupp & Spencer, in press; Spencer & Rupp, 2006). Based on a theoretical model grounded in the multifoci model, affective events theory (Weiss & Cropanzano, 1996), and fairness theory (Folger & Cropanzano, 2001), we have hypothesized that customers are a viable source of justice and that injustice coming from customers increases employee emotional labor. We have further predicted that this effect is mediated by discrete emotions and fairness-related counterfactual thinking. Two laboratory experiments and a field study show support for this model.

Proposition 2. Workplace justice has multiple targets, including individuals and groups of individuals, and internal and external stakeholders. Employees may be influenced by justice treatment targeted to them individually and by justice treatment targeted to their coworkers and other groups of employees; their own behaviors may also have justice implications for other organizational stakeholders.

Our second proposition is based on the notion that organizations are integrated systems with interdependent stakeholders. Thus employees not only receive justice treatment from different parties themselves, but also observe and hear about justice treatment targeted to others. Do they even care about how others are treated? Why do they care? Who cares most? Do they want others to be treated fairly? Or do they prefer others to be treated unfairly? How do they compare others' treatment with their own treatment? While extant justice climate literature sheds some light on these issues, we are far from knowing all the answers.

We are excited to see a stream of new research examining these topics. For example, based on equity theory (Adams, 1965) and fairness theory (Folger & Cropanzano, 2001), Colquitt (2004) proposed that individuals compare their own procedural justice experience with others' procedural justice experience and respond most favorably when the two match. The results revealed individuals exert higher levels of performance when both self and others were treated fairly, especially in more interdependent teams and for benevolent individuals in terms of equity sensitivity. Extending this study, Liao et al. (2005) proposed that the extent to which employees care about others' justice treatment depends on their cooperation- versus competition-oriented social values. The results suggest that perceptions of others' justice do matter, but that individual differences exist in how individuals react to others' justice; in particular, competitive individuals have less positive attitudes and behaviors when others were treated fairly.

Another aspect of this proposition is that organizational events and employee behaviors influence the justice perceptions of external stakeholders, such as shareholders, customers, communities, and so on (Aguilera, Rupp, Williams, & Ganapathi, in press). Existing justice research has primarily been internally orientated, focusing on the targets within organizations. A growing, but as yet still limited, body of research is starting to move beyond organizational boundaries. For example, given that we are in a service economy, fierce market competition identifies customers as one of the most important groups of organizational stakeholders. Customers expect to be treated fairly in service encounters (Clemmer & Schneider, 1993). For example, Conlon and Murray (1996) found that companies' responses to product complaints, such as accepting responsibility for the problems and providing coupons and reimbursements, influenced customers' fairness perceptions and satisfaction.

In a recent study, Liao (in press) examined the role of front-line customer service employees' behaviors in handling customer complaints, also known as service recovery performance (SRP), in conveying a just image of service organizations and achieving desirable customer outcomes. Results from a field study and a laboratory study demonstrated that making an apology, effective problem solving, being courteous, and prompt handling positively influenced customer-perceived justice, which further influenced customer satisfaction and loyalty. In contrast, service failure severity and repeated failures reduced the positive impact of some dimensions of SRP on customer satisfaction, and customer-perceived justice again mediated these moderated effects.

What has not been examined in these studies is justice climate from the customers' perspective, or customers' *shared* perceptions about how they are treated in service encounters. A high level of agreement among customers would indicate a consistent level of high- or low-quality service, and a low level of agreement would indicate inconsistent service experienced by different customers. This unique area of research offers the opportunity to integrate internal and external organizational stakeholders, draw on theories from multiple disciplines, and examine the interplay of management practices, organizational climates (e.g., service climate, justice climate), service provider characteristics, and customer characteristics.

Proposition 3. Global justice climate may be useful for the prediction of important workplace outcomes, but not until we understand how justice climates interact.

As we stated earlier, we absolutely agree with the assertions of Ambrose and Schminke (this volume) that a return to the basics might be needed with regard to the dimensionality of justice. We could certainly subdivide the construct of justice in many ways, but this parsing might leave us with a multitude of highly correlated variables that provide little added value over a more parsimonious model. We would take this argument even further to remind readers of the arguments of Law and colleagues (Law & Wong, 1999; Law, Wong, & Mobley, 1998), which state that we often set up our theoretical arguments at the construct level (e.g., general justice); make hypotheses, measure variables, and run analyses at the dimension level (e.g., distributive, procedural, interactional justice); and then interpret our findings back at the construct level (e.g., general justice). Law and colleagues have shown that different results can be obtained depending on the level of analysis examined.

That said, whereas a return to a more type-free general justice construct might both be useful and provide more parsimony, collapsing across sources bears problematic implications. We should not expect all parties within an organization to treat an employee or a group of employees in the same manner. Furthermore, the preliminary research we have conducted on this issue suggests that multifoci justice (climate) may not be compensatory. The relationship is complex and aggregating across foci might cloud interesting psychological phenomena or, at worse, produce canceled-out, nonsignificant, or spurious results.

Proposition 4. Both global and specific justice climates may be necessary to understand how justice climate forms, unfolds, and stabilizes over time.

Earlier in this volume, we presented a model of justice climate emergence. We argued that individual differences, environmental characteristics, and climate contingencies create a lens through which employees perceive individual events at work (referred to as event justice). These event perceptions, over time, lead to more general perceptions about the average level of fairness present in the workplace (referred to as social entity justice). When coworkers come together, socialize, share information, and accumulate collective experiences, a climate for justice forms that represents shared perceptions regarding treatment and climate contingencies regarding norms for the reward and punishments for fair/unfair behaviors.

This is a dynamic, multiactor psychological and sociological phenomenon. A single justice study might enter this dynamic system at multiple places in the model. Depending on the point of entry, the level of specificity at which we measure our justice construct will vary greatly. At one point of the model, it may be fruitful to measure actual events, and employees' responses to them. At another point in the model, it may be of interest to see how these event judgments combine to create more stable perceptions of fairness. Here is a place where we might strive to understand whether employees aggregate event perceptions by type (outcomes, procedures, interpersonal treatment) or by source (supervisor, organization, coworkers, customers). If source is an important differentiator of these more general justice perceptions (which we believe it is), then we might also seek to understand how a change in one actor (e.g., a new boss, a merger with another company, reassignment to a different team) changes fairness perceptions in the overall system.

In sum, there is a time and place for specific measures of justice, and a time and place for global measures of justice. As researchers, we should strive to choose the type and level of specificity, dimensionality, and measure based on the particular research question. Once this decision is made, we should then strive to consistently theorize, hypothesize, measure, analyze, and interpret at that predetermined type/level of dimensionality (Law & Wong, 1999; Law et al., 1998).

Proposition 5. Climate *for* justice forms among managers, can be measured by behaviors (reported by subordinates), and can be trained.

We wholeheartedly agree with Ambrose and Schminke (this volume) that exploring a climate *for* justice might represent a fertile undertaking. We have yet to thoroughly explore how expectations surrounding fair treatment form, and how fair and unfair behaviors might be reinforced or punished in the workplace. Does a climate surrounding the importance of fairness lead to more fairness behaviors? Can a climate for justice be created in an organization that leads to heightened actual and perceived employee justice? What might be the boundary conditions placed on such phenomena?

One area of research that might be integrated with such a pursuit is that of justice training. Three studies have shown that management can be effectively trained to be more fair. Such interventions have been validated by considering the changes in subordinates' justice perceptions before and after their managers were trained (Rupp, Baldwin, & Bashshur, in press; Skarlicki & Latham, 1996, 1997). Future studies might extend this research to test whether contingencies for fair treatment can be formally created, disseminated, and, in essence, "trained," and if such interventions might increase workplace justice.

CONCLUSION

In closing, we thank Cropanzano and colleagues, and Ambrose and Schminke, for their thought-provoking comments. In this rejoinder, we integrated and expanded on the ideas presented in their and our earlier chapters in this volume, and we advanced five propositions concerning the source, target, type, specificity, and emerging process of justice climate. We suggest that the time has come to begin looking more seriously at the process of justice and the way in which it unfolds over time. We hope these discussions inspire further theoretical development and empirical investigation of justice climate. For example, in a just-published study using conversational data, Roberson (2006) provides evidence that team sense making (i.e., the use of social cues to interpret unexpected or ambiguous events) is an important element in the creation of justice climate. This work is just the beginning. We eagerly await subsequent justice climate research that will push our understanding of this important topic forward.

REFERENCES

Adams, J. S. (1965). Inequity in social exchange. In: Berkowitz L. (Ed.), *Advances in exper-imental social psychology* (Vol. 2, pp. 267–299). New York: Academic Press.

Aguilera, R., Rupp, D. E., Williams, C., & Ganapathi, J. (in press). Putting the S back in corporate social responsibility: A multi-level theory of social change in organizations. *Academy of Management Review.*

Ambrose, M. L., & Arnaud, A. (2005). Are procedural justice and distributive justice concep-tually distinct? In: J. A. Colquitt & J. Greenberg (Eds), *Handbook of organizational justice* (pp. 85–112). Mahwah, NJ: Lawrence Erlbaum Associates.

Ambrose, M. L., & Schminke, M. (this volume). Examining justice climate: Issues of fit, sim-plicity, and content. In: F. Dansereau & F. J. Yammarino (Eds), *Research in multi-level issues.* Oxford: Elsevier.

Bashshur, M., & Rupp, D. E. (2006). Dealing with multiple sources of justice climate: A response surface methodology approach. Paper presented at the 21st annual conference for the society for industrial and organizational psychology, Dallas, TX.

Bashshur, M., Rupp, D. E., & Christopher, J. (2004). Theoretically-based strategies for defining and measuring justice climate: Implications for multi-level research in organizational justice. Paper presented at the 64th annual meeting of the academy of management, New Orleans, LA.

Campbell, D. T., & Fiske, D. W. (1959). Convergent and discriminant validation by the mul-titrait–multimethod matrix. *Psychological Bulletin, 56,* 81–105.

Clemmer, E. C., & Schneider, B. (1993). Managing customer dissatisfaction with waiting: Ap-plying social-psychological theory in a service setting. In: T. A. Swartz, D. E. Bowen & S. W. Brown (Eds), *Advances in service marketing and management* (Vol. 2, pp. 213–229). Greenwich, CT: JAI Press.

Cohen-Charash, Y., & Spector, P. E. (2001). The role of justice in organizations: A meta-analysis. *Organizational Behavior and Human Decision Processes, 86,* 278–321.

Colquitt, J. A. (2004). Does the justice of the one interact with the justice of the many? Reactions to procedural justice in teams. *Journal of Applied Psychology, 89,* 633–646.

Colquitt, J. A., Noe, R. A., & Jackson, C. L. (2002). Justice in teams: Antecedents and con-sequences of procedural justice climate. *Personnel Psychology, 55,* 83–109.

Colquitt, J. A., Wesson, M. J., Porter, C. O. L. H., Conlon, D. E., & Ng, K. Y. (2001). Justice at the millennium: A meta-analytic review of 25 years of organizational justice research. *Journal of Applied Psychology, 86,* 425–445.

Conlon, D. E., & Murray, N. M. (1996). Customer perceptions of corporate responses to product complaints: The role of explanations. *Academy of Management Journal, 39,* 1040–1056.

Cropanzano, R., & Ambrose, M. L. (2001). Procedural and distributive justice are more similar than you think: A monistic perspective and a research agenda. In: J. Greenberg & R. Cropanzano (Eds), *Advances in organizational justice* (pp. 119–151). Stanford, CA: Stanford University Press.

Cropanzano, R., Byrne, Z. S., Bobocel, D. R., & Rupp, D. E. (2001). Moral virtues, fairness heuristics, social entities, and other denizens of organizational justice. *Journal of Vocational Behavior, 58,* 164–209.

Cropanzano, R., Goldman, B., & Folger, R. (2003). Deontic justice: The role of moral principles in workplace fairness. *Journal of Organizational Behavior, 24,* 1019–1024.

Cropanzano, R., Li, A., & James, K. (this volume). Intraunit justice and interunit justice and the people who experience them. In: F. Dansereau & F. J. Yammarino (Eds), *Research in multi-level issues.* Oxford: Elsevier.

Cropanzano, R., Slaughter, J. E., & Bachiochi, P. D. (2005). Organizational justice and black applicants' reactions to affirmative action. *Journal of Applied Psychology, 90,* 1168–1184.

Folger, R. (2001). Fairness as deonance. In: S. W. Gilliland, D. D. Steiner & D. P. Skarlicki (Eds), *Research in social issues in management* (Vol. 1, pp. 3–33). Mahwah, NJ: Lawrence Erlbaum Associates.

Folger, R., & Cropanzano, R. (2001). Fairness theory: Justice as accountability. In: J. Greenberg & R. Cropanzano (Eds), *Advances in organizational justice* (pp. 89–118). Stanford, CA: Stanford University Press.

Folger, R., Cropanzano, R., & Goldman, B. (2005). What is the relationship between justice and morality? In: J. A. Colquitt & J. Greenberg (Eds), *Handbook of organizational justice* (pp. 215–245). Mahwah, NJ: Lawrence Erlbaum Associates.

Goldman, B. (2003). The application of reference cognitions theory to legal-claiming by terminated workers: The role of organizational justice and anger. *Journal of Management, 29,* 705–728.

Hayashi, Y., Rupp, D. E., & Shin-ichiro, H. (2006). The multifoci social exchange model of justice: A Japanese investigation. Paper presented at the 21st annual conference for the society for industrial and organizational psychology, Dallas, TX.

Hofmann, D. A., & Stetzer, A. (1996). A cross-level investigation of factors influencing unsafe behaviors and accidents. *Personnel Psychology, 49,* 307–339.

Holub, A. S., Rupp, D. E., & Spencer, S. (2006). Justice and emotional labor: The moderating effect of perspective taking. Paper presented at the 21st annual conference for the society for industrial and organizational psychology, Dallas, TX.

Kozlowski, S. W. J., & Klein, K. J. (2000). A multi-level approach to theory and research in organizations: Contextual, temporal, and emergent processes. In: K. J. Klein & S. W. J. Kozlowski (Eds), *Multi-level theory, research, and methods in organizations: Foundations, extensions, and new directions* (pp. 3–90). San Francisco, CA: Jossey-Bass.

Law, K. S., & Wong, C. S. (1999). Multidimensional constructs in structural equation analysis: An illustration using the job perception and job satisfaction constructs. *Journal of Management, 25,* 143–160.

Law, K. S., Wong, C. S., & Mobley, W. H. (1998). Towards a taxonomy of multidimensional constructs. *Academy of Management Review, 23,* 741–755.

Liao, H. (in press). Do it right this time: The role of employee service recovery performance in customer perceived justice and customer loyalty after service failures. *Journal of Applied Psychology.*

Liao, H., & Rupp, D. E. (2005). The impact of justice climate and justice orientation on work outcomes: A cross-level multifoci framework. *Journal of Applied Psychology, 90,* 242–256.

Liao, H., Rupp, D. E., Ko, J., Nam, K., & Bashshur, M. (2005). How they are treated matters too, sometimes: Self-focused justice perceptions and individual differences as moderators of other-focused justice effects. Paper presented at the 20th annual conference for the society for industrial and organizational psychology, Los Angeles, CA.

Naylor, J. C., Pritchard, R. D., & Ilgen, D. (1980). *A theory of behavior in organizations.* New York: Academic Press.

Ng, Z. W., Rupp, D. E., & Drasgow, F. (2005). Justice climate as a moderator of the conscientiousness–contextual performance relationship. Paper presented at the 20th annual conference for the society for industrial and organizational psychology, Los Angeles, CA.

Payne, R. L., & Pugh, D. S. (1976). Organizational structure and climate. In: M. D. Dunnette (Ed.), *Handbook of industrial and organizational psychology* (pp. 1125–1173). Chicago: Rand McNally.

Roberson, Q. M. (2006). Justice in teams: The activation and role of sensemaking in the emergence of justice climates. *Organizational Behavior and Human Decision Processes, 100,* 177–192.

Rupp, D. E., Baldwin, A. M., & Bashshur, M. (in press). Teaching organizational justice: Developmental assessment centers as a tool for translating abstract concepts into concrete behavior. *Psychologist Manager Journal.*

Rupp, D. E., Bashshur, M., & Liao, H. (this volume). Justice climate past, present, and future: Models of structure and emergence. In: F. Dansereau & F. J. Yammarino (Eds), *Research in multi-level issues.* Oxford: Elsevier.

Rupp, D. E., Bashshur, M., Smith, R. S., Mattern, K., Spencer, S., Holub, A. S., Credé, M., & Baldwin, A. (2004). Person and situational antecedents to social exchange-based justice effects: A consideration of multiple perpetrators. Paper presented at the 19th annual meeting of the society for industrial and organizational psychology, Chicago, IL.

Rupp, D. E., & Cropanzano, R. (2002). Multifoci justice and social exchange relationships. *Organizational Behavior and Human Decision Processes, 89,* 925–946.

Rupp, D. E., & Spencer, S. (in press). When customers lash out: The effect of customer interactional injustice on emotional labor and the mediating role of discrete emotions. *Journal of Applied Psychology.*

Salancik, G. J., & Pfeffer, J. (1978). A social information processing approach to job attitudes and task design. *Administrative Science Quarterly, 23,* 224–253.

Schneider, B. (1975). Organizational climates: An essay. *Personnel Psychology, 40,* 437–454.

Schneider, B. (1990). The climate for service: An application of the climate construct. In: B. Schneider (Ed.), *Organizational climate and culture* (pp. 383–412). San Francisco, CA: Jossey-Bass.

Skarlicki, D. P., & Folger, R. (1997). Retaliation in the workplace: The roles of distributive, procedural, and interactional justice. *Journal of Applied Psychology, 82,* 434–443.

Skarlicki, D. P., & Latham, G. P. (1996). Increasing citizenship behavior within a labor union: A test of organizational justice theory. *Journal of Applied Psychology, 81,* 161–169.

Skarlicki, D. P., & Latham, G. P. (1997). Leadership training in organizational justice to increase citizenship behavior within a labor union: A replication. *Personnel Psychology, 50,* 617–633.

Skitka, L. J. (2003). Of different minds: An accessible identity model of justice reasoning. *Personality and Social Psychology Review, 7,* 286–297.

Skitka, L. J., & Bravo, J. (2005). An accessible identity approach to understanding fairness in organizational settings. In: K. van den Bos, S. W. Gilliland, D. D. Steiner & D. P. Skarlicki (Eds), *What motivates fairness in organizations?* (pp. 31–48). Greenwich, CT: Information Age Publishing.

Spencer, S., & Rupp, D. E. (2006). Angry, guilty and conflicted: Injustice towards coworkers heightens emotional labor. Paper presented at the 21st annual conference for the society for industrial and organizational psychology, Dallas, TX.

Tajfel, H., & Turner, J. C. (1979). An integrative theory of inter-group conflict. In: W. G. Austin & S. Worchel (Eds), *The social psychology of inter-group relations* (pp. 33–47). Monterey, CA: Brooks/Cole.

Turner, J. C. (1985). Social categorization and the self-concept: A social-cognitive theory of group behavior. In: E. J. Lawler (Ed.), *Advances in group processes* (Vol. 2, pp. 77–122). Greenwich, CT: JAI Press.

Wanous, J. P. (1977). Organizational entry: Newcomers moving from outside to inside. *Psychological Bulletin, 84,* 601–618.

Wanous, J. P., Stumpf, S. A., & Bedrosian, H. (1979). Job survival of new employees. *Personnel Psychology, 32,* 651–662.

Weiss, H. M., & Cropanzano, R. (1996). Affective events theory: A theoretical discussion of affective experiences at work. In: B. M. Staw & L. L. Cummings (Eds), *Research in organizational behavior* (Vol. 18, pp. 1–74). Greenwich, CT: JAI Press.

PART VI:
ABOUT THE AUTHORS

ABOUT THE AUTHORS

Joseph A. Alutto is dean, Max M. Fisher College of Business, as well as executive dean of the Professional Colleges, The Ohio State University. He holds the John W. Berry, Sr., Chair in Business. From 1976 to 1990, he was dean of the School of Management, State University of New York at Buffalo. He has published more than 70 articles in leading academic journals and serves on a number of corporate and public sector boards, including Nationwide Financial Services, United Retail Group, Inc., and M/I Homes.

Maureen L. Ambrose is professor of Management in the College of Business at the University of Central Florida. She received her Ph.D. from the University of Illinois at Urbana-Champaign. Dr. Ambrose's research interests include organizational justice, employee deviance, and ethics. Her work has appeared in numerous journals.

Adam D. Bailey is a doctoral student in management at Texas Tech University. His research focuses on understanding how the economic productivity of organizations and communities can be enhanced. He is particularly interested in understanding the effects of social institutions and management policies on economic productivity.

Michael Bashshur is a graduate student in the Industrial Organizational Psychology program at the University of Illinois at Urbana-Champaign. His primary research focus is on the interrelationship of organizational context and individual differences and their effects on individual and organizational behavior.

Allen C. Bluedorn is the Emma S. Hibbs Distinguished Professor and Chair of the Department of Management at the University of Missouri-Columbia. He received his Ph.D. in sociology from the University of Iowa. For more than two decades, time and temporal matters in organizations have been his scholarly focus, which led to the recent publication of his book on the subject, *The Human Organization of Time: Temporal Realities and Experience* (Stanford University Press, 2002).

J. Christian Broberg is a doctoral student in Organizational Behavior at Texas Tech University. He received his B.A. from Brigham Young University and his M.B.A. from the University of Arizona. His research interests include shared and emergent leadership, system dynamic approaches to complex organizational phenomena, and conflict management within teams.

C. Shawn Burke is a research scientist within the Institute for Simulation and Training at the University of Central Florida, where her research has examined team adaptation, multicultural team performance, team performance under stress, and the development of training tools for multicultural team leaders. Previously, she worked at the Army Research Institute for the Behavioral and Social Sciences.

Jennifer L. Burke is a research scientist at the Institute for Safety Security Rescue Technology, University of South Florida. Her interests include human–robot interaction, team processes and performance in distributed systems, and e-leadership. Dr. Burke's research has been funded by NSF, DARPA, and ARL.

Jan Cannon-Bowers, Ph.D. recently left her position as the US Navy's Senior Scientist for Training Systems to join the School of Film and Digital Media and Institute for Simulation and Training at the University of Central Florida as an associate professor. Her research interests are in technology-enabled learning and synthetic learning environments. To date, she has been awarded several grants to support this work, including two awards by the National Science Foundation. Dr. Cannon-Bowers has published over 100 scholarly works.

Jeffrey M. Conte is an associate professor in the Department of Psychology at San Diego State University. He received his Ph.D. in Industrial and Organizational Psychology from Penn State University. His research interests include personality predictors of job performance, measurement of emotional intelligence, factors associated with health and stress in the workplace, and the measurement and validity of temporal constructs. His research has been funded by the National Institute of Mental Health. He is coauthor with Frank Landy of *Work in the 21st Century: An Introduction to Industrial and Organizational Psychology*. His research has appeared in numerous journals.

Michael D. Coovert is professor of Psychology at the University of South Florida. His interests include team performance, methodology, and quantitative issues. Dr. Coovert has in excess of 60 publications and has received several awards for teaching and research excellence.

Russell Cropanzano is the Brien Lesk Professor of Organizational Behavior in the University of Arizona's Eller College of Management. His research focuses on perceptions of organizational justice as well as on the experience and effects of workplace emotion. Dr. Cropanzano has authored more than 80 scholarly articles and chapters.

Gerald F. Goodwin is a research psychologist at the U.S. Army Research Institute for Behavioral and Social Sciences, assigned to the Leader Development Research Unit (LDRU). His current research focus is on leader and team effectiveness issues, particularly with regard to the joint, interagency, and multinational context.

James G. (Jerry) Hunt (Ph.D., University of Illinois at Urbana-Champaign) is the Paul Whitfield Horn Professor of Management, Trinity Company Professor in Leadership. He is a former editor of *Journal of Management* and *The Leadership Quarterly*. He founded and edited the eight-volume leadership symposia series, and has authored or edited some 200 books and journal publications. His current research interests include processual approaches to leadership and organizational phenomena and the philosophy of science of management.

Keith James is professor of Psychology at Portland State University. He studies Native American community sustainability, creativity/innovation in organizations, workplace social identity, and workplace health. He has been a Fulbright Fellow and a Fulbright Distinguished Scholar and is a Sequoah Fellow of the American Indian Science and Engineering Society.

Kimberly S. Jaussi is an assistant professor of Organizational Behavior and Leadership in the School of Management at Binghamton University and a fellow in the Center for Leadership Studies. She received her doctorate from the Marshall School of Business at the University of Southern California. Her research interests include unconventional leader behavior, creativity and leadership, strategic leadership, organizational commitment, and identity issues in diverse groups.

Joan H. Johnston received her M.A. and Ph.D. in Industrial and Organizational Psychology from the University of South Florida. She is a research psychologist at NAVAIR Orlando Training Systems Division, and she is responsible for managing human performance and military training systems research programs.

Andrew Li is a doctoral candidate at the University of Arizona. His research interests include organizational justice, cross-cultural issues in management, and impression management.

Hui Liao is an assistant professor of Human Resource Management in the School of Management and Labor Relations at Rutgers University. She received her Ph.D. in Human Resources and Industrial Relations from the University of Minnesota. Her primary research areas include customer service focused Human Resources Management, workforce diversity, workplace justice, multi-level theory and method, and group dynamics. Her work has appeared in numerous journals.

Sara A. McComb is an associate professor of Operations Management in the Isenberg School of Management at the University of Massachusetts, Amherst. Dr. McComb's research interests are in the area of cross-functional project teams, particularly team communication and shared mental models. Her research is funded by the National Science Foundation and the Office of Naval Research and is published in journals such as *IEEE Transactions on Engineering Management* and the *Journal of Engineering and Technology Management*.

Heather A. Priest is a Ph.D. candidate in Human Factors Psychology at the University of Central Florida, working at the Institute for Simulation and

Training. She has presented her work at national and international conferences and has also published them in journals including *Ergonomics and Design* and *Human Factors and Ergonomics in Manufacturing*.

Richard Reeves-Ellington is currently Professor Emeritus in the School of Management at Binghamton University, where he has served as associate dean and acting dean. He has also taught at the American University in Bulgaria and Sofia University in Bulgaria as a Fulbright Senior Scholar. His fields of interest revolve around cross-cultural aspects of global organization, marketing, and business strategy. He has served on the Fulbright Selection Committee for Southeast Europe (acting as chair for one year), the Muskie Foundation for students from the Confederation of Independent States, and the Fulbright Senior Scholars Program. His initial 33-year career in the pharmaceutical industry included 19 years in Asia, Europe, and Latin America.

Joan R. Rentsch, professor of Management and director of the Industrial/ Organizational Psychology Program at The University of Tennessee, earned her Ph.D. in industrial/organizational psychology from the University of Maryland. Dr. Rentsch's research interests include cognition in teams and organizations, the measurement of cognition, team processes, multicultural perspective-taking, and workplace absence.

Michael A. Rosen is a Ph.D. student in the Applied Experimental and Human Factors Psychology program at the University of Central Florida and has been a graduate research assistant at the Institute for Simulation and Training since Fall 2004. His research interests include individual and team decision making, human–computer interaction, and team performance.

Deborah E. Rupp (Ph.D., I/O Psychology, Colorado State University) has been a faculty member at the University of Illinois at Urbana-Champaign since 2002. She holds appointments in both the Department of Psychology and the Institute of Labor and Industrial Relations. She conducts research in the areas of workplace justice, corporate social responsibility, and managerial assessment and development. Her work has appeared in many of the field's top journals and research series. In 2005, she was awarded the Douglas W. Bray and Ann Howard Award from the Society for Industrial and Organizational Psychology for her international assessment center research focused on leadership development and has a forthcoming book on the topic. In addition, she serves on the editorial boards of *Organizational Behavior and Human Decision Processes* and *Journal of Management.*

Eduardo Salas is Trustee Chair and professor of Psychology in the Department of Psychology and the Institute for Simulation and Training at the University of Central Florida. He has more than 20 years of research experience on team training, simulation-based training, and team effectiveness and has published more than 300 articles, chapters, and papers on those topics.

Marshall Schminke received his Ph.D. from Carnegie Mellon University and is currently a professor of Management at the University of Central Florida. His research interests include organizational justice, ethics, and work climate. He has published a book on business ethics, and more than 40 articles and book chapters.

John F. Sherry, Herrick Professor and Chair of Marketing at the University of Notre Dame, is an anthropologist who studies the sociocultural dimensions of consumption. He is a Fellow of the American Anthropological Association and the Society for Applied Anthropology, a past President of the Association for Consumer Research, and a former Associate Editor of the *Journal of Consumer Research.*

Erika E. Small is a doctoral candidate in industrial and organizational psychology at The University of Tennessee, Knoxville. She is an assistant professor in the Department of Business at York College of Pennsylvania, teaching primarily leadership and organizational behavior courses. Her research interests include team leadership, trust, and team cognition.

Kevin C. Stagl is an organizational consultant with Assessment Technologies Group (ATG) and formerly served as a research scientist at the Institute for Simulation and Training (IST). At ATG and IST, his program of research has spanned the spectrum of team issues, with an emphasis on fostering team leadership, performance, development, and adaptation. The lessons learned and best practices distilled from this effort have appeared in many scholarly outlets such as the *Journal of Applied Psychology, Leadership Quarterly, Organizational Frontiers Series,* and *International Review of Industrial and Organizational Psychology*. He received his Ph.D. from the University of Central Florida.

Mary J. Waller is professor of Team Dynamics in the Department of Organization and Strategy, University of Maastricht (The Netherlands). She earned her Ph.D. in Organizational Behavior from the University of Texas at Austin. Her program of research focuses on individual and team perceptions and behaviors during time-pressured, complex, or unexpected situations, and includes field studies in the aviation and nuclear power industries. Her work is published in various academic volumes and journals.

SET UP A CONTINUATION ORDER TODAY!

Did you know that you can set up a continuation order on all Elsevier-JAI series and have each new volume sent directly to you upon publication? For details on how to set up a **continuation order**, contact your nearest regional sales office listed below.

To view related series in Business & Management, please visit:

www.elsevier.com/businessandmanagement

The Americas
Customer Service Department
11830 Westline Industrial Drive
St. Louis, MO 63146
USA
US customers:
Tel: +1 800 545 2522 (Toll-free number)
Fax: +1 800 535 9935
For Customers outside US:
Tel: +1 800 460 3110 (Toll-free number).
Fax: +1 314 453 7095
usbkinfo@elsevier.com

Europe, Middle East & Africa
Customer Service Department
Linacre House
Jordan Hill
Oxford OX2 8DP
UK
Tel: +44 (0) 1865 474140
Fax: +44 (0) 1865 474141
eurobkinfo@elsevier.com

Japan
Customer Service Department
2F Higashi Azabu, 1 Chome Bldg
1-9-15 Higashi Azabu, Minato-ku
Tokyo 106-0044
Japan
Tel: +81 3 3589 6370
Fax: +81 3 3589 6371
books@elsevierjapan.com

APAC
Customer Service Department
3 Killiney Road #08-01
Winsland House I
Singapore 239519
Tel: +65 6349 0222
Fax: +65 6733 1510
asiainfo@elsevier.com

Australia & New Zealand
Customer Service Department
30-52 Smidmore Street
Marrickville, New South Wales 2204
Australia
Tel: +61 (02) 9517 8999
Fax: +61 (02) 9517 2249
service@elsevier.com.au

30% Discount for Authors on All Books!

A 30% discount is available to Elsevier book and journal contributors on all books *(except multi-volume reference works)*.

To claim your discount, full payment is required with your order, which must be sent directly to the publisher at the nearest regional sales office above.